Chechnya – Russia's 'War on Terror'

The Russo-Chechen wars represent the bloodiest conflict in Europe since the Second World War. Making international headlines only after some 'terrorist spectacular', the conflict remains unresolved, despite President Putin's claim to have 'normalised' the situation. This book provides a comprehensive overview of the war and the issues connected with it. It examines the origins of the conflict historically, and traces how both sides were dragged inexorably into war in the early 1990s. The work discusses the two wars (1994–1996, and 1999–2006), the intervening truce and Putin's policy of 'Chechenisation', and shows how a downward spiral of violence has led to a mutually-damaging impasse from which neither side has yet been able satisfactorily to extricate itself. Theories of conflict, especially theories of terrorism and counter-terrorism, are applied and, in conclusion, some alternative resolutions are proposed that might lead to a more just and lasting peace in the region.

John Russell is a Senior Lecturer in Russian Studies and Peace Studies at the University of Bradford.

BASEES/Routledge series on Russian and East European studies

Series editor:
Richard Sakwa, Department of Politics and International Relations, University of Kent

Editorial committee:
Julian Cooper, Centre for Russian and East European Studies, University of Birmingham
Terry Cox, Department of Central and East European Studies, University of Glasgow
Rosalind Marsh, Department of European Studies and Modern Languages, University of Bath
David Moon, Department of History, University of Durham
Hilary Pilkington, Department of Sociology, University of Warwick
Stephen White, Department of Politics, University of Glasgow
Founding editorial committee member:
George Blazyca, Centre for Contemporary European Studies, University of Paisley

This series is published on behalf of BASEES (British Association for Slavonic and East European Studies). The series comprises original, high-quality, research-level work by both new and established scholars on all aspects of Russian, Soviet, post-Soviet and East European Studies in humanities and social science subjects.

1 **Ukraine's Foreign and Security Policy, 1991–2000**
Roman Wolczuk

2 **Political Parties in the Russian Regions**
Derek S. Hutcheson

3 **Local Communities and Post-Communist Transformation**
Edited by Simon Smith

4 **Repression and Resistance in Communist Europe**
J.C. Sharman

5 **Political Elites and the New Russia**
Anton Steen

6 **Dostoevsky and the Idea of Russianness**
Sarah Hudspith

7 **Performing Russia – Folk Revival and Russian Identity**
Laura J. Olson

8 **Russian Transformations**
Edited by Leo McCann

9 **Soviet Music and Society under Lenin and Stalin**
The baton and sickle
Edited by Neil Edmunds

10 **State Building in Ukraine**
The Ukrainian parliament,
1990–2003
Sarah Whitmore

11 **Defending Human Rights in Russia**
Sergei Kovalyov, dissident and
human rights commissioner,
1969–2003
Emma Gilligan

12 **Small-Town Russia**
Postcommunist livelihoods and
identities: a portrait of the
intelligentsia in Achit,
Bednodemyanovsk and Zubtsov,
1999–2000
Anne White

13 **Russian Society and the Orthodox Church**
Religion in Russia after
Communism
Zoe Knox

14 **Russian Literary Culture in the Camera Age**
The word as image
Stephen Hutchings

15 **Between Stalin and Hitler**
Class war and race war on the
Dvina, 1940–46
Geoffrey Swain

16 **Literature in Post-Communist Russia and Eastern Europe**
The Russian, Czech and Slovak
fiction of the Changes, 1988–98
Rajendra A. Chitnis

17 **Soviet Dissent and Russia's Transition to Democracy**
Dissident legacies
Robert Horvath

18 **Russian and Soviet Film Adaptations of Literature, 1900–2001**
Screening the word
Edited by Stephen Hutchings and Anat Vernitski

19 **Russia as a Great Power**
Dimensions of security under
Putin
*Edited by Jakob Hedenskog,
Vilhelm Konnander,
Bertil Nygren, Ingmar Oldberg
and Christer Pursiainen*

20 **Katyn and the Soviet Massacre of 1940**
Truth, justice and memory
George Sanford

21 **Conscience, Dissent and Reform in Soviet Russia**
Philip Boobbyer

22 **The Limits of Russian Democratisation**
Emergency powers and states of
emergency
Alexander N. Domrin

23 **The Dilemmas of Destalinisation**
A social and cultural history of
reform in the Khrushchev era
Edited by Polly Jones

24 **News Media and Power in Russia**
Olessia Koltsova

25 **Post-Soviet Civil Society**
Democratization in Russia and the
Baltic states
Anders Uhlin

26 **The Collapse of Communist
Power in Poland**
Jacqueline Hayden

27 **Television, Democracy and
Elections in Russia**
Sarah Oates

28 **Russian Constitutionalism**
Historical and contemporary
development
Andrey N. Medushevsky

29 **Late Stalinist Russia**
Society between reconstruction
and reinvention
Edited by Juliane Fürst

30 **The Transformation of Urban
Space in Post-Soviet Russia**
*Konstantin Axenov, Isolde Brade
and Evgenij Bondarchuk*

31 **Western Intellectuals and the
Soviet Union, 1920–40**
From Red Square to the Left Bank
Ludmila Stern

32 **The Germans of the Soviet
Union**
Irina Mukhina

33 **Re-constructing the Post-Soviet
Industrial Region**
The Donbas in transition
Edited by Adam Swain

34 **Chechnya – Russia's 'War on
Terror'**
John Russell

Chechnya – Russia's 'War on Terror'

John Russell

Routledge
Taylor & Francis Group

LONDON AND NEW YORK

First published 2007
by Routledge
2 Park Square, Milton Park, Abingdon, Oxon OX14 4RN

Simultaneously published in the USA and Canada
by Routledge
270 Madison Ave, New York, NY 10016

Routledge is an imprint of the Taylor & Francis Group, an informa business

© 2007 John Russell

Typeset in Times by Wearset Ltd, Boldon, Tyne and Wear
Printed and bound in Great Britain by TJI Digital, Padstow, Cornwall

British Library Cataloguing in Publication Data
A catalogue record for this book is available from the British Library

Library of Congress Cataloging in Publication Data
A catalog record for this book has been requested

ISBN10: 0-415-38064-2 (hbk)
ISBN10: 0-203-94666-9 (ebk)

ISBN13: 978-0-415-38064-5 (hbk)
ISBN13: 978-0-203-94666-9 (ebk)

To Anna Politkovskaya, just one of the countless innocent victims of this wretched war, the latest chapter of a tragic conflict long needed by nobody save the powerful few.

Contents

Preface   x
Acknowledgements   xiv
Abbreviations   xvi
Glossary of Chechen and Russian terms   xvii

1 Introduction   1

2 The roots of violence in the Russo-Chechen conflict:
   identifying Galtung's Conflict Triangle   10

3 A tragic history: unresolved contradictions in the
   Russo-Chechen relationship   29

4 Of wolves and werewolves: demonisation in the
   Russo-Chechen confrontation   53

5 Wars by any other name: Yeltsin's 'restoration of
   constitutional order' and Putin's 'counter-terrorist operation'   69

6 9/11, Chechnya and the war on terror   89

7 Entrepreneurs of violence   110

8 The paths not taken: the Russian failure to reach a
   political solution in Chechnya   131

9 The international dimension   149

10 Conclusion   168

Notes   175
Select bibliography   220
Index   237

Preface

The foaming Terek rushes on
His stony shores between,
And there the wicked Chechen creeps
And whets his dagger keen.
('Cossack Lullaby', 1840,
by Mikhail Lermontov)[1]

On the night of 9/10 July 2006, the fundamentally divergent careers of two of the most charismatic and controversial figures in the Islamic world came to an end in equally dramatic fashion. In the final of soccer's World Cup in Berlin, Zinédine Zidane's belligerent head-butt and subsequent sending-off was watched by thousands of millions worldwide on TV and online. Given his oft-stated passion for the 'beautiful game' and penchant for laptop computers, it would have been surprising had Shamil Basaev, the notorious mastermind of the Beslan school siege in September 2004, also not wanted to see Europe's 'match of the decade'. In fact, at this very time, the one-legged leader of the irreconcilable Chechen resistance was busy elsewhere planning the latest and, as it would turn out, last strike against the Russian authorities. Later that night, in the remote village of Ekazhevo in Ingushetia, in the far south-east corner of the continent, Russia's proclaimed number one terrorist was blasted to bits by, according to which version you believe, the accidental detonation of his own explosives or a sophisticated counter-terrorist operation by Russian special forces.[2]

Despite condemnation by the rest of the world for responding so violently in his farewell match to deliberate Italian provocation, Zidane returned to France a national hero. By the same token, although Basaev's death was greeted world-wide with relief and acclaim, his legendary status in the Chechen cultural narrative is assured for the proven ability, in his people's eyes, to retaliate against Russian aggression time and again by hitting back and bloodying the nose of the oppressor.[3] Zidane's mother, we learn, was proud of her son for standing up for her family's honour. One suspects that the survivors of Basaev's family, so many of whom were killed in a Russian bombing raid on his home village of Vedeno on 3 June 1995, immediately before he gained worldwide fame for the first of his audaciously brutal hostage-taking acts, will be proud that one of their kin chose to perpetuate the longstanding Chechen tradition of fighting against rather than submitting to their most hated oppressors.

Zidane's specific legacy to young Muslims will be the reflected glory of one of their own, exhibiting skill and talent in international sport at the highest level, a near perfect role model for those that seek to emulate him. Basaev's legacy, on the other hand, is likely to be his 'Book of a Mujahiddeen',[4] written in March 2004 and serving as a textbook, much as did the works of Che Guevara,[5] Régis Debray[6] and Carlos Marighela[7] before him, for those wishing to follow the revolutionary path. For some this route, understandably, will appear more accessible than the heights to which Zidane aspired and, overcoming all odds, conquered.

One might predict that the course and outcome of the 'war on terror', not just in Chechnya but throughout the Islamic world, may well be determined by which of these legacies – that in the secular world represented by professional soccer or that in a post-secular world epitomised by *jihad* – proves more appealing and relevant to disaffected young Muslims worldwide.

Although, unquestionably, Zidane would hardly wish to be bracketed with an international terrorist carrying on his conscience the deaths of so many children, the mixed messages about the 'legitimate' limits of provocation and retaliation in both cases remain equally open to interpretation by opposing sides. As such they represent the dilemma of acceptable 'ends' and 'means'; the lengths to which it is permissible to go to get one's way that appears to be afflicting so many aspects of life in the post-9/11 world, dominated as it currently is by mutual insecurity, fear and loathing generated in the ongoing 'war on terror' and a growing perception that the twenty-first century is seeing 'greed' rather than 'need' evermore overtly dominate throughout the world, in sport (in the form, for example, of doping) as in international relations.

Basaev's demise, clouded in the kind of mysterious circumstances to which Russia-watchers have become accustomed, came at a most opportune time for Vladimir Putin, as the Russian president prepared to host the G-8 leaders in his home city of St Petersburg. The removal of this last symbolic leader of Chechen resistance, according to the Kremlin, would surely bring peace at last to the beleaguered Southern region. For the long-suffering Chechen people reactions will be mixed. There is no doubt that Basaev's brutal *modus operandi* and flirtations with *Wahhabism* – the strict form of Islam imported into Chechnya by Arab mercenaries – were not supported by the majority of ordinary Chechens, so that many will be breathing a sigh of relief that their most infamous son is dead. At the same time, however, there are few that expect his death to change dramatically the situation in Chechnya, let alone bring an imminent end to their misfortune.

Basaev, for all of his headline-grabbing audacity was, in the final analysis, more of an *éminence grise* lurking behind all aspects of the confrontation than a central figure in the overall scheme of the Russo-Chechen conflict. He bore with pride the name of Imam Shamil, resistance hero of the Great Caucasian War in the nineteenth century; masterminded (but not directly participated in) the two major terrorist 'spectaculars' of the second war (the hostage crises of Dubrovka in 2002, and Beslan in 2004); led the irreconcilable opposition to 'Chechenisation' – the questionable political settlement imposed by the Putin regime. Basaev in many ways was the embodiment of the 'demonic' Chechen, so feared by Russians since they first came across this war-like mountain people almost three centuries ago, the 'bogey-man' seared terrifyingly into the minds of generations of Russian children through the words of Lermontov's popular 'Cossack Lullaby' quoted above.

Equally importantly, the negative image of Basaev, culminating in the Beslan school siege, was used by both Russian and Western leaders to reduce the Russo-Chechen confrontation into one of 'good' versus 'evil', ignoring the complexity and different layers of conflict involved. It has been left largely to what might be termed the 'values community' of scholars, journalists and human rights activists both within Russia and across the world to focus, much to the displeasure of the present incumbent in the Kremlin, on the malign role of successive Russian and Soviet administrations in this long-running tragedy.

For the war in Chechnya has been a tragedy not only for the Chechen people, several hundred thousand of whom has been killed, injured or left homeless by the conflict; not only for the once sizeable Russian-speaking population of Chechnya and neighbouring territories which has fled the violence in tens of thousands; nor the million-plus Russian service personnel who have endured the physical and psychological traumas of Chechnya. The real tragedy is for the Russian Federation itself: in the name of maintaining at any cost Russia's great power status by ensuring its territorial integrity, the Chechen conflict appears to have been the touchstone with which the Putin administration has whittled away the rights and liberties of Russian society to a free media, a division of powers, the rule of law and an active, multinational citizenry operating within an efficiently-functioning market economy – the very life-blood of democracy.

Far from enhancing the security of Russian citizens, paradoxically, Putin's 'counter-terrorist' operation in Chechnya appears to have produced right across the Northern Caucasus the very terrorist organisations that purportedly he initially set out to eradicate. While he could claim with some justification that he was provoked into declaring a 'war on terror' in Chechnya by Basaev's invasion of Dagestan and the apartment blasts of 1999, the Russian president should know that one of the basic strategies of insurgent terrorism is to provoke over-reaction. When this assumes the form of a 'war *of* terror' it will tend to provoke, in its turn, unintended consequences. Basaev, after all, is thought to have turned to terrorism in the form of hostage taking only after 11 of his close relatives had been killed in the Russian bombing raid on his home village mentioned above. Without seeking to justify or condone in any way his subsequent acts of violence, one nonetheless has to ask the question: What would Zidane, you or I have done in such provocative circumstances?

This, in turn, leads to the even more important question facing Russia today. Eleven years on, Basaev is gone, but in that time how many more younger and potentially even more dangerous Basaevs have been created by Russia's indiscriminate and disproportionate use of force in Chechnya and beyond?

Maisons, France

Acknowledgements

Although this book has been an unusually lone effort, it has relied on the contribution of so many people that it would take up half of the book to name them all. Most will be aware of the debt I owe them, but others may not realise how helpful they have been. Let me restrict my heartfelt thanks, therefore, primarily to my wife, for patiently accepting the priorities that the writing of this book imposed and to my family for giving me the time and space required; to the academic, administrative and technical staff in my home departments at the University of Bradford for their understanding and assistance; and to the hundreds, possibly thousands, of colleagues, students, experts and others from all walks of life all over the world who have advised me, at times argued with me but always encouraged me in this work.

Finally, thanks to the good people of Maisons in Aude (France) for affording me the friendship, hospitality and tranquillity required to complete this book. The view from my window of Mont Tauch, hardly the rugged flanks of the Caucasus, but a mountain nonetheless, daily inspired me to attempt to scale this personal summit. The scale of the challenge, the effort required and finally the exhilaration of attaining my goal, I am glad to report, was every bit as rewarding as climbing the mountain itself.

The publishers would like to thank the following for permission to reprint their material: J. Russell (2002) 'Exploitation of the "Islamic factor" in the Russo-Chechen conflict before and after 11 September 2001' *European Security*, 11:4, pp. 96–109. Available online at www.tandf.co.uk/journals; J. Russell (2002) 'Mujahedeen, Mafia, Madmen...: Russian perceptions of Chechens during the wars in Chechnya, 1994–1996 and 1999–to date', *Journal of Communist Studies and Transition Politics*, 18:1, pp. 73–96. Available online at www.tandf.co.uk/journals; J. Russell 'Terrorists, bandits, spooks and thieves: Russian demonisation of the Chechens before and since 9/11', (2005) *Third World Quarterly*, 26:1, pp. 101–116. Available online at www.tandf.co.uk/journals; J. Russell (2006) 'Obstacles to Peace in Chechnya: the scope for international involvement', *Europe-Asia Studies*, 58:6, pp. 941–964. Available online at www.tandf.co.uk/journals; J. Russell (2005) 'A War by any other name: Chechnya, 11 September and the War on Terrorism', in R. Sakwa (ed.), *Chechnya: from the Past to the Future*, London: Anthem Press, pp. 239–264.

Available online at www.anthempress.com; J. Russell (2006) 'The impact of Chechnya and the "War on Terror" on British–Russian relations', in Hanna Smith (ed.), *The Two-Level Game: Russia's Relations with Great Britain, Finland and the European Union*, Helsinki: Aleksanteri Institute, pp. 67–85. Available online at www.kikimora-publications.com; J. Russell (2005) 'Basayev: the Beast of Beslan?', in Stephen D. Shenfield's Research Report, *Chechnya and Russia: A Post-Beslan Symposium*, 29, January. Published online as *JRL Research and Analytical Supplement*, at www.cdi.org/russia/johnson/ 9024.cfm; Anonymous poem (2006) 'We are Wolves', quoted in M. Gammer *The Lone Wolf and the Bear: Three Centuries of Russian Defiance of Russian Rule*, London: Hurst & Co. p. v. Available online at www.hurstpub.co.uk.

Thanks to Anton Russell (www.apraze.com) for cartographic assistance on p. xix.

Abbreviations

APN	*Agentstvo Politicheskikh Novostei* (Political News Agency)
CIS	Commonwealth of Independent States
CPSU	Communist Party of the Soviet Union
CSM	Committee of Soldiers' Mothers
FSB	*Federal'naya Sluzhba Bezopasnosti* (Federal Security Service)
GRU	*Glavnoe Razvedovatel'noe Upravlenie* (Military Intelligence Directorate)
KGB	*Komitet Gosudarstvennoi Bezopasnosti* (Committee for State Security)
MID	*Ministerstvo inostrannikh del* (Ministry of Foreign Affairs)
MOD	(Russian) Ministry of Defence
MVD	*Ministerstvo vnutrennikh del* (Ministry of Internal Affairs)
NTV	Independent Television
OMON	*Otryad Militsii Osobogo Naznacheniya* (Special Purpose Militia Unit)
ORT	All-Russia Television
OSCE	Organisation for Security and Cooperation in Europe
PACE	Parliamentary Assembly of the Council of Europe
PONARS	Program on New Approaches to Russian Security (Washington DC)
RF	Russian Federation
RFE/RL	Radio Free Europe/Radio Liberty
RSFSR	Russian Soviet Federative Socialist Republic
SVR	*Sluzhba vneshnei razvedki* (Foreign Intelligence Service)
VTsIOM	*Vserossisskii Tsentr po Izucheniyu Obshchestvennogo Mneniya* (All-Russian Centre for the Study of Public Opinion)

Glossary of Chechen and Russian terms

Abrek	Chechen 'bandit of honour'
Adat	Customary law of Chechnya
Aul	Mountain village
Borz	Wolf (name given to Chechen soldiers)
Boyevik (pl. *boyeviki*)	Name given to Chechen fighter(s) by Russians
Chekist	Member of Russian/Soviet secret police
Dedovshchina	'Hazing' or bullying in Russian armed forces
Derzhavnost'	The philosophy that holds that Russia should remain a great power.
Djamaat	Nowadays a religion-based organisation uniting the fighters of neighbouring villages.
Djigit	Mounted Chechen warrior
Ekho Moskvy	'Echo of Moscow', an independent Russian radio station
Gazavat	Holy War
Gosudarstvennost'	The philosophy that maintains that the Russian state should be strong
Kadyrovtsy	Members of Ramzan Kadyrov's security forces
Kinzhal	Traditional Chechen dagger
Klanovost'	Clan mentality
Kontraktnik	(Russian) contract soldier
Marsho	Chechen for 'freedom'
Mufti	Chechen spiritual leader
Mujahideen	Islamic resistance fighters
Mukhadjirstvo	The great deportation (refers to 1864)
Narodnost'	The quality of identifying oneself as part of the Russian people often rendered as the 'national principle'
Naqshbandiya	The more centralised and disciplined of the two major pathways (see *tariqat*) of Sufism in Chechnya
Nokhchallah	The Chechen code of honour
Polpred	President's plenipotentiary representative in the seven federal districts of the Russian Federation

Qadiriya	The more individualised of the two major pathways of Sufism in Chechnya
Shari'a	Islamic law
Siloviki	Members of the Russian 'law and order' ministries
Spetsnaz	Russian special forces
Sufism	A mystic interpretation of Islam popular throughout the North Caucasus
Tariqat	A pathway or order within Sufism
Teip	Chechen clan
Vertikal'	The vertical structure of executive power favoured in Russia
Wahhabism	A strict version of Islam imported to Chechnya by Arab fighters in 1995
Wird	A sub-division (brotherhood) of a *tariqat*
Zachistki	Sweeps or clean-up operations in Chechen villages
Zikr	Traditional Chechen religious ceremonial dance
Zhurnalyugi	Journalist 'scumbag' (term of abuse used by *siloviki*)
Zindan	Dungeon used for holding hostages

Chechnya and its surroundings

1 Introduction

Today for me Chechnya is a people
who have gone through the worst of the worst,
the most bloody and sickening war,
which is devastating the planet.
This is not the only war in the world
but it is the most bloody in the sense that
there is no other people in the world
who over the last ten years have lost
between a quarter and a fifth of their population.
I know that the Chechens as a nation are not so numerous,
but if we compare the overall numbers of Chechens
with the number of those killed and wounded
and the number of children who have been killed,
then it has to be the worst thing that is happening on our planet today.
And it is horrendous that this is happening
with the silent agreement of the whole world.

(André Glucksmann, 2005)[1]

Readers will be well aware that this is by no means the first book devoted to the Russo-Chechen wars. Indeed, unlike the creators of the majority of works on the first war (1994–1996), this author has no frontline experience in Chechnya (or, elsewhere for that matter!) and, for a number of reasons, he has not been able to make a first visit to the conflict zone since the beginning of the second war late in 1999, when he first began to research this topic. There would be little utility, therefore, in trying to retread ground that has already been so well covered on such aspects as the pre-history of the conflict,[2] a chronological examination of the events of the first and second wars,[3] and detailed accounts of such terrorist 'spectaculars' staged by the Chechens as those at Dubrovka and Beslan.[4]

However, in order to complement this select body of existing research, new approaches and insights are always welcome. For, whatever Kremlin spokespersons might say, the problem of Chechnya has not been resolved and solutions are still urgently required to tackle what remains a major humanitarian disaster. What this author can offer is an intimate knowledge of Russian society and the

Russian language, the experience of numerous earlier visits to the Caucasus and a background in the highly relevant discipline of the study of terrorism and, more recently, a reinvigorated interest in conflict resolution.

These research tools, plus an extensive and intensive reading in English, Russian and, in translation, Chechen material from a wide range of sources, speaking on the topic at home and abroad and engaging in discussions, conversations or email exchanges on this topic with a representative collection of academics, combatants, hostages, human rights activists, journalists, lawyers, medical and military personnel, ordinary citizens, politicians and students from all over the world, prompt me to offer this book as a contribution to the ongoing debate on Chechnya.

With this monograph I hope to help answer one of the questions that has cropped up most frequently when I am discussing the topic, be it in St Andrews in Scotland or Rostov-on-Don in Russia: Why is it that the continuing saga of one of the most horrific human tragedies of the past decade in Europe has failed for the most part to stir the conscience of liberal society across a continent that avowedly seeks to define itself by its commitment to human rights, social justice and the rule of law?

If this question was already being raised after the first Russo-Chechen War,[5] with the international attitudes to the Russian invasion of Chechnya found wanting for being 'weak, lax and confused',[6] how much more relevant is it now, after the Russians have repeated their attempt to resolve the Chechen conundrum by force and, in so doing, placed the conflict alongside those in Palestine, Kashmir and Iraq as a *cause célèbre* for disaffected Muslims across the world, including those within our own societies, encouraging extremist elements within those communities to employ terrorism as the means to achieve their ends? The essence of the question remains, therefore, is Russia fighting in Chechnya a war *on* terror or conducting a war *of* terror?

Moreover, have Russia's actions, as a result of the conflict in Chechnya, set a precedent with which, by appearing to share interests with major democratic powers, authoritarian regimes such as that under Putin might feel tempted to conclude that, as long as it is conducted under the guise of the 'war on terror', they can employ force with impunity to crush any separatist or oppositional movements within their borders? Some of the suggested answers to these questions that I have formulated in this book may well be disturbing for readers, particularly for my generation, brought up in the immediate aftermath of the Second World War and thus, perhaps, generally more inclined towards policies of peace and reconciliation than, apparently, are those of our coevals who actually wield political power (George W. Bush's sixtieth birthday in July 2006 occurred exactly one month before my own).

As to my own position, inevitably, for a Western scholar committed to facilitating an end to this appalling conflict, in the interests of both Chechen and Russian peoples, I have to admit that this study has involved overcoming a fundamental moral repugnance to the violence employed in both acts of terrorism and the war of which they formed part. My primary aim, however, is not to seek to equate, let alone justify, any of this violence; my task is rather to explain it and to place it in a context that lends itself to rational analysis. Although I am highly critical of Russian policy in Chechnya, my argument is not with Russia per se, and certainly not with the Russian people, so much as with the philosophy behind the conduct of the worldwide 'war on terror', which the Putin administration appears to have adopted from the outset. My approach might be categorised, therefore, as deontological, in a world in which, unfortunately in my view, consequentialist philosophies increasingly appear to dominate.

Let us not delude ourselves, however. All over the world violent conflicts happen – sometimes out of need (competition for scarce political, economic and social resources), sometimes out of creed (the incompatibility of different ways of life living side by side or within a single community) but mostly, it would seem, through greed[7] (when private, group or even national interests are placed above any notion of the common good or 'right'). Whereas propaganda has often been employed to justify conflicts arising out of 'need', just as religious and nationalist discourse has for those emanating from 'creed', less attention appears to have been paid to the methods by which those that wish to profit from violent conflicts (whom I have called 'entrepreneurs of violence')[8] satisfy, feed and justify their 'greed'.

Naturally, 'entrepreneurs of violence' are unlikely to admit to such self-serving motives as 'greed', tending rather to cloak their justifications in terms of 'need' and/or 'creed', and thus resorting to propaganda, religious and nationalist discourse where possible. What I would suggest distinguishes such 'entrepreneurs of violence' is their capacity for the 'demonisation of the other', dehumanising not only their opponents, but also, when deemed necessary, their critics at home, a form of structural violence that not only incites but condones all too readily the violent behaviour that has come to characterise the Russo-Chechen conflict.

So great is the demand for peacekeeping, peacemaking and peacebuilding in cleaning up the mess created by so many 'greed-based' violent conflicts that 'peace' itself, rather like both anti- and counter-terrorism,[9] is in danger of becoming a kind of business: Should we talk already, indeed, of 'entrepreneurs of peace'? More and more, it would seem, the parameters of what can be done in a given conflict situation lie more in the realm of what can best be wrung out of a situation, rather than what with goodwill might be possible, let alone, in the name of humanity, desirable. Chechnya remains a graphic example of this.

Rather than opting for the traditional approach of beginning with a history of the Russo-Chechen confrontation and working through it chronologically, therefore, I have commenced this study with this point of disconnection: between what may rationally be proposed by those seeking to resolve this violent conflict and what might reasonably be expected to be achieved in practice in the short, medium and long term. By applying in the second chapter Johan Galtung's Conflict Triangle to the Russo-Chechen conflict, I seek to trace the origins of the widespread and horrific violence that has characterised the ongoing Russo-Chechen conflict, already arguably the most costly war on the European continent since the Second World War, in terms of civilian and military losses and displaced persons.

However, applying conflict resolution theory to the Russo-Chechen conflict manifestly is not in itself enough to make progress towards peace. Clearly, without the requisite goodwill of the conflicting parties, including recognition that the ability to compromise is a strength not a weakness, there is little prospect of constructing a win-win situation for both Chechens and Russians in Chechnya. Moreover, without adequate pressure from, if not leaders of the international community, then from other influential representatives of world public opinion, who are sufficiently aware of the complexities of this multi-layered conflict,[10] there is little real hope of doing much more than temporarily freezing the confrontation at a level of violence 'tolerable' to all except those at the receiving end.

Accepting this constraint, through the analysis of cultural contradictions between the Russians and the Chechens and between each and the contemporary world, I will attempt to discover what gives rise to and sustains the attitudes on all sides that have sanctioned a scale of violent behaviour that appears to make this long-running and seemingly endless confrontation as intractable as the conflict in the Middle East.

In seeking to apply theories of conflict resolution, international terrorism and counter-insurgency to the Russo-Chechen confrontation, the aim is not only to trace the stages along the road that led to the outbreak of the current conflict, which to my mind was eminently avoidable, but also to attempt to find for all parties concerned peaceful pathways out of the impasse into which the tit-for-tat violence of the confrontation has driven them.

Thus the third chapter, devoted to the historical background of the conflict, concentrates on the cultural contradictions between the Russians and Chechens, breaking up the conflict into what I regard as its components. These are identified as the clash of a 'modernising' with a 'traditional' society; a classical struggle between an 'imperial' power[11] and a 'colonised' people currently being fought around the competing (although not irreconcilable) claims of 'territorial integrity' and 'self-determination'; violence stemming from the absence of law and order in Chechnya, which I have called 'the black hole' of lawlessness;[12] and, finally, issues directly related to the 'war on terror'. This I perceive to be merely a part of the broader contradictions emanating from a US-led drive towards a new world order based upon globalisation that has gathered both pace and intensity since the tragic events of 11 September 2001.

The issue of demonisation, or the 'politics of naming', is highlighted in the fourth chapter, analysing Russian perceptions of the Chechens over the centuries, so many of which appear to be alive and operative in the current conflict, but concentrating on the subtle (and not so subtle!) shifts in the use and abuse of propaganda and other forms of information warfare between the Yeltsin and Putin regimes. Strictly speaking, the 'information' or 'propaganda' war might be characterised as a fifth conflict within the Russo-Chechen confrontation and thus belongs to the previous chapter. However, I take the view that it constitutes the means through which the Putin administration has highlighted the 'war on terror' and downplayed the other conflicts.

The fifth chapter also applies a comparative analysis; in this instance to the different wars waged by Yeltsin (1994–1996) and Putin (1999 to date) under equally euphemistic labels, respectively, the 'restoration of constitutional order' and a 'counter-terrorist' operation. This analysis focusses not so much on the detailed events of these wars, which have been covered more than adequately in other works, but on why the public support in Russia collapsed for Yeltsin when his Chechen policy left the confrontation in a dead-end, but continued to back Putin despite his Chechen policy also failing to deliver the anticipated victory in his 'small, victorious war'. This chapter concludes with an analysis of the policy of 'Chechenisation', which the Putin administration seeks to pass off as a 'political' solution, even though it entailed the physical elimination of such 'legitimate' leaders of the separatist opposition as Aslan Maskhadov.

The following chapter introduces the key turning point of 9/11, with the subsequent declaration of a 'war on terror'. Russia's new-found common interests with the US-led coalition of the willing had a profound impact on the way that the Russo-Chechen conflict was perceived in the worldwide Islamic community, on the one hand, and much of the rest of the world, on the other. The so-called 'Islamic factor' has been exploited, it will be argued, not just by the Putin administration to cover a shameful list of war crimes against the Chechen population, but also by leaders of Western states who, for their own narrow interests, seek to deflect attention away from the blatant violation of elementary human rights in this corner of Europe.

This chapter also looks at the various counter-terrorist options open to the Russian leadership. While recognising that in countering insurgencies such as that in Chechnya the secret is in developing the correct mixture of approaches, involving elements of both counter-terror ('hard' options characterised primarily at eradication and the employment of terror against terror) and anti-terror ('soft' options relying more on policies of containment and which address the root causes), Russia's performance in this confrontation will be evaluated along with that of other countries engaged in comparable conflicts. The phenomenon of 'complexity fatigue' is offered here as a possible explanation for the apparent unwillingness of Western civil society to engage fully with the real situation in Chechnya. Also introduced is the concept of 'traumatised' democracies in the wake of major terrorist attacks.

The 'entrepreneurs of violence' on all sides form the focus of attention in the seventh chapter. However, the very nature of the secretive, behind-the-scenes manoeuverings on the Russian side does not lend itself easily to analysis. By way of contrast the intriguing individual characters on the Chechen side offer a topic for research that is hard to resist. Thus, while the figure at the apex of Russia's *vertikal'* of power – President Vladimir Putin – could be analysed as an individual, Russian 'entrepreneurs of violence', more often than not, can only be viewed as a collective. Putin's 'dirty work' – including the neutralisation and even physical elimination of the opponents to his Chechnya policy – is carried out, with or without his knowledge, by nameless and faceless minions. However, the leaders of the competing factions among the Chechens can hardly be accused of hiding their lights under a bushel, allowing plenty of scope for an examination of the degree to which such prominent personalities as the late Shamil Basaev from the 'irreconcilables' and Ramzan Kadyrov from the pro-Kremlin forces may be categorised as prime examples of 'entrepreneurs of violence'.

Having concluded that 'Chechenisation' does not represent the basis of a genuine long-term political settlement, I will examine in the eighth chapter the failure of the Russian side to reach a political solution that not only is acceptable to all sides concerned but also is capable of moving the Russo-Chechen conflict away from violent politics and onto the path of peacemaking and peacebuilding. This chapter considers the position of Akhmed Zakaev, whose extradition trial in London in 2003, in which I was called as an expert witness by his defence team, served in so many ways not just as an example of the differing values and structures of Russian and Western society, but also as an intriguing case study with which to analyse the 'terrorist versus freedom fighter' debate. Although a strong case could have been made for studying in this context instead the position of the late Aslan Maskhadov, former President of Chechnya-Ichkeria, he was never given the opportunity, unlike Zakaev, of having his role in the conflict examined by an independent court. As may be said equally of Basaev, Maskhadov's story provides material enough for a separate book.

The ninth chapter examines the international dimension of the conflict, analysing a selection of those factors contributing to violence identified in Chapter 2 and seeking to explain why no peace proposal offered from without has so far met with the approval of the Kremlin. Although this reluctance to engage seriously in talks about talks about peace in Chechnya has led to a degree of impatience in Western countries with Putin's inability to reach a political solution acceptable to all sides, significantly, it has not been allowed thus far to damage bilateral relations between Russia and her Western partners, as is demonstrated by a case study of the Russo-British relationship. On the other hand, this failure has encouraged those representing the evident, albeit all too often latent, public interest that exists in Western societies to demand answers from their political leaders as to what exactly is happening in the North Caucasus, why more is not being done to stop the misery and what might be the consequences if nothing is done.

The tenth and concluding chapter will seek to summarise the answers to the array of complex questions posed in this Introduction. First and foremost of these is why a conflict of this scale and intensity has been 'swept under the carpet' and what are the consequences for all of us of such indifference to suffering and violence? In other words, in which ways might what continues to occur in Chechnya and the rest of Russia affect the way we live outside this war-torn region? For example, to what extent might Western passivity over successive post-Communist Russian regimes' penchant for the *à la carte* removal of perceived political opponents[13] be perceived as a contributory factor in the selective killing of such critics as Anna Politkovskaya,[14] one of the bravest and most highly-principled professional journalists that I have ever had the honour to meet?

For just one of the many paradoxes of the Russo-Chechen conflict is that, although it is rarely, nowadays, raised as an issue at summit meetings involving President Putin, it continues to inspire numerous attempts, of which this book is one, at explaining just what is going on in and around Chechnya. Although views expressed on Chechen terrorism range from thinly-disguised support to outright condemnation, the overwhelming majority of these works is united in criticism of Russian conduct in virtually all aspects of this conflict.

Such interest in Chechnya might be explained by Russia's role in the global 'war on terror'. For the Russians are by no means the only military power currently engaged in hostilities against a much weaker foe which believes that the application of even more force, the concomitant lack of discrimination and proportionality notwithstanding, will surely bring their adversaries to the realisation that it is folly to continue such an unequal struggle. Indeed, it could be construed that Russia was employing in Chechnya the same strategy adopted by both the coalition forces in Afghanistan and Iraq and the Israelis in Palestine.

In practice, it seems patently obvious to the outside observer that such a strategy, on the contrary, tends to harden and spread the resistance. Those Afghans, Chechens, Iraqis and Palestinians that currently are on the receiving end of this strategy (as well as, to a greater or lesser extent, their co-religionists living in states that condone and support it), could be forgiven for concluding that the post-9/11 'war *on* terror' seems at times more like a Western-inspired 'war *of* terror' against Islam. It is this very ambiguity produced by Russia's 'war on terror' in Chechnya that constitutes a theme that runs throughout this book.

Interest in the Russo-Chechen conflict lies also in the peculiarly Russian and Chechen attitudes and behaviour that it has brought to light. Against a background of massive casualties on all sides, the brutality of the seizure of hostages displayed in Moscow and Beslan has been matched only by the apparent opportunism and heavy handedness of the Russian rescue attempts. When such 'terrorist spectaculars' are not grabbing the world's attentions, the daily drip of horror stories of abductions, beheadings, dungeons, extrajudicial murders and torture create a picture of a 'black hole' of lawlessness, which cannot augur well for the future prospects of either Russia or Chechnya.

At the same time, the increasing power of the *siloviki* – leading members of the ministries of law and order – under Putin, himself formerly a career KGB official and director of its successor organisation, the FSB, raises the question as to how far this has led to an enhancement of the role of 'dirty tricks' by the secret services in order to achieve desired results, and what are the consequences for human rights in Russia and Chechnya as a result?

For example, the blatant Russian manipulation of Chechen elections since 2003 embodies this approach, while recalling some of the worst aspects of Stalin's Soviet-style 'democracy' and giving grounds for some to perceive that all of Russia is fast becoming like Chechnya. One of the leading activists in the *Memorial* human rights group in Moscow – Aleksandr Cherkasov – writing on 'The War in the Caucasus and Peace in Russia',[15] takes Putin to task for overseeing in Russia a slide into lawlessness towards a totalitarian past, identifying Chechnya as the touchstone for this process.[16]

It is not difficult to agree with his particularly damning indictment of Russia's manipulation of information, when he states: 'It has to be understood that the Russian authorities give words Orwellian meanings. Counter-terrorism is a word that has come to be used to avoid recognition of political problems and as a pretext for state terror. Denial of the existence of separatism as a political aspiration supports the use of counter-terrorist terminology as cover for a war against separatists. In fact such problems are political and ought to be tackled by Russia politically'.[17] If, as Cherkasov and many commentators both in Russia and the West believe, 'Chechnya is a war against Russian democracy',[18] in upholding those principles which we hold claim to define our way of life, whose side should we be on?

Thirdly, there remains the significant question of the future in geopolitical terms of the 'post-Soviet space'. Having overtaken Saudi Arabia in oil production[19] in a world becoming increasingly dependent upon its energy supplies, will Russia employ both 'hard' and 'soft' strategies in order to force its will upon its neighbours in the 'Near Abroad'? While at the same time firmly rejecting the European template for democracy in favour of its own more authoritarian variant, Russia has served notice of its intention to remain a key player in world affairs for the foreseeable future. Moreover, by portraying itself as being on the front line of the clash between Western civilisation and Islamic fundamentalism, Russia wishes to remind its, at times seemingly, unappreciative Western allies not only of the sacrifices it has made so far, but also of its potentially central role it has to play in this confrontation in the future.

The Russo-Chechen conflict falls also into the category of what nineteenth-century Russian thinkers might have called the 'cursed' questions: Why does the bloody, tragic story of Russo-Chechen relations appear to bear out so graphically Winston Churchill's dictum that 'each time history repeats itself it does so with more catastrophic results'?[20] How is it that the Chechens and more surprisingly still, the Russians, have not drawn appropriate lessons from the three centuries of conflict between them? Why have successive Russian (and Soviet) administrations appeared determined to suppress by force this manifestly irrepressible mountain people and why do significant numbers of Chechens refuse to submit to the will of their numerically vastly superior northern neighbours?

The final question concerns the contemporary, post-9/11 world. Has the insecurity produced by the threat of terrorism (and exploited opportunistically for their own narrower interests by leaders of democratic as well as authoritarian regimes) so reordered the priorities of modern humane societies that a deaf ear and a blind eye may easily be turned to the most blatant human rights violations as long as they are perceived to be necessary in order to reduce that threat? If perceptions are to become the determining factor in winning public approval for such policies, what responsibilities then should devolve onto both the media and the broader 'values' community, not just in Russia, but throughout the international community as a whole?

This book attempts to answer these and the many related questions arising from the Russo-Chechen confrontation; a conflict that is in danger of becoming not just a byword for gratuitous violence, but also for a profoundly disturbing indifference by the civilised world to the suffering of innocent, ordinary people.

2 The roots of violence in the Russo-Chechen conflict

Identifying Galtung's Conflict Triangle

Chechnya is our collective neurosis,
our collective diagnosis.
Vladimir Putin is one of us.
      (Andrei Piontkovsky, 2003)[1]

Johan Galtung, one of the founding fathers of conflict resolution, identified the three components of this new discipline as peacekeeping, peacemaking and peacebuilding.[2] Although it is generally held that these represent three consecutive stages of conflict resolution, there is some acknowledgement that sometimes peacemaking, or even peace-enforcement, has to precede peacekeeping and that there is, of necessity, a considerable overlap between all three stages.[3] Thus, the United Nations Organisation's concept of peacemaking is directed more at cessation of hostilities,[4] whereas Jean Paul Lederach's vision of peacebuilding[5] encompasses elements of both peacemaking and conflict prevention; an attempt, perhaps, to transform the conflict triangle into a circle of resolution.[6]

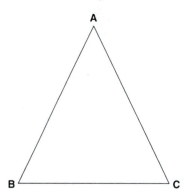

A = attitudes (structural violence) – processes – peacemaking
B = behaviour (direct violence) – events – peacekeeping
C = contradictions (cultural violence) – invariants – peacebuilding

Figure 2.1 Galtung's Conflict Triangle.[7]

As indicated in Figure 2.1, Galtung identified different forms of violence to characterise each stage: direct, structural and cultural, indicating that the first related to behaviour (events), the second to attitudes (processes) and the third to contradictions (invariants). Whereas many of the contradictions on the Russian, Chechen and both sides are manifestly not invariants (e.g. colonisation, territorial integrity, occupied homeland and underdevelopment), their persistence over time has allowed all parties concerned to regard them as permanent.

Table 2.1 provides salient examples of these categories in the context of Russo-Chechen relations:

A short description of each of these factors is given below. In attempting to identify the three most likely sources for the violence in the Russo-Chechen conflict, I have concluded that the factors listed below may be categorised as violence emanating from:

1 unresolved elements traditionally found in the Russo-Chechen relationship;
2 the absence of aspects of a 'modern civil society';
3 the post-9/11 world order, including the 'war on terror' and the post-secular discourse, as well as elements of US-led globalisation;

Table 2.1 Comprehensive list of factors illustrating the application of Galtung's Conflict Triangle to Chechnya which relate to either the Russian or Chechen side, or to both[8]

Behaviour (events) Direct violence Peacekeeping	Attitudes (processes) Structural violence Peacemaking	Contradictions (invariants) Cultural violence Peacebuilding
On the Russian side		
Chechen syndrome	Caucasophobia	Colonisation
'Disappearances'	Chauvinism	*Derzhavnost'*
Disproportionate force	Demonisation	Geopolitics
Ethnocide	Intolerance of diversity	*Gosudarstvennost'*
Indiscriminate violence	Suppression	Russian Orthodoxy
Zachistki (sweeps)	*Vertikal'* of power	Territorial integrity
On the Chechen side		
Banditry	Cultural narrative	Asymmetry
Guerrilla warfare	*Adat*	Diaspora
Intifada	'Freedom' cult	Islam
Ritual beheading	Militarised clans	'Mountain' people
Terrorism	Self-Determination	Occupied homeland
Warlordism	*Shari'a*	Survival
On both sides		
Arbitrary brutality	Clientelism	Absence of *Rechsstaat*
Extrajudicial killings	Corruption	Globalisation
Hostage-taking	Extremism	Post-secular discourse
Intimidation	Impunity	Underdevelopment
Protection rackets	'Might' over 'right'	War on Terror
Torture	Xenophobia	Weak civil society

Many of the contributory factors listed in Table 2.1 will derive from two or even all three of these categories. A fourth category, which cuts across all of the three above, might be usefully identified as violence stemming specifically from the increased significance of post-9/11 of the so-called 'Islamic factor'.

Direct violence (behaviour)

On the Russian side

Chechen syndrome[9] – This represents an acute form of post-traumatic stress disorder suffered by a significant proportion of the million-and-a-half Russian personnel[10] that have served in Chechnya and have either suffered injury or abuse themselves or witnessed and in some cases participated in gross violations of human rights. The syndrome can manifest itself in alcohol and drug abuse, psychological problems and outbursts of extremely violent behaviour upon returning home. One 'cure' appears to be signing up as a *kontraktnik* (contract soldier) and returning to the conflict in Chechnya with predictably violent outcomes for all concerned. Although analogous to the Vietnam, Afghan and Gulf War syndromes, the Chechen variant appears to stem primarily from the ambiguous and ill-defined relationship between the Russians and the Chechens (with the former killing the latter, ostensibly, in order to persuade the latter to remain Russian!), and the extraordinary lack of concern shown by the Russian authorities for the welfare of their troops (manifested elsewhere in the prevalence of *dedovshchina* – the 'hazing' or bullying of new conscripts).[11]

'Disappearances'[12] – These are a distinctive feature of the conflict in Chechnya. Poorly-paid Russian military personnel 'earn' money by abducting Chechens at checkpoints and then ransoming them, dead or alive, back to their relatives. Subsequently, these violations became closely linked to the *zachistki* (sweeps; see below). Obviously, such forms of violence against the civilian population would be far less likely to occur in a fully-functioning modern society in which the military is held accountable by civil institutions.

Disproportionate force[13] – Although this is expressly forbidden in international law by the concept of *jus in bello*,[14] it has long been a prominent feature of Russian/Soviet conflict resolution. The asymmetry built into the post-9/11 'war on terror' appears to have excused, if not sanctioned, this strategy in the struggle against insurgent terrorism allowing Russia to deflect criticism of such actions in Chechnya.

Ethnocide[15] – This relates to the attempt to suppress and eradicate a way of life or ideology. If virtually the entire population is targeted, because it embraces the norms embodied in the way of life under attack, it becomes difficult to distinguish policies of ethnocide from those of genocide. Many would argue that this has characterised Russian/Soviet treatment of the Chechens for much of the past 300 years.

Indiscriminate violence[16] – The obligation to discriminate between combatants and civilians, not to employ disproportionate force, is enshrined in international law under the concept of *jus in bello*. This, too, has long been honoured in the breach in Chechnya by successive Russian and Soviet administrations, but any international criticism has been significantly compromised by the flagrant breaches of this principle by other ostensibly democratic states in the worldwide 'war on terror'.

Zachistki[17] – 'Sweeps' or 'clean-up operations' represent another distinctive feature of the Chechen conflict. Russian troops surround a village suspected of collaborating with the Chechen fighters, meting out summary justice to anyone they come across. As such operations rarely caught any genuine Chechen fighters they became feared as a reprisal for allegedly aiding the insurgents or as yet another opportunity for federal personnel to plunder the possessions of the civilian population in Chechnya. The rise of Chechen suicide bombing between 2000 and 2004 has been expressly linked to the intensification of this form of violence.[18]

On the Chechen side

Banditry[19] – The *abrek*[20] has a long, illustrious and generally positive history in the Chechen collective memory, somewhat akin to that of such 'outcasts' as Robin Hood, highwaymen or poachers in English social history. As Richard Sakwa has written: 'Banditry has deep roots in Chechen tradition, and for many, was less a crime than a social tradition, which not only encapsulated resistance to a specific occupier but also represented resistance to the very idea of authority itself'.[21] The *abrek* has been a source of intense irritation to successive Russian and Soviet regimes which have all sought to eradicate a phenomenon considered to be a manifestation of the backwardness of traditional Chechen society.

Guerrilla warfare[22] – The mountainous terrain of much of Chechnya south of the Terek River[23] makes it an ideal territory from which to conduct a guerrilla war, a fact which the Chechens have taken advantage of repeatedly during their 300-year-old confrontation with Russians intent on conquering their land. The 'legitimacy' of guerrilla warfare as distinguished from 'terrorism' goes to the heart of the 'terrorist versus freedom fighter' debate and is just one of many features of attitudes to insurgency and self-determination that appear to have undergone a sea change since 9/11. In an open letter, dated 10 March 2003, to President George W. Bush, two of the most prominent Soviet-era dissidents ask, not altogether disingenuously, whether under the discursive terms of the current 'war on terror', George Washington would be regarded as a 'terrorist' or a 'freedom fighter'.[24]

Intifada[25] – This is the generic name given to the alternative to guerrilla warfare for the active resistance living in towns and camps controlled by the invading force. Clearly the demonstration effect of the two popular uprisings by Palestinians in settlements occupied by the Israelis may be seen to have been at work here, although such strategies under various names have historically been adopted by those resisting occupiers.

Ritual beheading[26] – This is one of the more grisly features brought to the conflict by the Chechen side and one clearly influenced by the demonstration effect of this kind of execution elsewhere in the *jihad* (e.g. Afghanistan, Iraq). This apparent reversion to pre-modern atavism serves to differentiate and polarise communities in conflict.

Terrorism[27] – Few insurgent movements have not resorted to terrorism in some form as a tactic, rather than a strategy, in their usually asymmetric struggle with the forces of *status quo*. Since 9/11, of course, the whole concept of 'terrorism' appears to have shifted exclusively to the insurgent side, the notion of far more deadly 'state' terrorism (unless referring to 'state-sponsored' terrorism) having been effectively ignored.

Warlordism[28] – This represents the classic role for local entrepreneurs of violence in states lacking a sound legal basis and strong civic society, enabling them to maintain and consolidate their power through violence. Although Afghanistan and Sudan are most often quoted as examples, this form of politically-based violence was especially evident during Chechnya's second period of de facto independence between 1996 and 1999.

On both sides

Arbitrary brutality[29] – Observers of this conflict from outside the region have been shocked at the sheer scale and intensity of the arbitrary brutality that characterises this confrontation. War correspondent Anthony Lloyd wrote of the first conflict: 'Chechnya blew the bell off the end of the gauge, and revealed an extreme of war to me that I had no conception of. Afterwards my understanding of conflict was never quite the same again. It was indeed a glimpse from the edge of hell'.[30] The prevalence of 'might' over 'right' and a widespread feeling of impunity added to the lack of a law-governed state on either side tends to make this form of violence the rule rather than the exception.

Extrajudicial killings[31] – Prevalent due to the same reasons as above. Despite rulings from the European Court of Human Rights[32] the Russians have refused to accept responsibility for such killings. For their part, the traditional blood feud of the Chechens tends to 'justify' such killings, a tradition apparently upheld to this day by Ramzan Kadyrov. In an interview during which he speaks of hunting down Basaev, Kadyrov says: 'When we find him, I want to lead that operation and kill him myself. It's our way, revenge'.[33] Writing about the Chechen 'law of vendetta', Aleksandr Solzhenitsyn wrote: 'We Europeans, at home and at school, read and pronounce only words of lofty disdain for this savage law, this cruel and senseless butchery. But the butchery is perhaps not so senseless after all. It does not sap the mountain peoples, but strengthens them.'[34] In her last article published before being shot dead in Moscow, Anna Politkovskaya had accused the pro-Kremlin Chechen forces under Ramzan Kadyrov of copying the actions of undercover Russian security forces 'death squadrons' by employing extrajudicial killing and torture as a means of eliminating, neutralising or intimidating opponents to their rule.[35]

Hostage-taking[36] – Although the Dubrovka and Beslan incidents captured the attention of the world's media, low-level hostage taking (unlawful detentions) had long been practised by both sides. For the Chechens this represented a return to pre-modern forms of behaviour – the ransoms demanded (and paid) for hostages spurring this grisly form of business. The Russians responded by systematically kidnapping Chechen civilians and ransoming them back for money, dead or alive, to their relatives. Both sides illegally held hostages in *zindans* (underground dungeons) or, in the Russian case, in 'filtration' camps (see below). Evidence that the Russian forces and their Chechen supporters are responsible for a significant proportion of these kidnappings was provided in June 2005 by Alu Alkhanov, then pro-Russian President of the Chechen Republic, who admitted that 'out of all kidnappings, those carried out by federal forces are around 5–10 per cent. This is a big drop on previous years'.[37] Moreover, the deliberate targeting, for kidnap, by Chechens loyal to the federal forces of family members of leaders of the Chechen resistance, most notably those of Aslan Maskhadov has been well-documented.[38] This so-called 'counter hostage-taking' appears to be one of the manifestations of Chechen-on-Chechen violence that has followed Putin's policy of Chechenisation.[39]

Intimidation[40] – A commonly-found phenomenon in societies lacking crucial aspects of modern society, in which 'might' (solving problems by force) virtually always takes precedence over 'right' (seeking solutions on the basis of justice). In this respect the vast majority of ordinary Chechen civilians, particularly refugees, have been caught between the 'rock' of separatist Chechen resistance and the 'hard place' of pro-Russian suppression (by both Russians and their Chechen supporters).

Protection rackets[41] – Again a familiar aspect of conflict and post-conflict situations, in which protagonists used to getting their own way by force, continue such tactics because a combination of the lack of legal or civic constraints and the absence of economic alternatives encourages them to. Usually involves the illegal trafficking of narcotics and other contraband, prostitution and illegal rent-seeking.

Torture[42] – Although categorically banned by international conventions, the Russians and Chechens are by no means the only combatants to use this form of violence widely. As with other aspects of the Russo-Chechen conflict, this appears to have been condoned post-9/11 by the coalition fighting the 'war on terror'. On the Russian side the worst places of torture were the ad hoc detention centres called 'filtration' camps, particularly the notorious Chernokozovo camp outside Grozny.[43] It is believed that Anna Politkovskaya was murdered because she was about to publish a full exposé of the involvement in torture and kidnapping of the pro-Moscow Chechen security forces under Ramzan Kadyrov.[44] Given the Byzantine nature of Kremlin (not to mention Chechen) politics, however, this by no means indicates for certain that she was murdered at Kadyrov's behest.

Summary

As has been demonstrated, there is a strong case for concluding that virtually all of the violence common to both sides stems from the absence of aspects of a 'modern' society, with only the acceptance of torture as a 'legitimate' means of warfare (despite it being banned by international conventions) and, possibly, the arbitrary nature of the brutality employed stemming from the 'consequentialist' school of the post-9/11 world order. By the same token, virtually none of the violent behaviour common to both sides, I would argue, stems from traditional bilateral cultural elements (in the broadest sense to cover political, economic and social components).

On the Russian side perhaps only the disproportionate use of force can be attributed to the post-9/11 world order, although, like the indiscriminate nature of the violence inflicted on Chechen civilians, even this could be seen to derive more from Russian tradition. Apart from the 'Chechen syndrome', all other Russian manifestations of violent behaviour listed would appear to stem from a mixture of traditional values and the absence of a law-governed state. The same could be said of the banditry, guerrilla warfare and warlordism on the Chechen side. Clearly, however, the 'Islamic factor' comes into play, albeit retrospectively in some cases, in the ritual beheading, *intifada* and terrorist tactics used by Chechen militants, the last two also being connected to the post-9/11 world order.

Overall, however, most violent behaviour in the Russo-Chechen conflict appears to stem directly from the absence of aspects of 'modern' civil society. Insofar as Russia under Putin appears to be regressing in this respect, much of the violence must be put down to his failure, perhaps even unwillingness, to create a modern, law-based society in Russia. Insofar as his handpicked leader in Chechnya, Ramzan Kadyrov, seems to embody most of the attributes of an 'entrepreneur of violence' (see Chapter 7), unfortunately, there appears little prospect of the policy of 'Chechenisation' (see Chapter 5) leading to the kind of society in Chechnya in which such violent behaviour becomes the exception rather than the norm.

Structural violence (attitudes)

It should be stressed here that although modern psychology offers little evidence to support the proposition that attitudes themselves determine behaviour, there is no doubt that the former can condone, justify and incite the latter. More importantly, these attitudes can be exploited, consolidated and exaggerated by 'entrepreneurs of violence' in order to provoke and sustain violent behaviour, not only among those on their side but also on that of their opponents.

On the Russian side

Caucasophobia[45] – A quintessentially Russian form of racism aimed at all peoples of Caucasian origin, whom the Russians label as 'blacks' (*cherniye*) or 'black-arses' (*chernozhopy*). Due partly to the prominence of Caucasians in the 'black' and 'grey' markets, there exists a strong tendency for Russians to perceive these 'incomers' as 'thieves', 'bandits' and mafiosi. Fully 42 per cent of Russians polled in August 2006, were for restricting the activities in Russia for peoples originally from the Caucasus.[46]

Chauvinism[47] – Embodies the concept of 'Russia for the Russians', which gained currency after the collapse of the Soviet Union. Although Chechens and other nationalities in the North Caucasus are nominally citizens of the Russian Federation, inevitably there is a widespread perception among non-Russian peoples of their second-class status. This also represents the distinctive concept of Russian nationalism; as two contemporary Russian commentators put it: 'Russian nationalism, it has been pointed out, unlike other nationalisms in the world does not have a "modernising" element and, therefore, any reformist programme will be perceived in Russia as "anti-Russian" and "anti-national"'.[48]

Demonisation (the 'politics of naming')[49] – The application of propagandistic elements of information warfare since the end of the Cold War has seen a rise of this long-recognised form of structural violence, although it has seemingly been a feature of Russian attitudes towards the Chechens from the very beginning of this confrontation. This aspect of the conflict is examined in some detail in Chapter 4.

Intolerance of diversity[50] – A peculiarly Russian (and Soviet) phenomenon which tends to justify such manifestations of direct violence as persecution of political religious or cultural dissidents, minorities and even entire peoples. The perceived 'goal' of uniformity, in order to preserve the integrity and power of the Russian state, tends to justify any means being employed to achieve this. The rise of the influence of the *siloviki* under Putin appears to have reinforced this trend.

Suppression[51] – Again, this represents a distinctively Russian strategy for dealing with opposition, there being little tradition or experience throughout the long history of Russia's relationship with the Chechens of employing alternative, non-violent means for resolving conflicts. Clearly, this strategy has not just been employed against the Chechens (one thinks of the fate of the Cossacks, for example, under Russian imperial and Soviet power, epitomised by Khrushchev's use of tanks to resolve what essentially was an industrial dispute in the Cossack 'capital' of Novocherkassk in southern Russia in 1962).

Vertikal' of power[52] – Seemingly the preferred form of administration of both the Russian authorities and the Russian public in which virtually all power is invested in a single line of authority in the executive branch. This form of administration is justified by the priorities of maintaining Russia's great power status and its territorial integrity at any cost, but is hardly an appropriate policy for an avowedly federal state.

On the Chechen side

Cultural narrative[53] – The collective 'folk' memory of a people, commemorating its victories, tragedies, heroes and villains. Particularly strong historically among people struggling to regain a separate identity or territory (e.g. Jews, Palestinians, Poles) and/or those engaged in a long, asymmetric struggle against more powerful neighbours (Baltic peoples, Basques, Irish). Usually disregarded or underestimated by the oppressing side, as has clearly been the case in Chechnya.

Adat[54] – The code of traditional rules and laws by which many of the North Caucasian peoples live. It includes the blood feud, reverence for one's ancestors and a strict code of honour (*nokhchallah*).[55] The practice of *adat* is not always fully consistent with the fundamentalist interpretation of *Shari'a* introduced to Chechnya and supported by the *Wahhabites*, giving rise at times to conflict between both sets of adherents.

'Freedom' cult[56] – This is a central but underestimated (by the Russians) aspect of Chechen self-identity that resists the imposition of alien rule. As important to the Chechens as is, for example, the right to roam freely is to the Roma. The French philosopher, André Glucksmann, has written in this context: 'Beauty is the beauty of freedom. That is what people delight in with the Caucasus, that is what becomes a torture in all the Chechen wars. Chechnya is an example of freedom, of dignity and an example for the whole Russian population.'[57]

Militarised clans (teips[58]) – These were the principle form of organisation along blood and territorial lines in traditional Chechen society prior to the deportation of 1944, when *tariqats* and *wirds* came into their own. Since the return of Chechens to their homeland in the 1950s, *teips*, however, have formed the basis of many Chechen criminal gangs and formed the basis of the military resistance to the Russians in the first war (1994–1996). The clans have increasingly been overtaken in significance in recent years by the *djamaat* – a religion-based organisation uniting the fighters of neighbouring villages.[59]

Self-determination[60] – From the nineteenth century, this European concept has manifested itself as an alternative nationalist expression of the 'freedom' cult. Although the Chechens would appear to fulfil most of the criteria for international recognition of their independence, their claim has been greeted with as little enthusiasm as that of the Kurds, Kosovars and Tibetans. Some critics have argued that the very idea of a Chechen nation state is counter-productive. For example, Arjun Appadurai claims that, for peoples like the Chechens, this inability 'to think their way out of the imagery of the nation-state is itself the cause of much global violence because many movements of emancipation and identity are forced, in their struggles against existing nation states, to embrace the very imagery they seek to escape.'[61] Others, such as the Russian political observer, Sergei Markedonov, have argued that it was Stalin's deportation of the entire Chechen people that created the brand of Chechen nationalism that has the strength to demand self-determination.[62]

Shari'a[63] – The pronounced shift in Chechen society from a set of rules based on tradition and custom *adat* to the adoption, as an alternative to the Russian legal system, a stricter interpretation of *Shari'a* law, coinciding with the popularisation of the notion of the 'clash of civilisations' and followed by the post-9/11 new world order has had a pronounced effect on the sympathy and support lent to the Chechen cause both by the Muslim world, on the one hand, and the wider international community, on the other.

On both sides

Clientelism[64] – The favoured alternative to contract-based political, economic and social relationships in states lacking developed market economies, pluralistic political systems and a strong civic society. This form of relationship would appear to lend itself equally to both the 'warlordism' of the Chechens and the *vertikal'* of power of the Russians. Dmitry Kozak, Putin's *polpred* in the Southern Federal District (which includes Chechnya) has branded the leaders of the North Caucasus republics as 'venal and compromised' and characterised their power as based on 'corporate extended family groupings'.[65]

Corruption – This represents one of the most serious obstacles obstructing both Russia's and Chechnya's progress towards a law-based society. Rampant at all levels from soldiers and *boyeviki* at checkpoints to ministers, oligarchs and warlords. In Transparency International's Corruption Perceptions Index for 2005, Russia shared a lowly 126th place in the world, along with Albania, Niger and Sierra Leone;[66] in the Freedom House ratings for 2005 the level of corruption in Russia remained high at 5.75 on a scale of 1 (lowest) to 7 (highest).[67] Sergei Markedonov characterises the Russian state as thinking in 'money-grubbingly short-termist' (*rvacheski siyuminutniye*) categories.'[68]

Extremism[69] – The tolerance of extremist views, both at the popular and state level, appears more in line with traditional Balkan, rather than contemporary European, norms. This mindset tends to project complex issues in stark black-and-white terms, leading to polarisation and justifying an upward spiral of atrocities. Like so many features of the Russo-Chechen conflict, this factor has been profoundly influenced by the post-secular discourse after 9/11.

Impunity[70] – Respectable international human rights organisations have consistently catalogued gross violations of international law by all sides in the Russo-Chechen conflict. For example, according to a *Memorial* report of June 2003 of the 177 criminal investigations launched against Russian servicemen by the Russian Military Prosecutor's Office from September 1999 to June 2003, only nine went to trial.[71] The impunity with which the 'entrepreneurs of violence' on all sides operate ensures that it is the exception rather than the rule when somebody is held to account for their 'war crimes'. The attempt by PACE to institute a Chechen war crimes tribunal (to address war crimes committed by both sides) in April 2003 met with insufficient sympathy or support among Council of Europe member states.[72]

'Might' over 'right'[73] – Societies in which 'might' operates to the virtual exclusion of 'right' may be categorised as authoritarian or even totalitarian, the very opposite of democratic governance. By the same token, within such societies, those sections of the population relying for their security on 'right' to counter 'might' tend to be perceived as impotent. Both Russian and Chechen societies currently would appear to fit this pattern.

Xenophobia[74] – Distrust of outsiders tends to be a traditional feature of both Russian and North Caucasian societies, although both have also a long tradition of hospitality towards trusted guests. Given the prominence in the current Russian administration of *siloviki* – particularly those, like the Russian president, with a background in the intelligence agencies – this factor has become much more pronounced since Putin's accession to power in 1999.

Summary

As with 'behaviour', the explanation for the attitudes common to both sides differ considerably to those held by the Russians, on the one hand, and the Chechens, on the other. Clearly, the rampant clientelism and corruption stem from the absence of a modern law-governed state with a fully-functioning market economy, as to some extent, does the impotence of 'right' over 'might' throughout Russian society.

However, the post-9/11 world order appears to have sanctioned, to some extent, the triumph of 'might' over 'right' as long as the ends can be perceived to justify the means. Thus, since the launch of the 'war on terror' in virtually every society, basic human rights have had to be curtailed in the face of the perceived intensity and credibility of the new threat. Elements of xenophobia and extremism may also be seen to emanate from this new world order, although both have been a traditional feature in Russian and Chechen society.

On the Russian side the new world order might be held to be partly responsible for the perceived need both to suppress and demonise opponents, although both have a long tradition in Russia's relationship with its minority cultures. The *vertikal'* of power, Caucasophobia, chauvinism and intolerance of diversity, although all with deep roots in the Russian tradition, might be seen as leftovers from an earlier age that would be likely to disappear were Russia to embark more wholeheartedly on the path of democracy.

On the Chechen side, matters are complicated by the perceived radicalisation of the 'Islamic factor' post-9/11. Thus, certain features of *adat*, *Shari'a* and the Chechen cultural narrative might be held to indicate the absence of aspects of a modern society, as, undoubtedly, could be the persistence of militarised clans. However, all of these features derive also from Chechen cultural traditions, as do the freedom cult and, in part, the striving for self-determination. The last-mentioned, along with the more militant aspects of *Shari'a*, have been overtaken to some extent by the new world order, which, post-9/11, appears to give precedence to territorial integrity over self-determination and tends to oppose militant manifestations of *Shari'a* law.

Thus, one could conclude, the structural violence embedded in the attitudes of each side stems largely from unresolved cultural contradictions, whereas the structural violence and attitudes shared by both tends to emanate from the new world order and the absence of aspects of modern society.

Cultural violence (contradictions)

While it should be stressed that contradictions occur in any relationship, be it between two persons or two (or more) nations, the overwhelming majority of such contradictions may be resolved without recourse to violence through such tried and tested conflict resolution mechanisms as negotiations and compromise. Only when one side attempts to coerce the other by force does violence tend to occur. What is notable in the centuries-long Russo-Chechen confrontation is how few times genuine negotiations and compromises have been employed and how quick and frequent has been the resort to coercion and, consequently, violence.

On the Russian side

Colonisation[75] – This factor has long been recognised as giving rise to such forms of structural violence as *apartheid*, racism and slavery and is generally held to be inimical to a healthy, functioning democracy. The stubborn refusal of Russia to acknowledge the colonial conquest of the Northern Caucasus in the nineteenth century has left a major cultural contradiction unresolved between the Russian and Chechen peoples. Vassily Klyuchevsky, the great nineteenth-century Russian historian wrote that: 'Russia's entire history was a history of colonizing new lands'.[76] The essence of the problem is that, alone of all the great European empires, Russia has never come to terms with decolonisation. As Aleksei Malashenko, of Moscow's Carnegie Centre pointed out, as long ago as June 2000,[77] Russia's interest in Chechnya is logical only if Russia continues to regard itself as an empire.

Derzhavnost'[78] – This relates to the quintessentially Russian concept that maintains that Russia is, and must remain a great power (*derzhava*). Much stronger under the Putin administration than under that of Yeltsin, the conflict in Chechnya appears to have become the touchstone for the success of this, in some respects, retrograde ideology and permits his use of such absolutist discourse as 'victory at all costs'. The importance of this concept to the current administration's view of Russia is best summed up, perhaps, by President Putin's remark on 4 September, 2004 (the day after the resolution of the Beslan hostage-taking crisis), when he declared: 'We showed ourselves to be weak and the weak get beaten.'[79]

Geopolitics[80] – The geostrategic location of Russia on the Eurasian land mass to the immediate north of the 'arc of Islamic fundamentalism', together with the vast energy resources at its disposal in an increasingly energy-dependent world, means that national and bloc 'interests' will tend to take cognisance of Russia's potential importance at the expense of holding it to account for its idiosyncratic understanding, in practice, of 'values', which are very likely, on occasions, to create cultural contradictions between Russia and the Western world.

Gosudarstvennost'[81] – This is another time-honoured Russian concept (dating, perhaps, from the rise of Muscovy, which in turn inherited the concept from the 'Golden Horde') that holds that only a strong, centralised state (*gosudarstvo*) can keep the vast territory of Russia together. This ideology tends to justify both the *vertikal'* of power and the suppression of any non-conformist ideas, characteristics of successive Russian and Soviet regimes which appear to be making a strong come-back under Putin. The US journalist and seasoned observer of the Russian scene, David Remnick, wrote of the Russian president in October 2003: 'Putin is, first and foremost, a *gosudarstvennik* – a "statist" – who values the growth and stability of Russia before all else.'[82] The Russian political commentator Pavel Felgenhauer has used the same term in describing Putin.[83]

Russian orthodoxy[84] – Not the religion per se, despite its revival under both Yeltsin and Putin, so much as the Russocentric view of the world that gives rise to such phenomena as an intolerance of diversity, the belief that the ends justify the means and the conviction that Russia's cause is just, whatever the outside world thinks of it. The religious component of this phenomenon was replaced temporarily during the Soviet period by essentially Russian interpretations of Marxism-Leninism.

Territorial integrity[85] – Closely linked to the concepts of *derzhavnost'* and *gosudarstvennost'*, the very future of the Russian state is held to depend upon maintaining at all costs the present borders (and, where possible, clawing back adjoining former Soviet territories). This leads to the bizarre contradiction by which the Russians refuse international intervention in its 'domestic' conflict with Chechnya, while simultaneously interfering quite openly in the internal affairs of such neighbours as Georgia and Moldova. After Beslan, Russian Foreign Minister, Sergei Lavrov, speaking to the UN General Assembly on 23 September 2004, reaffirmed: 'We will not let anybody encroach on the sovereignty of our state.'[86] It is worth noting here that, although this concept is not compatible with 'secession' it could accommodate such notions as 'self-determination' and 'autonomy'.[87]

On the Chechen side

Asymmetry[88] – Since the collapse of the USSR and in anticipation of the rise of China, the USA has reigned supreme as the world's only remaining superpower. This has meant that all conflicts involving the United States have by definition been asymmetrical. By extension, all wars between state powers and insurgent opponents (including that between Russia and Chechnya) have tended to be asymmetrical. As Yasser Arafat might have put it: 'They, having an air force, bomb us from above; we, lacking such a force, bomb them from below.' The absence of any attempt to equate 'state' terrorism with 'insurgent' terrorism is one of the defining features of the post-secular discourse and allows the Russians to present all forms of violent Chechen resistance as 'terrorism', while excusing all of their own violent actions as a necessary component of the 'war on terror'.

Diaspora[89] – A contributory factor often underestimated by the Russians and involving not only those Chechens exiled to Turkey and the Middle East in the great *mukhadzhirstvo* (expulsion) in the nineteenth century, but also those within the former Soviet Union and, subsequently, throughout the Western world, who have left Chechnya to seek alternative lives. All, to a greater or lesser extent, carry with them the Chechen cultural narrative (parallels here may be drawn with the Armenian, Irish or Jewish diasporas). Unfortunately, Chechen control of aspects of the 'grey' and 'black' economies in post-Soviet Russia have led the Chechen diaspora in Russia to be stereotyped as mafiosi, rather than as offering legitimate modern role models to young Chechens that might compete with the violent alternatives offered by the field commanders and warlords.

Islam[90] – Both the *Sufi*[91] and *Wahhabi* (Salafist)[92] variants of Islam might be perceived as attempts by the Chechens to maintain their religion in a hostile environment; the former, arguably, providing better protection from the ubiquitous intrusiveness of the Soviet regime and the latter from the scale of outright violence of successive post-communist Russian administrations. Certain Russian commentators have identified Islam as the 'New Marxism', filling the ideological void for peoples from a Muslim cultural background left by the collapse of the Soviet Union.[93]

'Mountain' people[94] – Despite the relative success of the Chechen diaspora in adapting to life in modern societies and the positive aspects of Russian/Soviet colonial rule in terms of education, health and access to the world outside, the Chechens remain closely committed to their distinctive way of life as indigenous 'mountain' people. The UN Commission for Human Rights Draft Declaration on 'The Human Rights of Indigenous Peoples' states in Article 31, that: 'Indigenous peoples, as a specific form of exercising their right to self-determination, have the right to autonomy or self-government in matters relating to their internal and local affairs, including culture, religion, education, information, media, health, housing, employment, social welfare, economic activities, land and resources management, environment and entry by non-members, as well as ways and means for financing these autonomous functions.' The Declaration has yet to be adopted by the UN General Assembly.[95] Far from being afforded the right to be different within their own territory as has happened, for example, to Inuit peoples in Canada and Lapps in Finland, the Russian message to the Chechens through the centuries has effectively remained 'change or perish'.

Occupied homeland[96] – One of the many paradoxes of the post-9/11 world order is that the very countries who, due to their own historical experiences, one would reasonably expect to be most sensitive to the concept of an 'occupied homeland', namely the USA, Israel and Russia, appear stubbornly to reject the possibility that their current opponents (the Afghans/Iraqis, the Palestinians and the Chechens, respectively) might share such feelings every bit as strongly, if not even more keenly. As noted above, Chechnya has not only from time immemorial been the homeland of the Chechens, but also it remains alien territory to the Russians sent to fight there.

Survival[97] – Much of the ferocity and intensity of the Chechen resistance may be attributed to the fact that for most Chechens the conflict with Russia is perceived as a struggle for survival not just in the physical sense, but also as regards their distinctive way of life. On the day-to-day individual level this translates into behaviour such as that described by Anna Politkovskaya: 'But the main concern for everyone – absolutely everyone, without exception – remained refining the art of survival in the midst of organised mass repressions'.[98] On the level of the Chechen people as a whole, given the record of their treatment by the Russians, such a belief lends credence to such absolutist Chechen slogans as 'Freedom or death',[99] which, in turn, is used to 'justify' such extreme forms of terrorism as suicide bombing and suicidal acts of hostage-taking. One eminent Chechen academic has suggested that: 'The Chechens are a unique people and we should be entered into the Red Book' [of endangered species JR].[100]

On both sides

Absence of Rechsstaat (law-governed society)[101] – The apparent deliberate failure of the Putin administration to complete Russia's anticipated transition to a law-governed state accounts for many of the contradictions that remain unresolved between the Russian Federation and the rest of the developed world. Whereas Russian and Western 'interests' might coincide, 'values', at least until the onset of the war on terror, rarely did. This gives an element of credibility to the arguments of critics in the West whose Russophobia has outlasted the collapse of the USSR. Andreas Gross, the rapporteur on Chechnya to the Parliamentary Assembly of the Council of Europe (PACE) reported in September 2004 (in the wake of the Beslan hostage taking, which he resolutely condemned) that: 'The absence of the rule of law in Chechnya prevents the development of a humane and democratic society.'[102]

Globalisation[103] – This US-driven template for the twenty-first century has produced its discontents, both within Western societies and in the world at large. Based on a materialistic, consumer-driven view of the world and presented as the only way forward for 'democratic' societies, it has mobilised the opposition of those who do not or cannot share either the vision or the benefits promised. Perceived by its critics to be based on 'greed' and not 'need', it tends to benefit the 'haves' to the detriment of the 'have-nots', with predictable consequences. Since 9/11, this has become increasingly entwined with the war on terror.

Post-secular discourse[104] – This represents the considerable shift since 9/11 away from universal 'values' towards specific 'interests', expressed in the new terminology of the 'war on terror' and the 'clash of civilisations'. In the Internet age, information warfare in the form of propaganda and demonisation has assumed a role in conflict that is second only to the military element. That this shift has worked to the benefit of Russia and to the detriment of the Chechen separatists is illustrated by the Chechen journalist, Timur Aliev's comment: 'In fact, the term "rationality" is not very instrumental in understanding processes governing Russian society. Unlike Europe, our state lives by interests, not values'.[105]

Underdevelopment[106] – Can apply to the political system and society in general, but is understood here as relating to the economy. Mature societies, which operate within the rule of law, tend to rely on a smoothly-functioning market economy, largely meritocratic and devoid of clientelism and corruption. Societies that have not yet reached this level inevitably tend to rely upon 'might' rather than 'right' in settling unresolved contradictions. This would certainly appear to be endemic throughout all levels of officialdom in Russia and Chechnya (both on the pro- and anti-Russian sides).

War on terror – The fact that this strategic concept of dubious military value has gained currency and legitimacy since 9/11 serves as an example of the power of post-secular discourse. Sir Michael Howard was among the first to point out the folly of declaring a 'war' on terrorism, concluding that: 'I can think of no policy more likely, not only to indefinitely prolong the war, but to ensure that we can never win it'.[107] This point is also made by Grenville Byford who writes 'Wars have typically been fought against proper nouns (Germany, say) for the good reason that proper nouns can surrender and promise not to do it again. Wars against common nouns (poverty, crime, drugs) have been less successful. Such opponents never give up. The war on terrorism, unfortunately, falls in to the second category'.[108] That 'state' terrorism is excluded from any definition of this concept means that those on the receiving end of the 'war *of* terror' being waged against insurgent peoples can rely on neither justice nor support from those waging that war. Russia is not alone in using this as a cover with which to breach with impunity international conventions governing *jus in bello*.

Weak civil society[109] – One of the dilemmas for what might be termed the 'values' community worldwide is that they currently represent the views of just a small minority of both Chechen and Russian people. For example, in August 2006, only 1 per cent of Russians polled were convinced that they influenced political and economic life in Russia, whereas 56 per cent were adamant that they exercised no such influence.[110] The dilemma thus arises as to whether one should stick to one's principles and adopt a deontological approach to conflicts such as that between Russia and Chechnya or should one be a hard-nosed realist and admit that neither the time nor the place is right for such well-meaning liberal interventions? The problem facing advocates of a strong civil society in transitional states is that only the state tends to be in a position to legislate for a civic society (as Putin has with his Civic Forum)[111] whereas in a fully-functioning democracy political, economic and social institutions tend to reflect the freely-expressed will of its citizens. For those Russians and Chechens that share our belief that a strong civil society should be a necessary component of a modern democratic state, these are tough, even dangerous, times indeed.

Summary

Virtually all of the contradictions on both the Russian and Chechen sides represent unresolved contradictions that are cultural in the broadest sense (i.e. to include political, economic and social factors). Arguably, on the Russian side, such features as *derzhavnost'* and *gosurdarstvennost'* are as much outdated in terms of the modern world as is colonisation. The aforementioned post-9/11 preference for territorial integrity over self-determination undoubtedly has strengthened Russia's hand in this respect as, thanks to the enormous energy resources at Russia's disposal, has the element of geopolitics and the concomitant shift in international relations from 'values' to 'interests'.

On the Chechen side, any self-identification as a 'mountain' people clearly implies aspects of a pre-modern society that might be accommodated in a state more enlightened in such matters than currently is Russia. As Harsha Ram points out in characterising the cultural clash between the Russian state and the Chechen highlanders in the nineteenth century:

> By refusing assimilation into the territorial boundaries and rationalizing power of the Russian state, the Chechens were thus said to cling to a natural condition where liberty is indistinguishable from anarchy, and the freedom fighter from the criminal.[112]

Although both anarchy and crime clearly flourish in Chechnya to this day, it is the Russian failure to recognise, in this confrontation, any elements of 'liberty' or 'freedom fighting' that undoubtedly has exacerbated and prolonged the overall conflict.

The adherence to Islam manifestly has had a significant impact since 9/11 upon the way the Chechens and their struggle with Russia have been perceived by the outside world. The same could be said of such core features of the post-9/11 world order as globalisation, the post-secular discourse and, most prominently, the 'war on terror' – Russia, somewhat fortuitously, finding itself on the 'right' and the 'separatist' Chechens, sometimes to their bewilderment and frustration, on the 'wrong' side.

However, on the basis of the evidence produced here, I would argue strongly that it is the lack of any tradition in either Russian or Chechen society of a law-governed state, a developed economy and a strong, independent civil society that allows entrepreneurs of violence on all sides, within the parameters set currently by the new world order – characterised by globalisation, the post-secular discourse and the war on terror – to exploit cultural contradictions that manifestly could be overcome without violence.

Conclusion

Taking into account all the factors discussed above, it might seem incredible to any interested outside observer that the Russo-Chechen conflict is routinely presented both in Russia and the outside world as one that is, first and foremost, part of the global contemporary clash between the 'civilised us' and the 'uncivilised them', all too often shorthand for the clash of civilisations between what are often carelessly and less than accurately referred to as 'Western secularism' and 'Islamic fundamentalism'.

By totally ignoring unresolved cultural contradictions stemming largely from the imposition by force of Russian colonial rule on the Chechens a century and a half ago, first the Yeltsin, and now the Putin administration have ensured that at best a temporary lid is forced onto the cauldron containing these very real contradictions, which will continue to boil away inside until the pressure becomes unstoppable. Moreover, it is difficult not to agree with Lilia Shevtsova, of Moscow's Carnegie Centre, who concludes that 'contradictions between Russia and the West will grow in proportion to Moscow's efforts to restore its great-power status'.[113]

As indicated, most of these cultural contradictions could be resolved through negotiations and compromise. That they are not is due not only to the influence on all sides of the entrepreneurs of violence, who maintain and stoke up the attitudes that condone such violent behaviour, but also by the self-interested policies emanating from the new world order, particularly since 9/11. Many of these attitudes are specifically proscribed by international conventions and agreements which all signatories are meant to abide by. That such undertakings are routinely ignored by leaders of most of the member states that have signed up to them makes them, at least on the moral plane, every bit as culpable in the continuation of the tragedy in Chechnya as are the leaders of the Russian Federation.

For virtually all of the violent behaviour exhibited by both sides can be justified within the terms of this new world order, be it the 'no negotiations with terrorists' mantra issuing from the Kremlin on the Russian side or 'Shari'a is the only law that true Muslims need obey' from the militants on the Chechen side – both equally as intolerant of compromise and negotiations as the other.

The vast range of opinion in Russia and Chechnya between these absolutist positions effectively is being ignored, whereas it is patently obvious that this is where a resolution satisfactory to all but the extremists on either side is to be found.

Since its introduction in 2000 Putin's policy of Chechenisation has generated an additional set of cultural contradictions between those Chechens that accept the inevitability of the asymmetric relationship with Russia and those that insist on some form of autonomy for Chechnya. Although this has led to the introduction of, specifically, Chechen forms of violence on both sides of the confrontation, they can be understood only within the overall context of the Russo-Chechen confrontation.

Thus, the fact that the pro-Russian Chechen forces under Ramzan Kadyrov and Sulim Yamadaev continue to terrorise the Chechen population with intensified sweeps of their own, extrajudicial killings, torture and intimidation and kidnapping relatives of known opponents,[114] would appear to argue against Galtung's theory of structural violence – for clearly these Chechens are not imbued with the same Caucasophobia that afflicts their ethnic Russian allies (many of whom, indeed, continue to look down on them).[115]

However, insofar as these Chechens shared with their Russian allies an arrogance of power, greed to use that power to enrich themselves, a carte blanche of means to achieve their ends with effective impunity, and yet, a fear of violent retribution from the 'irreconcilables', they could be seen to be reacting to the asymmetry in Russo-Chechen relations, pragmatically, by working on the side, and adopting some of the values and attitudes, of those whom they consider the more powerful against those (a significant proportion of the Chechen people) that they claim to represent.

What we are left with is a paradoxical situation. For Chechenisation in the short term appears a means, in theory at least, for both sides to achieve their strategic goals: Russia maintaining its territorial integrity and Chechnya running its own affairs. However, this arrangement is likely in the medium to long term to further complicate the already challenging search for resolution of the contradictions between the two peoples. Moreover, more recently there has appeared disturbing evidence of a further blurring of traditional cultural contradictions between the Russians and the Chechens in the other direction, as ethnic Russians disillussioned with life under successive post-Soviet regimes, have taken up the Islamic cause.[116]

So, in the absence of any meaningful involvement by the international community other than helping to pick up the pieces of Chechnya's shattered economy, environment and civil infrastructure, the prospects for the immediate future look grim for 'Europe's darkest corner'.[117]

Behaviour will continue to be determined by those exercising power in their narrow private interests, attitudes will continue to sow seeds of enmity between the two sides and the cultural contradictions from which they derive will continue to remain unaddressed. A perfect recipe, one might conclude, for the indefinite continuation of the Russo-Chechen conflict.

3   A tragic history

Unresolved contradictions in the
Russo-Chechen relationship

From my personal experience as Foreign Minister of Chechnya – in which capacity my main duty is to explain to outsiders the nature of the Chechen conflict – I
would say that the biggest obstacle to being understood is ignorance of the
history of the conflict.

(Ilyas Akhmadov, 2006)[1]

On 22 April 1395, when Tamerlane finally defeated Tokhtamish, the leader of
the Golden Horde, by the River Terek, near to the site of the present-day capital
of Chechnya, Grozny, the 'Scourge of God' and 'Sword of Islam' might have
smiled to think that, exactly 600 years later, this insignificant and remote outpost
of his fabulously wealthy Eurasian empire would still be savagely fought over in
the form of asymmetrical warfare quite alien to him.[2] That Amir Temur (as he is
called in contemporary Uzbekistan) 'whose name had been alternately suppressed and vilified for seven decades by the Soviets',[3] should become a national
hero as soon as the Uzbeks had thrown off their 'colonial yoke' with the collapse of the USSR in 1991, should have sent a warning signal to any Russian
leader seeking to maintain, by force, any part of the former Empire. However,
the fact that this and the many similar signals provided by the long history of
Russian military expansion went unheeded goes a long way towards explaining
why post-Communist Russia stumbled so clumsily into renewing the violent
conflict in Chechnya and is finding it so difficult to develop an acceptable exit
strategy.

Ironically, these signals have been picked up by concerned individuals from
Russia's human rights community who appear to understand the need to learn
the lessons that the history of the Russo-Chechen confrontation has to offer. In a
characteristically sober manner, Aleksandr Cherkasov from Moscow's *Memorial* organisation pleads that the lessons of history be heeded in the conflict in
Chechnya: 'History cannot be altered. But we can try to understand it and learn
from it.'[4] For those seeking a peaceful resolution of this conflict, one of the frus-
trating mysteries of the entire Russo-Chechen confrontation is just why so few
military and political leaders have managed to grasp this simple truth.

For, as I hope to demonstrate in this chapter, it should be manifestly obvious to anyone who cares to acquaint themselves with its history that the confrontation between the Chechens and the Russians is both complex and multi-faceted. It contains elements not only of a cultural conflict between an imperial ideology and a mountain people fighting for survival, and a classic asymmetric struggle between a colonial power and an occupied people seeking self-determination, but also represents a 'black hole' of lawlessness in which 'might' rules over 'right'.

One cannot but concede, nonetheless, that the conflict has also become just one of the many settings in which the struggle for the 'new world order' is being fought. However, it is disingenuous in the extreme to allow, first the Yeltsin, and then the Putin administration to reduce such a complex conflict into a simple fight to the finish between a 'civilised' power (representing 'us') and 'terrorists' (representing 'them').[5] That they have been allowed so to do also helps to explain why successive Russian administrations have tended always to seek in Chechnya a military rather than a political solution.

Historically, the Russians have consistently portrayed their relationship with the Chechens as a force for good, from its so-called *mission civilatrice* in the nineteenth century to the equally euphemistic 'counter-terrorist operation' in the twenty-first century. Yet, running through the history of Russo-Chechen relations like a red thread is the opposing concept of the Russians being the perpetrators, indeed oft-times, instigators of violence, and not just, as they would have us believe, the victims of violence and terror from the savage and warlike Chechens.

Thus, from the very beginning of Russia's attempts to conquer the mountain tribes we learn that, as early as the 1780s, the Russian commander in the Caucasus – Lt-Gen. Pavel Potemkin – concluded that the only way to subdue the Chechens was to exterminate them completely![6] Prior to the first Russian incursion in the eighteenth century, the Chechens had already won a fearsome reputation for being the most skilled and daring raiders, sweeping down from the mountains to steal livestock, hostages, women and slaves. It was at the request of the Georgians in 1805 that Imperial Russia set out to finally suppress the Chechens. In this respect, the Chechen case resembles that of the Native American Indians, as the language employed in the first tentative attempts by Russia to bring the Chechens under their control tends to indicate.

For example, in 1806, in the first agreement of this campaign to be signed by Chechen elders with Russian General Khudovich, setting out the terms upon which the Chechen people might become subjects of the Russian Empire, one clause states: 'Finally, if the Chechens do not refrain from carrying out raids, they must expect to be completely exterminated and destroyed.'[7]

Such attitudes led inexorably to the events of 27 September 1819, when the Russian General Sysoev ordered his troops to massacre all men, women and children in the Chechen village of Dadi Yurt,[8] a tragedy seared into the cultural memory of the Chechens as firmly as the Stalinist atrocity at Khaybakh during the 1944 deportations, but barely remembered, if it all, in Russian history books.[9] Of course, such selective forgetfulness is by no means the preserve of

Russians alone, as the victims of comparable atrocities such as those at Deir
Yassin and Wounded Knee would testify.[10]

That General Sysoev and his men were merely following the orders of their
commander, Aleksei Yermolov,[11] is evident in the 'Proconsul' of the Caucasus's
assertion that: 'I desire that the terror of my name should guard our frontiers
more potently than chains or fortresses, that my word should be for the natives a
law more inevitable than death.'[12]

Yermolov's view of the Chechens was particularly dismissive, they being, in
his opinion, the 'basest of the bandits who attack the (Caucasian) Line ...
Chechnya might rightly be called the nest of all the bandits'.[13] In 1818, he wrote
to Tsar Aleksandr I warning that 'he would find no peace while a single
Chechen remained alive'.[14]

One should not forget, of course, that Yermolov was a man of his time and
that his views would not have differed greatly from many of the empire-builders
and frontier fighters of the early nineteenth century. However, by the standards
of modern discourse, the Proconsul's imperial arrogance does stand out for its
rigid absolutism, best summed up, perhaps, in his statement that:

There has been no precedent yet of someone being able to force a Chechen
to fight his co-tribesmen; but the first step towards this has already been
taken and it has been impressed upon them that this will always be
demanded of them.[15]

What would the Proconsul have made of Akhmad and Ramzan Kadyrov, the
Chechens who almost 200 years later would finally put into practice his strata-
gem?[16]

One cannot help but read histories of Russia's initial conquest of Chechnya
and subsequent attempts by successive Russian and Soviet administrations to
suppress its irrepressible inhabitants without marvelling at the crude and repetitive nature of the mistakes made, of which the following represent merely the
most striking:

1 Underestimating the fighting capacity of the Chechens.
   The first military defeat suffered by Peter the Great's Russian troops at the
   hands of the Chechens near Enderi in 1722,[17] appears to bear all the hallmarks of the same underestimation of the capacity of the Chechens to fight
   that the Russian political scientist and regional specialist Emil Pain noted
   272 years later in 1994, just prior to the outbreak of the first war. When he
   was asked during an interview about the Russian Army generals' level of
   anticipation of the likely consequences of military intervention at the commencement of the first Chechen War, Pain replied:

   When I was a member of the Experts Council and the Presidential
   Council, I sometimes met with those people who were in charge of the
   campaign, including (army generals), and when I was asking them that

question it was absolutely clear that they didn't have any real plan, that they had not even taken into account such an obvious thing as the possibility of a fierce and massive armed resistance.[18]

2   The over reliance of force at the expense of political means.

This is best exemplified by Prince Chernyshev, the Russian Minister of War's observation in the wake of the stunning reversal suffered in Chechnya by Russian troops under General Grabbe in June 1842, that: 'The system of our activity, being based exclusively on the use of the force of arms, has left political means completely untried.'[19] Over 150 years later, after the Russian defeat in the first war, Russian human rights activist, Sergei Kovalev, and Moscow-based Chechen businessman Malik Saidullaev were complaining of exactly the same thing.[20] As Saidullaev has concluded: 'Unfortunately, the same mistake was made again and again and again. Russia kept choosing the same option – force. Force cannot work.'[21]

3   The acceptance of massive losses among Russian troops.

One Russian source claims that the nineteenth century conquest of the Northern Caucasus cost the lives of 145,000 troops (most of who died from sickness).[22] Calculating Russian casualties in the latest decade of conflict, Valentina Melnikova, of the Russian Soldiers' Mothers Committee released the figure of 25,000 deaths on 4 May 2004, during an interview on the radio station, *Ekho Moskvy*.[23] By way of comparison, there were 14,751 combat deaths during the Soviet invasion of Afghanistan (1979–1989). The same source cites 8,943 Russian combat deaths in the two Chechen wars up until the end of 2001.[24]

4   The failure to make any distinction between Chechen *abreks* (bandits of honour) and common criminals.

As Gammer has noted:[25]

> Before contact with Russia *abreks* were fugitives from justice usually escaping a vendetta hiding high in the densely forested mountains. During the 'great *gazavat*' [1830–1859 JR] the term acquired a negative meaning in Russian usage and of course a positive one among the Chechens, of a highlander, in many cases a fugitive from Russian law, fighting the Russians.

This ambiguity continued into the Soviet period. As a young Chechen who joined the Bolsheviks commented: 'the authorities terrorized the peaceful population, and the *abreks* terrorized the authorities. Obviously the people regarded them as fighters against the persecutions and atrocities of the authorities.'[26]

Neither of the situations described would be alien to contemporary Russian attitudes to the Chechen *boyeviki*, especially to such leaders as Aslan Maskhadov, who, despite having been widely recognised as the legitimate leader of the Chechens in Russia and beyond, was regularly referred to by military and political representatives of successive Russian regimes as a criminal and a terrorist and, as such, was assassinated by Russian special forces.

5　The consistent failure to bide by agreements made with Chechen leaders.

Such treachery appears to have become a standard Russian tactic from the early stages of their relationship with the Chechens. Gammer comments on an incident in November 1820, which 'not only taught the Chechens – and other Caucasians – not to trust the Russians, but also increased their contempt and hatred for their new uninvited neighbours'.[27] This trend would have appeared to reach its apogee in the Soviet period, giving rise to the Chechen proverb 'to lie like the Soviets';[28] in the context of the current conflict, the most striking example of this would be the Russian–Chechen Peace Treaty signed in Moscow on 12 May 1997 by Presidents Yeltsin and Maskhadov, which undertook 'to reject forever the use of force or threat of force in resolving all matters of dispute'.[29]

Moreover, there is evidence that assurances given to the hostage-takers at Dubrovka in October 2002 that negotiations with a senior Russian official (Viktor Kazantsev) were about to commence, were merely a ruse to catch the terrorists off guard.[30]

6　Recourse to actions likely to provoke a *gazavat* (Holy War).

It is hard to disagree with Gammer's observation that: 'It is perhaps no coincidence that in 1785, two years after the massacre of the Nogays, Sheikh Mansur, the first Imam (leader) of resistance, began his activity' [i.e. launched the first *gazavat*].[31] In the current conflict, no less a personage than Djokhar Dudaev, the first President of Chechnya-Ichkeria, blamed Russian excesses for provoking a *gazavat*[32] (first called for in 1995, ironically, by the then Mufti, Akhmad Kadyrov, who in 2000 was to become Putin's handpicked architect of Chechenisation).

That such traumatic episodes in the collective memory of the Chechens as the crushing by 1864 of their resistance to Russian expansion at the end of the Great Caucasian War and the deportation to Kazakhstan and Siberia of the entire nation by Stalin in 1944 for 'collaboration with the enemy',[33] should be dismissed from the calculations of the Russian authorities in launching their 'small victorious war',[34] seems with hindsight both foolhardy and grossly negligent. Such great-power arrogance was epitomised in the alleged remark made by Russian Defence Minister Pavel Grachev on 27 November 1994 – the day after the disastrous attack on Grozny by Russian 'mercenaries' had been repulsed – that a single parachute regiment could take Grozny in two hours.[35] Yermolov would have been proud of the sentiment, if not of the disastrous outcome.

The most deep-rooted of these historical aspects were largely of a cultural nature, stemming from a clash between a traditional and a modernising civilisation.[36] In Chechnya, some distinctions may be drawn between *adat* and *Shari'a*. Many aspects of Chechen culture, which the Russians perceive as Islamic, and therefore alien, are, in fact, traditional customs. A good example of this might be the Chechen identification with the fighting qualities of the wolf or, indeed, the blood feud.

Of course, some aspects did have profoundly political and geopolitical ramifications (not least the imperial ambitions of successive Russian and Soviet regimes and the subsequent expectation, on the part of the Chechens, of the same rights to self-determination as those enjoyed by Estonia, Georgia or Turkmenistan). Moreover, these factors need to be understood in the context of not only a collapsing empire, but also a disintegrating superpower. The emergence of, and increased emphasis upon, the so-called 'Islamic factor' since the collapse of Communist ideology and Soviet patriotism in 1991 needs to be set in the context of all former Soviet peoples, including the Russians and the Chechens, establishing new national and cultural identities with which to fill the ideological vacuum.[37]

That for the ethnic Russians this included the integrity of a Russian Federation, in which they had become a significant majority, inevitably had consequences for all non-Russian citizens.[38] For many Russians, the attractiveness of their new, smaller homeland, alongside the promised benefits of democracy, a free market economy and a law-governed state, was the apparent resolution of the 'Islamic question', which had been perceived as a growing menace to Slavic numerical superiority in the last years of the USSR. Nonetheless, given birthrates that are low among Russians and high among minorities from a Muslim cultural background, it is estimated that, within 25 years, approximately one in three citizens of the Russian Federation will be Muslim.[39]

However, the Russian Federation, although still a multicultural entity, is markedly less so than was the USSR. Despite its Eurasian landmass, the loss of the Central Asian republics made the new Russia a much more Eurocentric country in cultural terms. It appeared to promise its citizens (both Russian and non-Russian) a new, prosperous and voluntary commonwealth based on democratic principles. To the extent that it failed to deliver, it is not surprising that the discourse of the Russians became more traditional (nationalistic and authoritarian), leaving the disaffected and defiant to find a new discourse of their own. Paradoxically, although in traditionally Muslim cultural areas of the former USSR, Islam predictably became the new discourse, in the Central Asian republics the nationalist and authoritarian successor governments combined these discourses to help ensure the pre-eminence of secular over militant Islam in that region.

A similar mix of nationalist, authoritarian and Islamic discourse enabled an accommodation to be reached with Tatarstan and other republics within Russia containing titular nationalities of a nominally Muslim cultural background, including all of Chechnya's neighbours in the North Caucasus. Few would argue that the Chechens were less secular or Eurocentric than these neighbours or the Tatars. The Russian political commentator, Pavel Felgenhauer, noted at the outbreak of the first war that: 'Most Chechens drink, eat pork, and don't really know the Koran.'[40] Even the current leader of the Chechen resistance, Doku Umarov, admitted in an interview with Andrei Babitsky that he did not really know how to pray before the conflict with Russia.[41] The problem would appear to be the 'unfinished business' of determining the exact relationship between the Chechens and the Russians in the post-Soviet (post-colonial) era. Both sides had scores to settle. As David Remnick, an experienced American observer of the Russian scene concluded at the end of the first war:

> In the Russian imagination ... Chechnya is an obsession, an image of Islamic defiance, an embodiment of the primitive, the devious, the elusive. For more than three centuries, the czars and the general secretaries – and now a democratically elected president – have tried to obliterate the Chechens, first by war on horseback, then by deportation in cattle cars, and now by heavy artillery bombardment and carpet bombing.[42]

For the Russians, Chechnya seemed to provide the 'small, victorious war', which would put right any number of wrongs, from the ignominious defeat in the Afghan War to the loss of the Cold War. Vadim Dubnov, one of the few out-spoken critics of the second war in the Russian press, noted that:

> The Chechens are paying, in a sense, for everything, for the Baltics, for the Black Sea fleet, for Georgia trying to get into NATO, for Gorbachev and Shevardnadze.[43]

For the Chechens, the disintegration of the Soviet Union represented an his-toric opportunity for the small mountain republic to escape from its perceived structurally repressive relationship with Russia (not least the forced incorpora-tion into the Russian and Soviet empires and the deportations of the Second World War) and to attain an element of political and cultural self-determination, what they would call 'freedom'. The role of the concept 'freedom' in the Chechen psyche, it is argued, is as central as it is to the Roma, exemplified in the traditional form of Chechen greetings. Explaining the importance of this concept, Moshe Gammer notes:

> *Marsho* – freedom – is the central concept in both Chechen culture and the Chechen psyche. Although Chechen nationalists attach to it modern polit-ical connotations, traditionally its meaning went far beyond that of either the Western or Islamic connotation of the word. In the Chechen language the word also contained the connotation of 'peace' and 'well-being'. This is clearly demonstrated in daily greetings: welcoming a male guest Chechens say '*marsha woghiyla*' ('*yoghiyla*' to a woman; literally 'enter in freedom'). Good-bye is '*marsha ghoyla*' (go in freedom). Sending regards Chechens say '*marshalla doiytu*' (wish freedom to ...) and proposing a toast they say '*Dala marshall doila*' (May God provide freedom).[44]

In identifying the spiritual source of Chechen resistance to the Russians, Gammer adds that: 'accepting Russian rule was to the Chechens more than losing freedom in the Western sense of the word: it was losing one's manhood and – more important –one's soul'.[45] Again one hears echoes of similar sentiments expressed by indigenous peoples from the Aborigines in Australia to the Native Indians of America, the 'small' peoples of the Russian Far North and the Zulus of South Africa.

However, for all the history of antagonism between them, there is evidence that the majority of both the Chechen and Russian people were opposed to the idea of fighting against each other before the first war. For example, the fact-finding commission for International Alert reported from Chechnya in 1992 that:

> Any conversation of more than 15 minutes with a Chechen touches on the humiliation they suffered at the hands of successive Russian governments, starting with the period of Tsarist expansion into the Chechen lands in the 18th century, continuing through the deportation to Central Asia in February 1944, and culminating in failure of the Soviet state to return property to them when they were allowed to return in the late 1950s, or compensation for losses and sufferings during their Central Asian exile. On the other hand, we heard surprisingly few comments that characterised Russians as a people in unreservedly negative terms or berated Russians now living in Chechnia for arrogant behaviour. Resentment against what Chechens regard as colonialisation in Tsarist times and Stalinist repression during the Soviet era does not translate into rancour against the current Russian component of the republic's population, who for the most part are seen as victims of the Soviet system, like everyone else who lived under it.[46]

The problem at the end of the first war was not just that few, if any, of the outstanding issues in the long-running confrontation between Russia and Chechnya had been resolved satisfactorily, but also that it had spawned new elements that were to shape the second conflict. Thus, the centuries old clash of cultures between the mountain tribes of Chechnya and the 'civilising' ambitions of the conquering Russians remained unresolved, and both the Chechen quest for self-determination and the Russian imperative of territorial integrity unfulfilled. Moreover, the lawlessness, and the resultant arbitrary brutality and impunity for those causing it, was exacerbated by the Chechen victory in the first war.[47]

The new elements to emerge from the first conflict were Islamic fundamentalist terror; part of what Mary Kaldor has termed 'regressive globalisation' (the exploitation of aspects of globalisation for narrow ideological, economic and political interests)[48] and a new understanding of the importance of 'information warfare'.[49] It was the first of these two new elements that placed the Chechens on the 'wrong' side of the post-9/11 world order and the acquired skill in the second that allowed the Russians to present the entire conflict under the label of a 'counter-terrorist operation', effectively ignoring the very real contradictions left unresolved in the other three areas of the Russo-Chechen confrontation.

Let us examine in turn each of these four overlapping conflicts within the overall confrontation between Russia and Chechnya.

Traditional versus modernising societies

While it would be incorrect and patronising to describe Chechen society in the twenty-first century as anything other than 'modernising', there are aspects of traditional Chechen culture that have yet to be accommodated adequately within either the form of modernisation that the Soviet Union/Russia has attempted to impose or the blueprint for globalisation emanating from the USA in the post-Cold War era. Foremost among these are the lack of a resolution of the precise relationship between the Chechens and the Russians, and the failure to date of Chechen society to establish a viable, normative state, capable of operating successfully within the contemporary world environment.

Manifestations of these traditional aspects of Chechen society, particularly the gruesome practice of ritually severing the heads or otherwise mutilating hostages held in primitive *zindans* (dungeons), can and have been utilised by the Russians to consolidate a negative image of all Chechen opponents as savage bandits and to thus facilitate the depiction of rebel leaders as terrorists. Videos of these atrocities are widely available on the Internet, being used by the Chechen side for raising funds and morale, by the Russians (and then by CNN), to demonise their enemy. The Russian film, *Voina* (War), opens with a scene in which a Chechen commander, using the traditional *kinzhal* (dagger), severs the head of a Russian officer, for whom he has paid a substantial sum in order to 'redeem' a blood vendetta. Since 9/11, of course, such traditional practices, perceived by the modern world as medieval, barbaric and evil have made it much easier for Putin to characterise his opponents in Chechnya as being on the 'other side' in both the global war against terrorism and the 'clash of civilisations'.

Similarly, although its role in Chechen society undoubtedly has been exaggerated,[50] the traditional *teip*, as a social institution, can be seen to have facilitated both the defence of Chechnya once hostilities had commenced and the emergence of strong, local warlords, who often combined military with criminal activities. The *teip* thus presents itself simultaneously as a positive feature in the Chechen perception and a negative throwback to times of pre-modern savagery in the eyes of the Russians.

Parallels may be drawn between the Chechens' struggles to maintain their distinctive way of life against foreign oppressors, bent upon bringing them to submission, with those of the Scottish Highlanders against the British Redcoats.[51] The difference was that, once the perceived threat from the Jacobites had been removed, not only were Scottish 'modernisers' given an opportunity to compete on more or less equal terms with their English counterparts, but also, commencing with the romantic novels of Walter Scott and culminating in the reign of Queen Victoria, there appeared a positive, albeit highly stylised and sanitised, cult of the symbols of highland life (bagpipes, clan tartans, dirks, Highland Games, deer hunting).[52] Moreover, Scottish regiments became the pride of the British army. Taken together, these measures went a long way to offset the traumatic folk memory of the Highland clearances and the ruthless suppression of the Gaelic language and traditional way of life. In other words, the transition from traditional to modern society was achieved partly by defining a new relationship between the English and the Scots from which both could be seen to have benefited.

Unsurprisingly, it is with the Scottish Highlanders before their defeat by the English that the Chechen fighters themselves like to identify. An American mercenary fighting on the Chechen side notes that *Braveheart*, Hollywood's romanticised portrayal of the Highlanders, was the favourite video among the Chechen fighters with whom he was hospitalised, stating that: 'we watched it at least once every couple of days'.[53]

Elements paralleling these processes may be detected in the Russo-Chechen relationship, from the romantic descriptions of Chechen *djigits* (mounted warriors) by Lermontov and Tolstoi to Soviet successes in codifying the Chechen language and establishing a modern system of education. Paradoxically, due to the popularity in translation of the works written during the Great Caucasian War (1817–1864) by Pushkin, Lermontov and Tolstoi, Western readers prior to the Russo-Chechen wars, and to some extent right up until 9/11, tended to share the same highly-romanticised perception of the freedom loving, savage, yet brave and honourable Chechens and their fellow mountain peoples with that of the Native American Indians as portrayed by James Fennimore Cooper's *Last of the Mohicans* (1826) or the Scottish Highlanders in Walter Scott's *Rob Roy* (1817).

What all three groups represent, of course, is the romantic writer's nostalgia for a traditional tribal/clan-based way of life, tinged with regret that its suppression and extinction are inevitable given its incompatibility with the demands of modernising, 'civilised' societies. Quoting Hayden White, Harsha Ram traces the appearance in Western culture of the fictionalised 'Noble savage' or 'Wild Man Within' to the late seventeenth century, identifying the function of this image as serving as 'a positive contrast to the coercive norms of European civilization',[54] in other words 'freedom' as the Chechens and other indigenous peoples would understand the concept.

The grim reality was that the military confrontation with modern civilisation, in these three cases, led to defeat followed by the *mukhadjirstvo* (deportation) for the Chechens, the Removal Acts for the Indians and the clearances for the Highlanders, all effectively destroying the old way of life. A common experience, too, was that the injustice, brutality and unequal struggle that accompanied the suppression of the natives, however much this was justified by the perpetrators, left those on the receiving end with a sense of collective cultural superiority over the invading 'barbarians'. This is graphically described by Lev Tolstoi in *Hadji-Murat*, his tale set in Chechnya in the 1850s.[55]

For their part, the Russians, although sharing a positive perception of the *djigit*, have always counterbalanced it with the negative 'bogeyman' image of the 'wicked Chechen' who 'whets his dagger keen' in Lermontov's famous 'Cossack Lullaby' (see p. x).[56] Although the average Russian would be hard put to distinguish between a Cherkess or Kabardinian (let alone an Ingush) and a Chechen, it is the Chechens that have entered the Russian imagination as the epitome of this negative perception. This is not just because they are the most numerous of the North Caucasian ethnic groups, but also because even the neighbouring mountain peoples regard them as being the most aggressive and uncompromisingly hostile to Russian rule.

The ambiguity of the Russians' perception of the Chechens is perhaps best summed up by the evolution of the word *abrek*. In Lermontov's time this evoked the image of a lone armed and mounted outlaw resisting Russian rule, traditionally portrayed, rifle in hand, alone on a hilltop silhouetted like a wolf against the moon.[57] Yet, by the beginning of the twentieth century the term had acquired the less positive connotation of a *blagorodnyi razboinik* (noble robber).[58] By the time Soviet power had been consolidated, following fierce Chechen resistance, first to the Bolshevik Revolution, then to the collectivisation of agriculture and, finally, to alleged support for the Nazi invaders, this word had become a totally negative 'enemy of the people'.[59] The Russian message to the Chechens over the centuries appears to have remained: 'abandon your old ways or perish'.

Unsurprisingly, the mainstream cultural narrative[60] of the Chechen people is based firmly on brave resistance, led by charismatic leaders (from the theocratic Imam Shamil to the 'international terrorist' Shamil Basaev) to any attempt by the Russians, or any other nation, to extinguish their desire to live as they choose. Moreover, the abiding folk memory for all Chechens remains the tragedies of the diaspora after the First Caucasian War, the forceful suppression of their indigenous *adat*, and the deportation of the entire Chechen nation by Stalin during the Second World War.[61]

The strength of anti-Russian feeling in the Chechen cultural narrative begs the question: Why the Chechens and not, for example, the Dagestanis, Cherkess or even Ingush?[62] Al'fred Koch, a Russian observer, notes that the initial blame is sometimes even laid on Tamerlane, who, in his aforementioned devastation of the Caucasus, drove the Chechens from their agricultural communities and 'normal' existence in the plains and foothills into the highest mountains where they survived as best they could. Yet he goes on to note that Tamerlane did the same to other Caucasian mountain peoples who have not proved to be so irreconcilable to Russian rule.[63] Others, such as Sergei Markedonov, claim that the Chechens had perfected, better than any of the mountain peoples, the 'raiding' or 'plundering' system (*nabegovaya sistema*) that the Russians were determined to crush in the Caucasus.[64]

One Western academic, Robert Bruce Ware, has concluded that, even among the Caucasian mountain people, the Chechens are feared and renowned for their ferocity, brigandage and aggression, and, as such, must shoulder much of the blame for their current condition. He has, for some time, been virtually a lone voice in the West on this issue. As far back as 2000 he co-authored, with Ira Straus, an article in the *Christian Science Monitor* drawing attention to Western media bias *against* the Russians over Chechnya, stating:

> We in the West are naive to think that the choice in the Caucasus is between the massive human rights abuses committed by Russians in Chechnya and

no human rights abuses. The real choice is between the current Russian abuses and the massive abuses previously committed by Chechen groups in Dagestan and other areas near the Chechen border.[65]

The Chechen 'Eurasianist' Khozh-Akhmed Nukhaev has even suggested that the mountainous area of Chechnya, home of 'the staunchest bearers of the pre-modern national traditions, refuting any form of statehood whatsoever' be turned into a kind of tribal reservation separated from Russia by a 'modern' Chechnya on the plains.[66] The leading Russian ethnologist, Sergei Arutyunov, has also advocated such a division of Chechnya,[67] as in September 1994, even before the first conflict had begun, did Emil Pain, Director of the Centre for Ethnopolitical and Regional Studies in Moscow.[68] Voices have also been raised in Russia advocating the construction of a wall, in order to keep out of Russia Chechen bandits, terrorists and thieves, similar to that being built by the Israelis on the West Bank![69]

On the other hand, the Russian obsession with the eradication of the spirit of freedom among the Chechens, has been long identified, but never satisfactorily explained. As the two authors of an article published in Russia during the second conflict have claimed:

> The impression has been created that our authorities have a sort of drug addiction to everything connected with Chechnya. And sometimes they react irrationally to it.[70]

One might suggest that in the current conflict this stems, to a large extent, from the specific mindset of the *siloviki*[71] – elite leaders in the Russian ministries of 'law and order', such as the Federal Security Service (FSB), the Ministry of Internal Affairs (MVD), the Ministry of Foreign Affairs (MID) and the Foreign Intelligence Service (SVR).[72]

The Russian sociologist, Ol'ga Kryshtanovskaya, estimated that there are currently 4.5 million *siloviki* in Russia,[73] and that while their proportion in the national leadership, governmental and regional elites has risen from 3.7 per cent under Gorbachev to 25.1 per cent under Putin, in the top leadership the figures are 4.8 per cent and an astounding 58.3 per cent, respectively![74]

People from such a background can hardly be expected to comprehend, let alone value, the cultural importance to Chechens of what they call 'freedom'. The philosophy of this group would appear to include such quintessentially Russian concepts of *derzhavnost'* (belief in Russia as a great power) and *gosudarstvennost'* (belief in the power of the state) of those that traditionally have run Russia, that demands conformity and submission, while suppressing dissidence or anarchy in any form. In his first state of the union address as President, in July 2000, Putin claimed that authority 'should rely on the law and a single, vertical line of executive power',[75] an unusual arrangement, to say the least, in a country ostensibly organised according to a federal principle which requires, at the very least, a genuine division of powers, real power for the subjects of that federation and control over the networks of power manipulated by the centralised security forces.[76]

On the other hand, those 'modernist' Chechen leaders who had succeeded in Soviet/Russian society, such as the former President of Chechnya-Ichkeria – the late Aslan Maskhadov – Ruslan Khasbulatov or Akhmed Zakaev, and who might be expected more easily to see the conflict from both sides, represent precisely the kind of mediator that was deliberately excluded from the political process in Chechnya, in effect after 9/11, but totally after the Dubrovka hostage-taking drama in October 2002.

In terms of state formation, Chechnya, in its two brief periods of de facto self-government (1991–1994 and 1996–1999), appeared incapable on its own to establish the foundations of a viable system. In this it was not helped by the obstructive policies of Russia.[77] Since 9/11, there has been genuine concern in the West that an independent Chechnya would become a 'failed' state like Afghanistan and Lebanon when they, too, were run by a collection of feuding warlords; the Bush administration having made quite explicit the linkage between such states and terrorism.[78]

In the absence, during these two periods, of Russian forces, a common enemy against which Chechens could unify, local warlords were quite capable, for their own parochial interests, of undermining attempts to establish effective national institutions, norms and hierarchies; Igor Porshnev, correspondent of *Interfax-Vremya,* wrote in July 1999:

> The 'mountain generals' do not want Maskhadov's contacts with Moscow to succeed, as this would strengthen the positions of the Chechen leader. Analysts believe that the field commanders need to maintain the status quo under which Maskhadov controls no more than 20 per cent of the republican territory and armed formations. Each field commander wants to be the king of his province – Arbi Barayev in Urus-Martan, Shamil Basayev in Vedeno, etc.... If field commanders pooled forces, they would have easily got rid of Maskhadov, but they have no such plans so far.[79]

The crucial failure of the Chechen warlords to help Maskhadov construct the foundations of a modern 'normative' state can thus be seen as critical not only in encouraging the Kremlin to eradicate this 'nest of terrorism', as Yeltsin had previously sought to stamp out Dudaev's 'criminal free-zone', but also in allowing the West to undermine Maskhadov's legitimacy by withholding any recognition of his regime. Although this must be seen as a failure on the part of the Chechen nationalist movement, there is little evidence to suggest that a more conciliatory approach would have met with more sympathy from the chastened and bitter Russian power elite. It might, however, have applied a brake to the rapid erosion of such understanding and support as had been forthcoming from the Western public.

Self-determination versus territorial integrity

The Chechens are by no means the only nation to have missed out, due to the countervailing right of territorial integrity for all existing states, on the self-determination that is enshrined in international law as the right of all peoples. In Western Europe separatist and irredentist groups which have taken up the armed struggle for their cause are routinely labelled 'terrorist' (the Provisional IRA, ETA, the FLNC in Corsica, etc.) on the basis that peaceful alternatives to violence (via the ballot box) exist. Further afield things are more ambiguous. If one accepts that the Kurds and the Kosovars have equal rights to self-determination, it is hardly consistent to label the PKK a terrorist enemy and the KLA an ally in the struggle for 'freedom'. Similarly, on what criteria, other than self-interest, did the West support *Falintil*, the armed rebel group in East Timor, but not the Chechens, the Tamils or the Uighurs?

Thus far, in the twenty-first century, the right of all peoples to self-determination, invoked in sporadic waves during the nineteenth and twentieth centuries as successive great empires collapsed, has been overridden by the right of existing states to territorial integrity. Consequently, Chechens share the fate of Kashmiris (India), Kurds (Turkey), Tibetans and Uighurs (China) and many others in having seemingly 'missed the boat' with respect to self-determination.

The last wave of new independent states appeared with the more or less simultaneous collapse of the three federations of the former socialist bloc in Central and Eastern Europe (the USSR, Yugoslavia and Czechoslovakia). Even so, some peoples failed to achieve self-determination (for example, the Abkhaz in Georgia, the Albanians in Macedonia and the Ruthenians in Slovakia). In the only remaining federation, Russia moved to prevent a repeat of the disintegration of the USSR by insisting on territorial integrity. Whether this was to preserve the integrity of a new democratically inclined multinational state of Russia made up of a federation of willing constituent peoples, or to shore up by force the remnants of a Russian empire remains to this day a point of contention among Russians and outsiders alike.

In the event, only Tatarstan and Chechnya stood firm. Tatarstan eventually came to an acceptable accommodation with Moscow and Chechnya fighting a seemingly successful war of secession. However, as we have seen, the failure of the international community to recognise the independence of Chechnya-Ichkeria lent legitimacy to Russia's claim, upon reinvading Chechnya in 1999, that the rebellious republic remained part of the Russian Federation.

Whereas the Tatar cause was weakened to some extent by the existence of a diaspora spread right across Russia and the fact that the Republic of Tatarstan is surrounded by Russian territory, the Chechens could argue that they met all conditions set by Stalin, on the basis of which the right of secession had been granted to the 15 former Union Republics: (a) that they had a population of a million or more; (b) that the titular nation comprised the majority; and (c) that they shared a border with a foreign state (in Chechnya's case, Georgia). The central dilemma should be, therefore, which right takes precedence, that of self-determination or that of territorial integrity?[80] In the case of Tatarstan, the accommodation reached indicated that the latter held sway, whereas in the case of Chechnya, the Chechens attempted to impose the former, the Russians responded by applying even greater force in order to achieve the latter.

However, it is important to note that it was the disproportionate and indiscriminate application of force by the Russians, not Dudaev's pre-emptive push for independence, characterised by Aleksandr Lebed' as a 'mafia squabble at state level',[81] that caused the overwhelming majority of Chechens to perceive this conflict as the defence of their right to self-determination – a partisan war that is recognised as such by even the Russians; *The Russia Journal* in March 1999, i.e. before the second war started admitted as much when it claimed:

> The point is that those who fight against invaders, even the worst criminals, are defenders, and this status justifies the use of any means, including terrorism.[82]

This does not necessarily mean that the Russo-Chechen conflict should be viewed only as a classical war of liberation (decolonisation) akin to that fought by the Algerians against the French in the 1950s and 1960s. To begin with the Mediterranean Sea divides France and Algeria, so that states such as China, Sri Lanka and Turkey that are also faced currently with secessionist movements on territory contiguous to their own provide a closer parallel. Nonetheless, the battle for Algeria's freedom clearly contains lessons for those seeking to resolve the Russo-Chechen conflict.

Had the Russians adopted a more nuanced and sensitive approach to Chechen cultural and political assimilation instead of imposing brutally a uniform system of rule, Chechnya would probably have developed a normative state structure that would have allowed it to modernise while coexisting comfortably within Russia's orbit. Rather, once General Yermolov and his successors had crushed the brave and heroic resistance under Imam Shamil in 1859, the Russians exacted a savage revenge by exiling hundreds of thousands of mountain people, including Chechens, to Turkey and parts of the Middle East. The *mukhadjirstvo* (deportation) of 1864 rankles still with Chechens in a way that the Turkish massacres do with Armenians. This national humiliation, though, was followed in 1944 by an even worse tragedy that, to this day, remains prominent in the cultural narrative of the Chechen people: Stalin's deportation in cattle trucks of the entire Chechen nation to Siberia and Kazakhstan. The fact that 50 years later, in 1994, the Russians used heavy artillery and carpet bombing against Chechen towns and villages, ostensibly to 'restore constitutional order', and then repeated the exercise in 1999, this time as part of a 'counter-terrorist operation', merely consolidated further in the view of Chechens the repetitive nature of Russian brutality from Yermolov to Yeltsin.

There is no doubt that Chechnya was colonised by Russia in the nineteenth century as a result of the Great Caucasian War (1817–1864), at about the same time as were the now independent Central Asian states. Not surprisingly,

Chechens claim the same right to self-determination as their co-religionists in Central Asia. Even some Russian commentators have noted the paradox of Stalin's division of the USSR apparently remaining valid internationally after the collapse of the Soviet superpower. For example, ex-Gorbachev aide Yuri Maltsev of the Mises Institute writes:

> But surely Chechens or Tatars or Dagestani have as much right to nation-hood as, say Estonia, Armenia or East Timor. The Chechens are a colonized people who have been conducting a struggle against imperial Russia and the imperial Soviet Union for more than 200 years. It is amazing that Stalin's Constitution is still a valid legal document for the Bush administration refusing to recognize the right of the oppressed nationalities of Russia for self-determination.[83]

However, it is argued that, since Chechnya in 1991 was still part of, and contiguous to, Russia, a more appropriate analogy is provided by the relationship between England and Scotland. The English Redcoats finally defeated the Scottish Highlanders more than a century before the Russian conquest of Chechnya. Assimilation followed, initially by co-opting the Scottish aristocracy but, eventually, by admitting all Scots as more or less equal partners into the new class-based industrial society of Great Britain. Although only gaining the right to self-determination in 1998, it is now established that the Scots and not the British as a whole should determine Scotland's status in future.

The Chechens have no such right. The new 'Putin' constitution effectively bans pro-independence parties and would only allow Chechnya to leave the Russian Federation if a majority of Russian citizens agreed.[84] The simple truth is that Russians consider Chechen territory to be an inviolable part of Russia, regard Chechen oil as their own and see the multinational people of Chechnya as belonging to the Russian Federation, irrespective of whether the Chechens like it or not.

All of the evidence indicates that, far from being Islamic fundamentalists, most Chechen fighters have taken up arms in order to resist occupation by what they perceive as invading, hostile forces, a right enshrined in international law. Again, all that is required to address this element of the conflict is for the Russians to agree that the Chechens have a *prima facie* case for self-determination that needs to be dealt with. It could well turn out that a degree of autonomy, along the lines, perhaps, of that enjoyed by Puerto Rico vis-à-vis the US, would more than satisfy the bulk of Chechnya's war-weary inhabitants. However, by refusing to acknowledge any Chechen claims for self-determination, the Russians are ensuring that this key aspect of the conflict will remain unresolved.

The 'black hole' of lawlessness

The absence thus far of any concentrated and coordinated battle against the widely documented phenomenon of lawlessness in Chechnya renders this facet of the war central to this study as its very existence highlights the difficulty in resolving any of the other conflicts that make up the Russo-Chechen War. In the context of this war the problem of lawlessness is an excellent example of how a continuation of the armed struggle benefits the few to the detriment of the many. That this applies to both sides in the conflict is scant consolation to the long suffering civilian population of Chechnya or, indeed, to the much abused, traumatised Russian troops that have served in this horrendous conflict. Stories of corruption, of Russian Army generals and Chechen field commanders working hand in glove, of arbitrary brutality and impunity from prosecution of those carrying it out, of illegal drug trafficking, extortion, hostage taking and kidnapping for ransom, of large-scale criminal fraud, are all so common as to give the impression that there remains no semblance of a law-governed state in Chechnya.[85] All this, of course, occurs against a background of the disproportionate and indiscriminate use of military force against civilian populations.

One of the psychological obstacles to tackling this 'black hole' remains the widespread Russian perception of the Chechens as a lawless nation. This, of course, reached its apogee when Stalin deported the entire Chechen nation in 1944. Although Stalin used the epithet of 'enemies of the people' against millions of individuals during his reign of terror, he was selective in collectively punishing whole peoples, as he did the Chechens and other minorities before, during and after the Great Patriotic War (1941–1945). Apart from the Chechens, the Ingush, Balkars, Karachai, Kalmyks, Bulgarians, Greeks, Meskhetian Turks, Crimean Tatars were deported en masse from their traditional areas of settlement in the Caucasus/Black Sea region, all for allegedly collaborating with the enemy. Other national groups, e.g. the Volga Germans, Poles, Koreans and Baltic peoples, were also deported in large numbers from other parts of the USSR.[86] Along with the mass deportations to Turkey and the Middle East in 1864, the injustice of the enforced exile to Siberia and Kazakhstan in 1944 of every last Chechen man, woman and child is etched deeply in the collective cultural narrative of the Chechen people.

It has been argued military considerations can hardly have justified Stalin's actions. The military case is undermined albeit by the fact that between 20,000 and 40,000 Chechens fought on the front-line in the Great Patriotic War (1941–1945).[87] Over 300 Chechens and Ingush fought in the heroic defence of the Brest fortress in the summer of 1941, one of them, Magomed Uzuev, being made posthumously a Hero of the Soviet Union for his exploits.[88] There may have been, however, an ideological logic to Stalin's deportation of entire peoples. Steven T. Katz writes:

> The Stalinist program of complete cultural conversion through migration ... directly and indirectly caused up to 500,000 deaths. It is therefore a paradigmatic instance of ethnocide facilitated through mass murder. But it was neither intended, nor did it become in practice, an example of physical extermination of a minority nation. The intent was to destroy a variety of minority cultures and the ambitions built upon them, rather than to murder all the members of a specific people.[89]

Yet, in effect, Stalin's so-called 'socialist culture' was a thinly disguised version of the Russian culture that the Chechens had fought so hard for so long to resist. Paradoxically, therefore, it led to a strengthening in exile of the Chechen self-reliance and the social structures that helped sustain this.[90] Unsurprisingly, the return to Chechnya failed in itself to resolve the Russo-Chechen relationship, the Russians still demanding assimilation to Soviet 'proletarian' norms and the Chechens seeking to restore their *adat* and *nokhchallah*.[91]

Unequipped or unwilling to follow the opportunities in the oil industry or collectivised agriculture available in the Soviet Chechen-Ingush Autonomous Republic, many Chechens turned to the nascent 'grey' and 'black' economies that were to thrive in the USSR under Brezhnev. This produced considerable profits for the Chechens and resentment from the Russians, who felt that they were being ripped off.

Stephen Handelman, in his book on post-Soviet crime, notes the perceptive remarks of Captain Yury Nikishin of the Moscow Organised Crime Squad, in explaining the link between the deportations and the Chechen gangs' penchant for crime:

> They had a strong clan system, based on family ties.... Every Chechen youth was taught to obey and respect his elders and distrust outsiders. They were also addicted to firearms as a way of settling disputes or merely demonstrating prowess.... They seemed to me very similar to the Sicilian mafia.... When the Chechens were finally permitted to return after the war, they discovered that their best land had been occupied by strangers. What else could many of them do but turn to crime? ... It was a logical step to turn their clans into criminal groups.[92]

As the power and influence of the Chechen gangs grew, the transition into the stereotype of Chechens held by both the authorities and the public in Russia from that of *abrek* to that of *vor* (thief) or *bandit* (bandit) was not at all difficult. By the time the Soviet system collapsed in 1991, it was widely recognised that, of all the mafia groups: 'The most successful were the Chechens and their hallmark was extreme violence.'[93]

Certainly, the Chechen mafia, established in the major Russian cities, was well placed to exploit the opportunities afforded by the post-Soviet transition to a market economy. However, as Handelman makes clear: 'Yet for all their money, even the Chechens were, in the end, only junior partners in the (Russian) military's expanding operations.'[94]

If Chechens have reasons aplenty to wish to be rid of direct Russian rule, then the Russians can point to Chechnya's abject failure, in its two phases of de facto independence (1991–1994 and 1996–1999), to create viable state institutions capable of tackling the wave of anarchy, crime and religious fundamentalism that subsequently engulfed it. That Russia did all that it could to exacerbate Chechnya's plight during these periods, rather than helping it to develop these institutions, represents yet another missed opportunity by Russia to come to terms finally with its reluctant and rebellious southern neighbour. By claiming that the actions of Chechen separatists stemmed from a cultural tendency towards 'banditry', the Russian authorities consolidated the deep-seated anti-Chechen prejudices held by many Russian people.

Events in Iraq over the past few years have shown that the absolute priority in countering insurgency is to establish security and order for the overwhelming majority of citizens within a disputed territory. Clearly a degree of law and order is necessary for the observation of human rights, but the wholesale preponderance of might over right in Chechnya has led, in the view of most of its citizens, to the rule of tyranny.[95] Of all of the aspects of the Russo-Chechen conflict, this is the one that the Russians and Chechens together, without any assistance from the outside world, could begin to address immediately. One can only conclude that Putin is either not strong enough or not sufficiently willing to oppose those high-placed vested interests within his political and military elite that are benefiting from the anarchy in Chechnya.

The 'war on terror' and the Islamic 'factor'

Of course, since 9/11 the defining cultural contradiction between the Chechens and the Russians has been the former's adherence to Islam. Primarily manifested before the current round of the conflict in Sufism, a populist and grass-roots pathway within Islam ideally suited to survival in an authoritarian system.[96] It has been attacked both by Russian intransigence and by an uncompromising form of authoritarian Islam – *Wahhabism*. On an ideocratic, financial and military level, the latter has been more successful than Sufism in countering the kind of aggression unleashed on Chechnya by the Russian federal forces[97] – a fact which has been exploited both by outside sponsors and mercenaries and by the more extremist Chechen warlords. The failure to re-establish Sufism at the expense of *Wahhabism* as the preferred form of Islam among Chechens represents another major obstacle in the path of peace in Chechnya.

Since 9/11, the 'Islamic factor' as a cultural contradiction has played a disproportionate role in the Russo-Chechen conflict [98] and is portrayed by the Putin administration as the single most important contributory factor to the violence in Chechnya. In this, the Russian president is aided by the fact that, in three of the cultural contradictions that affect both sides (globalisation, the post-secular discourse of 'good versus evil' and the war on terror), Russia finds itself on the 'right', and Chechnya on the 'wrong' side. Arguably, however, it is the shared experience of both Russia and Chechnya of the lack of a law-governed state, a smoothly functioning market economy and a robust civil society that place both on the 'wrong' side.[99] Clearly, any significant improvement in Russia of any of these three factors would considerably increase the chance of changing attitudes in order to achieve peace in Chechnya. To the extent that Putin appears to be obstructing progress in these areas, he, too, could be portrayed as an 'entrepreneur of violence' (see Chapter 7).

Nowhere is this more apparent than in Putin's dealings (or lack of them) with representatives of the Chechen independence movement, who clearly fall into the category of 'legitimate' (in the eyes of the Chechens and much of the world community) resistance rather than that of terrorist. Thus, Aslan Maskhadov, whose election as President of Chechnya-Ichkeria was regarded internationally as more legitimate than either of those of his pro-Russian successors Akhmad Kadyrov or Alu Alkhanov, in the wake of Beslan (September 2004), was raised to an equivalent demonic status as that of the acknowledged mastermind of the atrocity – the 'international terrorist' Basaev. Unlike the situation following the death of Basaev in July 2006, the Kremlin's euphoria at Maskhadov's assassination by Russian forces on 8 March 2005 was not shared by the international community. Indeed, even 62 per cent of Russians polled felt that Maskhadov's body should be handed back to his relatives for a proper Muslim burial, rather than being interred in an unmarked terrorist grave, as the authorities in Moscow stubbornly insisted.[100]

Almost certainly, Maskhadov would have been willing to compromise on some form of Chechen autonomy that fell short of outright independence. However, Moscow was unwilling to risk putting Maskhadov or any of his representatives before the Chechen electorate. Furthermore, political parties advocating Chechen independence were expressly banned from participating in the November 2005 elections to the Chechen legislature.[101]

By insisting that members of the Chechen independence movement are nothing more than terrorists, Russia has come into collision with both the UK and the USA, the independent judiciaries of which refused to extradite to Russia Maskhadov's envoys in the UK (Akhmed Zakaev) and the USA (Ilyas Akhmadov). The British courts have 'exacerbated' this stand-off by also refusing to extradite Putin's erstwhile supporter but now leading critic abroad, Boris Berezovsky. As the reason given for granting asylum, in both the Zakaev and Berezovsky cases heard in London, was the lack of prospects of a fair trail by a Russian judicial system that is not sufficiently independent of executive power, one can identify Russia's frustration at the UK's 'double standards' in the fight against international terrorism as emanating from a lack of understanding as to how the separation of powers works in a democratic society. By the same token the screening in both countries (Channel 4 in the UK,[102] ABC in the USA[103]) of televised interviews with Shamil Basaev led to furious protests by Russian foreign ministry officials and the closure after more than 40 years of the ABC office in Moscow

As events in Northern Ireland, since the Good Friday Agreement, have demonstrated, no matter how deep the cultural contradictions and how bitter conflicting attitudes might be, the popular attraction of an outcome that appears to offer peace after decades of the most arbitrary violence is not to be underestimated. There is evidence that both the Russian and Chechen populations would welcome precisely such an outcome. In August 2006, more than two-thirds (68 per cent) of those polled would prefer peace talks with the Chechens against just 18 per cent favouring Putin's policy of a continuing war,[104] proportions that indicate that, since 2000 when it became obvious that the second war, too, had failed to achieve a quick and easy victory, Russian citizens have favoured by at least two-to-one peace negotiations over a continuation of the fighting. The only exceptions to these proportions have occurred in the immediate aftermath of the Dubrovka and Beslan sieges.

This is illustrated in Table 3.1. Even allowing for the upsurge in support for a 'military solution' following each of these 'terrorist spectaculars', especially the Beslan siege of 2004, the average proportion of those Russians supporting the continuation of the war in Chechnya more than halved in the period 2000–2005. However, if one takes February 2000, as the high point of the Russian public's support for the war, then it declined from 70 per cent[105] over the five-year period to a level of just over 21 per cent.[106]

By April 2006, support dropped to an all-time low of 17 per cent, rising slightly to 18 per cent on the second anniversary of the Beslan siege (1 September 2006).[108] Evidence of the yearning for peace in Chechnya is provided by the results of an opinion poll reported by *Interfax* on 2 February 2006, indicating that 86 per cent of Chechens 'link the achievement of peace, stability, justice and order' with the activities of the current (pro-Russian) Chechen authorities'. However, in an earlier survey of Russian and Chechen public opinion, it was found that, although 78 per cent of Chechens polled wished to remain part of Russia, 61 per cent of these believed that Chechnya should have a greater degree of autonomy than any other part of the Russian Federation.[109]

That Putin refused steadfastly to heed the clear message from his electorate, which had twice given him a clear mandate to represent them in negotiations with the separatists, lends weight to the theory that the Russian president, or perhaps his closest advisors among the *siloviki*, for their own narrow political, perhaps even, economic interests, do not wish the conflict to end any time soon.

Conclusion

Historically, then, the relationship between the Russians and the Chechens has been characterised by the Russian willingness to use overwhelming might to suppress the Chechen's distinctive understanding of freedom and the Chechens

Table 3.1 Annual average percentage of Russians polled favouring a continuation of the Chechen War, 2000–2005[107]

Year	%
2000	46.6
2001	33.6
2002	30.4
2003	24.6
2004	27.9
2005	21.5

sporadically fighting back while stubbornly refusing to submit to Russian rule. Given the asymmetry of the human and military resources in this confrontation, it is not surprising that the Russians have managed to subdue the Chechens for much of the past 200 years. Although it could be argued that, unlike the Nazis' attitudes to *Untermenschen*, neither the Russians nor the Soviets wished to physically exterminate the Chechens, but rather to resettle and re-educate them *en masse*, such has been the scale of arbitrary brutality that has been employed collectively against them as a people, that one might forgive the Chechens for failing to draw this fine distinction between 'genocide' and 'assimilation'.

Despite the undoubted progress towards modernity made by Chechens within the Russian and Soviet Empires, their experience has been, in many respects, akin to that of indigenous tribes in the Americas, the Arctic and Australasia, or the Roma in Europe. Their traditional way of life was suppressed and replaced forcibly by often unsuitable 'modern' norms. The sharp contrast between, on the one hand, Russia's 'single vertical of power', its rigid class system and an arrogance characteristic of great powers, while, on the other, Chechnya's *teip* system headed by regional warlords, its local *adat*, and the passionate defence by its people of their freedom, given the circumstances, was a recipe for conflict.

It should be emphasised here, however, that not all cultural contradictions are in themselves violent; most, however, do call for mechanisms of conflict avoidance and resolution, many of which appear to be absent in the Russo-Chechen conflict. For example, although many peoples have been more or less successfully colonised, sometimes by the most violent of means, e.g. aboriginal peoples, indigenous peoples such as Native American Indians, clan-based peoples such as the Scots, the Chechens appear to have never accepted the finality of either the Russian occupation of their territory or the supremacy of Russian over Chechen values. The key, it seems to me, is the extent to which the peoples thus colonised are able to adapt to, flourish in and even to some extent control their lives within the new political entity.

In the Chechen case Russian Imperial and Soviet rule did bring some benefits of modernity: education, healthcare, literacy, access to the wider world of scientific advance, etc. However, the suppression of the distinct Caucasian way of life, the Chechen's cult of 'freedom' and the brutality that accompanied, first Russian, then Soviet occupation have left an open wound in Russo-Chechen relations, felt most keenly by the 'recipients' but almost totally disregarded by the 'donors' of Russia's *mission civilatrice*.

Historically, Russia has sought to impose internal stability throughout its territory by means of prescriptive ideologies: in the nineteenth century, through the three main principles of the Russian Empire (autocracy, orthodoxy and *narodnost'* – the national principle); replaced in the USSR by the one-party rule of the Communist Party of the Soviet Union, Marxist–Leninist orthodoxy and Soviet patriotism. In both cases, however, this stability proved to be illusory and both belief systems produced instead severe repression (the Tsarist 'prison of nationalities' and Stalinist terror) and, eventually, collapse.

In the Putin era, it would appear that orthodoxy (in the sense of an intolerance of diverse opinion) has been largely restored and that the *gosurdarstvennost'* of the ruling *siloviki* has become the new 'autocracy'. The national principle appears to have been superseded, perhaps temporarily, by *derzhavnost'*. Again, the aim appears to be internal stability, a key aim of the *siloviki*, whereas the likely outcome will be repression, which serves the interests of neither the Russian people nor the wider international community. It cannot be denied that these foundations of Putin's state are supported by large sections of the Russian public, poll after poll shows that the three most (indeed only) trusted institutions in Russia today are the Presidency, the security services and the Russian Orthodox Church, although 'oligarchs, bankers and financiers' replace the church when Russians are asked to name the most influential organisations in Russian life.[110]

While Russia has every right to consider itself a world power and its enormous energy resources alone will probably ensure that it remains one, it should be discouraged, for example, from playing the 'energy' card in an attempt to regain its former hegemony over the 'Near Abroad'. More importantly, it should not be allowed to sign up to the principles of European institutions if it has no intention of observing them.

Similarly, a strong, centralised state with highly-personalised power invested in an executive leader may be held to have served well, in the past, the world's largest country and may be the optimum way of maintaining the territorial integrity of the Russian homeland. Yet the imposition of a Russian-style *vertikal'* of power is bound to provoke conflict in a Chechen society traditionally preferring horizontal power structures based on clan and territory.

It is, first and foremost, Russia's intolerance of diversity, stemming perhaps from a strict interpretation of its understanding of orthodoxy, which leads to an insistence on imposing its values – if necessary by brute force – that is preventing a lasting solution being found to the conflict in Chechnya. It is instructive to note that neither Russian Orthodoxy under the Tsars nor Marxism–Leninism under the Soviets could accommodate the 'heretical' views of, respectively, Lev Tolstoi and Aleksandr Solzhenitsyn, arguably the most quintessentially Russian writers at either end of the twentieth century.[111]

Finally, Russia's geopolitical view of the world must be taken into account. Clearly it is in Russia's national interest to remain the dominant player in the 'Near Abroad' and maintain an influence over Caspian energy reserves and transit routes. The events along Russia's southern border – from Abkhazia to Afghanistan – must provoke the Russians to question US and NATO strategy in the region. Having already endured Western intervention in Georgia, Tajikistan and Ukraine, President Putin must be painfully aware that a military and political victory in Chechnya is necessary both to prevent similar occurrences in the Northern Caucasus and to preserve the territorial integrity of the Russian Federation.

However, the brutal means by which this victory is being sought has ensured that any genuinely free and fair election in Chechnya would result in the defeat of the Kremlin's choice,[112] a situation reminiscent of that pertaining in the

Peoples' Democracies during the Cold War era. This creates a window of opportunity for outside influence in the region. As was the case during periods of heightened tension in East–West relations during the Cold War, if they seek to bring an element of stability and predictability into their relations with Russia, then Europe, the USA and NATO would be well advised to be more open and frank about the scope and limits of their interests in the Caucasus region. For its part Russia needs to be reminded that internal repression not only tarnishes its reputation internationally, but also stokes up the likelihood of future domestic conflict.

Of the cultural contradictions emanating from the Chechen side many stem from the very asymmetry of their confrontation with the Russians. For example, greater clarification is required from the UN as to the exact trade-off in rights between the territorial integrity of existing states and the self-determination of indigenous peoples perceiving themselves to be fighting for their very survival against a more powerful occupying force: the experiences of East Timor, Kosovo, Kurdistan, Kuwait, Palestine, Taiwan and Tibet tend to confuse rather than clarify what constitutes acceptable defence.

Moreover, it is by no means clear, in the current international system, to what extent aboriginal, nomadic and mountain-dwelling peoples are obliged to embrace unquestioningly the 'benefits' of modernisation and to what lengths they might legitimately go to defend their traditional ways of life.

In this, as in so many other aspects of the Russo-Chechen conflict, Russia would do well to study the experiences of other societies in dealing with comparable problems. By continuing to ignore these contradictions, the Russians are effectively ensuring that the recurring spirals of violence that have characterised the Russo-Chechen relationship from the outset will at best be temporarily suppressed and at worst will seriously weaken the prospects of ever constructing a genuinely multicultural federative state in Russia.

4   Of wolves and werewolves

Demonisation in the Russo-Chechen confrontation

You are really wolves
But you had not the guts for it.
You were grey,
Once you were brave,
But you were handed scraps
And became slaves.
You are glad to serve and flatter
For a crust of bread,
But the leash and chain
Are your prize – and well deserved!
Tremble in your cages
When we are out hunting!
Because, more than any bear,
We wolves hate
Dogs

('We are wolves',
anonymous Chechen poem)[1]

As was clearly demonstrated in a broad-ranging collection of articles published in 2005 in the journal *Third World Quarterly*,[2] demonisation, or the 'politics of naming', has long been and remains a feature of warfare all over the world. Of course, this phenomenon has rarely been the preserve of just one side in any given conflict. This certainly holds true in the Russo-Chechen relationship. Thus, the Chechens call Russians *barany* (sheep)[3] or *svinya* (pigs),[4] justifying in their own minds, perhaps, not just the killing of their opponents, but also, to the horror of Russian and Western audiences alike, their ritual slaughter with the *kinzhal* – the traditional Chechen dagger. As becomes apparent from the sentiments of the above poem, the other name routinely given to the Russian is *sobaki* (dogs).[5]

Moreover, Shamil Basaev habitually used the term *Rusnya* to refer to Russia,[6] perhaps seeking simultaneously to be derogatory and to equate it, albeit phoneti-cally, with *Chechnya* – the name imposed on the Chechen homeland by its Russian colonisers (*Nokchiin mokhk* being the name of their homeland in the Chechen language).[7]

However, in asymmetric conflicts such as that between the Russians and the Chechens, it tends to be the resort to demonisation by the incomparably stronger side – in this case the Russians – that attracts more attention. The fact that virtually every child in Russia knows by heart Lermontov's 'Cossack Lullaby' with its 'evil Chechen', quoted in the Preface, emphasises both how deeply ingrained in the Russian consciousness is the negative image of this far from numerous mountain people and what a disproportionate impact the Chechens have had in the last two centuries on Russian life.

Russian demonisation of leaders of the Chechen resistance appears to have commenced from the outset of the Russo-Chechen confrontation, when Sheikh Mansur became the first in a long line of charismatic Chechen rebels to be targeted by the Russians with what we would now call Russian 'information warfare'. Moshe Gammer writes:

> Using terms such as 'false prophet', 'cheat', 'tramp', 'rebel', 'savage' and 'wild beast', the Russian propaganda effort painted a highly negative picture of Mansur. This picture would endure in Russian and – with two or three exceptions – in Soviet historiography; a fact that perhaps suggests that successive regimes in St Petersburg and Moscow considered Mansur – or rather what he stood for – no less dangerous after his death than when he was alive.[8]

For 1785 one could read 2005, and for Mansur – Maskhadov,[9] indeed it is claimed that even their bodies were treated with equal irreverence by the Russians.[10]

In an earlier work on the Russo-Chechen conflict, I used the categories 'Mujahideen', 'Mafia', 'Madmen' to describe Russian perceptions of the Chechens.[11] These terms paraphrase the typology of 'terrorists' as 'crusaders, criminals or crazies' made in 1976 by Frederick J. Hacker, an American psychologist.[12] As will be seen in this chapter, these stereotypes were exploited by the Russian press to demonise the Chechen resistance in both wars.

However, in assuming that the term 'crusader', in distinction to 'criminal' and 'crazy', has an overall positive connotation to the Western mind, its replacement by the term *mujahideen* is problematic. For, although the Afghan *mujahideen* were supported by the West in their struggle against Soviet troops, their role in the rise of the Taliban in that country, transformed in Western eyes the term from a positive 'freedom fighter' into a negative 'terrorist', a view finally confirmed by the events of 9/11 and the subsequent invasions of Afghanistan and Iraq. Russia can also be accused of double standards, the USSR having supported anti-Western insurgencies as 'national liberation movements', whereas the majority of Russians recognised neither the Afghan resistance, nor the Chechen conflict as anti-imperialist.

Hacker argues that the self-perception of revolutionary groups as 'crusaders' ('freedom fighters') is just as important a factor in conflict resolution as the classification by the authorities of such insurgents as 'criminals' and/or 'crazies' ('terrorists'). His approach has been used to good effect by police hostage nego-tiators,[13] but has been dismissed by some theorists of terrorism as too simplistic. It serves to highlight the dangers of ignoring the perceptions of the other side, a key component of 'structural violence' (injustices perceived to stem from the dominant order).[14] According to this concept, insurgency (direct violence) is per-ceived by the authorities solely as a security issue to be dealt with by 'legitim-ate' forces of law and order, whereas the insurgents may view direct violence as the only means of liberating their people from a structurally unjust system (apartheid, imperialism, slavery, etc.).

Although Yeltsin and his entourage routinely characterised Chechen sepa-ratists as terrorists, bandits, criminals and madmen, in the first war there was widespread understanding among the Russian public that Chechens perceived their struggle as one of national liberation. Few salient lessons appeared to be drawn by the Russian authorities from Western experience of domestic insur-gency or the turbulent history of Russo-Chechen relations. In an article in the *Washington Post* in September 1995, Yo'av Karny questioned whether this was due to 'cultural condescension or sheer racism', adding that:

> Sadly, few questions have been raised in Russia about the demonization of the Chechens. Few lessons have been drawn from the failure to respect a different culture, an attitude that precludes any attempt to understand it and thus coexist with it.[15]

Perhaps the supreme example of the insensitive arrogance on the part of Kremlin leaders towards one of their subject peoples was the naming of the Soviet operation to deport the Chechens in February 1944 *chechevitsa* (lentil), clearly playing on the nearness in sound of this word to *chechentsy* (the Russian word for Chechens).[16] However, whereas the packing tightly into railway trucks and the transportation of 'goods' over thousands of miles might be held to be an acceptable mode of transport for a sack of pulses, few would agree that it is befitting treatment of any human being, let alone an entire people, including old folk, women and children.

Dudaev blamed the Russian invasion for the emergence of a radical form of Islam in his country.[17] This radicalisation of the insurgents by the time of the second war explains, to a large degree, the erosion of sympathy for the Chechens both in Russia and the West. The Russian press exploited this, carry-ing articles, headlined in Arabic fonts (that echoed the Nazi use of Gothic script) and carrying titles such as *Dnevnik terrorista* (Diary of a Terrorist)[18] and *Nalozhnitsa vakhkhabitov* (Concubine of the *Wahhabites*),[19] which preyed on the fear in the Russian psyche of Islamic fundamentalism and played a big part in demonising the Chechens as the 'other'.

Of course, as we have seen in Chapter 3, the acceptance of Russia's aims in these wars depends upon whether one considers the Russo-Chechen conflict as one of the last anti-colonial wars of liberation or as a case of terrorism within a friendly state. The means employed by Russia to achieve her ends in Chechnya have evoked bitter criticism from non-governmental organisations both abroad and within Russia, notably from the human rights organisation *Memorial*.[20] *Memorial* has produced a number of books and reports on the Chechen conflicts, holds and attends conferences and maintains a most informative website.[21]

A number of human rights groups in the West produced lengthy reports on both the first and second conflict. The Organisation for Security and Cooperation in Europe (OSCE) was the most influential international organisation to monitor consistently the human rights situation in Chechnya in the first war and was even instrumental in securing the peace that ended that conflict. As Russia only joined the Parliamentary Assembly of the Council of Europe after the end of the first war, that body could not take significant action against perceived violations of human rights by the Russians in the earlier confrontation. However, during the second conflict, this organisation has been in the forefront of bringing pressure to bear on the Russian authorities over violations of human rights in Chechnya.[22] It has signally failed, however, to bring sufficient pressure on the governments of its member countries to persuade them to take firm action against Russia over Chechnya.

Significantly, whereas the response of foreign governments has been muted in both wars, that of the Russian public has swung from hostility and shame, the first time round, to at best indifference, and, at worst, active encouragement for the hardest of lines to be taken in the second war. For example, a poll taken in the early stages of the second conflict revealed that fully 64 per cent of Russians wanted all Chechens out of Russia and favoured the bombing of Chechen towns and settlements.[23]

The Economist, even before the outbreak of the first war, demonstrated the lack of international sympathy for Chechen independence:

> Chechnya has gained an international reputation, not as a gallant little nation struggling against Kremlin imperialism, but as a tinpot dictatorship with gun-mad gangsters prone to vendettas and shining sports cars.[24]

Whatever the degree of justification for such stereotyping of the Chechens, implicit in the above quote, such sentiments go a long way towards explaining the failure of any major state either to recognise Chechnya's independence or to condemn without qualification Russia's excesses, despite ample evidence of the extreme and widespread abuse of fundamental human rights by the federal forces in both wars.

One might have anticipated that official Russian perceptions of Chechen militancy would be as stereotyped, subjective and judgemental as those held by Western governments in relation to their own revolutionary groupings, but the role of TV and the press was less predictable. In the event, media coverage of the first war proved a major political factor being, on the one hand, subject to official manipulation and guilty of propagating some of the crudest stereotypes of Chechens and yet, on the other, sufficiently critical of the Russian authorities' conduct of the war to ensure that throughout its duration this conflict remained hugely unpopular with the Russian public. The first survey of public opinion conducted in Moscow in January–February 1995 found that 72 per cent of respondents disapproved of the conduct of the war, and that 94 per cent got their information on events in Chechnya from central Russian TV.[25]

The feeling allegedly was widespread among Russian generals that victory in the first war had been snatched from them 'by journalists, liberals, or Jewish Masons',[26] whereas it was the military's lack of openness that, in the opinion of both Russian and Western observers, helped maintain public opinion against the war and, eventually, led to the federal defeat.[27] Russian military commanders, with the full backing of the Kremlin leadership, ensured that no such freedom would be granted to either domestic or foreign press during the second war, which as a result proved to be significantly less unpopular among the Russian public, despite the failure for a second time to secure the anticipated quick and decisive victory. A key role in this was the representation, not only of the Chechens as the enemy, but also of those at home and abroad who supported them as 'accomplices of the enemy' (*posobniki vraga*). One commentator has identified these as including:

> within the country – Duma politicians, journalists (journalist scumbags), human rights activists, soldiers' mothers, corrupt officers and generals, and the first Russian president.

External 'accomplices' are held to include among others: 'Islamists, Georgians, Western intelligence services.'[28]

Unsurprisingly, those 'positive' heroes of the war in Chechnya portrayed by the Russian media generally had little time for such people and perceived the situation in more black-and-white terms. Thus, one factor which did not change, at least in the initial stages of the second war, was the deliberate blurring in the official media of concepts of 'us' (i.e. Russian federal troops) and 'them' (Chechens), the latter being subject to, as we shall see, particularly crude forms of demonisation.

While such demonisation of the foe by governments and the media is by no means unknown in the West,[29] the Chechen wars provided both the Russian authorities and the mass media with novel challenges. To begin with, officially, Chechens were regarded as Russians (*rossiiskie*), along with Buryats, Chuvash, Tatars, etc. – not ethnic Russians (*russkie*), but with homelands within the Russian Federation.[30] Thus, Russian officials and journalists were not strictly accurate in referring to 'our' troops and 'their' fighters.[31] Moreover, Dudaev, in common with the Chechen military commander Aslan Maskhadov and many of the Chechen field commanders, was a fluent Russian-speaker and had served with distinction in the Soviet armed forces.

'Demonisation' is one of the semantic nuances that characterise the emotive 'terrorist versus freedom fighter' debate,[32] which has embraced virtually every insurgent leader in the postwar world, from Yasser Arafat to Nelson Mandela. The ambiguity this engenders may be seen in Russian perceptions of leading figures in the Chechen resistance: the commander of the Chechen forces in the first war and elected president in the second, Aslan Maskhadov; the leading Chechen field commander, Shamil Basaev; and the Arab mercenary, Khattab.[33]

Perceptions, for example, of Basaev, who was to emerge in the second war as Russia's wanted 'Terrorist No. 1', in the first war ranged from 'an ideological terrorist' and 'a butcher' to 'Chechnya's greatest war hero', 'cybernetic super-star' and 'a rebel with a cause'. A Russian reporter writing of Basaev at the commencement of the second war pleaded: 'Call him what you will – a bandit, a romantic, a murderer. Only not a terrorist.'[34]

In the second war, on the then still independent Russian TV station – NTV – Gennady Troshev, the Russian general who, in 1999, led the federal forces back into Chechnya (where he was born), openly denounced Maskhadov, Basaev and Khattab as 'terrorists'.[35] Khattab, in particular, the 'demon from hell', or 'genie in a jeep',[36] with Che Guevara-style combat fatigues, flowing locks and beard, represents the ambiguity of perceptions; he might easily have been regarded, according to one's viewpoint, as either an archetypical 'terrorist' or a classic 'freedom fighter'.

Demonisation so dehumanises the opposition as to mitigate responsibility, in the perception of both 'our' forces and 'our' public, of killing 'them'. In this vein, General Mikhailov (who experienced both wars in Chechnya) in an inter-view for an American journal referred to Chechen fighters as 'monkeys' and regretted that: 'One cannot make "whites" out of Chechens.'[37] Pogroms and round-ups of Chechens were further symptoms of the 'Chechenophobia' that surfaced in both conflicts.[38]

The Russians were liberal in their use of the epithets 'criminal' and 'crazy' and their synonyms in describing their Chechen opponents, laying special emphasis on Mafia connections and drawing attention to a fanaticism bordering on madness. The 'criminal' label was pinned to the Chechens, first and fore-most, due to the identification of their *teip* system with that of the Mafia.[39] The link between the deportations and Chechen involvement in organised crime has been well documented. However, some Russian journalists have taken this stereotyping to embarrassing extremes. Yury Mogutin is reported as writing in the journal *Novy Vzglyad* (New Viewpoint) that the Chechen nation 'had given the world absolutely nothing except international terrorism and the drugs busi-ness', adding that 'any Russian feels towards the Chechens a zoological, genetic, animal hatred'.[40]

That certain Chechen players on both sides of this conflict did indeed boast criminal records, should not obscure the fact that the credentials of the Russian side, right up to ministerial level, were hardly unimpeachable in this respect. The popular Chechen field commander, Ruslan Gelaev, is an example, as was the former pro-Russian Mayor of Grozny, Beslan Gantamirov, who was literally plucked from Lefortovo prison in Moscow – where he was serving time for embezzlement – for the job.

The 'crazy' element of insurgency stems from a conflation of 'a-normal' with 'abnormal' behaviour, in that those involved actively oppose the accepted 'rules' and 'norms' of society that any 'rational' person would regard as 'reasonable'. A clear distinction is thus drawn between the noble but non-threatening Chechen warrior (*djigit*) and the bloodthirsty and dangerous rebel (*bandit*).

Further grounds for questioning the sanity of leading Chechen protagonists stemmed from perceptions of their slightly ridiculous posturing, megalomania and illusions of grandeur. This is evident not only in the 'tinpot' presidential conduct of independent Chechnya-Ichkeria's first elected head of state, Djokhar Dudaev,[41] but also in the bragging of his son-in-law and field commander Salman Raduev, who was described by his own side as 'possessed'[42] and by Russian observers as 'loony'.[43] Raduev, for example, threatened both Yeltsin and former Prime Minister Chernomyrdin with a trial by *Shari'a* court and public execution in Grozny![44] In the second war it was the ascribed fanatical adherence to fundamentalist Islamic practices that provided the richest source of Chechen 'craziness'.

Chechen leaders, in the conflict with Russia, employed declarations by Muslim fighters of the *gazavat* as a rallying call. As we have seen, it was the chosen architect of Putin's policy of Chechenisation – Akhmad Kadyrov – who first declared a *gazavat* on Russia in 1995.[45] The Russian authorities exploited such calls to enhance the pejorative portrayal of their enemy as 'terrorists' as well as 'bandits' and 'fanatics'. 'Crusaders' entered the discourse of the more militantly religious Chechen fighters as a derogatory term for their Russian opponents.[46]

This mixture of criminal brutality and religious fanaticism has been exploited fully by the pro-Kremlin media. As Yuri Maltsev of the Mises Institute reports:

> Russian government propaganda (following the best traditions of Soviet indoctrination and employing the same people) was and is trying to portray all Chechens as criminals and fanatics. Chechens are portrayed possessing special 'national' characteristics: 'brutality, sadism, fanaticism and fascism.' Chechens are even accused of 'making Russians drunk by giving them vodka'.[47]

Although the brigand portrayed in Lermontov's verse fits the image of the Chechen, held by most Russians, after the bombing campaign, it would be wrong to suggest that, historically, this has been the only stereotype of the Chechen. Lermontov himself, along with Pushkin, Tolstoi and other giants of Russian literature, who participated in the Caucasian War of 1817–1864, left also a much more positive image of the wild, freedom-loving, hot-blooded mountain warrior that still appeals strongly to the romantic side of the Russian imagination, in much the same way as does the braveheart image of the Scottish Highlanders to the Anglo-Saxon mentality.

The parallel may be taken further as both the Highland Regiment and the 'Savage Division' (immortalised in Eisenstein's *Oktyabr'*; and made up largely of Chechen, Ingush and Dagestani mountain men)[48] became prized units within, respectively, the British and Tsarist imperial armies and handed down traditions of military prowess that survived the break-up of both empires.[49] Despite Soviet charges that the Chechens were a nation of collaborators with the Nazis, there is ample evidence that many Chechens had fought with distinction on the Soviet side in the Great Patriotic War of 1941–1945.[50] Moreover, the first president of Chechnya-Ichkeria, Djokhar Dudayev, for example, had been a general in the Soviet Air Force (and is credited with the elaboration of carpet-bombing techniques during the Soviet–Afghan War)[51] and his successor, Aslan Maskhadov, reached the rank of colonel in the Soviet Army (and was serving in Vilnius when the TV tower was stormed in January 1991).[52]

The years of the wolf: Russian demonisation under Yeltsin, 1991–1999

In both Scotland and Chechnya, what these romantic portrayals of mountain men obscure is the inhuman manner in which they were hunted down like animals, almost to extinction, by government forces. In Scotland the animal that comes to mind is the proud and noble stag, in Chechnya it is the wolf – a fearsome but worthy enemy, cunning, fierce and untamable, but wild and dangerous enough to warrant only death and destruction. These parallel perceptions: the Chechen's instinctive need to fight for self-preservation and the Russians' desire to exterminate resistance among the mountain peoples have resurfaced nearly 150 years later.

The identification of the Chechens, by themselves and by the Russians, with wolves became a central feature of this war of images between 1994 and 1999. A Chechen fighter was proud to be called a *borz* (wolf) and strove to uphold the spiritual affinity between the *abrek* and the courageous, lone wolf silhouetted against the moon. The Chechens have adopted the wolf as a national symbol, it being portrayed on the flag and coat of arms of independent Chechnya-Ichkeria and appearing in the very first line of the Chechen-Ichkerian national anthem.[53] Significantly, the new national anthem commissioned under Akhmad Kadyrov's pro-Russian regime erased any mention of the wolf, which was removed also from the new flag and coat of arms.[54]

The Russians, drawing on the powerful impact of the wolf on the Russian mentality, from the protagonist in the fairy tale to the source of machismo pleasure in the wolf-hunt, have seized upon this identity with relish. Not only was the conflict against the Chechens likened at times to a wolf-hunt, but also various Chechen military leaders were given lupine epithets: Aslan Maskhadov – 'the wolf with a human face',[55] Shamil Basaev – 'the lone wolf',[56] and Salman Raduev – 'the loony wolf'.[57]

The most enduring literary portrait of a Chechen is that provided by Lev Tolstoi in his short story *Hadji Murat*, set in Chechnya in the 1850s during the Great Caucasian War. Whereas the murderous and destructive raid on the Chechen *aul* (village) is perceived in this tale by the Russian troops as little more than an exhilarating hunting party, the reaction of the Chechens described by Tolstoi expresses the perspective of the victims eloquently:

Nobody spoke of hate towards the Russians. The feeling which all Chechens large and small experienced was stronger than hate. It was not hate, but a refusal to accept these Russian dogs as people and such repugnance, loathing and bewilderment at the clumsy cruelty of these creatures that the desire to destroy them, like the desire to destroy rats, poisonous spiders and wolves, was as natural a feeling as that of self-preservation.[58]

Chechens from the village of Samashki expressed virtually identical emotions (also calling the Russian troops 'dogs') in April 1995, after Russian federal forces had perpetrated one of the bloodiest excesses against civilians of the entire 1994–1996 war,[59] an act of barbarism repeated in February 2000 in the village of Katyr Yurt.[60]

A British officer travelling through Chechnya in the 1850s noted similar sentiments of disgust among the local population at Russian excesses:

> The wanton brutality of the soldiers to the inhabitants, in their line of march, disgusted even those tribes who would have been willing to remain friendly, and all learned unmistakably what they had to expect from Russian rule.[61]

He recorded also a detailed characterisation of the mountain people encountered in Chechnya:

> The Caucasian character has all the good and the evil features common amongst semi-savage mountaineers. Possessed of the most daring courage ... frugal and temperate in their ordinary habits; honourable and affectionate in their domestic relations; they are, nevertheless, to an enemy, or, indeed, to an outsider of any kind, both ruthless and bloodthirsty, seeming to be actuated by but two motives – love of bloodshed and love of gain.[62]

A Russian observer in that region at approximately the same time was less even-handed, venturing that the Chechen nation was remarkable:

> for her love of plunder, robbery and murder, for her spirit of deceit, courage, recklessness, resolution, cruelty, fearlessness, her uncontrollable violence and unlimited arrogance.[63]

Some observers fear that the conflicts have eroded some of the Chechens positive traits. Sergei Kovalev, one of the leading Russian human rights activists, notes with dismay the growing *machismo* of the Chechen fighters, accusing them of behaving like gangsters, trying to outdo each other in brutality because they feared to appear weak, hinting that, because of this, their flag should depict not a wolf but a jackal.[64] The Abkhaz writer, Fazil' Iskander, regrets the disappearance of respect for older and wiser heads among the younger Chechen warlords.[65]

The changing of Russian perceptions of the Chechens and the conflict in Chechnya is reflected in opinion polls: by September 2000, only 15 per cent of Russians thought that the Chechens were fighting for independence, against 38 per cent for money, 22 per cent for revenge and 16 per cent due to their aggressive nature.[66] That only 16 per cent of Russians considered the war in Chechnya as *the* major political event in Russia in 2000 exemplifies public indifference to the conflict.

Similarly, in an opinion poll taken in 2005, asking respondents to name the most important event in Russia in 1995, the taking of Grozny in the first Chechen War had slipped from first place with 55 per cent in 1995 to 40 per cent ten years later, whereas the unsolved murder of the popular investigative journalist, Vladislav List'ev, had risen in the same period from 35 per cent to 48 per cent. Significantly, however, the importance of terrorist acts had risen in retrospect over the decade: the hostage-taking incident at Budennovsk from 17 per cent to 29 per cent and the bomb attacks in Moscow and Vladikavkaz from 6 per cent to 22 per cent.[67]

At the same time, Russians are aware that the longer the war drags on the more Chechens will take up arms against them. Vadim Dubnov admits:

> Today we are fighting against those who a year ago were hoping that work would appear and money for a new house, and that's why they cursed their radicals for invading Dagestan. And if we don't start to work with them today, then tomorrow they will be twice as many and, the day after tomorrow, their already grown children will regard it as a disgrace not to join their ranks.[68]

He highlights a growing awareness among Russians of how alien the Chechens have become[69] and sees no chance of early reconciliation:

> How can those that have forgotten everything live alongside those who have lost feelings of pain and danger, but remember everything?[70]

From its declaration of independence in October 1991 until the outbreak of the first war in December 1994, Chechnya was de facto independent. Russia was more concerned with its internal problems and was faced with a greater security threat on its borders, the civil war in Tajikistan, than that posed by the Chechens. By 1993, the Chechens were alone in refusing to sign the new Russian Constitution, even the Ingush having broken away in 1992 to join the Russian Federation. In 1994, when the Yeltsin administration finally had the opportunity to turn its attention to its rebellious southern republic, a series of botched armed insurrections and coups were launched, culminating in the humiliating capture and destruction, in November 1994, of a column of Russian tanks masquerading as Chechen oppositionist forces. On 11 December 1994, Yeltsin launched a full-scale land and air attack on Chechnya to 'restore constitutional order', culminating in the disastrous assault on the Chechen capital, Grozny, on New Year's Eve.

Once it was obvious that Yeltsin would not achieve the quick victory in Chechnya that he sought, public opinion in both Russia and the West turned sharply against the Russian federal forces. The disproportionate use of massive air power and artillery to flatten Grozny, ostensibly to 'save' its citizens, the incompetence of the Russian Army and the heroic resistance of the Chechen defenders were all played out in front of the world's (and Russia's) media, with the result that support for the Chechen 'underdog' against the Russian 'topdog' was widespread.

Yeltsin's attempts to brand the Chechen resistance as 'bandits' or 'terrorists', the regime 'criminal', and its leader Djokhar Dudaev as 'mad' sounded like hollow rhetoric to a considerable proportion of the Russian population, some 70 per cent of whom remain opposed to the war throughout.[71] Because the Chechen fighters spoke Russian and were much more accommodating to both Russian and Western journalists and human rights activists than were the federal forces, the insurgents got more than their fair share of positive reporting and were generally held to have won the propaganda war during the 1994–1996 conflict.

The years of the werewolf: Russian demonisation of the Chechens under Putin, 1999–to date

The Chechen wolf theme had so caught the public imagination in the first war that it was quite easy for the media to resurrect it when fighting broke out again in 1999. This time, however, it was against the background of Russia's own 'Black September' after which the public mood swung decisively against the Chechens.

In the aftermath of the apartment house bombings in Moscow and other Russian cities in September 1999, *Izvestiya* headlined one of its reports of a Chechen connection 'Wolf tracks'[72] and *Argumenty i fakty* featured on its front page a pack of rabid wolves under the headline: 'The Chechen wolves have been driven back to their lair, but for how long?'[73] It was alleged by that the Russian guards at the notorious Chernokozovo detention camp in Chechnya would terrify male Chechen prisoners by calling: 'Wolves, the hunters have come', before dragging them out and raping them.[74]

On 1 February 2000, the campaign by the Russian federal forces to rid Grozny of Chechen fighters was called 'Operation Wolf Hunt'.[75] One of the crack Russian counter-terrorist units was called the *volkodavy* (the wolfhounds).[76] Playing upon this theme, a popular Chechen song of the first campaign by Timur Mutsuraev, referred to Dudaev's *boyeviki* as *Volki bez granits* (Wolves without frontiers),[77] which also featured as the title of an article by Marina Strukova published in *Zavtra* on 22 September 2004. Memoirs of Russian soldiers fighting in the Chechen campaigns also reflected this theme, Nikolai Astashkin's *Po vol'chemu sledu* (Following Wolf Tracks) being just one example.[78]

Although the ordinary Russian soldiers had already picked up on the wolf theme in the first conflict, as is usually the case in such counter-insurgent operations, the troops soon came up with their own names for their opponents. Among these were *dukhi* (spooks),[79] because of the way the Chechen fighters would appear as if from nowhere, especially at night and melt away again in the darkness; *chichi*[80] and *chekhi*[81] (both shortened and distorted variants of *chechentsy* – the Russian for Chechens). 'Chichi' was also the name of the monkey known to all Russian children in Kornei Chukovsky's celebrated children's book, *Doktor Aibolit* (Doctor Ouch).[82] The 'monkey' theme was quite popular among troops, even officers, for instance, General Mikhailov going on record to foreign correspondents calling the Chechen fighters *obezyany* (monkeys).[83] Finally, the religious element in the confrontation was reflected in the name *modjakhedy* (mujahideen) applied to Chechen fighters by Russian troops.[84]

The Russian population at large, however, continued to call Chechens, as they did all other inhabitants of the Northern Caucasus *cherniye* (blacks), *chernozhopy* (black arses) or by the euphemistic acronym 'LKN', meaning *litso kavkazskoi natsional'nosti* (a person of Caucasian nationality). The Russian journalist Sergei Sossinsky wrote in the English-language periodical *Moscow News*:

> Most city residents of peasant origin in Russia blame Jews or 'Caucasians' (people who come from the Caucasus) for all their woes. Despite the fact that Caucasians (being Caucasians) are largely white-skinned, common Russians call them blacks or black asses. Police officials have even come up with a term 'a person of Caucasian nationality.'[85]

Angry and ashamed at their force's capitulation in the first war, and horrified at independent Chechnya-Ichkeria's slide into savage anarchy in the inter-war period, under Maskhadov, a leader who appeared incapable of stopping the excesses of the Chechen warlords, Russian public opinion was not minded to be magnanimous to its southern neighbours.

A shocking sequence of *Shari'a* beheadings and torture of Russian and foreign hostages by the Chechens, which were captured on videos and widely distributed by both sides for propaganda reasons, stoked up anti-Chechen feeling among the Russian public and reinforced calls for a 'crusade' against these Islamic fundamentalists.

The symbolism of this was not lost on Aleksandr Nevzorov, the Russian arch-nationalist and TV director, who, in a gruesome and emotionally-charged scene in his film *Chistilishche* ('Purgatory'), had the stereotypically wolf-eyed Chechen commander order his *mujahideen* to crucify the captured young Russian tank crewman.[86] This revealed how easily, in Russia today, pent-up frustrations, anger and injured national pride can be harnessed against a designated enemy, particularly if the foe can be presented as a threat to Russia by alien forces, in this case Islamic fundamentalists. The screening by Channel 2, on Russian TV, on the weekend prior to the invasion of Chechnya that signalled the outbreak of the second war, of a gruesome video depicting a stereotypical black-bearded Chechen fighter cutting the throat of a young blond Russian soldier, served to raise to fever pitch the demands for revenge against Chechnya.[87]

This abhorrence at the perceived evil savagery of the Chechens led to the Russian media introducing the term *oborotni* (werewolves) to describe the Chechen rebels.[88] Although not etymologically connected to the wolf in Russian, it did represent a transitional shift in the Russian perception of the Chechens from a wild animal to something as equally inhuman but much more sinister.

Of course, manifestations of such atavistic behaviour not only confirm the prejudices of ordinary Russians against Chechens, but can also lead to the exploitation of the victims for religious and nationalistic purposes. Thus, Yevgeny Rodionov, a 19-year-old conscript border guard, beheaded in Chechnya on 23 May 1996 (his birthday) after 100 days in captivity, reputedly being held by Arbi Baraev, has apparently become something of a saint in his home town of Kurilovo (west of Moscow) and his grave, there, a site of pilgrimages from all over Russia.[89]

It should be stressed, however, that the Caucasian peoples, in common with the Balts, generally accept the asymmetry of their relationship with Russia as a fact of life and one that has to be accommodated and, at times, just tolerated. Thus, Chechnya's neighbours have all more or less resigned themselves to the fact that, however they might yearn for self-determination, if not independence, it really is not worth the suffering that would be required to achieve this. In Chechnya's case the brutality of periodic Russian attempts to crush their distinctive way of life appears to have pushed the Chechens almost uniquely towards choosing the path of resistance rather than that of resignation.[90]

The first Russo-Chechen War (1994–1996) and the de facto independence of Chechnya-Ichkeria from 1996 until 1999, culminating in the ill-judged *Wahhabi* incursion into Dagestan, actually reinforced this preference for peaceful coexistence with the Russians among the North Caucasian peoples. Paradoxically, it is the effects of Caucasophobia on all Caucasians during the second war (1999 to date) and the extension of sweeps into neighbouring territories (e.g. Dagestan and Ingushetia) that appear to have radicalised the opposition to Russian rule across the North Caucasus.

However, elements of the Chechen resistance (from Akhmad Kadyrov to Aslan Maskhadov) came to the realisation that an accommodation with the Russians short of independence had to be made in order to save the Chechen people from further suffering and, perhaps, themselves from annihilation; a fully pragmatic choice in the circumstances (although both, in the event, were assassinated within a year of each other). Yet, because the Kremlin was unwilling to recognise even moderate Chechen oppositionists as anything other than terrorists, those who took a pragmatic line were caught potentially between a rock and a hard place; the Russians would target them if they did not cooperate, just as surely as would the 'irreconcilable' Chechen opposition – led by Shamil Basaev – if they did.

At the same time the existence of a relatively successful and thriving

Chechen diaspora indicates that the Chechens can survive and flourish in modernising societies. As has been the case with the Baltic States, Armenia, Lebanon and elsewhere, successful academics, business men and women, politicians and sporting celebrities in the diaspora can provide important alternative role models for aspiring Chechen youngsters to the gun-toting warlords of the Chechen resistance or, indeed, the pro-Russian forces under the supreme warlord Ramzan Kadyrov. Certainly, on the basis of countless conversations I have had with a broad range of Russians from taxi drivers to academicians, it must be said that far too many of them still tend to cling to the stereotype of successful Chechens as no more than criminal mafiosi.

Putin, to his credit, albeit belatedly, did come recognise during the course of the second conflict the incongruity of stereotyping the Chechens as a nation of bandits, on the one hand, while seeking to keep them as Russian citizens on the other. On 25 June 2002, Putin finally admitted that: 'Our task is to destroy this image [of Chechens] as terrorists.'[91]

One of the more bizarre attempts by the Putin administration to make Chechens feel part of Russia was the official encouragement of the *Terek* soccer team from Grozny, which won the Russian Cup in 2004, represented Russia in 2004–2005 in the UEFA Cup and was received by President Putin at an official reception in the Kremlin. Rebel Chechen websites have likened the role of the club's patron – Ramzan Kadyrov – to that of Uday Hussein vis-à-vis the Iraqi soccer team.[92] However, despite understandable euphoria among Chechens at this unexpected boost to their international profile, there remained widespread scepticism in Russia about the significance of a team that boasted only a handful of Chechen players and that played its home games in Pyatigorsk, in southern Russia, well outside of the Chechen Republic.[93]

Much to the dismay of Kadyrov and his team, *Terek* finished sixteenth and last in the Russian premier league in 2005, but not before the young Chechen deputy prime minister had written to President Putin protesting at the anti-Chechen bias displayed by Russian referees![94] This sporting setback was made all the more difficult for Chechens to swallow by the fact that the premiership title was won that season by CSKA Moscow – the Russian Army team.[95]

Conclusion

The dilution of *narodnost'* as a concept representing the unity of identity of all citizens of the Russian Federation is well illustrated in the Russo-Chechen conflict. Imposed throughout the Russian Empire and, under the guise of 'Soviet patriotism' and 'Friendship of the Peoples', the USSR, this concept has fallen foul of the 'Russia for the Russians' syndrome in the post-Soviet period. In July 2005, 58 per cent were moderately or decisively for the concept of 'Russia for the Russians' and 32 per cent against; proportions that had not changed significantly a year later.[96]

A poll conducted by the Russian Academy of Sciences' Centre for the Study of Xenophobia shortly after the Beslan siege in 2004 found that 55.8 per cent of those polled regarded 'non-Russian nationalities' as a threat to the security of Russia.[97] In a poll published in *The Economist* in February 2005,[98] it was revealed that 52 per cent of Russians would rather Chechens did not live in Russia (40 per cent preferring a Russia with no 'Caucasians' at all). Indeed, many Russians feel much closer to the 25 million ethnic Russians living in the 'Near Abroad' than they do to the half as numerous non-Russian citizens of the Russian Federation. Given the Chechen cultural narrative, Russian chauvinism, Caucasophobia and the attendant demonisation of the Chechens, there is little prospect of the average Chechen sharing a sense of *narodnost'* with the Russians.

In the first war, the arbitrary brutality of the federal forces was kept in the public consciousness in Russia and abroad and the Russian authorities admitted that it had 'lost' the battle for the hearts and minds. As Aleksei Malashenko and Dmitry Trenin from the Carnegie Institute have noted:

> The Chechen campaign of 1994–1996 was the first 'televised war' in the history of Russia. The 'picture' presented of this war played an enormous role in changes for the worse in attitudes to the Russian military machine.[99]

Even before the commencement of the second war, Putin's administration was successfully manipulating both the domestic and international mass media coverage. By drawing on lessons learned from NATO's information war in Kosovo, elite 'liberal' opposition was marginalised and discounted, while popular support was maintained.[100] As a result, the second war only made the headlines, both domestically and internationally, when the Chechens launched a 'terrorist spectacular', along the lines of the Moscow theatre siege of 2002, the suicide bombings of 2003, or the Beslan school siege in 2004, hardening convictions at home and abroad, particularly in the wake of 9/11, that the conflict was, indeed, part of the global struggle against terrorism.

The role of the 'information war' is seen, therefore, as crucial in dissuading both Russian and world opinion from perceiving the renewed conflict for what, in essence, it was: a series of overlapping conflicts that included the fight against terrorism but also involved a continuation of the battle for Russian territorial integrity, an attempt to control the black hole of lawlessness that independent Chechnya-Ichkeria had become and, insofar as the generals were itching for revenge for their humiliating defeat in the first war, a clash of culture in which the 'civilised' Russians could tame the 'savage' Chechens. The impact of this media manipulation was not lost on the more observant of Russian commentators:

> In contrast to the previous war in Chechnya, this one has failed to evoke indignation among Russians. The public seldom hears the bad news from Chechnya, Russian losses aren't regularly disclosed and major media report only the deadliest attacks. The government makes it virtually impossible for journalists to work in Chechnya except in close coordination with the military. The media are banned from reporting interviews with the rebels.[101]

Through skilful manipulation and control of the Russian mass media and by not missing a chance to remind the world of Russia's membership of the global alliance against terror,[102] Putin's administration effectively has removed all other elements of the war in Chechnya from the political agenda at home and abroad. Should the Russian mass media step out of line, retribution can be swift, as *Izvestiya* editor Raf Shakirov found in September 2004, when he was obliged to resign after allowing publication of explicit but disturbing pictures of the Beslan siege.[103]

Putin's policy of demonising the Chechens certainly had borne fruit. While it might be anticipated that the more backward-looking Russian generals still yearn for a 'Caucasus without Caucasians',[104] it is extremely disturbing to note how such views have spread throughout Russian society. The phenomenon of 'Caucasophobia' among ethnic Russians appeared to be spreading fast and, by October 2002, Lyudmilla Alekseyeva, Chairperson of the Moscow Helsinki Group, had identified it as:

> Definitely the most serious problem that Russia is faced with today. It is very widespread among the population in general, at all levels.[105]

Later that month the very heart of Russia's capital was struck by the tragedy of the Dubrovka theatre siege, a horrendous event that, in common with the subsequent Beslan school siege in September 2004, served only to exacerbate anti-Chechen sentiment among the broader Russian public.

Paradoxically, it is claimed that it is because Putin is so in step emotionally with the bulk of the Russian people that, for better or worse, he shares the same prejudices against, and negative attitudes towards the Chechens in particular, and Caucasians in general.[106] Therefore, as long as Putin or a like-minded *silovik* is in power in the Kremlin, there is unlikely to be much attention paid to addressing the deep-seated attitudes that spawn so much of the violent behaviour in Chechnya, let alone a genuine attempt to resolve centuries-old cultural contradictions between the two peoples.

It is difficult to imagine Vladimir Putin, or any similar Russian president offering the Chechen people a Willy Brandt-style apology for the wrongs historically visited upon them by successive Russian and Soviet regimes. Given the tortured history between the peoples, even this gesture, small in itself, might go a long way towards healing the wounds of the past centuries.

5   Wars by any other name

Yeltsin's 'restoration of constitutional order' and Putin's 'counter-terrorist operation'

'Only a fool could think that a war is going on in the North Caucasus,' remarks a character in Rudakov's book *The Chechen Mafia*, 'for the war is going on throughout Russia, because there are funerals in Vologda, and in Khabarovsk, and in Yakutsk.'

(Quoted by Galina Zvereva)[1]

The Chechen wars of 1994–1996 and 1999 to date have played a significant role in determining the outcome of Russia's three post-Soviet presidential elections, and, insofar as Vladimir Putin was Boris Yeltsin's nominated successor, effectively thrice (1996, 2000 and 2004) saved the presidency from the so-called 'red-black' coalition of communists and nationalists. Others have pointed out that it has been precisely the two Chechen campaigns that have set back prospects for Russia's transition to democracy.[2]

On becoming Russia's second democratically elected president on 26 March 2000, Putin followed Yeltsin's example by successfully playing the 'Chechen' card during the election campaign. By July 1996, Yeltsin had persuaded enough Russian voters (misguidedly, it turned out) that his war in Chechnya could not be lost, to beat convincingly in the second round his communist opponent, Gennady Zyuganov.[3] Nearly (crucially, not exactly) four years later[4] in Russia's last truly competitive election, Putin defeated the same opponent in the first round by convincing enough of this electorate that his war in Chechnya must be won, whatever the cost.

The major difference was that Yeltsin saved his presidency by climbing to victory from an all-time low personal rating in early 1995,[5] when the war was going very badly, whereas the tough stance vis-à-vis the Chechens that Putin adopted from the very beginning of his presidential campaign,[6] assured him of solid support throughout.[7]

The macho language that accompanied this new stance is epitomised in Putin's promise, made on 24 September 1999, to hunt down the terrorists wherever they might hide: 'we will waste them even in the shithouse' (*i v sortire zamochim*). In 2002, I asked Anna Politkovskaya, who was in London for a talk at the City University, how best to translate Putin's notorious threat and she suggested that I use the language (jargon) of the 'barrack room or prison' (*serzhantsko-ugolovnyi*). This corroborates Sergei Kovalev's earlier description of 'the argot of the criminal world'; he rendering this phrase as a promise to 'bury them in their own crap'.[8]

It could be claimed that Putin won the presidency precisely because he promised victory in Chechnya;[9] certainly, the second Russo-Chechen War provided the launch pad that thrust him into power in March 2000.[10] Gone, apparently, were the ambiguous Russian attitudes towards the Chechens that dogged Yeltsin's war of 1994–1996. For, as has been well documented, neither the Russian nor Chechen peoples had sought war in 1994. Due to the personal and political shortcomings of both Dudaev and Yeltsin, however, and almost certainly against the wishes of both of their electorates, the two sides stumbled into all-out confrontation. Yeltsin needed a 'short, victorious war' to re-establish his popularity and the Chechens, once invaded, rallied around Dudaev to resist Russian occupation. Bizarrely, Grozny, home to a significant proportion of Russians in Chechnya was subjected to carpet bombing raids by the Russian air force, hardly a policy, one might conclude, that is likely to win the hearts and minds of those targeted, let alone persuade them of the benefits of Chechnya staying in Russia.

Russians leading the war effort in Chechnya could have drawn on a substantial body of theory and information that might have caused them to temper their perceptions of the Chechens and their aspirations, thus avoiding the public humiliation at home and abroad generated by the brutality and ineptitude with which the campaigns were fought and, finally, lost.

For the 1994–1996 war in Chechnya represented the first conflict on Russian territory to be covered in detail by the newly liberated Russian media. This lesson was one of the few that were learned by the Russian authorities,[11] which in the second war managed the media more effectively,[12] although they could not prevent a battle for hearts and minds fought out mainly over the Internet.[13]

The language factor was important also in that, in the first conflict, Russian journalists were afforded greater access to the Chechen forces than to their 'own' side, and were in a position to understand and relay, if not sympathise with the Chechen point-of-view.[14] In the second war, Russian journalists seeking objective information from the 'other' side might expect the sort of treatment meted out to the Radio Liberty journalist Andrei Babitsky, who was 'traded' by the Russian military to Chechen kidnappers.[15] Not only was *Novaya gazeta* correspondent, Anna Politkovskaya, imprisoned by Russian troops and threatened with rape and execution,[16] but was also apparently poisoned in September 2004 when on her way to negotiate the release of children held hostage in Beslan.[17] That in October 2006 even this courageous professional journalist was shot dead outside her Moscow apartment demonstrates both the danger inherent in being an investigative reporter in Russia and the lengths that powerful entrepreneurs of violence will go to silence their critics.

A similar 'lesson' was provided by the fate in the inter-war period of the NTV reporter, Yelena Masyuk, whose purportedly pro-Chechen reports from the first war and alleged friendships with Maskhadov and Basaev did not prevent her being held hostage between the two conflicts.[18] The ORT (All-Russia TV) reporters, Roman Perevezentsev and Vyacheslav Tibelius were also among those Russian journalists kidnapped by Chechen warlords in this period, their release being paid for, allegedly, by Boris Berezovsky.[19]

Similarly, Western journalists and human rights activists, who were, pretty much, able to roam at will during the first conflict, were obliged in the second war either to enter Chechnya illegally (and run the risk of being taken hostage by Chechen warlords or killed by the Russians) or to go under the protection and tight control of the federal forces and thus be constrained in what they might see and report. Inevitably, the picture of the second war presented to the international community under such restraints was markedly less comprehensive than that offered in the first.

Although the humiliation suffered by the Yeltsin leadership as a result of the debacle of sending Russian troops to Chechnya in the guise of mercenaries in late 1994 served immediately to trigger the first war in Chechnya, there was evidence that the Russian authorities had wanted to take action against Dudaev's 'criminal regime' as soon as was logistically possible and politically expedient. This was possible only after the threat of civil war within Russia had receded following the events of October 1993.

That Yeltsin's use of tanks against his own parliament did not result in any meaningful degree of international censure, no doubt emboldened him to rely on the application of overwhelming force in his campaign against Chechnya the following year. His opportunistic use of the 'Chechen' card during the 1996 presidential election campaign enabled him, with the help of the oligarchs controlling Russia's mass media and with the tacit support of his Western allies, to see off the communist threat, albeit, almost certainly, by dubious means.[20]

Fedor Burlatsky suggests that 'the Chechen war once again demonstrated that, since cannons disbanded the Russian Supreme Soviet on 4 October 1993, Russia has had an authoritarian regime'[21] However, it was because of the overriding view, shared by the Russian leadership, oligarchs (who owned most of the media) and by the West, that Boris Yeltsin be re-elected President of Russia, that a conflict was allowed to break out in the south-eastern corner of Europe that was to exceed even the Bosnian War in ferocity, intensity and the scale of abuse of human rights. By way of comparison, Frederick C. Cuny (an American aid worker who, shortly thereafter, lost his life in mysterious circumstances in Chechnya) claimed that, whereas the highest level of firing recorded in a single day in the Bosnian capital of Sarajevo was 3,500 heavy detonations; a colleague counted in Grozny in February 1995, 4,000 detonations per hour.[22]

How ironic that Grozny, saved from Nazi occupation in the Second World War by the German defeat at Stalingrad, should suffer destruction on the scale of that city, and that the Russians, so supportive of the Republicans in the Spanish Civil War, should elect the first government in Europe to launch airraids against one of its own cities since Franco's Luftwaffe-backed bombing of Guernica in 1937.[23] The worst civil disorder in Western Europe since the Second World War, in Northern Ireland – a country of approximately the same size and population as Chechnya – in 30 years between 1968 and 1998 accounted for just over 3,000 deaths (i.e. 100 per year). The 21 months of the first conflict in Chechnya resulted in between 45,000 and 100,000 deaths (about 2,000 to 5,000 per month).[24]

Yet, for all the notice Western governments paid, in public at any rate, to the conflict, Chechens might well have concluded that they could have been wiped out before anybody took preventative action. Anatoly Khazanov was one of the many Russian commentators on the war that drew attention to: 'Russia's readiness to continue, if necessary, the war to the last Chechen, to force them into submission.'[25]

Yeltsin had to contend with a mass media covering Russia's first televised war, a public that was generally hostile to that war, an active and vocal opposition reminding the Kremlin of the contradiction in an internal civil war of bombing and shelling on such a massive scale ones 'own' citizens and cities, and armed forces that were poorly-trained, poorly-paid and poorly-equipped for the task in hand.[26] Moreover, the Russians were being faced, and killed, with their own equipment, obtained for the most part from the former Soviet military bases in the country.[27] The last Soviet Defence Minister – Yevgeny Shaposhnikov – claimed that Grachev had signed in May 1992 a directive giving the Chechens half of the armaments left in Chechnya following the collapse of the USSR.[28]

Although there was general acceptance of Yeltsin's objectives in overthrowing Dudaev: (a) the desire to curb and contain throughout Russia the power of the Chechen mafia; (b) to re-establish government control over the oil pipelines running through Chechnya; and (c) to counter in Russia the centrifugal forces that had brought about the collapse of the USSR,[29] the means employed were considered to be far too excessive. Few were fooled that these were merely manoeuvres to 'restore the constitutional order' in Chechnya. Daily TV footage and graphic reports in newspapers made it clear that this was a very dirty war.[30] Perhaps, the most haunting memory of this first war was the lengths to which the Russian soldiers' mothers were obliged and prepared to go to determine the fate of their sons and recover their bodies.[31]

Whereas the 1999 campaign aimed, with public support, to counter the Chechens with the full might of Russia's armed forces, the 1994 conflict had been launched by Yeltsin's advisors with a tragic underestimation of the fighting capability of the Chechen armed detachments, led by a President (Dudaev) and field commanders (e.g. Aslan Maskhadov), who had not only been trained in the conventional Soviet armed forces, but, in the case of Shamil Basaev, by Soviet military intelligence – the GRU.[32] Basaev had fought in 1992 on the Russian side in Abkhazia's war against Georgia (as had Ruslan Gelaev). The loss of over 1,000 largely untrained conscript Russian troops in the initial attack on Grozny on New Year's Eve in 1994 exposed mercilessly the miscalculations by Russian generals.[33]

Only after the Russian armed forces had pounded Chechnya with heavy weaponry from the air and ground and had, by the summer of 1995, virtually defeated the Chechen fighters, did the latter resort to actions that could be termed terrorism, rather than acts of war. Thus, the seizure of a hospital and over a thousand hostages in Budennovsk in June 1995[34] by Basaev and the copycat operation in Kizlyar/Pervomaiskoye in January 1996[35] by Raduev, both occurred at times when the Russian Army was very much in the ascendancy.

That both raids, despite the heavy loss of life among civilian hostages, were perceived as propaganda coups by the Chechens and as ignominious defeats by the Russians, only serves to emphasise the utility of such actions to rally sagging morale and to increase the pressure on those conducting an unpopular war. The humiliating sight of a Russian prime minister yielding to the demands of a Chechen warlord live on Russian TV was, however, not to be forgotten either by the Russian public, or by one Vladimir Putin, who has gone on record, after the Dubrovka siege, as saying: 'There will be no more Khasavyurt, no more Budennovsk.'[36]

Yet because he had seen off successfully the communist threat, Yeltsin was not even made to suffer unduly the terrible irony, in August 1996, of the Russian forces' final defeat in the Chechen capital, Grozny, at the very moment that he was being sworn in as President.[37] The excessive budget deficit, however, swollen by the cost of the war and of 'paying back' the oligarchs whose support had ensured his re-election, contributed significantly to Russia's economic crash just two years later in August 1998, from which point Yeltsin's popularity plummeted.[38]

Moreover, the Russian armed forces' humiliating defeat at the hands of the Chechens had seriously weakened Yeltsin's credibility as a leader. Although, the Khasavyurt Peace Accord, signed by Maskhadov and Lebed' on 31 August 1996, froze the resolution of the constitutional issue of Chechnya's status until 31 December 2001, it did lead to the withdrawal of all Russian troops by the end of that year, leaving Chechnya de facto independent and, of course, victorious. Yeltsin characterised this time frame as allowing for the wounds to heal and for emotions to be replaced by common sense.

The Khasavyurt Accords were given legal force in the Peace Treaty signed by Presidents Yeltsin and Maskhadov in Moscow on 12 May 1997, Yeltsin claiming that this brought to an end 400 years of hostility between the peoples. The first point of the treaty obliged both sides 'to renounce forever the use of force in resolving any disputed questions', while the second point committed them to build their relations 'in accordance with generally recognized principles and the norms of international law'.[39] The signing of the Accord, therefore, came to represent in retrospect a temporary high point of Russo-Chechen mutual understanding, which soon began to unravel. There was little else, in the circumstances, that Yeltsin could do at this juncture, but there is no doubt that several of his team and a significant proportion of the *siloviki* overall were determined to reverse this humiliation in Chechnya at the earliest opportunity. This opportunity occurred in the summer of 1999 when Putin was nominated Russian Prime Minister in the wake of the invasion of Dagestan by Basaev and Khattab.

Whereas President Yeltsin's campaign (1994–1996) for the 'restoration of constitutional order' was perceived generally, in Russia and abroad, to be little more than a fig-leaf for a war aimed at preventing Chechnya's secession, Putin's equally euphemistic 'counter-terrorism operation' (1999 to date), has not been subjected to the same disparagement. Indeed, Putin has managed, albeit not entirely successfully, to have, retrospectively, the entire Russo-Chechen conflict perceived as part of the global war against terrorism. This has enabled him not only to conflate notions of 'a just war' (*jus ad bellum*) with those of 'a justly fought war' (*jus in bello*),[40] but also to eradicate memories of Yeltsin's 'bad' war, by presenting the entire confrontation with the Chechens as, if not a 'good', then certainly a 'necessary' war.

Even this assault on Russia's southern border, however, on its own would not have mobilised sufficiently Russian public opinion for an invasion of Chechnya. This had been called for since March 1999 by the then Interior Minister, Sergei Stepashin, who claimed that: 'Russia has reached the limit of its tolerance for Chechnya's orgy of crime.' He also said: 'A full-scale military operation is out of the question now, as it would lead to huge losses',[41] but that 'in line with international practice, the bases and strongholds of these terrorists will be eliminated'.[42]

Although overridden by then Prime Minister, Yevgeny Primakov, it does appear that a contingency plan for the invasion of Chechnya had been in place at least by July 1999,[43] US officials having been warned by Russian military sources of an impending attack as early as April of that year.[44] Stepashin replaced Primakov as Prime Minister in May 1999 and became head of the Federal Anti-Terrorist Commission the following month (with Vladimir Putin, head of the FSB, and Vladimir Rushailo, Interior Minister, as his deputies).[45] In August, during the crisis in Dagestan, Putin replaced Stepashin in both posts and the push towards war accelerated.

The threat to Russia's territorial integrity posed by an independent Chechnya-Ichkeria seemed to have persuaded the new Kremlin leadership that resolute action must be taken and that the Russian public be made fully aware of the threat facing them.[46] Moreover, there was genuine concern that the United States was ready to exploit any power vacuum on Russia's extensive southern flank.[47] Western experts and journalists invited to Putin's summer residence at Novoye Ogarevo, outside of Moscow, in the wake of the Beslan siege noted how convinced Putin was that Western secret services were trying to bring Russia to her knees.[48]

In any event, the bombing of apartment blocks in Moscow, Volgodonsk and Buinaksk in September 1999 came either at an extremely fortuitous juncture, or with a helping hand from the Russian security services;[49] unanswered questions about the 'bomb' discovered in Ryazan' on 22 September adding fuel to the fire of 'conspiracy'.[50] Certainly, both Maskhadov and Basaev denied any involvement in these bombings, whereas Basaev had readily owned up to the subsequent Dubrovka and Beslan attacks in 2002 and 2004, respectively.[51]

None of those tried and imprisoned for the bombings have turned out to be Chechens, the perpetrators appearing to be Karachai and Dagestani militants allegedly acting under the orders of the Jordanian Khattab and the Egyptian Abu Ammar, who led the small Arab presence among the Chechen fighters, and who were both killed in the second conflict.[52] Non-Russian estimates of the number of Arab mercenaries fighting in Chechnya rarely exceed 300.[53] Even Russian military sources sometimes concur with this figure, claiming that one-fifth of Chechen fighters are Arabs, but assessing the total strength of the opposition at only 1,500 men.[54] However, the very presence of these 'international *jihadists*' on Chechen soil was enough to establish a link, however tenuous, between the rebels and al-Qaeda.

This did not deter Russian public opinion from blaming the Chechens. Angry and ashamed at their forces capitulation in the first war, and horrified at independent Chechnya-Ichkeria's slide into savage anarchy in the inter-war period, under Maskhadov – a leader who appeared incapable of stopping the excesses of the Chechen warlords – Russians were not minded to be magnanimous to their southern neighbours.

At the same time a degree of disenchantment with Maskhadov's Chechen regime could be noted in Western countries. It is instructive to look at the way the mood swung in Britain, during the inter-war period, against the Chechens. At the governmental level the launch of the then Foreign Secretary Robin Cook's initiative of a foreign policy with a moral dimension coincided with the seizure, in July 1997, by Chechens, of British aid workers Camilla Carr and Jon James.[55] Moreover, their release, brokered, and allegedly paid for, by the Russians in September 1998[56] was followed that December by the discovery in Chechnya of the severed heads of four employees of a British telecommunications company.[57]

Such acts of barbarism seriously undermined at both official and public levels such goodwill as had accumulated in Britain towards what had been perceived generally as the brave Chechen resistance against overwhelming odds in the first war with Russia (1994–1996). However, due primarily to the disproportionality and indiscriminate nature of the violence visited upon the Chechen people by federal forces in that first conflict, British condemnation was motivated more by Russia's appalling conduct of the war, rather than by any desire to see a new, inherently weak, unstable and Muslim mini-state appearing in the vicinity of the oil-rich Caspian Sea.

However, if Boris Yeltsin's credentials as a 'democrat' had been irretrievably tarnished in the West by the time of the outbreak of the second war in Chechnya in October 1999, those of his eventual successor – Vladimir Putin – were met with a degree of cynicism from the start, as the following contemporary account reveals:

> The prospect of another full-scale war in Chechnya prompted Western governments to issue statements of concern over Russian tactics against rebels in the breakaway republic. But there appeared to be little appetite among outside powers to intervene in the conflict with anything more than public complaints. The Russian government benefits from this criticism,

because it allows Russian leaders to portray themselves as standing up for Russia against the West at no cost. Some observers connect the course of the war with the appointment of Prime Minister Vladimir Putin in early August 1999. It is widely believed in Russia that the war has something to do with the presidential election coming up in mid-2000. With Yeltsin's approval rating standing at something like two percent in the polls, Putin won public support that he couldn't get any other way. Russia's public expected the Chechen issue to be resolved for good, and the present intervention enjoys the support of practically all political forces in Moscow.[58]

The Chechen forces were driven out of Dagestan after heavy bombing by Russian aviation of the villages at the centre of the *Wahhabite* movement. A series of bombs placed in apartment blocks in the south of Russia and Moscow would appear to be revenge attacks for this, by Dagestani militants. Despite the lack of proof, the atrocities were immediately blamed on the Chechens. Vladimir Putin's infamous threat to 'wipe out the terrorists even in the shit-house', helped win him the epithet of 'iron' Putin[59] and send his popularity sky high.

There is little doubt that Putin's intemperate language exactly caught the mood of the traumatised and enraged Russian population. It seems probable, therefore, that the Moscow bombings were the key link in a chain of events that not only led to the second Chechen War, but also replaced an unpopular and ailing president with one of the *siloviki*'s own – a career Chekist who could be relied upon not to reign in his generals.

State Duma Security Committee Chairman, Viktor Ilyukhin, complained in November 1999 that President Yeltsin was totally unpredictable and claimed that: 'A "fifth column" of Yavlinskii, Kiriyenko and Borovoi was acting to terminate the counter-terrorist operation.'[60]

By August 1999, therefore, Putin had advantages that had not been available to Yeltsin in 1994:

a   an embittered military elite which had felt betrayed by both politicians and the Russian media in the 1994–1996 war and which, in 1999, sought to restore Russia's battered military reputation without interference from either source;[61]

b   in three years of de facto independence the Chechen regime had not only failed to gain international recognition, but, through a series of high profile kidnappings[62] and gruesome murders[63] of Westerners (and Russians), and a series of public executions under the newly-imposed *Shari'a* law,[64] had alienated, further, the West and diluted any romantic notions among Russians as to the rectitude of the Chechen cause;

c   the presence on Russian soil of foreign Islamic militants, the *Wahhabites*, who were portrayed as representing the same threat to Russian democracy as fundamentalists such as Osama Bin Laden did to the West.[65]

Moreover, he had the precedent of NATO's 'clean' bombing campaign against Yugoslavia during the Kosovo crisis,[66] the surgical nature of which not only compared favourably with the clumsy butchery of Yeltsin's Chechen adventure but also appeared to give a 'green light' to military attacks on civilian targets.

Another crucial difference between Yeltsin's and Putin's Chechen campaigns was that the first war was bungled from the start, whereas the second was well planned and conducted initially with a higher degree of professionalism.[67] It became bogged down when success in establishing a security zone prompted the Russian generals to finish the job by chasing the Chechens into the hills and engage once more in a protracted guerrilla war.

Much has been made, in respect of the mystery surrounding the exact reasons for launching the second war, of two articles in *Nezavisimaya gazeta*: one (12 October 1999) in which Vitaly Tret'yakov hinted that the Chechens had been lured into invading Dagestan; and the second (14 January 2000) in which Sergei Stepashin, a former prime minister and one of those directly responsible for launching the first Chechen War, revealed that an invasion of Chechnya had been planned since March 1999![68] At this time, it should be stressed, it was reported that 82 per cent of Russians polled agreed that Chechnya should be allowed to separate from Russia in one form or another.[69]

Although Russia's political and military structure wished to take decisive action against this perceived threat on its southern border, public opinion in Russia, disenchanted with the cost – economically as well in terms of human losses – would have to be won over. It is for this reason that conspiracy theories abound both about the luring of Basaev and Khattab's *Wahhabite*[70] fighters into Dagestan in August 1999 and the bombings, ostensibly by Chechens, of apartment blocks in Moscow and other Russian cities. A further possible turning point for Russia was the abduction, and subsequent murder, in Chechnya of its Minister of Internal Affairs, General Shpigun, in March 1999. As we have seen, former Russian Prime Minister, Sergei Stepashin, claimed that plans to reinvade Chechnya were drawn up from this date.[71]

The lessons drawn from the 1994–1996 war had undoubtedly influenced, also, the development of Islamic culture right across the Russian Federation; towards the end of the first war, the American journalist, James Walsh, suggested that: 'Whatever form it ultimately takes, Islam's reawakening across Russia is being shaped by the hammer and fire visited by Moscow on breakaway Chechnya.'[72]

As a result, when the terrorist bombings in the late summer of 1999 were presented as bringing the threat of Islamic terrorism to the heart of Russia, and the second Chechen campaign as not a war but a 'counter-terrorist operation', this inevitably drove a wedge between Russia's ethnic Russian population and non-Russian Muslim citizens of the Russian Federation. After the apartment house bombs in September 1999 there was support for full-scale military attacks on Chechen towns and villages from a Russian public not minded at that time to anticipate that this 'operation' would involve using weaponry banned by international conventions against the Chechen civilians (Air Force Chief Konakov claimed that thermobaric bombs, for example, were used only to: 'flush fighters out of mountain gorges'),[73] or that every month of the conflict would claim hundreds more Russian lives.

The following incident gives a flavour of the near-hysterical sense of insecurity among Russian citizens after these bombings. In a brutally frank admission at the annual conference of the British Association for Slavonic and East European Studies (BASEES), in Cambridge, in April 2000, during a discussion on Chechnya and the Russian presidential elections in which I was presenting a paper, a representative from the Central Public Opinion Institute in Moscow (VTsIOM) ventured, to the evident shock of many in the audience, that most Russians thought that the only solution to the Chechen conflict was the 'elimination of, albeit, the male half of the Chechen population!'

Small wonder, therefore, that in the aftermath of the invasion of Dagestan and the apartment house bombings that preceded the second war there were calls both for a 'strong hand'[74] and punishment for Chechens and Chechnya.[75] Putin, albeit thanks mainly to the suspiciously high degree of manipulation involved, undoubtedly had the overwhelming support of his people to invade Chechnya. What had changed from the first conflict is that the Russian public remains indifferent to the fact that this war, too, has ground to the same bloody stalemate.

Fortunately for Putin, the March 2000 elections came before all but the most perspicacious of Russian commentators were aware of the dead-end into which Russia's Chechen policy had been driven again. He won the elections easily in the first round. An opinion poll in the same month revealed that 89 per cent of Russians were weary of the war in Chechnya. Putin thus had a unique opportunity and a mandate to reach a political settlement at this juncture, but appeared unwilling to face down his generals, who were calling for ever more extreme measures to be taken against the enemy and their families. General Vladimir Shamanov, in June 2000, excused the killing of the wives of Chechen fighters, asking: 'How do you tell a wife from a sniper?'[76] A year later, General Gennady Troshev, called for the public hanging of captured Chechen fighters, explaining: 'This is how I'd do it: I'd gather them all on a square and string up the bandit and let him hang, let everyone see.'[77]

Once Putin had given way and allowed Russian forces to raze Grozny and attack the heartlands of Chechen resistance in the mountains, the war became a humanitarian disaster, not just for the civilians of Chechnya, who suffered from the disproportionate and indiscriminate force employed against them, but also for the million and a half federal troops that have fought so far in this conflict, for whom the arbitrary brutality and sense of virtual impunity became part of their everyday life in Chechnya.[78]

Tight control over the media and access to Chechnya was the most effective way that Putin could hide from the public actions that, by any objective criteria, would appear to deserve investigation as war crimes. Early examples of these were the declaration issued by the Russian military on 6 December 1999 that: '[t]hose who remain in Grozny after December 11 will be viewed as terrorists and bandits and will be destroyed by artillery and aviation',[79] the atrocities at Katyr Yurt in February 2000,[80] and the violations routinely occurring at the notorious Chernokozovo filtration camp.[81]

As a result, the fact that neither the political, nor the military leaders of Russia, in their zeal to eradicate such 'terrorists', appear to dwell overlong on the distinction between ordinary Chechen civilians and the 'terrorists' hidden in their midst, has by no means, during this second war, met with the overwhelming disapproval of Russian public opinion. For example, an opinion poll of 18 March 2002 by *Glasnost' Media* indicated that the Russian population was exactly split (47.41 per cent each) over the military or peaceful resolution of the Chechen conflict (5.18 per cent did not know). Indeed, a disturbingly high proportion of 4.43 per cent still advocated 'nuking' the entire territory! Of even more concern is the fact that as many as 23.28 per cent expressed the wish to wipe Chechnya, with all the Chechens, from the face of the earth![82]

This near hysteria facilitated Putin's task of fostering the perception internationally that all those who take up arms to oppose its policies were Islamic terrorists and were part of the same war on international terror launched by the USA in the wake of the 9/11 attacks. This allowed President Bush to require that Maskhadov choose, in effect, between Khattab and Putin,[83] in a situation in which a democratic plebiscite among Chechens would have preferred, almost certainly, a third option.

The role of the Russian media in maintaining and consolidating public support for the Russian conduct of the conflict in Chechnya during the second war was crucial. During the first Chechen War an independent Russian media ensured that a just and lasting resolution of the conflict was kept on the agenda on behalf of a sceptical Russian public. By the start of the second war, Russian generals and politicians had learnt the utility of a tame and dependent press, safe in the knowledge of a public thirst for revenge against the Chechens, in particular, and Islamic fundamentalists in general.[84]

The 'honeymoon' of the Russian public with Putin's Chechen policy reached its apex in February 2000, by which time what was to prove to be an all-time high of 70 per cent of those Russians polled supported continuing the war to a victorious conclusion.[85] Likewise, 67 per cent of the Russian public supported the campaign to expel the Chechen fighters from Grozny in February 2000,[86] during which three leading Chechen field commanders – Khunkarpasha Israpilov, Aslanbek Ismailov and Lechi Dudaev – were killed and Shamil Basaev lost a foot.[87] With the taking of Grozny, however, the long guerrilla war in the mountains commenced.

Significantly, a year after taking over as Prime Minister – after the bombing in Moscow in the Pushkin Square subway in August 2000 – Putin declined to pin the blame on the Chechens for what turned out to be a 'turf war' between Moscow criminal gangs.[88] By then, of course, Putin was President, the war in Chechnya had been relegated from the front pages and the Russian public appeared indifferent to the excesses committed by their troops against Chechen civilians.

The war was by no means over, however. This was testified to by the fact that the death count among Russian federal troops was continuing to creep towards the official total of 3,826 killed in the first conflict. The official death toll for the first year of the second war was 2,472, at a rate of 206 a month, higher than that of the 21-month-long first war.[89]

That the Russian federal forces had only nominal control of Chechen territory was highlighted by a report, dated 6 March 2001, by the Glasnost Foundation in Moscow that Chechen field commanders Basaev, Khattab, Baraev and others were meeting in Grozny (!) to plan a spring offensive with 3,500 fighters.[90]

The concentration of power in the hands of the *siloviki*-led executive under Putin's *vertikal'* led to the effective marginalisation of opposition in politics, business and the media.[91] Insofar as Putin's rise to power and initial popularity among the Russian electorate was linked so closely with events in Chechnya, any political, media or human rights opposition that might draw attention to the manifest failure of his policies in the North Caucasus was perceived to represent a real danger.

However, because, as we have seen, this widespread political support had been won in the wake of the series of bomb blasts in apartment buildings in Moscow and other Russian cities in August–September 1999, that had left over 300 civilians dead the pressure on the 'terrorists' had to be maintained. The suspiciously convenient timing for the new Russian Prime Minister of these atrocities, matched with Putin's handling of their aftermath led many in the West to conclude that, even if the Russian president himself might be blameless of orchestrating the bombings, 'rogue elements' within his security forces most probably were not.

For example, the theory that the Chechens had carried out the 1999 bombings was never proven but was ruthlessly exploited. Thus, prior to the bombings, in 1998, the term 'Chechen trail' (*chechenskiye sledy*) had been used just ten times by the news section of ITAR-TASS. In 1999 this went up to 34 usages and, in 2000, to 46.[92] Moreover, the Putin administration was unable to halt persistent rumours of FSB involvement in the thwarted Ryazan' bombing. A similar lack of transparency in the aftermath of both the Dubrovka (October 2002) and Beslan (September 2004) atrocities has done little subsequently to dispel the doubts of 'conspiracy' theorists who continue to suspect 'dirty tricks' in high places.[93]

In a recently published book,[94] John B. Dunlop exposes these conspiracy theories suggesting what amounts to Russian war crimes with the forensic skill, tenacity and sources of an investigative detective. He declines to sit on the fence between the 'conspiracy theory' and 'cock-up' explanations for the Russian special services' dismal performance at the two highest profile hostage-taking incidents of the current conflict, pointing implicitly to 'dirty tricks' at the highest levels of the Putin administration. Dunlop's findings, published earlier online by The Jamestown Foundation (on Beslan)[95] and Radio Free Europe/Radio Liberty (on Dubrovka),[96] lead the reader to the following uncomfortable conclusions that:

1   at Beslan it was the Russian special forces that had started the firing at the school;[97]
2   the security forces employed thermobaric *Shmel'* flamethrowers and tanks[98] in the assault to free the children trapped inside the school's gymnasium in Beslan;
3   at Dubrovka the FSB, it is implied, had 'staged' the hostage-taking crisis to undermine peace processes that were promising a genuine political settlement negotiated with the Chechen separatist leadership.[99]

While it would be naive to pretend that security services in any country are immune from carrying out 'dirty tricks' in the 'national interest', one intuitively hesitates in accepting that even a state like Russia – ruled by former or existing security officials – would take matters quite this far. Suffice it to say, that there are influential individuals both in Russia and outside who believe it could, including many of the respected Russian, American, German and British investigative reporters on whose Dunlop's enquiry is largely based.

At the diplomatic level, of course, such considerations could hardly be aired in public. However, even by the time Putin had become acting President on 1 January 2000, it was already clear that his 'counter-terrorist operation' in Chechnya was going to lead to a second all-out assault on the rebellious territory and its population. This ensured that Russia's human rights record would resurface as the main area of concern and criticism from all levels of Western society, including the government. In Britain it was assumed, as Robin Cook noted in May 2000, that 'Russia's protection of human basic rights would affect the sort of bilateral relationship it could expect with Britain'. Recalling this four years later, he added:

> This was just five months after Vladimir Putin came to office. The shrinking of democratic space in Russia since then has been marked. It is now time that we in Britain and Europe examined the policies needed to re-engage Russia in finding a path to modernization of a democratic rather than an authoritarian character.[100]

However much Cook's sentiments in 2004 may have echoed those seeking to uphold Britain's 'values' in Chechnya, both Putin's use of the term 'counter-terrorism' to describe the renewed conflict in Chechnya and his warning of an 'arc of Islamic fundamentalism from Kosovo to the Philippines'[101] were to acquire a new resonance after the attacks on the USA of 11 September 2001. In the post-9/11 world it became increasingly difficult to separate 'values' from 'interests' in a seemingly global conflict between 'them' and 'us'.

Whatever the truth as to who was to blame for the apartment bombings, the impact on the Russian population was similar to that on the US population after 11 September. Demands for revenge up to and including a nuclear attack on Chechnya were aired and Putin had won a mandate for the toughest possible response against the rebellious republic.[102] The losers, undoubtedly, were the ordinary Chechens themselves, who must have cursed Basaev and Khattab for their ideological fantasies. The legitimate government of Chechnya, under Maskhadov, lost out too, for it became collectively *persona non grata* as far as the new administration in Moscow was concerned. The winners, undoubtedly, were Putin and his team of military advisors, who now had a virtual carte blanche to resolve the Chechen problem militarily once and for all, albeit under the guise of a 'political' solution.

Chechenisation – Putin's 'endgame'?

A curious feature of the Russo-Chechen conflict is the lengths that successive Russian administrations have gone to avoid depicting the confrontation as a 'war', while everywhere else in Russia, Chechnya and the rest of the world, it is routinely referred to as the 'Russo-Chechen War' or the 'war in Chechnya'. The expert evidence brought on behalf of the Russian Government in the recent extradition case in London against Akhmed Zakaev, placed great emphasis on the fact that the conflict between Russia and Chechnya was not a war, an argument ultimately rejected by the British judge.[103]

Yet, even Marshal Viktor Kulikov, speaking in the debate, in July 2002, on changing the law 'On Veterans', with a view to extending the law to include those who had fought in Chechnya, stated: 'You can say what you like, but it is undoubtedly a war.'[104] Likewise, the legal expert Vadim Solov'ev wrote:

> On the one hand, the official line is that a peaceful situation exists in Chechnya and adjoining regions. On the other hand, troops are obliged to conduct full-scale combat operations and must be constantly ready to fend off "mountain warriors" as was done many years ago, when Russia was bringing the Caucasus under its domination. Back then this sort of thing was called a war, but nowadays it is ludicrously described as the 'restoration of constitutional order'.[105]

On the other hand, by August 2004, journalist Vadim Rechkalov was admitting that, although bloody skirmishes would continue, the full-scale war had come to an end.[106]

As the conflict dragged on inconclusively, stories reappeared of Russian atrocities against the Chechen civilian population. A series of reports by NGOs in Russia (*Memorial*) and abroad (Médecins sans Frontières, Amnesty International, Prague Watchdog, Human Rights Watch, etc.) collated a whole series of gross abuses of human rights in the conflict, carried out overwhelmingly by the federal side. Of particular concern were the sweeps of Chechen towns and villages, looking for Chechen fighters, which resulted in the disappearance, torture and death of civilians.

Russian society, too, was feeling the impact as hundreds of thousands of veterans of the Chechen campaigns returned to Russia scarred with the 'Chechen syndrome', the result of witnessing or directly participating in the brutal treatment meted out in Chechnya.[107]

Putin, like Yeltsin before him, was trapped without any obvious exit strategy or endgame, short of total military victory or admission of defeat. Unlike his predecessor, he was not about to countenance the latter. In this he was generally supported by the Russian public, perhaps because they had been traumatised by the insecurity generated by the series of terrorist bombings of the apartment blocks in the late summer of 1999 and sought, once and for all, a resolution of the Chechen 'threat'.

By mid-2000, however, a new direction was clearly needed if the second war was not to end in the same way as the first. This new direction came to be called 'Chechenisation'. The policy of Chechenisation of the conflict in Chechnya was begun in June 2000 with the appointment of former resistance fighter and Mufti, Akhmad Kadyrov as Putin's head of administration in the republic. The policy, first proposed in 1995 by then presidential advisor Emil Pain,[108] offered a way out of this impasse for both the Kremlin and their Chechen allies: pro-Russian Chechens would now conduct the 'anti-terrorist' campaign (and control their share of the illicit economy that flourishes in Chechnya) and Putin would be spared much of the unwelcome, albeit half-hearted, international condemnation of the inhumane treatment of Chechen civilians by Russian troops.

In effect, the new policy was presented as a political solution to the problem of Chechnya. However, it was one that excluded political forces seeking a future for Chechnya outside of Russia. As will be seen in the following chapter, after 9/11, these forces could be presented as no longer being separatists, but members of the international *jihad* against civilisation.

The fact that, far from being a political *solution*, Chechenisation was the only way, not involving Russian armed forces, that Putin could achieve the basic Russian objective of keeping Chechnya as part of Russia is well understood in the international community. Andreas Gross of PACE, for example, in a report delivered in 2004 complained:

> President Putin announced a political solution already in January 2000 as a member of a delegation to the Council of Europe. Politics does not mean the realisation of one's own will without military measures, but it is the attempt to understand and make compromises.[109]

On 22 November 2002,[110] shortly after the 2002 Dubrovka siege (and, significantly, after 9/11) Putin set in motion his own three-step programme, to commence with the holding, early in 2003, of a referendum in Chechnya on a new constitution, which would ban all political parties advocating Chechen independence,[111] and, at the same time, remove any possibility of negotiations on Chechnya's future by all opponents of Putin's plan. It was not apparent at this time that this would include the physical elimination, by means of political assassination, of such leaders of Chechnya-Ichkeria as its elected president, Aslan Maskhadov (8 March 2005)[112] and his successor Abdul-Khalim Sadulaev (17 June 2006).[113]

The Kremlin has now carried out all stages of this programme, holding on 23

March 2003 the referendum despite protests from within Russia and from the international community. The holding of such a referendum in conditions of war led to the resignation of Lord Judd, rapporteur for Chechnya, and a member of the Parliamentary Assembly of the Council of Europe (PACE). A number of respectable monitoring organisations boycotted the elections for the same reason. French and British journalists on the spot at the time recorded irregularities. Oleg Mironov, head of the Russian human rights organisation, *Memorial*, claimed that an atmosphere of fear and terror had been created in Chechnya ahead of the referendum. Villages that declined to vote for the referendum were threatened with the dreaded *zachistki* (sweeps). Thousands of Russian federal forces stationed in Chechnya were allowed to participate in the vote. Shortly after the results were announced, President Putin claimed that Russia's last serious problem had been solved.[114]

The incredible turnout and figures for voters in support of the Constitution were reminiscent of the worst days of the Soviet communist regime. Officially the turnout for this referendum was 89.48 per cent, with 95.97 per cent approving the Constitution. The title of the International Helsinki Federation for Human Rights report on this event –'The Constitutional referendum in Chechnya was neither free nor fair'[115] – sums up the international 'values' community's response to Putin's 'political' initiative.

The second stage of Putin's policy, in October 2003, was to arrange the holding of new presidential elections in Chechnya. Obviously the preparations for this were so controlled and coordinated as to ensure that no one of a separatist persuasion would be allowed to participate in these 'democratic' processes, which as a result were also recognised as neither free nor fair.[116]

For example, an opinion poll conducted in Chechnya between 20–25 June 2005 by the 'Validata' organisation revealed the Moscow-based Chechen businessman Malik Saidullaev was favoured as president by 20.1 per cent of respondents, former Speaker of the Supreme Soviet, Ruslan Khasbulatov by 19.2 per cent, State Duma deputy Aslambek Aslakhanov by 17.6 per cent and Akhmad Kadyrov by just 12.5 per cent.[117] In the event Kadyrov won with more than 82.5 per cent of the vote,[118] all of his main contenders being either persuaded not to stand or disbarred, Saidullaev as late as 11 September![119]

On 9 May 2004 (on Victory Day once more), the newly-elected president Akhmad Kadyrov was assassinated in a bomb blast at a stadium in Grozny, an act for which Shamil Basaev claimed responsibility.[120] As soon as Putin had made clear that Kadyrov's successor would also be a Kremlin-approved candidate, even Aslan Maskhadov was moved to threaten that any such 'Chechen president' would be the target of future assassination attempts.[121] Elections to appoint his successor, scheduled for August 2004, witnessed the same shenanigans, and Putin's choice – the former Chechen Interior Minister, Alu Alkhanov – was duly elected, albeit in the midst of a series of savage terrorist attacks, culminating in the Beslan school siege of 1–3 September, and with 'only' 73 per cent of votes cast, significantly less than the percentage garnered previously by Kadyrov.[122]

The manifestly clear impossibility of holding democratic elections in such conditions led to most of the world community treating the whole process with some scepticism. As Andreas Gross of PACE commented:

> These impressions show the validity of the argument, that democratic elections cannot be held under such circumstances: no freedom of movement, very limited freedom of expression, general climate of fear and intimidation.[123]

However, as Chechenisation was the only 'political' solution on the table, even Gross had to admit that the election of Alkhanov could serve as a stabilising factor in Chechnya and has ruled out any talks about Chechen independence or separatism for the next 15 years.[124]

Finally, in the third stage of Putin's attempt to 'normalise' the situation in Chechnya, on 27 November 2005 parliamentary elections were held in which the most popular political party in Russia, United Russia, won a majority of seats.[125] Even within the parameters of the Kremlin-imposed control, there was room for some local chicanery: Ruslan Yamadaev being illegally replaced by Ramzan Kadyrov as the local representative of the victorious party.[126] Thus the Russian *vertikal'* of power was imprinted on a Chechen society for which a genuinely parliamentary form of government, based on the clan system, might well have been the optimum means of incorporating traditional Chechen norms into the twenty-first century. Stanislav Belkovsky from the Institute of National Strategy, for example, is on record as saying:

> The model of one-man management, as history shows, has never been successful in Chechnya; only a polycentric model, a parliamentary republic ensuring a balance between the most influential clans, is appropriate there.[127]

As it is, all power in Chechnya is vested in one man, Ramzan Kadyrov, and the *teip* to which he belongs – the *Benoi*, which also includes Chechen President, Alkhanov, chair of the Chechen State Council, Taus Djabrailov and Moscow businessman, Malik Saidullaev.[128]

The toothless and sham nature of the new Chechen parliament was revealed in July 2006 when, against the background of such deep-rooted antagonisms, these representatives of the Chechen people in their 'wisdom' repaid Putin's 'concern' for the Chechens by proposing that he be allowed to run for the Presidency in 2008, for a third term, a remarkable example of failing to articulate the real wishes of their constituents, for many of whom Putin remains the embodiment of 'absolute evil'.[129]

This indicates, however, how successful Putin's policy has been in splitting the Chechen camp and shifting the violence from Russian on Chechen and vice versa to Chechen on Chechen. This essential feature of Chechenisation was encapsulated in a comment contained in a *Médicins Sans Frontières* report in August 2004, which characterised the new policy thus: 'The conflict appears to have become more of an internal civil war between rival Chechen factions, instead of a war for independence.'[130]

It is not surprising, therefore, that another feature of the Chechenisation phase of the conflict has been the way in which outside influences have conspired to prompt both the pro-Russian pragmatists and their 'irreconcilable' opponents to break deep-seated Chechen cultural taboos. For example, the former – appear to have been influenced by Russian norms – are increasing the incidence of Chechen killing Chechen (remember Yermolov!) and the latter were clearly influenced by *Wahhabite* ideology when resorting to female suicide bombers in the period 2000–2004.[131]

Through cognitive consonance and dissonance,[132] each side only perceives the 'war crimes' of the other, thus intensifying the structural violence embedded in their respective attitudes. This, in turn, makes it all the more difficult to dispassionately assess the fundamental contradictions in the current relationship between Chechens and Russians and leads to the irrational prominence of such uncompromising and maximalist positions as 'freedom or death' (for the Chechen separatists), 'victory or paradise' (for the *Wahhabites*) and 'victory at all costs' (for the Russians).

If one perceives Chechenisation as Russia's last attempt to impose its will on Chechnya – (by means of manipulated elections, concentrating all power in the hands of a single pro-Putin Chechen leader) – then that policy careered off the road with the assassinations of Akhmad Kadyrov in May 2004 and Aslan Maskhadov in March 2005.

Kadyrov represented the 'strong man' figure (in the mould of Saddam Hussein) and had the political know-how to balance his own interests with those of the Kremlin. He probably could even have cut a deal with Maskhadov to split the Chechen opposition between a relative 'moderate' leader with some vestiges of legitimacy and the irreconcilable elements, led by Basaev, an admitted international terrorist with a declared interest in a wider *jihad* in the North Caucasus.

The choice of Alu Alkhanov, unlike his predecessor, a supporter of the federal forces since the outbreak of the first war in 1994, as Putin's preferred appointee to replace Akhmad Kadyrov,[133] provides evidence that the Kremlin is not yet prepared to trust the political judgement of Chechen voters.[134] In this, Putin is being very hard-nosed and pragmatic: in an opinion poll taken in the summer of 2004, fully 81 per cent of those polled in Chechnya characterised Russia's Chechen policy as 'completely ineffective' or 'not very effective'; 66 per cent thought Chechens had taken up arms to resist the actions of Russian forces and only 14 per cent for the struggle for independence.[135]

It would seem that it remains beyond the wit of the Russian leadership to comprehend that an engagement with representatives of broad sections of Chechen society, to work out optimum state structures, which would acknowledge that Chechnya's traditional system of power is devolved to its regions and would reflect the centrality of *adat* in the Chechen way of life, would reduce the impact of Islamic fundamentalism and the strict implementation of *Shari'a* law in Chechnya.

Conclusion

Insofar as Russia's 'Chechenisation' policy, in effect, devolves responsibility for the conduct of the conflict in Chechnya to those Chechens that accept the formal recognition of Russia's territorial integrity, Russia's key strategic goal has been achieved. However, the tactics employed to achieve this goal have proven sufficiently counterproductive as to question whether the ends really have justified the means. The massive civilian losses and displacements, the arbitrary violence visited upon ordinary Chechens by federal troops and their Chechen allies have added a further black page to the Chechen cultural narrative, dominated as it already was by centuries of heroic resistance to Russian brutality.

Moreover, the imposition of a Russian-style *vertikal'* on a society traditionally favouring a balance of power among tribal and regional groupings has led to a potentially dangerous concentration of might in the hands of one person – Ramzan Kadyrov – whose reign of intimidation and terror has hardly endeared himself to the international community, let alone a Chechen population that has been brutalised by war and violence for more than a decade. Nonetheless, the the fact that he has the Kremlin's backing has left Kadyrov as the only game in town.

Paradoxically, the brutal Russian tactics of suppression and the Chechen employment of equally savage tactics after having apparently achieved independence led Western governments, including that in Britain, to seek a political solution that would bring an end to Russian brutality while offering the Chechens some semblance of autonomy that fell short of outright independence. The only alternative to Russian sovereignty over the territory was therefore held to be some form of international oversight by the UN or the Organisation for Security and Cooperation in Europe, a task that neither organisation, nor individual governments were keen to promote. As the only political solution offered by Putin has been Chechenisation,[136] it has proven difficult for the British or any other Western government to do much more than offer this clearly unsatisfactory policy lukewarm support.

In a democratic society with a strong independent media, questions would have been aired on behalf of a public concerned over the costs and wisdom of the policy of Chechenisation. Under Putin's authoritarian system, however, the Russian public is not consulted and it seems quite content for Putin to act in its name if it means reducing the likelihood of further Chechen attacks.

Nonetheless, a few brave voices of protest have been heard, complaining that the policy is nothing more than 'hidden' separatism,[137] 'systemic' separatism[138] or 'Separatism-lite'[139] and asking:

> What does Chechen power in the guise of Ramzan Kadyrov have in common with the Russian juridical space and for what, in any case, did we conduct a years-long counter-terrorist operation that cost many thousands of lives.[140]

As has been ruefully noted, Russia's policy of Chechenisation, investing all power in the Kremlin's chosen placeman, has in effect turned into

'Kadyrovisation'[141] Anyone wishing to find gainful employment in Chechnya has a stark choice between joining the irreconcilable rebels in the hills and signing up for Kadyrov's paramilitary forces. The result is that up to half of these forces – the so-called *kadyrovtsy* – are made up of former rebels, hardly a sound basis for a stable future. In October 2005, Alu Alkhanov admitted that 7,000 former *boyeviki* made up, almost, half of the forces of law and order in Chechnya.[142] The series of amnesties promulgated by the Russians, initially aimed at protecting Russian servicemen from facing war crimes' tribunals, are now effectively being handled by Kadyrov himself, thus making loyalty to him, rather than to Russia, the main criterion for a pardon.[143] Again, this hardly represents a policy for long-term stability.

Meanwhile, such an influential commentator as Mikhail Remizov, president of APN's Institute of National Strategy, has categorised the system operating in Chechnya under Kadyrov's rule as 'developed feudalism', warning that this is an essentially expansionist phenomenon which could manifest itself both in the concentration of all levers of power in Chechnya in the hands of its leader and in the attempt by the Putin administration to use Kadyrov and his methods to 'pacify' the Islamist opposition throughout the North Caucasus.[144]

Both outcomes are inherently dangerous for Russia. For if corrupt politicians, poverty and unemployment feed the roots of Islamic extremism, as the Russian historian Boris Sokolov has suggested, then Kadyrov's rule is likely to strengthen, not weaken the impact of Muslim fundamentalists in the region.[145] For, as Anna Politkovskaya had already perceptively remarked:

> The side-effects of Chechenization today are also perfectly obvious to anyone following developments in the region. First and foremost it has facilitated the emergence and consolidation of a Muslim underground, not only in Chechnya, but in other regions of the Caucasus as well.[146]

6   9/11, Chechnya and the war on terror

If you were distressed by the killing of your nationals in Moscow, remember ours in Chechnya

(Osama bin Laden, 2002)[1]

The first war in Chechnya presented post-Soviet Russia with its first example of a domestic insurgent movement for self-determination. The bombing campaign that hit Moscow and other Russian cities in late August/early September 1999, which led directly to the second war, gave ordinary people in Russia their first taste of modern-day international terrorism. Hostage taking raids in Budennovsk (June 1995) and Kizlyar/Pervomaiskoe (January 1996), classic acts of terrorism perpetrated in the first war, neither had the same impact as the bombings in the Russian capital, nor their international dimension.

Concepts such as 'terrorism' and 'freedom fighting' give rise to strong emotions and do not lend themselves readily to objective scrutiny. Yet they lie at the heart of the Russo-Chechen conflict. Galtung would recognise in the Russo-Chechen relationship many aspects of 'structural violence', i.e. injustices perceived to stem from the dominant order. According to this concept, insurgency (direct violence) is perceived by the authorities solely as a security issue to be dealt with by 'legitimate' forces of law and order, whereas the insurgents may view direct violence as the only means of liberating their people from a structurally unjust system (apartheid, imperialism, slavery, etc.).

What such a theory helps us to understand is why nations fight against all the odds for self-determination. More controversially, it helps explain why, armed with the ideology of an international *jihad*, suicide bombers martyr themselves and why, indeed, people fly aeroplanes into skyscrapers. It is this common feature – that of a fundamentalist Islamic ideology – that allows parallels to be drawn between Chechnya, Palestine and September 11. It is worth noting here the symbolic linkage between the respective 'Black Septembers' of Russia in 1999, Israel in 2000 and the USA in 2001.

The danger of giving too much weight to this theory is that ends might be used to justify any means, as Basaev's account of the events of Beslan tends to demonstrate. However, the cost of ignoring it is to assume that violent conflicts can be resolved without addressing, or even recognising, the root causes.

The Forum on Early Warning and Early Response lists as its first 'dangerous assumption in responses to terrorist attacks': 'The management of the symptoms of terrorism, rather than tackling the root causes of conflict that foster the growth of terrorism, is sufficient to defeat terrorism'. Assumption 9 is: 'Terrorism can be defeated militarily. The lessons from history that military responses strengthen the resolve of terrorist groups and their supporters can be ignored.'[2]

We have seen in the previous chapter how the bombing of apartment houses in Moscow and elsewhere in Russia in the late summer of 1999, 'traumatised' Russian public opinion in seeking a quick and decisive cure for their insecurity.

That the bombings, carried out by, according to whom you believe, Chechens[3], other Caucasians,[4] Arab mercenaries,[5] FSB agents,[6] criminal gangs or anarchists, could so rally public opinion behind Putin's strategy as to tarnish all opposition voices in political circles, the media[7] or among human rights activists with the stigma of lack of patriotism, represents a turning point in the Russian public's attitude to the war in Chechnya.

A feature of Putin's war was the relative lack of vocal opposition from Russia's own human rights lobby. Galina Starovoitova, a leading critic of the 1994–1996 war had since been assassinated. Sergei Kovalev, Yeltsin's most powerful critic in 1994–1996, and Yelena Bonner, widow of Andrei Sakharov, although both expressing forcefully their opposition to the renewed war in Chechnya, had lower public profiles by 1999.

Putin exploited this new-found enthusiasm for a military solution to the Chechen conflict by calling for 'victory at all costs', balancing in absolutist rhetoric the slogan of the irreconcilable Chechen opposition of 'Freedom or death'. The hyperbole in this latter traditional rallying call, though not unusual in the discourse of self-determination and national liberation, has taken on sinister new associations since September 11, from when it has often been interpreted to mean 'Death or Paradise'.

The timing of the terrorist attacks on New York and Washington, like those on Moscow just two years earlier, was extremely fortuitous for Putin. The events of September 11, retrospectively, appear to have justified Russia's longstanding claim that the West was not only underestimating the 'plague of the twenty-first century' – international (Islamic) terrorism, but also ignoring the existence of 'an arc of Islamic fundamentalism from Kosovo to the Philippines'.[8] On 2 March 2000, for example, *Agence France Presse* quoted the Kremlin spokesman on Chechnya – Sergei Yastrzhembsky – as stating that: 'The West does not understand the circumstances of terrorism in Russia. No country in the world has confronted terrorism on such a grand scale.'

Russia has been catapulted into a key support role in America's war against terrorism in Afghanistan and has also taken every opportunity since the World Trade Centre attacks to present its conflict with the Chechens, which it has always characterised as a counter-terrorist operation, as a component of the coalition's overall struggle with Islamic insurgents.[9] Western leaders have responded by toning down significantly their criticism of Russian actions in Chechnya, acknowledging tacitly President Putin's carte blanche in dealing with not only the Chechen rebels, but also the civilian population in the war zone. Within a fortnight of 9/11, the then German Chancellor – Gerhard Schroeder – had stated that: 'As regards Chechnya, there will be and must be a more differentiated evaluation in world opinion,'[10] a sentiment soon to be repeated by the then Secretary General of NATO, George Robertson, who commented that 'we have come to see the scourge of terrorism in Chechnya with different eyes'.[11]

In the perception of many of its citizens, Russia has been restored to its predestined role as the first line of defence in the 'clash of civilisations', defending the Western way of life against the threat of, traditionally the 'Yellow' but now, the Islamic 'Green' Peril.[12] Since September 11 this claim is no longer dismissed in the West as mere post-Great Power posturing.

On the other hand, the events of 11 September 2001, inevitably have affected attitudes towards all Muslims in the former Soviet Union. A political analyst at the Hoover Institution at Stanford University claimed that:

> The September 11 terrorist attacks in the United States and Putin's support for the US-led war against terrorism is interjecting new and potentially explosive tension back into Russia's inter-ethnic relations.[13]

In that the events of 11 September have allowed Russia to join the USA as a strategic partner in the war against international Islamic terrorism, the attacks on New York and Washington have worked very much to Putin's advantage. As the conflict dragged on throughout 2000 and 2001 with no victory in sight, public opinion in Russia was beginning to turn against the war in Chechnya. *Le Monde* reported on 6 April 2001, that for the first time since the launch of the second war in October 1999, the percentage of Russians opposed (46.4 per cent) to Moscow's Chechnya policy exceeded the percentage for (42.8 per cent). The *Interfax* news agency reported on 1 February 2002, that a majority (51 per cent) of Russians now favoured peace talks over Chechnya.[14]

Although levels of support for the war among the Russian public have not regained those of the early months of the conflict in 1999/2000, Putin's newly-found status as an ally of Bush, Blair and other Western leaders has consolidated his personal popularity ratings. According to the All-Russian Centre for the Study of Public Opinion (VTsIOM), support for Putin as President rose from 56 per cent in July 2001 to 65 per cent in October 2001.[15] Although the percentage of Russians who trusted Putin dipped to 32 per cent in January 2005 in the wake of the unpopularity of his cash-for-benefits policy,[16] his approval rating climbed back up in time for his hosting of the G-8 in his home city of St Petersburg, in July 2006, to stand at 79 per cent.[17]

In October 2002, following a period during which polls declared that the Russian public was almost two to one against the continuation of the war in Chechnya, the Moscow theatre siege and Putin's tough stand in resolving it led to a surge in support for the President's policy of seeking a military solution. For the first time since 2000, those favouring a continuation of the war (46 per cent), exceeded those opting for peace talks (45 per cent).[18] The same trend could be discerned after the Beslan hostage-taking incident in September 2004.

Perhaps a clue to the Russian leadership's post-9/11 thinking on Chechnya is provided by John B. Dunlop's assertion that:

> Following the stillborn initiative of November 2001, the Kremlin had apparently jettisoned the idea of holding any negotiations whatsoever with moderate separatists in favour of empowering its handpicked candidate for Chechen leader, former mufti Akhmad Kadyrov. This tactic, said to be backed by Aleksandr Voloshin, the then presidential chief of staff, soon became known as 'Chechenization'. Other elements among the top leadership of the presidential administration, such as the two deputy chiefs of staff, Viktor Ivanov – a former deputy director of the FSB – and Igor Sechin, as well as certain leaders in the so-called power ministries, for example, Federal Security Service (FSB) Director Nikolai Patrushev, were reported to be adamantly opposed both to Chechenization and, even more so, to holding talks with moderate separatists; what they wanted was aggressively to pursue the war to a victorious conclusion. If that effort took years more to achieve, then so be it.[19]

Such a collective mindset might well perceive the crushing of terrorists at all costs to be more important than the lives of their own civilians, be they theatre-goers or schoolchildren. Certainly, one way to deflect any criticism from even allies in the coalition against terror abroad, after 9/11, would be to present these acts by extremist elements in the Chechen resistance as not only part of a worldwide terrorist assault, but also as representative of all factions of Chechen society opposed to Chechnya remaining part of the Russian Federation. Of course, another way of dispelling such doubts would be for the Kremlin to provide frank and open details of these 'counter-terrorist' operations or to allow a semblance of independent inquiry, a course of action the Putin administration resolutely refuses to take.

Any examination of the impact of September 11 on the Russo-Chechen War needs to pay particular attention to public attitudes towards the 'Islamic factor'[20] in Russia and the West. We have analysed already the crude stereotyping and demonising of the Chechens, in which I described how, in the course of two brutal wars, Russian popular stereotypes of the Chechens had been manipulated in such a way as to replace a generally positive perception of the noble and free mountain man – the *djigit* – into, first, a dangerous and bloodthirsty criminal (bandit) and, subsequently, into a crazed and fanatical terrorist of an Islamic fundamentalist persuasion.[21]

Chechnya endured in the interlude between the two wars a diplomatic, economic and military blockade, which, significantly, did not extend to high-level contacts of a decidedly criminal nature. This led, perhaps inevitably, to a significant rise in the profile of a more sharply-defined religious orientation, portrayed in the Russian media as one of the most extreme forms of Islamic fundamentalism – *Wahhabism* – and backed up with open displays in Chechnya of actions perceived in the West as being of either an atavistic or fundamentalist character.

In three years of de facto independence of the Chechen regime, a series of high-profile kidnappings occurred. It was estimated that kidnappings throughout the region in 1997 earned the Chechen bands at least $20 million.[22] A secession of gruesome murders of Westerners (and Russians) also took place. In December 1996, six Red Cross workers were killed and in December 1998, the severed heads of four British Telecom engineers were discovered.[23] Such horrific events together with a series of public executions under the newly-imposed *Shari'a* law alienated further the West and diluted any romantic notions among Russians as to the rectitude of the Chechen cause. Moreover, the presence on Russian soil of foreign Islamic militants, the *Wahhabites*, could be, and was, portrayed by the Russian media as representing the same threat to Russian democracy as fundamentalists such as Osama bin Laden did to the West.[24]

Rather than encourage the growth of that particularly benign type of secular Islam to which the overwhelming majority of Chechens, including their first president – Djokhar Dudaev – aspired,[25] there appears to be some evidence that the elements in the Russian leadership provoked the *Wahhabite* incursion into Dagestan in August 1999,[26] if not the apartment house bombs in Moscow and elsewhere.

On 14 December 2001, Berezovsky claimed that the FSB had organised the apartment house bombings in Moscow and Volgodonsk, as well as the 'training exercise' in Ryazan in September 1999.[27] This claim had been made much earlier by several Western and Russian journalists and was the subject of the Channel 4 Dispatches programme, *Dying for the President*, screened on 9 March 2000. As early as July 1998, the journalist Andrei Piontkovsky had predicted that: 'a couple of urgently organised terrorist acts in Moscow' might lead to a State of Emergency being declared and 'a second small, victorious war' could be launched.[28]

Clearly, under international law, the Russian authorities were entitled, even obliged to take action, not only over Dagestan, but also over the lawlessness in Chechnya. The problem was Russian public opinion. Whatever one thinks of the web of conspiracy theories surrounding the bombings in Moscow and Volgodonsk, there is no doubt that they changed fundamentally the Russian population's attitude to dealing with the Chechen problem once and for all. In this sense the explosions in the capital had a similar impact in hardening the Russian public's demand for both action and revenge, as did the September 11 attacks on the American popular consciousness and, arguably, the Palestine suicide bombings on Israeli public opinion. Certainly, the events in Chechnya, Dagestan and Moscow were sufficiently linked in the perception of the average Russian citizen as to give an unambiguous 'green light' to Putin's invasion of Chechnya, ostensibly to root out international terrorism. In the period leading up to the invasion, those urging restraint and caution or raising doubts were pilloried in the mass media as traitors.

It has become a truism that the events of September 11 ushered in a new epoch. Since then the world has been trying to come to terms with the twenty-first century with political tools inherited largely from the twentieth, nineteenth and even eighteenth centuries. Such was the impact of the attacks on New York and Washington that all conflicts are viewed by the Western alliance through the prism of the war on terrorism. Thus, if in Chechnya, Western criticism was confined largely to human rights and other NGOs prior to September 11, after the suicide attacks on New York and Washington, Western leaders including Bush and Blair have gone out of their way to draw parallels between the Russian and American experience of combating Islamic terror, utilising the same formula that the coalition was not against 'Islam' or the 'Chechen people', but against the cancer of international terrorism. This was most notable during Putin's visit to President Bush's ranch in Texas in November 2001.[29]

Subsequent attempts by sympathisers with the plight of the civilian population, refugees, those non-combatants opposed in principle to a continuance of Russian rule in Chechnya to call Russia to account for its excesses, have fallen foul of President Bush's catch-all 'he who is not with us, is against us' (paradoxically one of Stalin's more memorable formulations). This simplistic hard-line approach to counter-terrorism, which goes against more than 30 years of accumulated theory, perversely, has met with the overwhelming support of the public, not only of Russia, but also of Israel and the United States of America.

This has been achieved not least through the utilisation of lessons learned in the first so-called 'Media War' – the Kosovo crisis. Media-trained 'spin doctors' have targeted popular news channels and tabloid newspapers, effectively marginalising those who seek to negotiate the complexities of these issues in a rational and considered manner. Thus, a legitimate struggle for national self-determination, if it occurs on the territory of a strategic partner of the West, can easily and deliberately be confused with international terrorism, leading to an even greater sense of injustice in those areas that have fallen victim to this policy and, effectively, throwing such peoples into the arms of the extremists, the only forces perceived to be capable of opposing such power.

In this sense, one result of the insecurity engendered by September 11 is that the public in the West, especially in the USA, appears to have 'shelved', one hopes only temporarily, its own values, prioritising instead the perceived overarching interest of a need for security, characteristic, already, of Israeli and Russian societies.

This apparent paradox stems from the contradiction inherent in the concept of a war against terrorism, which, along with 'wars' against crime or poverty, is radically different from a war against a given country. This point has been made well by both Sir Michael Howard and Grenville Byford.[30]

Because of the acknowledged special conditions pertaining in war, acts that otherwise fulfil the criteria for being classified as 'terrorist' (such as the bombing of Hiroshima, the activities of the French resistance in the Second World War, assassinations of enemy leaders, etc.) are exempted. Indeed, one definition of an act of terrorism is 'the peacetime equivalent of a war crime',[31] implying that terror and war are incompatible. There is some utility to the Russians, therefore, in presenting the conflict as part of the war against terrorism (in which, by definition, only the other side can be accused of employing terror) rather than a war against Chechnya (in which the rules of war would apply to both sides).

Of course, this argument has only gained any broad support outside Russia since the attacks of 11 September 2001 and the subsequent declaration of war against global terrorism. Prior to that, the conflict in Chechnya was a cause for embarrassment, if not complaint, among Russia's Western partners and the target of considerable criticism from human rights organisations both in Russia and the West. Although these organisations, with the support of brave and outspoken public figures, have continued this criticism throughout the second war, the Russian public at large was converted to the new perception of the conflict two years earlier when the war in Chechnya (i.e. Russians fighting on Chechen soil) became conflated with the war against terrorism (i.e. Chechens bringing the war to Russia). Russians, therefore, suffer no psychological discomfort from the apparent contradiction that the country is engaged in one war with terrorism (which they support) and, simultaneously, another against the Chechen people (which they do not).[32]

Apart from the major hostage-taking incidents at Budennovsk in June 1995 and Kizlyar/Pervomaiskoe in January 1996, the concept of a war against terror was largely absent in the first confrontation, which was perceived generally as a war in the traditional sense. Indeed, during the first war, the leader of the Chechen armed resistance, Aslan Maskhadov, repeatedly asserted that: 'Never will we descend to terrorism. We are warriors, not assassins.'[33]

Further weight as to the true nature of the conflict is provided by the fact that the most successful feature film made of the conflict so far by a Russian director is called simply *Voina* (War).[34] The fact that a peace treaty was signed at the end of the first conflict, that internationally recognised elections were held in a de facto independent Chechnya-Ichkeria, that most combatants on both sides (except for those Chechens accused of leading the hostage-taking incidents) were offered an amnesty and that Russian soldiers who had fought in Chechnya have been accorded the status of war veterans, would all seem to emphasise the perception of the struggle as a war. The intensity of the fighting and the scale of casualties (by some estimates up to 100,000 deaths), would appear to confirm this.

When, in the wake of the apartment house bombings in Moscow, Buinaksk and Volgodonsk in September 1999, Putin launched the second war, it certainly contained the element of a 'counter-terrorist operation'.[35] Once the generals were given the go-ahead to flatten Grozny again and occupy the entire territory of Chechnya, however, Russia entered the same impasse of guerrilla fighting in the mountains and an *intifada* in the foothills and on the plains, with casualties on a scale similar to those of the first war.[36] As a result the nomenclature became every bit as inappropriate as that employed by Yeltsin, and public support for the war, predictably, began to wane.[37] It was events elsewhere in the world that came to Putin's rescue.

First, there was the outbreak of the al-Aqsah *intifada* in September 2000, characterised by the terrifying new phenomenon, in the context of the Arab–Israeli conflict, of suicide bombing.[38] The extremely tough and uncompromising stance taken against this new form of insurgency by the Israelis met with support and understanding in Russia, the population of which had been similarly traumatised by the terrorist attacks a year earlier. The concept arose of 'traumatised' democracies, in which ordinary citizens felt their security to be so threatened as to demand, whatever the cost to personal freedoms and without reference to the norms of international law, action that was rapid, resolute and immediately effective.

In the Israeli context, a former Lieutenant Colonel in the IDF has written:

> Israeli's misunderstanding of the new Palestinian way of war may come back to haunt them. Their perception of their enemy's weakness is likely to embolden them and encourage more broad punitive operations in response to future attacks. But Israel's military responses will eventually exhaust themselves, whereas the Palestinians will still have legions of willing 'martyrs'. In fact, despite defiant Israeli rhetoric insisting that there will be no surrender to terrorism, one can already see the opposite happening. Israelis are willing to pay an increasingly high economic and diplomatic price for increasingly short periods of calm. As a result, more and more people support panaceas such as unilateral separation – the building of walls, fences, and buffer zones to protect Israel's population centers from Palestinian wrath.[39]

The harder the leaders cracked down on terrorism in these societies, the higher their popularity rose; the short-term application of 'might' proving to be in electoral terms far more popular than any notions of 'right' or 'rational' political solutions.[40]

The appearance of 'traumatised' democracies coincided with the spread of what I term 'complexity fatigue',[41] a growing reluctance on the part of the public throughout the world to negotiate the extremely complex and undoubtedly difficult factors underlying such seemingly intractable conflicts as those in Northern Ireland, the Middle East, Kashmir, Kosovo or, of course, Chechnya. Simplistic, short-term 'fixes' based on force were clearly not without attraction either to those citizens who, apparently, preferred escapist entertainment to engagement with complex issues.

By way of a graphic example of this, the film director, Paul Mitchell, told me that his acclaimed documentary *Greetings from Grozny* was denied a screening on British terrestrial TV, not because of any censorship, but that it had been pointed out to him that the British public did not want to come home from work and be confronted with the tragedy and complexity of Chechnya when they could watch *Big Brother* or *Pop Idol*.[42] It would seem that the Russian public is not immune from such distractions, a Chechen separatist news agency in June 2006 accusing Yevgeny Petrosyan's popular entertainment show on Russian TV *Anshlag* (Sell-Out) of playing a similar role.[43]

Finally, in 2001, when it was the turn of the United States of America to suffer its 'Black' September on 9/11, the world's only military superpower joined the ranks of 'traumatised' democracies and the US population was quick to call for the same rapid, resolute and effective reaction demanded by their counterparts in Russia and Israel. Almost overnight, Russia had become a key ally of the USA and Israel in a common struggle – the global war on terrorism – against a common foe – Islamic fundamentalism. For Putin's Russia, this presented another golden opportunity.

Since 9/11, the Bali bomb of October 2002, together with a succession of domestic terrorist-related incidents, organised with or without the collusion of the Russian authorities, in Russia (especially the Moscow theatre siege later that month and the Beslan hostage-taking crisis of September 2004), and Chechnya (where the appearance of female suicide bombers has paralleled developments in the Middle East) has not only kept the anti-Chechen sentiments high among Russians, but done enough to persuade Western leaders that Chechnya is Russia's frontline in the war on terrorism.

Moreover, as we have demonstrated in the preceding chapter, Putin has had some success in splitting the Chechen opposition between those who can and those who cannot tolerate the influence of the *Wahhabis*. Insofar as Maskhadov had proved incapable of reigning in the excesses of Basaev and his allies, and had been obliged at times to move towards public reconciliation with them, the prospect diminished of the Russians ever accepting them as participants in any political solution.

The video of Maskhadov's meeting in July 2002 with Basayev and Khattab's successor as leader of the 'international' *Wahhabites*, Abu Al-Walid, before a Chechen flag, upon which Arabic script and swords symbolically had replaced the traditional Chechen wolf, was used to great effect by the Russian authorities to discredit the Chechen leader. Maskhadov, one can only speculate, made the video and a subsequent one in September 2002 (after the shooting down in August of the Mi-26 military helicopter with 121 Russian casualties, which was attributed to forces led by Abu Al-Walid) in order to secure much-needed funding from Islamic supporters abroad.[44]

Al-Walid, a Saudi-born fighter who had seen active service in Afghanistan, Bosnia and Tajikistan prior to arriving in Chechnya in 1995, was assassinated by Russian forces on 17 April 2004.[45] Russian sources had attributed many of the major Chechen attacks on military targets to Al-Walid, including assisting Khattab in his celebrated destruction of the 245th motorised rifle regiment in April 1996,[46] as well as the 27 December 2002 truck-bomb attack on the Chechen administrative building in Grozny (that killed 80) and even the 1999 Russian apartment-block bombings.[47]

This blurring of 'legitimate' military targets (which should not strictly be classified as terrorism) and attacks on civilians (which should) and the presence of Arab fighters in Chechnya enabled Putin not only to justify his policy of pre-emptive assassination of known leaders of the Chechen resistance, but also to highlight the links between the Chechen separatists and international terrorist organisations, thus allowing him to classify all resistance forces as 'terrorists'.

Putin's insistence that the entire Chechen War should be viewed through the prism of the global war on terrorism has not been harmed by a natural propensity to retrospectively reinterpret history in the light of subsequent events. With the end of the Cold War and after the attacks of 9/11, it no longer seemed unreasonable to claim that the real enemy of first the Soviet Union and then Russia was not the USA or NATO, but Islamic fundamentalism, with whom, it turned out, the successors to the Red Army had been fighting in Afghanistan, Tajikistan and Chechnya since 1979. Similarly, Putin's reference to the threat of Islamic-based terrorism contained in his interview with *Paris Match* on 6 July 2000: 'We are witnessing today the formation of a fundamentalist international, a sort of arc of instability extending from the Philippines to Kosovo', not only sounded far more convincing after 9/11, but also reminded the West how foolish it had been to ignore these early warnings. This message was underlined by the fact that links were ultimately discovered between Chechen militants and some of the suicide attackers of 9/11, as well as with their convicted co-conspirator, Zacarias Moussaoui.[48]

By the summer of 2001, only 22 per cent of Russians listed the largely forgotten war in Chechnya as a major concern; compared to 66 per cent mentioning rising prices, 59 per cent the level of poverty, and 41 per cent the rise in crime.[49] Although NGOs in the West continued to hammer Russia for gross human rights violations in their reports, the Western public appeared to be curiously disengaged from the suffering, a psychological state that I have termed 'complexity fatigue'. In the absence of any meaningful criticism from Western governments, Putin could continue to operate as he pleased in Chechnya.

However, given that by the spring of 2001, for the first time since the launch of the second war in October 1999, the percentage of Russians opposed to Moscow's Chechnya policy exceeded the percentage for, the al-Qaeda attacks on New York and Washington on 11 September 2001 came at a juncture that was extremely fortuitous for the Russian leader. Almost overnight, Russia became a key partner of the USA and its allies in the common struggle – the global war on terrorism – against a common foe – Islamic fundamentalism.

Members of the Putin administration were quick to draw the link between the Chechen rebels and Osama bin Laden, the Presidential aide, Sergei Yastrzhembsky, claiming that 800 fighters from the Middle and Far East had been in Chechnya at the start of the second war.[50] Despite denials by the Chechen side, and doubt cast by journalists covering Chechnya, who have estimated that there were never more than 300 'Arab' fighters in Chechnya, this version was accepted both by Western leaders and the Russian public.[51]

Since 9/11, with such powerful allies in the leadership of the 'Coalition of the Willing' as President Bush and Prime Minister Blair, Putin has been able to play shamelessly the 'Islamic terrorist' card every time Chechnya appears on the agenda, effectively deflecting any attack on his Chechen policy.

By April 2002, in his state of the union address, Putin felt secure enough to declare once more that the military phase of the war in Chechnya was over.[52] Predictably, within weeks, the rebels hit back to prove that it was not, choosing symbolically 'Victory Day' (9 May 2002), when a bomb planted at a military parade in the Dagestan town of Kaspiisk killed 43 soldiers and family members and injured more than 100. Although Dagestani rather than Chechen militants were subsequently arrested, they could still be portrayed as part of an Islamic terrorist alliance and an enraged Russian public blamed the Chechens.[53]

Despite hostility from the Putin administration, but in line with preferences indicated in Russian public opinion polls, prominent Chechens, Russians and Americans were meeting, in the summer of 2002 to elaborate a peace plan for Chechnya. Perhaps to counter these positive developments, on 25 June 2002, Putin finally drew a distinction between the civilian population in Chechnya and the rebels, by claiming:

> As far as the negative image of Chechens is concerned, the Chechen people are not to blame for anything. I think this is the fault of the federal center that the Chechen people were left to the mercy of fate at some point [...] Our task is to destroy this image [of Chechens] as terrorists.[54]

That no such tolerance was to be shown to any Chechen advocating a political solution other than that proposed by Putin was soon to become apparent. Thus, Kadyrov, who had fought the Russians in the first war, was, to all intents and purposes, granted a full amnesty, whereas such first war commanders as Turpal-Ali Atgeriev and Salman Raduev, who also took no part in the second war, were tried, sentenced and died, in less than transparent circumstances within a few months of each other in 2002, in Russian prisons.[55] FSB agents, meanwhile, as part of a series of preemptive strikes against the Chechen resistance, had apparently assassinated the Arab field commander Khattab, in April 2002.[56]

The murky circumstances around the Dubrovka siege in October 2002 have attracted as much speculation as had the Moscow bombings of 1999, with key questions about the Russian administration's handling of the whole operation still as yet unanswered. Whatever the truth, Putin came out of the affair well representing a triumph for the policy of demonisation. Although all but two of the 129 hostages and 41 hostage-takers were killed by the Russian special forces, Putin was absolved of blame by his Western allies, with three groups led by Basaev being added to the US State Department's list of terrorist organisations.

What the Chechens, other than the extremist elements led by the mastermind of the operation, Basaev, had to gain from this act, other than the highly improbable satisfaction of their sole demand – to end the war in Chechnya – is unclear. The prominence of the 'black widow' female hostage-takers, dressed in their black *hijabs*, made it easy to draw parallels between Palestinian and Chechen tactics. The first female Chechen suicide bomber would appear to have been Khaba Baraeva, sister of the notorious warlord, Arbi Baraev and aunt of the leader of the Beslan hostage-takers, Movsar. On 6 June 2000, she and Luisa Magomadova drove a truck bomb into a military building in Chechnya, killing themselves and two OMON soldiers.[57]

From this first incidence of suicide bombing by Chechens until the Beslan school siege in September 2004, nearly 1,000 were killed and almost 3,000 injured in 25 separate Chechen suicide attacks, all but five of which included women bombers, evidence enough for those seeking to prove that the imported *Wahhabite* ideology appeared to be turning Chechnya's independence struggle into part of the worldwide *jihad*.[58]

In reality, of course, the overwhelming majority of the Chechen population remains tired of war and disgusted at the terrorist tactics resorted to by the extremists. Speckhard and Akhmedova report the brother of a Chechen terrorist rationalising thus:

> Certainly, I feel pity for the hostages; they are not guilty in anything. But many civil Chechens were killed too. Our brothers and sisters did not have any other way. The government and army do not understand any other language, except for the language of force.[59]

If one needs further convincing that violence breeds violence then the data provided by Speckhard and Akhmedova is persuasive. Of the 34 suicide bombers interviewed by these two psychologists, no fewer than 30 had experienced the death, in the conflict, of at least one member of their immediate family, three had experienced the 'disappearance' after arrest of a close family member, and one had a family member who had been tortured.[60]

While by no means every relative of a victim of such repression becomes a suicide bomber, it would seem likely that all Chechens who have taken the path of becoming suicide bombers have experienced similar tragedies themselves, encapsulated in the oft-repeated statement by the Chechens who seized the theatre at Dubrovka that they were more keen on dying than their hostages were on living.[61] As a Russian expert at the Mises Institute noted, the Chechen terrorists' rationalisation of their act at Dubrovka was understandable, if misguided, summed up in this statement by one of the 'Black Widows':

> Every nation has the right to its fate. Russia has taken away this right from the Chechens and today we want to reclaim these rights, which God has given us (in the same way that he has given it to other nations). God has given us the right of freedom and the right to choose our destiny. And the Russian occupiers have flooded our land with our children's blood. And we have longed for a just solution. People are unaware of the innocent who are dying in Chechnya; the sheiks, the women, the children and the weak ones. And therefore we have chosen this approach. This approach is for the freedom of the Chechen people and there is no difference where we die, and therefore we have decided to die here in Moscow. And we will take with us the lives of hundreds of sinners. If we die, others will follow us – our brothers and sisters who are willing to sacrifice their lives (in God's way) to liberate their nation. Our nationalists have died but people have said they are terrorists and criminals. But the truth is Russia is the true criminal.[62]

Needless to say, such sentiments were not given extensive airing among the world's media, let alone that of Russia. Far from evoking any sympathy or widespread soul-searching, the act of terror at Dubrovka merely exacerbated the alienation of the Russian public to the values that the Chechens ostensibly were fighting for. The average Russian was more than ready to believe that the Chechens under Movsar Baraev were willing and able to blow up a theatre with more than 800 people in it. The prominence of the 'Black Widow' female suicide bombers reminded the public at home and abroad of the parallels between Palestinian and Chechen tactics in the international 'war on terrorism'.[63]

Putin moved immediately to put an end to the international peace plan process by seeking Zakaev's extradition from first Denmark and then, after his acquittal by the Danish court, the United Kingdom.

By cutting out the negotiations on the future of Chechnya all moderate opposition, Putin's policy effectively rendered impotent all those advocating diplomacy and inclusive negotiations as a means of reaching a political solution. Those intent on carrying on the fight switched their tactics to suicide bombing. In December 2002 trucks driven by suicide bombers destroyed the government headquarters in Grozny, killing 80, and in May 2003 a further 59 in Znamenskoye. Throughout 2003, female suicide bombers struck in Moscow, in southern Russia and in Chechnya. With over 300 dead, these attacks proved just as costly in human terms as the series of apartment blasts in September 1999.[64] Yet against this backdrop of unprecedented violence being visited upon the Russian heartland, Putin stubbornly refused to contemplate any other solution to the Chechen insurgency other than the total eradication of the rebel forces.

Four counter-terrorist strategies – a comparative analysis

At this point it would be useful to analyse the alternative counter-insurgency policies to eradication of the threat that Putin could have adopted.

Although Russia's one-dimensional approach to the conflict has drawn criticism from all sides – for being the policy least likely to lead to a just and lasting peace – there is little incentive for Putin to alter the status quo. He has a fresh mandate from his electorate, which backs his goal of eliminating all Chechen 'terrorists', and Russia's uncompromising attitude towards insurgents is consistent with the line taken by Israel against the Palestinians and the US-led coalition against al-Qaeda. It is, perhaps, only the manifest failure of the 'coalition of the willing' to establish stability in Iraq that has prompted the world community finally to heed the scepticism, and to call into question the wisdom of trying to reach political solutions through the application of massive military force.

The portrayal by leaders of complex conflicts as little more than battles between 'good' and 'evil'[65] can, through skilful manipulation of the media, garner the support of their threatened populations, particularly if they have suffered, as in Russia, Israel and the US, the trauma of a series of terrorist attacks during their respective 'Black Septembers'.[66]

However, as these 'wars' on terrorism drag on inconclusively, pressure is mounting on governments bent on a military solution to bring even more force to bear, until eventually, the hopelessness of such a one-track approach becomes obvious to all concerned. In evaluating the comparative utility of four different strategies that might be adopted to redirect Russia's Chechen policy towards achieving a peace that serves the interests of both the Chechen and Russian peoples, one must recognise that the successful implementation of such a policy would simultaneously remove a major obstacle to stability in the Caucasus.

The four-track approach, drawing on experience of other conflicts and counter-insurgencies around the world, provides a much more balanced, reliable and tested means of reaching a satisfactory accommodation than the costly, inherently unstable and dangerous one-track methodology employed hitherto by successive Russian administrations.

Strategy 1: eradication

Although the US-led coalition, following the example of Israel in its conflict with the Palestinians and the Russians in their dispute with Chechnya, is pursuing a policy aimed at the eradication of terrorism, as a strategy it belongs more in the realm of political rhetoric and propaganda, as opposed to practical counter-insurgency.[67] Its value is that it grants counter-insurgent forces virtual carte blanche to employ the most sophisticated weaponry and military forces against an enemy so ill defined as to cover, in effect, all who are perceived as opposing or might be deemed to be against the coalition. On the pretext that suspected terrorists might be hiding among the civilian population, attacks of such frequency and intensity have been launched against essentially civilian targets that, in Afghanistan, Chechnya, Iraq and Palestine, precise numbers of casualties are not routinely recorded.[68]

The manifest failure in any of these conflict zones to eradicate terrorism by purely military means does not appear to have deterred the proponents of the policy.[69] In normal times the killing of up to one-fifth of the population, mostly non-combatant civilians, as appears to be the case in Chechnya,[70] would attract withering criticism and demands for action from the world community. Since 11 September, however, times have been anything but normal.

The cost of eradication tends to be extremely high; estimates of the cost to the Russian economy of the war in Chechnya range from $1.3 billion dollars to $11.5 billions per year.[71] Although the rising price of oil and gas has meant that the Russian economy is better placed to withstand such expenditure, it is a moot point whether a genuinely democratic expression of Russian public opinion would share the same priorities as their President. As one Russian journalist has written:

> That's one of the underlying reasons for the war. It offers unlimited opportunity to steal from the state, since everything can be written off as due to the war. The money goes directly into the pockets of civilian and

military officials. In peacetime, embezzlement is difficult, but during a war everything is so much easier. The same thing is happening in Iraq, though the sums disappearing there are much larger. Like Russia, the United States has created a large budget hole through which a great deal disappears.[72]

Far from restricting the policy of eradication to Chechnya, the Russian authorities have given notice that they would hunt down 'terrorists' wherever they were located. In September 2004, just a few days after the conclusion of the Beslan siege, Colonel-General Yury Baluyevsky, chief of the Russian General Staff announced: 'We will take all measures to eliminate terrorists in any region of the world',[73] justifying, perhaps, in retrospect, the assassination in Qatar by Russian agents earlier that year of the former president of Chechnya-Ichkeria, Zelimkhan Yandirbiev.

Strategy 2: terror against terror

If the eradication of terrorism represents the 'reach' of advocates of military means in countering insurgency, then combating terrorism by employing terror tactics against the terrorists might be held to represent the 'grasp'. Like eradication, it has the propaganda value of reassuring one's domestic constituency that something is being done to tackle terrorism without appearing to be weak, conciliatory or irresolute. Tactically, it keeps the insurgents on the back foot as they become 'legitimate' targets, irrespective of international law and conventions.

Combating 'terror' with terror also relies heavily on military means, from overwhelming firepower to 'aggressive' interrogation, but it has the added advantage of access to a range of supportive non-military options (from policing to the rebuilding of social and economic infrastructures). As the experiences of Afghanistan and Iraq have shown, an over reliance on military choices to the detriment of non-military ones can have unwelcome and unintended consequences.

Two key concepts here are proportionality in the application of military might and discrimination as to whom it is to be employed against. If these factors are ignored, the civilian population among which the insurgents are hiding is just as likely to become a target, driving it effectively into the arms of its only perceived protector, the very 'terrorists' whom the counter-insurgency effort is seeking to destroy.

As just about every objective account of Russia's military campaign in Chechnya points to the disproportionate and indiscriminate use of force by federal troops,[74] one must conclude that this is precisely what has happened in Chechnya. The 'Chechenisation' of the conflict, far from making things better in this sphere, seems, if anything, to have exacerbated matters. The *kadyrovtsy* (led by Kadyrov's son, Ramzan) quickly acquired a reputation for brutal savagery, terrorising the civilian population even more than the Russian federal forces.[75]

With this policy of Chechenisation, Putin attempts to convince the Russian public and the outside world that the Chechen crisis is over. For example, in

June 2004, just days after the arms raid in Ingushetia, Putin claimed that 'normalization in Chechnya is well underway'.[76] Yet, the period from Putin's statement up to and including the Beslan siege in September 2004 saw the bloodiest series of attacks by the rebels since the beginning of the conflict, that left 425 dead and 500 wounded.[77]

A third key factor is the impunity with which combatants on all sides of the conflict can carry out the most arbitrary and brutal of crimes against civilians. With the notable exception of the Budanov case, in which a Russian tank commander was sentenced to ten years for raping and killing a teenage Chechen girl only after public protests against an earlier not guilty verdict,[78] successful prosecutions of Russian soldiers for war crimes have been rare. Even Chechen President Alu Alkhanov publicly expressed frustration at the failure of Russian courts to secure a conviction in the trial of Captain Eduard Ullmann, a Russian officer accused along with three soldiers under his command of killing six Chechen civilians in 2002.[79]

Until the problems of disproportionate and indiscriminate use of force and impunity with respect to war crimes are tackled, the strategy of terror against terror in Chechnya is likely to be as impotent as that of eradication.

Strategy 3: containment

By far the most tried and tested form of counter-insurgency since the Second World War has been that of containment.[80] The essential difference between this strategy and the preceding two is that military force is used only as a back-up to help ensure implementation of a wide range of measures, including policing, political, economic, social and diplomatic initiatives aimed at establishing law, order and security in the conflict zone. Its great benefit is that it allows to begin the slow and painful process of demonstrating to the civilian population that non-violent options are available to resolve their conflicts; transferring the battle, if you will, from the field to the mind, if not yet to the heart.

For this process to succeed, all of those who prefer a peaceful conclusion to the conflict need to be involved. This leads to the difficult and emotive phase of engaging with those who one has been fighting, politically and militarily, thus identifying, isolating and marginalising those diehard opponents of anything other than a military solution. It is apparent that if all of one's enemies are designated as 'terrorists', there is little prospect of success. But if the context in which the 'terrorists' took up arms is acknowledged, and the aim is to change that context, then there is every chance that 'crimes' committed as part of an armed confrontation will not be repeated once the conflict moves from the military to the political stage.

While admitting that direct comparisons are difficult to draw, Britain's experience in Northern Ireland has some relevance to the Russo-Chechen conflict. Granting an amnesty to those on both sides convicted of acts of terrorism, up to and including those who attempted to blow up the entire British government, led to a breakthrough in the demilitarisation of the conflict. Admittedly, the political conflict remains to this day disappointingly polarised, but at least the civilian population of Northern Ireland is free to go about the long and difficult task of rebuilding its fractured society. Applying this method to the Russo-Chechen conflict would imply engaging not only with all types of political opponents within Chechnya (such as Ruslan Khasbulatov or Malik Saidullaev), but also with leaders of the Chechen separatist resistance (like the late president of Chechnya-Ichkeria Abdul-Khalim Sadulaev or Akhmed Zakaev). This would have isolated within Chechnya such hard-line, so-called 'Islamic fundamentalist' insurgents as Shamil Basaev. However, even Basaev and his ilk should at least have been given the opportunity to reject the military struggle in favour of a peaceful political solution.

Clearly this strategy is fraught with difficulty. Moreover, it calls for compromise, patience, trust and forgiveness from traumatised populations on both sides. It is highly unlikely that Russia has the will or the resources to remedy the wrongs that it has imposed on the Chechen people over the past decade and before, so a degree of understanding and assistance from the world community is probably necessary to start this process. As long as the view that 'those who are not with us, are with the terrorists' – enshrined in the coalition's 'war on terror' – prevails, there is little prospect of such help being offered or accepted any time soon.

Strategy 4: addressing the root causes

Most of the root causes of the Russo-Chechen conflict have been identified during the course of this analysis, including the asymmetry between Russian-imposed modernisation and Chechen traditional societal structures, the impact of two brutal wars, characterised by disproportionate and indiscriminate use of force against the civilian population, the impunity with which war crimes have been committed against civilians, and the rampant lawlessness that allows the well-armed few on both sides to continue a conflict that is extremely beneficial to them but which represents a human tragedy on a colossal scale for the many.

These problems are basically between the Russians and the Chechens themselves and could be addressed, if not solved in the short term, given goodwill on both sides. To this list, though, have been added the even more complex issues arising from the 'war on terror': the problems associated with globalisation; the clash between Western and Islamic ideologies; the legitimacy of armed insurgency; the imbalance between the war-fighting capabilities of the US and its allies and those who oppose them; the growing gulf between the 'haves' and the 'have nots'; and the routine violation of international norms and conventions, by terrorists and state-controlled armies alike, under the pretext that 'the ends justify the means'.

One need not be a pessimist to conclude that the time, patience and understanding, let alone the considerable financial resources, required to address these root causes are not going to be readily forthcoming. At the same time, it is clear that an outcome in which the greatest number of people involved in the conflict has a genuine stake is the only one that will satisfy the world community, the Russians and the Chechens.

Some correlation has been established between the excesses of the federal side (now characterised by sweeps, but formerly by indiscriminate heavy artillery attacks and carpet bombing of inhabited areas) and those of the insurgents (characterised by acts of terror). While world leaders and the media are not inclined to equate the two, it has long been established in theories of terrorism that such repressive measures by government forces tend to provoke extreme responses from insurgents. As long ago as 1988, Alex Schmid set out the options available to state and non-state actors in a time of 'violent' politics; if the state resorted to such forms of violent repression for control of state power as assassination, state-terrorism (torture, death squads, disappearances, concentration camps) massacres, internal war or genocide one might expect the non-state actor to use violence to contest state power by means of terrorism, massacres, guerrilla warfare and insurgency.[81] Insofar as Russian behaviour in Chechnya may be perceived as falling within the parameters as defined by Schmid of 'state-terrorism', one might anticipate that the response from their Chechen opponents might include terrorism.

Disassociating herself from the consistently-expressed view of the Putin administration that all armed Chechen oppositionists are 'international terrorists', Ekaterina Stepanova has drawn a clear distinction between 'conflict-related' terrorism (such as that practiced by the Chechens) and the 'super-terrorism' or 'mega-terrorism' of groups such as al-Qaeda.[82]

At the same time, even the pro-Kremlin Chechens continue to share with their co-ethnics deep misgivings about the behaviour of Russian federal forces in Chechnya. As we have seen both Ramzan Kadyrov and Alu Alkhanov have spoken out forcefully against any release of Colonel Yury Budanov or Captain Eduard Ullman, respectively, and, in order to survive as an effective fighting force, his *kadyrovtsy* have been obliged to swell their ranks with former Chechen *boyeviki* (fighters), the loyalty of whom is suspect. Moreover, some of Kadyrov's former *boyeviki* are rumoured to have participated in Shamil Basaev's arms raid in Ingushetia in June 2004, which left more than 100 federal employees dead and provided much of the weaponry employed in the attack on the school in Beslan.[83]

Conclusion

It has been noted that three of the four different aspects of the Russo-Chechen conflict identified could be resolved through negotiations between the Russians and the Chechens themselves. The only one that makes this conflict of immediate concern to the international community as a whole, other than as a human rights issue, is its relation to the global confrontations that have dominated world politics since the end of the Cold War and, more specifically, since 11 September 2001.

Even if one rejects out of hand the notion of a 'clash of civilisations', one must admit that Russia and the Chechen separatists have found themselves on opposing sides with respect to some of the major divisions and issues in the post-Cold War era, including the North–South economic divide, the Judeo/Christian–Muslim schism and the war on terror. As a result, Russia can depict itself as broadly on the side of the US in its drive for globalisation, whereas the Chechens are easily perceived as constituting an obstacle to this goal. The terrorist attacks of 11 September 2001 have led to a conflation, encouraged by the administration of US President George W. Bush, of all of the disparate elements of globalisation. The skilful application of 'information warfare' has convinced large sections of a traumatised public that all who oppose any aspect of US foreign policy, be it the UN, 'Old' Europe or Osama bin Laden, are on the side of the 'terrorists'.

Recognising the utility of key elements of this approach, Putin, since 11 September 2001, has more or less successfully been able to portray Russia's conflict in Chechnya as being against Islamic fundamentalist terror,[84] which, in its turn, represents part of what Mary Kaldor has termed 'regressive globalization'.[85]

As the other three 'soluble' aspects of the Russo-Chechen conflict are rarely allowed to be discussed in the popular Russian media, and only occasionally attract the attention of the more liberal elements of the Western media, the only time that the conflict penetrates the consciousness of the world community is when the Chechens launch a 'terrorist spectacular' along the lines of the Dubrovka theatre siege of October 2002 or the seizure of the school in Beslan in September 2004. These, in turn, can be presented as 'proof' that all Chechen opposition to Putin falls within the realm of the 'war' on terrorism. Thus, the $10 million bounty placed on the heads of both Basaev and Maskhadov after the Beslan siege, equally 'justified', in the perception of Putin's administration, if not that of the rest of the world, the assassination of both.

In sum, because those aspects of the conflict that can be addressed are ignored, and the one remaining aspect depends on the successful outcome of the 'war' against al-Qaeda – in line with US policy, and in common with the Israeli–Palestinian confrontation and the war in Iraq – the entire Russo-Chechen conflict remains at an impasse without any obvious exit strategy but in danger of spilling over into the North Caucasus as a whole.

However, these tactics promise to deliver the Chechens (or at least those that side with Kadyrov) their key strategic goal, i.e. ridding their territory of Russian 'occupation'. For not only has the once considerable ethnic Russian community almost in its entirety left Chechnya, but the antagonisms between Russians and Chechens (not least the quintessentially Russian phenomenon of 'Caucasophobia'), the fear of terrorism and the unattractiveness of Chechnya under Kadyrov, virtually ensures that they will not return in any great numbers.

We are left with the paradoxical situation, that one Russian observer has characterised as 'a separatist Chechnya under the Russian flag',[86] in which both the Russian and Chechen sides could claim to have achieved their strategic goals in Chechnya. Insofar as this represents a 'political solution', it also meets the West's main concern in the Russo-Chechen conflict. However, such an outcome only lets Putin off the 'Chechnya hook' if he can prevent opponents airing the very obvious reservations towards his Chechen policies and its results. This is where his tightened grip over the political system and media in Russia comes in useful. It is hardly surprising that elements of Western civic society engaged with the conflict in Chechnya feel under no such constraints in exposing the shortcomings of this outcome and asking the obvious question; could not such an unsatisfactory conclusion have been reached more than a decade ago thus sparing hundreds of thousands of casualties, refugees and the spread of instability throughout the Northern Caucasus?

From the Chechen side, the 'victory' is even more dubious. Quite apart from the loyalty of the ex-rebels, the Kremlin's policy relies heavily on the ability of Ramzan Kadyrov to rule with an iron hand. Already the rebels have proven that they can upset such certainties; having assassinated Ramzan's father, the first architect of 'Chechenisation' – Akhmad Kadyrov. The rebels, led until July 2006 by Shamil Basaev, have resorted to terrorism as a tactic in order to achieve independence and are quite capable of threatening the monopoly of power of the younger Kadyrov. Moreover, the current deal excludes them from any legitimate political or economic role in Chechnya, so they are bound to project such power as they undoubtedly possess through illegitimate means.

This leaves those Chechen separatists who have inherited the Maskhadov legacy with a genuine dilemma. Those within the area, led until his assassination in 2006 by Abdul-Khalim Sadulaev, appeared to have joined forces with Basaev and declared a war front throughout the Northern Caucasus. Those isolated abroad, such as Zakaev and Akhmadov, are losing influence both in Chechnya, where they are increasingly regarded as being too distant from events on the ground,[87] and in their adopted homelands, where they form an 'awkward squad' that embarrasses their host governments from time to time (as when Zakaev spoke out of turn following the Nalchik attacks in October 2005).[88] On the other hand, the sheer rate of attrition among the leaders of the Chechen resistance will soon mean that those in the relative safety of the West will be the only representatives left to articulate the viewpoint of the 'moderate' resistance.[89] It remains to be seen whether a future British government will regard as expedient, in the broader national interest, Zakaev's extradition under tighter counter-terrorist laws.

The al-Qaeda attacks on New York and Washington on 11 September 2001 came at a fortuitous juncture for Putin. Not only did they justify, in retrospect, his warnings of 'an arc of Islamic fundamentalism from Kosovo to the Philippines', but also they allowed him to present himself as President George W. Bush's closest ally in the 'war on international terrorism'. His subsequently elevated international status more than made up in the minds of Russian voters for his disappointing handling of the Kursk affair a year earlier[90] and his policy towards the Chechen fighters (at least two-thirds of those Russians polled regularly disapproved of Putin's handling of this aspect of the war).[91]

Since 11 September 2001, Putin has not missed an opportunity to present the Chechen conflict as Russia's contribution to the war on terrorism and to label all members of the Chechen resistance as 'terrorists'.[92] Indeed, as we have seen, it was only on 24 June 2002 that Putin declared that not all Chechens are terrorists. By absolutising the conflict, he leaves little room or flexibility for a just and comprehensive political settlement.

The impact of 9/11 on East–West relations in general, and British–Russian relations in particular, was best encapsulated in the words of George Robertson – the former British Defence Secretary and then Secretary General of NATO – that 'we have come to see the scourge of terrorism in Chechnya with different eyes'.[93] Any vestiges of support for Chechen self-determination fell away far more dramatically at British governmental level than they did among the public at large, let alone among the human rights lobby.

Indeed, it was not just the Chechen insurgents who found themselves on the back foot in the aftermath of 9/11. After the attack on the Twin Towers and the Pentagon any hint of 'terrorist' activity, especially if connections could be traced to radical Islamic groups, immediately placed the perpetrators and their supporters on the 'wrong' side in the 'war on terror'. Thus, if groups such as the IRA and ETA felt constrained to eschew acts of violence that might be construed as terrorism, one can imagine the pressure on, for example, Palestinian and Chechen groups. When both groups resorted to suicide bombings, the form of attack which, since 9/11 had come to epitomise 'them' (radical Islamists) against 'us' (the 'civilised' world), they were hard put to retain the empathy, let alone the sympathy, of anyone other than those who understood the full complexity of their respective struggles.

Almost overnight, the Chechen cause had shifted away from one that appeared more or less analogous with that of Kosovo, to one that more resembled Palestine. At the same time, the Russian cause became more closely aligned to that of the USA and thus, through common membership of the 'Coalition of the Willing', to that of the UK. On receiving Putin at Chequers in December 2001, Prime Minister Tony Blair pointedly drew parallels between the bombings in Russia of 1999 and the events of 9/11.[94]

At the same time the shift away from secular values by the Chechen side, under the influence of the *Wahhabites*, but also due to the alienation from Western values of the emerging generation of Chechen resistance leaders, epitomised until his assassination in June 2006 by Abdul-Khalim Sadulaev, has led to a near total disenchantment among secular circles in the West with the Chechen cause. As has been noted, if Chechnya's first constitution, drafted under Djokhar Dudaev, resembled that of Estonia, where he had been based while serving in the Soviet Armed Forces prior to the collapse of the USSR, then that of any future independent Chechnya under the militant Islamists is likely to resemble more the constitution of Sudan.[95]

7   Entrepreneurs of violence

We are terrorists for them, and they are terrorists for us.

(Shamil Basaev, 2006)[1]

Lord Russell-Johnston, then President of the Council of Europe's Parliamentary Assembly (PACE) complained in an interview with *Le Monde* on 6 February 2001, that not one of the 40 states in the Council was willing to bring Russia before the European Court of Human Rights over violations in Chechnya. The temporary suspension of Russia from the Council in 2000–2001 had been more than offset by Western leaders appearing to close their eyes to the catastrophe in Chechnya.[2] The inconsistency of the West's position vis-à-vis Chechen independence has been recognised by perceptive Russian observers. Boris Kagarlitsky, for example, notes that:

> The situation in Chechnya is specific only in that the world community (in fact, the West), following its own interests, was prepared to recognize as independent Kuwait, and later, Croatia, Macedonia, Bosnia and other 'self-proclaimed' states.... But they were in no hurry to recognize Chechnya, insofar as the current Russian elite (in distinction from the elite, for example, of Serbia or Iraq) is a strategic partner of the West.[3]

This helps explains why the Russian leadership felt free to apply with impunity arbitrary and brutal force against the Chechens in both wars. As the Russian observer – Pavel Felgenhauer – noted towards the end of the first conflict:

> Obviously no reasonable world leader wishes to deal in the future with a totally unpredictable, but fully sovereign and independent, buccaneer Chechen Republic – a source of illicit arms and drugs, ruled by an assembly of Lebanese warlords in Grozny. The world is already full of rogue states, lunatic dictators and all-powerful drug cartels.[4]

The inept execution of the initial stages of the first war turned public opinion against the campaign, whereas the hysteria and fury generated by the 300-plus deaths in the apartment bombings in Moscow, Volgodonsk and Buinaksk[5] demanded a 'firm hand' to deal with the renewed Chechen 'threat'. Such figures of moral authority as Aleksandr Solzhenitsyn contrasted the 'stupidity' of Yeltsin's invasion, with the rectitude of Putin's.[6]

This allowed Putin to so manipulate public opinion into accepting a single, negative stereotype of the Chechens that, in a much better-organised and 'cleaner' initial campaign, he was able to reverse the results of that earlier war, despite subsequently visiting on the Chechen people the same scale of violence and provoking the same level of concern, if not condemnation, among his Western would-be allies.

It was this attitudinal shift, occasioned by public reaction to the terror bombing campaign, the subsequent attributing of blame to Islamic militants from the Caucasus and by association to the Chechens, followed by the invasion of Chechnya early in October 1999, that created for Putin the platform from which to launch his successful presidential campaign.

The part played by Basaev and Gelaev in the final rout of the federal forces in Grozny, in August 1996, served to heighten their prestige as national heroes in the eyes of the Chechen people and as daring 'Robin Hood'-type revolutionaries by broad sections of the Russian media.[7] One source even maintains that Basaev and Gelaev, just prior to the outbreak of the first war, had sought to hand over Dudaev to the Russians in exchange for promises not to invade.[8]

The Chechens were seen to be winning the 'propaganda' war, a victory virtually ensured by the propensity of the federal forces to regard aid workers, journalists and human rights activists as siding with the enemy. For example, the charitable organisation *Médecins sans frontières* (in Russian *Vrachi bez granits*), was called *Vragi bez granits* (Enemies without frontiers).

By the commencement of the 1999 campaign, both Basaev and Raduev had been thoroughly discredited in the Russian press, the former for his conversion to a militant form of Islam and his close friendship with the Arab *Wahhabite*, Khattab (who appears to have been trained in insurgency by Russian instructors),[9] and the latter through his participation in several high profile kidnaps and assassination attempts.

By the spring of 2000, Raduev had been arrested in Chechnya by the Russian authorities and Basaev had lost a foot to a land mine during the evacuation of Grozny. Khattab, an explosives expert, who had earlier lost some fingers while priming a bomb, had become the *bête noir* of the Russian federal forces, being responsible for the attack on the Pskov paratroopers that left 86 dead in April 2000, was eventually killed by Russian forces in a special operation in 2002.[10] These field commanders, as well as Maskhadov, Udugov and other Chechen leaders appeared to be in regular contact with powerful men close to the Russian Presidency, such as Boris Berezovsky,[11] thus providing further evidence that a renewed conflict was in the interests of both Chechen and Russian elites. Basaev swore on the Koran that Berezovsky had given him $3 million to finance the incursion into Dagestan,[12] which served, along with the apartment bombings, as the pretext for the second invasion of Chechnya.

The capture in March 2000 of Raduev[13] led to a scenario on Russian TV not dissimilar to that staged by the Turkish authorities when they paraded the Kurdish separatist leader Abdullah Ocalan. At the outset of the second war, *Izvestiya* had listed Ocalan alongside Basaev, bin Laden and the leader of Japan's *Aum Shinrikyo* cult in an article entitled 'Apostles of Terrorism'.[14] At this time a $1million price tag has been placed on Basaev's head[15] and demands were being made that Russian special forces should assassinate both Basaev and Khattab.[16]

It would appear that the economic, political and military elites of both sides played down the chances for a peaceful resolution and exploited instead the racial, cultural and religious differences between them in order to prosecute the conflict.[17] As we have noted, the late Aleksandr Lebed', who negotiated with Maskhadov the cease-fire that ended the first war, characterised the first conflict as a 'mafia squabble at state level', implying that its roots were 'primarily economic, then political, and only after that military'.[18] Certainly, the confrontation between the Russians and the Chechens acquired a symbolic importance for both sides way above that which the situation, objectively, merited.

The brutal and arbitrary conduct in that first war by the federal forces, which left tens of thousands of mostly Chechen civilians dead, served to sharpen these differences, as did the role, by August 1996, in defeating the Russian occupying forces by rebel commanders of a more fundamentalist Islamic orientation, such as the Chechens Basaev and Raduev and the Arab Khattab. Although the Russian government and its supporters in the media had raised the spectre of terrorism from the outset of the first war, it was only really brought home to the Russian population at large by the actions of such field commanders in the course of that conflict. Basaev and Raduev had launched spectacular 'terrorist' attacks (the seizure of hostages in Budennovsk in June 1995 and Kizlyar/Pervomaiskoye in January 1996, respectively), while Khattab pulled off a string of successful attacks on military targets, such as the ambush which culminated in the killing of 76 Russian troops at Yarysh-Mardy in April 1996.[19]

That all of these actions occurred when the federal forces were on the brink of rendering ineffective the Chechen armed opposition highlights not only the utility of 'terrorist' acts to shore up sagging morale at home during times of military weakness, but also the manner in which the 'success' of such acts erodes the sympathy for the underdog among the adversary's public. Again, as the events of September 11 have demonstrated graphically, while such acts are employed to dramatise the rebel cause, it tends to be the drama of the situation that attracts media and public attention rather than the cause itself. Thus, are the perpetrators of such acts regarded as martyrs for the cause by their supporters and as demonic and dangerous criminals by those who feel threatened by them.[20]

The Russian pretext for the 'counter-terrorist operation' launched in September 1999, was the incursion into Dagestan of *Wahhabite* militants. This action, led by Basaev and Khattab is the subject of numerous 'conspiracy theories' of Kremlin involvement.[21]

A war that started in 1994 as a squabble between corrupt elites has descended into one of the dirtiest conflicts that the European continent has witnessed, comparable only to the horrific civil wars in the former Yugoslavia for sheer human degradation and the violation of basic humanitarian rights.[22] Neither the UN, through its High Commission for Refugees, nor the EU, through the Council of Europe,[23] has been able to persuade governments to act on its recommendations vis-à-vis Chechnya. Russia has protested robustly whenever representatives of these international organisations have attempted to mediate in the conflict.[24] Even President Putin appears to be easily provoked on this subject, as demonstrated by his outburst in Brussels on 12 November 2002, most notably when he invited a French journalist asking probing questions about Chechnya to Moscow for a circumcision![25]

Those engaged in the war on both sides have suffered terribly; the Chechens from psychological, mental and physical traumas and the Russians from the dreaded 'Chechen' syndrome, the post-traumatic stress condition that affects a high proportion of the million and a half Russian troops that have served in Chechnya and which has created tens of thousands of human 'time bombs' in towns and villages across the Russian Federation, or, as a Russian journalist commenting on the collapse of the Russian Army in its anti-guerrilla war in Chechnya put it: 'Hundreds of thousands of criminalized soldiers who have passed through this filthy meat-grinder are now bringing the nightmare of that collapse to our city streets.'[26]

Since the Dubrovka hostage drama of October 2002, and arguably since 2000, Putin's only political solution appears to be a 'Chechenisation' of the conflict, transferring responsibility for countering the Chechen secessionists to pro-Moscow Chechens, initially under the dubiously-elected President Akhmad Kadyrov,[27] whom the award-winning *Novaya gazeta* journalist, Anna Politkovskaya, identified as 'Putin's Chechen clone'.

In the same interview during which Politkovskaya gave her assessment it was noted that Akhmad Kadyrov had called for Vladimir Putin to be made President for life![28] The particularly brutal strong-arm tactics employed by Kadyrov's feared Chechen police force[29] indicate not only that his legitimacy rests solely on support by the Kremlin, but also that strong traditional taboos have been eroded by the current conflict, such as Chechens killing other Chechens and Chechen women sacrificing themselves as suicide bombers. Yet, as *The Economist* commented on Kadyrov after his election,

> a weak leader in a lawless republic is likely to use any means he can to keep control. So Chechnya will carry on much as before: a corrupt, unstable mess of competing armed bands, fighting over oil, selling arms and terrorising the population.[30]

From the point of view of the Chechen warlords, the situation is reminiscent of Afghanistan, where, according to a Human Rights Watch report of December 2002:

> Warlords now represent the primary threat to peace and stability in the country.... The power of the warlords has made it impossible for (the government) to establish its authority much beyond Kabul. The enduring system of 'fiefdoms' ... reinforced by the policies of the US ... is simply not conducive to long-term stability or to the protection of human rights.[31]

The critical difference is that, in Afghanistan, the outside forces may be reluctant to intervene, but at least they are not as arbitrary, brutal, corrupt or involved as are the Russian occupation forces in Chechnya. The consequences for Chechnya, Russia and the world, may not be so different from those warned of by the US Council for Foreign Relations and the Asia Society vis-à-vis Afghanistan in the summer of 2003:

> Unless the situation improves, Afghanistan risks sliding back into the anarchy and warlordism that prevailed in the 1990s and helped give rise to the Taliban. Such a reversion would have disastrous consequences for Afghanistan and would be a profound setback for the US war on terrorism.[32]

It is useful to analyse briefly, in this context, the actions of two of Chechnya's most infamous 'warlords': the late Shamil Basaev, during his most notorious terrorist 'spectacular' at Beslan in September 2004 and Ramzan Kadyrov, since the assassination of his father, Akhmad Kadyrov, on 9 May 2004, the beneficiary and increasingly the architect of Putin's policy of Chechenisation.

Shamil Basaev – the butcher of Beslan?[33]

The official Russian version of the Beslan siege, broadly accepted by Western leaders if not by all sections of the media in the West, is that this was Russia's 9/11, the latest manifestation within its borders of the assault by international (Islamic) terrorists on innocent citizens in a law-abiding society. Members of President Putin's administration have argued the fact that those behind the hostage taking should target children on September 1, celebrated as the first day of school throughout Russia, demonstrates just how inhuman, fanatical and antipathetic to all decent human values the terrorists are. An intensified war on terrorism to eradicate all remnants of this threat, therefore, remains the Kremlin's policy towards not only militant Chechen supporters of the late Islamist Shamil Basaev, who claimed responsibility for the Beslan events, but also those moderate Chechen leaders, such as the late Aslan Maskhadov, Ilyas Akhmadov and Akhmed Zakaev, who openly criticised the hostage-taking and sought to distance themselves from Basaev.

In spite of overwhelming evidence to the contrary, any links with the long-running war in Chechnya or with the recent elections for a new president of Chechnya have been consistently underplayed.[34] Full responsibility for the violent death of over 300 hostages (more than half of them children) has been placed firmly, as was the case after Moscow's Dubrovka theatre siege in

October 2002, on the hostage takers. While one can empathise with those politicians and representatives of world public opinion who maintain that nothing can justify the violence inflicted upon these young hostages, it is surely worthwhile, if only to determine whether similar attacks might be anticipated or planned in the future, asking the question: why did Basaev do it?

Of course, if one is convinced that Basaev was merely a sadistic, bloodthirsty, mercenary fanatic bent on revenge and aiming to create as much mayhem as possible before the Russian federal forces finally caught up with him, then the answer is simple. However, he has long been recognised as one of the most able, audacious and adept guerrilla fighters of our age. Moreover, the history of insurgency, indeed, of modern warfare from Hiroshima to Fallujah, is littered with examples of the most brutal of means – from the perspective of the victims – being employed to ends that – in the view of the perpetrators – are considered honourable.

In his widely (though rarely in full) quoted open message of 17 September,[35] Basaev explicitly identifies the main goal of the Beslan operation as bringing an end to the war in Chechnya, an objective shared of course by many, both within Chechnya and beyond.

Basaev does not always use such rational argumentation as he exhibits in this message. Even allowing for any use of hyperbole to rally his own troops or satisfy sponsors abroad, some of his statements are so adorned with quotes from the Koran that it can be difficult for the non-Muslim to follow.[36] Moreover, there appears to be evidence that messages purportedly from Basaev are FSB fabrications out to discredit him in the eyes of Western audiences, as in this vituperative e-mail in English received by the Institute for War and Peace Reporting on 27 August 2004:

> Scoundrel Western crusaders, bogged down in lechery, and you, hoggish Jews, I have ordered my Muslim brothers and sisters, the Chechens, staying in your filthy countries to annihilate you without taking any compassion on you. The Russians have felt Allah's just anger on their skins already. Now it's your turn. The flame of Jihad will burn your abominable world, the world of unbelievers, to the ground. We will blow up your houses, ships, airliners, we will be killing you right in the streets of your impious cities and towns, for the death of lecherous, loathsome unbelievers occurs in accordance with the will of Allah. The way of Jihad is the way of true Muslims. Allah Akhbar![37]

So, rather than dismissing all of Basaev's messages as the ranting of a madman, I suggest, therefore, that we not only analyse carefully his interpretation of the Beslan siege but also attempt to assess how 'successful' the action was in the context of contemporary theories of terrorism.

Basaev called the Beslan raid Operation 'Nord-Vest', a clear reference to the previous hostage-taking incident at Dubrovka, often identified as 'Nord-Ost'. The name hints also that the raid was planned not in Nazran or Grozny (the capitals, respectively, of Ingushetia and Chechnya), which lie to the east of Beslan but from the forests of either southern Ingushetia, where significant numbers of *boyeviki* (fighters) were said to have their camp, or North Ossetia. Basaev was filmed on a video released on a separatist website during an attack on the arms store of Ingushetia's Ministry of Internal Affairs on 22–23 June 2004, in which he claims more than 570 *mujahideen* participated and that provided them with a significant amount of ammunition and weapons, many of which were recovered from dead fighters after the Beslan siege. In his letter, Basaev claims to have tested out the mines used in the operation in the forests near the village of Batako-yurt, which is some 20 kilometres to the north-west of Beslan.

The Dubrovka debacle, in turn, a failed reprise of Basaev's strikingly successful raid on the hospital at Budennovsk in 1995, ended with the hostage takers being fooled into believing that negotiations were about to ensue and surprised at the use of the gas that killed 129 hostages. There remain so many unanswered questions about this operation that one need not subscribe to conspiracy theories to suggest that we have not been told the full story.

In Beslan, Basaev clearly chose a tactic and a target designed to avoid a repeat of either of these perceived misjudgements at Dubrovka. A building full of children was less likely to be stormed; the local Ossetian population serving as a further deterrent and the welfare of the hostages was linked to the speed with which the demands made of Putin were met. Even the apparently sadistic refusal to allow the hostages any water, according to the evidence of eyewitnesses, came about only after the Russian authorities had deliberately underestimated the number of hostages at around 300 rather than the actual figure of over 1,100 (the large number of hostages being an important factor in the intensity of the threat posed by the insurgents).

Similarly, it is by no means clear that Basaev's assertion that the storm was initiated by the federal forces and not by the *boyeviki* firing into the backs of fleeing children is untrue. People who got out of the school said there was an explosion that blew a hole in a wall, through which they escaped:

> It was not clear whether the blast was caused by explosives laid by the hostage-takers, or whether it could have been done by the security forces. 'I was hiding in a house near the school, and my impression is that the storm did not start spontaneously; but rather that it was planned by the security forces,' said Elbrus, one of the local men who joined armed groups which formed outside the school.[38]

In his message, Basaev admits to committing three mistakes in the Beslan operation. First, he assumed that the Ossetians would form a human shield between the school and the troops, second, he took North Ossetian president Aleksandr Dzasokhov for a more independent and courageous man and third, he underestimated Putin's cruelty. This self-reproach indicates to me that he sought negotiations from a position of strength rather than the tactic of mass slaughter, this being almost invariably the case in major hostage incidents. His demands – an end to the war, Chechen independence and Putin's resignation – have been criticised as unrealistic and, therefore, as no more than a cynical ploy to force Putin's hand. However, a closer reading of the demands reveals that all are couched in terms of Chechen self-determination rather than Islamic hegemony and hedged with conditions, many of which actually address Russia's security needs.

It is this writer's belief, nonetheless, that Basaev did not expect his demands to be met, which raises the question as to what he hoped to gain. The answer lies, I think, in the main reason that so many insurgent movements resort to terrorism as a tactic: i.e. to dramatise their cause.[39] If one accepts, as Laqueur does, that 'if terrorism is propaganda by deed, the success of a terrorist campaign depends decisively on the amount of publicity it receives',[40] then like 9/11, the Beslan siege achieved one of its major goals. Yet, as with 9/11, the massive retaliation provoked by the terrorism would appear to have advanced neither the cause that we ascribe to these terrorists (i.e. the war between Islamic fanatics and the West) nor the military struggle itself.

However, if the aim was to remind the public in Russia and the West that Putin's Chechen policy has reached an intolerably bloody and brutal dead end and that no-one in Russia, let alone Chechnya, will be safe until a satisfactory political settlement is reached, then the Beslan siege, taken together with the earlier suicide bomb attacks on aircraft and public places in Moscow, at least partly achieved its objective.[41] Basaev states quite explicitly in his message that the suicide attacks on aircraft and the metro in Moscow in the run-up to Alu Alkhanov's victory were 'our vote ahead of time' in the presidential elections in Chechnya.

As for the inadmissibility of using innocent children as a pawn in this game, then I think that we have to be consistent and insist that any such blatant violations of international law and norms of war fighting, including those committed by 'our' side, have to be condemned and punished accordingly. I cannot be alone in recognising that, in the absence of any official statistics, even if the much-quoted figure of 35,000–42,000 Chechen children of school age killed in the fighting may be wildly exaggerated, the real numbers must be frighteningly high and totally unacceptable.

This is reflected towards the end of Basaev's declaration when he asks the whole world:

> All right, we are bad lads and you can wipe out 7,000 of us. But for what have you wiped out the remaining peaceful 250,000 and continue to wipe them out to this day? They fight against us without any rules at all with the direct connivance of the whole world so we are not bound to anyone by any obligations and will fight in a manner that suits us and is advantageous to us, by our rules. And if the world community genuinely does not wish that next time we seize in Russia a kindergarten, it should insist that Putin observes international law.[42]

As we have already noted, as long ago as 1988, terrorism expert Alex Schmid counterposed the options available to state and non-state actors in a time of 'violent' politics; if the state resorted to such forms of violent repression for control of state power as assassination, state-terrorism (torture, death squads, disappearances, concentration camps) massacres, internal war or genocide one might expect the non-state actor to use violence to contest state power by means of terrorism, massacres, guerrilla warfare and insurgency.[43] If one accepts, ignoring a post-9/11 definition that appears to exclude states from engaging in acts of terror, that this analysis still holds good today, the deal that Basaev appears to have been offering Putin is 'you stop your war crimes and we will stop ours', a rational strategy whatever one thinks of the morals involved.

The whole question of the rationality of terrorists has been the subject of much debate among experts on terrorism of late. Whereas some observers, like Robert Pape, conclude that 'suicide terrorism pays',[44] others, such as Max Abrahms, argue that 'terrorism is always a self-defeating strategy'.[45]

The key concept here appears to be 'strategy'. There are enough examples of the use of terrorism as a tactic towards a non-violent political end to conclude that it does work; on the other hand, terrorism as a strategy would appear to remain the preserve of ruling tyrants and revolutionary dreamers. It is appropriate to determine, therefore, whether Basaev perceived himself to be using terror as a tactic or a strategy and whether the Russo-Chechen conflict is based on Chechen self-determination versus Russian territorial integrity or is primarily part of an Islamic *jihad* against Western civilisation. My analysis of this message from Basaev indicates that he believes the former holds true in both cases.

If this is so, the question arises: Why cannot a political solution be brokered in Chechnya along the lines of that achieved in Northern Ireland? Let us put to one side the very real differences of scale, history and location and concentrate upon what the two scenarios have in common. In both cases there existed a clash of cultural traditions, a struggle for self-determination, the rule of might over right in virtually every aspect of life and recourse to extrajudicial violence on both sides. Only by engaging all those across the spectrum who wished to seek a non-violent political outcome, irrespective of the crimes committed in the name of the struggle, was the violence finally ended. While I am fully aware of how improbable it would be for an 'Ulster'-type solution to be applied in Chechnya (after all, even the Spanish government cannot bring itself to apply it to ETA), the principle, I feel, needs to be established.

Were such an approach to have been applied to Chechnya, however, it would soon have become apparent whether Basaev, let alone Maskhadov and his ilk, were interested only in the armed struggle. If, as I suspect, the population of Chechnya yearns for peace, then those intent on continuing the fight regardless would soon have been identified and marginalised allowing those that could best deliver peace, with requisite support from both Russia and the international community, to have come to the fore.

Of course, this in itself would not solve Chechnya's problems; after all, progress towards a political settlement in Northern Ireland has been painfully slow, not least because both sides need to show their own supporters that they are not to suffer the humiliation of surrender. To this must be added the complicating factor of the Chechen's code of honour, including the blood vendetta, the tension within Islam locally between *adat* and *Wahhabism*, the crippled economy and the poisoned and mined environment that the war will leave behind in Chechnya. For their part, Russians must come to terms with both their imperial past in the region and their Caucasophobia, if any North Caucasians, let alone the Chechens, are to feel comfortable remaining voluntarily within the Russian Federation.

Doing nothing is clearly not an option, for the Chechens, for the Russians or for the West. While Russians might claim double standards in that Western 'liberals' demand action from its government in Chechnya, but not, for example, from Spain's in the Basque country or Britain's in Northern Ireland, one must point out that neither the Spanish nor the British have resorted to pounding their domestic rebels with bombs from the air or heavy artillery shells from the ground. Nor are they terrorising the civilian population. One will find, however, that many of these same 'liberals' will charge the coalition forces in Iraq and Israeli forces in the Middle East with precisely such transgressions, in the firm belief that they are equally counterproductive and actually facilitate the growth of terrorism in these lands. For example, in a chilling account of America's war in Iraq, the experienced war reporter, Chris Hedges, warns:

> if we continue to allow force and violence to be our primary form of communication, we will not so much defeat dictators like Saddam Hussein as become them.[46]

In discussions with Russian military officials on lessons that might be drawn from the resolution of the violent conflict in Northern Ireland, I have been struck by how often the response has been to point out that it took the UK 30 years to bring an end to the troubles, so that Russia has still almost 20 years in which to sort out Chechnya. Even some of the parallels drawn between the two conflicts by Russian scholars can hinder rather than help understanding. Mikhail Alexeev, for example, makes the crude error of trying to equate Russian society's response to Basaev's invasion of Dagestan in 1999, which triggered the second war, with a patently hypothetical analogous situation in the UK:

> To comprehend the magnitude of public repercussions to these developments one has to imagine how the public of England would react to an attack by 600 Irish Republican Army (IRA) fighters on British Army positions in Northern Ireland![47]

In a fascinating series of articles in *Izvestiya*, published on five successive days in December 2004 and entitled '*Pochemy spetssluzhby ne mogut poimat'*

Shamilya Basayeva' (Why the security services cannot catch Shamil Basaev), Vadim Rechkalov proposed five reasons:

1   Popular support inside Chechnya.[48] This relates as much to Basaev's standing as a folk hero in Chechen society as to the fear of retribution from fellow Chechens, were Basaev to be betrayed to the Russians.
2   Well-hidden bases.[49] Although diagrams are provided of extremely secure and difficult-to-spot hideaways, the high proportion of ex-*boyeviki* among Kadyrov's forces in addition to sophisticated Russian surveillance equipment would appear to have compromised somewhat this aspect of Basaev's slipperiness.
3   Financial help from Russian and Chechen oilmen.[50] Most of the conspiracy theories regarding Basaev have him working in cahoots with both Russians and Chechens on the federal side.[51]
4   Considerable freedom of movement throughout the North Caucasus.[52] A military intelligence officer for the GRU claimed anonymously in January 2005, that the federal forces knew exactly where Basaev was, but that they were under strict orders not to capture him or eliminate him, just track him.[53] Moreover, Rechkalov points to the network of former comrades across the North Caucasus who fought alongside Basaev in, for example, Abkhazia.
5   The absence of any sound ideological basis for Russia's Chechen policy.[54] Apart from the mantras of 'territorial integrity' and the 'domino theory', this could best be described as nothing more than a desire for the restoration of centralised control.[55] The lack of clear direction is reflected also in soldiers' accounts of the war.[56]

We would do well to bear in mind the final threat to the world community in Basaev's message that 'this whole world will burn with a blue flame before we will turn our backs on our Freedom and Independence'. Giving such a seasoned protagonist a straight choice between a violent death and carrying on his destructive work never seemed to me to be the most rational of approaches. After his death in July 2006, predictably Basaev has become both a martyr and an example for impressionable young Chechens to follow; had he lived, there is every possibility that his attacks would have become ever more audacious and terrifying. The butcher of Beslan he may have been to most Russians and Westerners alike, but to how many others in the North Caucasus, in particular, and the Islamic world, in general, will he be remembered as the Che of Chechnya?

In this message and in interviews given since the school siege, Basaev has clearly tried to shift blame for the tragedy onto Putin and the local leadership in North Ossetia. Since Beslan, he not only honoured the ceasefire announced by Maskhadov in January 2005, but also appeared to accept the stated intentions of both of Maskhadov's successors, Abdul-Khalim Sadulaev and Doku Umarov, not to target innocent civilians.

After Sadulaev's assassination by Russian forces on 17 June 2006, which it is claimed led directly to the murder of the three Russian diplomats taken hostage in Iraq,[57] Basaev was appointed vice president of Chechnya-Ichkeria under Umarov,[58] simultaneously bringing together strands of the Chechen opposition to Kremlin rule and confirming the prevailing view outside Russia that, with the death of Maskhadov, the rebel leadership contained internationally-recognised terrorists rather than potential interlocutors in any peace process.

His last message before his death was to congratulate Iraqi *mujahideen* for eliminating their Russian hostages, possibly one slap in the face too many for Putin's *siloviki*. The ambiguity of Basaev's significance for Chechens is summed up, perhaps, by Akhmed Zakaev, now leading representative of the so-called 'moderate' wing of the Chechen resistance, speaking after confirmation that the controversial field commander was dead:

> There is simply no justification for what happened in the school and I know that Shamil Basayev regretted it in his heart and soul.... Yet I do not believe that history will remember Shamil Basayev primarily for Beslan, but for his 15-year fight against Russian occupation.[59]

The expressions of such equivocal sentiments towards such a figure of hate in Russia, of course, by one that the Putin administration still regards as a fugitive from justice, might well encourage his regime to reopen the question of Zakaev's extradition from the UK.

Ramzan Kadyrov – wolf-tamer or tyrant in a tracksuit?

Several Russian commentators were shocked to see Raman Kadyrov, in the wake of his father's assassination, turn up dressed casually in a sky-blue track-suit and trainers at the Kremlin for a televised meeting with the always smartly-dressed Russian President, Vladimir Putin.[60] Although some account must be taken of the tragic circumstances in which the meeting took place, the scene did little to dispel the impression that here was a young, inexperienced politician, who would have looked more at home in the dressing room of his beloved *Terek* Grozny football team than he did in the splendour of the Kremlin state-rooms. Nonetheless, it did represent a remarkable transformation for a young man who had not only, like his father, once taken up arms against the Russian federal forces, but also claims to have killed his first Russian when just 16 years old (i.e. sometime in 1991/92, before the outbreak of the first Russo-Chechen War!).[61]

On an equally chilling note, the footage of Ramzan reminded one that he had already built up a reputation in Chechnya as the strong-arm enforcer in charge of his father's security forces and was not about to surrender this power easily. However, because the Chechen Constitution stipulates that the President of Chechnya had to be at least 30 years old, Ramzan, who attained that age only on 5 October 2006, had little choice but to consent to Alu Alkhanov, from his own *Benoi* clan, being selected by the Kremlin to replace his father as head of state.

Whatever happens after he comes of presidential age, few believe already that he remains anything other than the most powerful individual in Chechnya.

It is this that makes his notoriety as a strongman all the more pertinent to the future of Chechnya under Chechenisation. An article published in *Die Welt* and translated into Russian, for example, alleged that even while Akhmad Kadyrov was alive, Ramzan had a prison in his house for torturing captured Chechens, who were already beginning to fear his so-called 'death battalions', even more than the Russian forces.[62]

Such was the negative impact of Ramzan's troops – the *kadyrovtsy* – that Andreas Gross, the Parliamentary Assembly of the Council of Europe's rapporteur on Chechnya was moved to observe at this time:

> Paradoxically, even the security troops of the late president Kadyrov have been a cause of fear among the population. This fear must be overcome and the people in Chechnya must be able to develop confidence and trust.[63]

Kadyrov's intimidatory style has not been confined to Chechnya. It was reported that in January 2005, a group of 150 of his armed men crossed into Dagestan and severely beat up local policemen in Khasavyurt who had been holding Kadyrov's sister, Zulai.[64]

Western journalists have been impressed, even somewhat intimidated, by Ramzan Kadyrov's extravagant exhibition of power. More allegations of his brutality against fellow Chechens as well as the description of his father being 'reviled by Chechens as a traitor', are to be found in an article by Nick Paton Walsh, published in the *Guardian* in January 2004.[65] After Kadyrov Junior was appointed Chechen Prime Minister in March 2006, Walsh wrote another article critical of Ramzan, entitled 'Land of the Warlords'.[66]

Mark Franchetti has also had published an interview with Ramzan Kadyrov entitled 'In the torture cell of Chechnya's tyrant',[67] which pictures the Chechen warlord with his pet tiger, one of several exotic pets kept apparently in the Kadyrov household. The BBC's Steve Rosenberg, also reported a less than comfortable meeting with Chechnya's strongman on *From Our Own Correspondent* in November 2005.[68] In yet another interview, with the BBC Russian Service's Artyom Liss, Kadyrov, pictured this time with a pet lion cub, claimed that the *kadyrovtsy* combined 'American uniforms, Russian weapons, Islamic beliefs and a Chechen spirit', a combination that made them, apparently, 'invincible'.[69]

Russian journalists, too, have been both fascinated and horrified by Kadyrov's *machismo*. Anna Politkovskaya, no admirer of his father, has written critically of Ramzan's brutality in *Novaya gazeta*. In one article, ironically entitled 'Ramzan Kadyrov – the beautiful face of Chechnya', Kadyrov is pictured, again dressed casually, with an extremely fierce looking guard dog (with a posse of armed human guards in the background).[70]

When Kadyrov appeared to make light of Maskhadov's assassination on 8 March 2005, by presenting it as a present to Russian and Chechen women on International Woman's Day, an astonished female Russian journalist retorted:

I can imagine that in England they might catch and kill (and kill while in detention) some hardened terrorist from the IRA, without having recourse to due legal process. But I absolutely exclude the possibility that some functionary of the British crown (and Ramzan Kadyrov is a functionary of the Russian Federation, if Chechnya, as the federal authorities confirm is a part of Russia) made an announcement that this was a present for English, Irish or Scottish women on St. Valentine's Day. Yet Ramzan Kadyrov advertised the operation to eliminate Maskhadov, carried out by special forces of the FSB, as a present to women on the 8 March.[71]

On the other hand, as might be expected, such qualities do find admirers, not least among segments of the Chechen population. An opinion poll in February 2006 in Chechnya claimed that 67 per cent of Chechens trust their young Prime Minister.[72] As one observer notes:

> Energetic campaigns by Kadyrov Jr aimed at stopping the 'moral decline of the Chechen nation' (like the banning of slot machines, casinos, the fight against prostitution, alcoholism, etc.) are especially popular with older Chechens, while his success at a relatively young age and his influence have secured him a certain admiration among young people, some of whom have even started to imitate him.[73]

Kadyrov has also inherited a pretty bleak economic situation for ordinary Chechens, with a 76.8 per cent unemployment rate among the Chechen working-age population.[74] He has had some success in extracting more funds from the Russians, although by way of comparison it is alleged that whereas just 64 million rubles have been spent on restoration of Chechnya in the last four years, 40 million rubles were devoted to the celebration of the 300th anniversary of Putin's native city – St Petersburg – alone.[75] Moreover, Kadyrov has not been slow to invest his own fortunes into both the staging of spectacular events, such as visits by celebrities like Mike Tyson[76] and Chechen beauty competitions,[77] as well as the rebuilding of Chechnya's shattered infrastructure.[78]

The young Kadyrov has alienated a number of powerful politicians, including, apparently, Dmitry Kozak, Putin's presidential plenipotentiary in the Southern Federal District (which covers the North Caucasus), with his unilateral actions on such issues as polygamy and the expulsion of charity workers from the Danish Refugee Council in the wake of the Mohammed cartoon crisis in early 2006.[79]

The most serious clash occurred on 28 April 2006, when it was reported that forces loyal to Ramzan Kadyrov fought a gun battle with the bodyguards of President Alkhanov. Two men were reportedly killed and three injured in the clash, clear evidence of the brewing power struggle between groups of pro-Russian Chechens who control the republic. The situation was exacerbated in that the exchange of fire happened during a meeting between Alkhanov and Sergei Stepashin, Putin's predecessor as Russian prime minister. The crisis was finally defused with the appearance of a third group of Chechen gunmen from the *Zapad* division, under the command of Said-Magomed Kakiev. It is reported that both Kozak and Putin subsequently were obliged to instruct the young Kadyrov quite bluntly to mend his ways.[80]

Potentially even more seriously, some Russians, including Vadim Rechkalov, suspect that he is in cahoots with fellow-Chechens on the anti-Russian side in ripping off funds from the federal budget.[81] This exemplifies the weakness inherent in allowing Kadyrov to run Chechnya via his clan; not only will the level of corruption remain high, but potential investors from the Chechen diaspora, let alone from Western countries, will be discouraged.[82]

Certainly Ramzan has followed his father in demanding extraordinary sums from the federal budget to be used for the rebuilding of Chechnya, justifying this with the comment that the Russians caused the destruction in Chechnya and now they are helping to clean up the mess. *Interfax* reported that, with his encouragement, the Chechen parliament refused the 19 billion rubles allocated to Chechnya in 2006 and requested 130 billion rubles instead![83] Moreover, Kadyrov is using his control over the Chechen mass media and, via his personal identification with Vladimir Putin, via the Russian mass media, to build up a positive image as the only option for Chechnya in the reconstruction period.

The potential risk of this to Russia might be the temptation to adopt a policy of 'Kadyrovisation' of all of the North Caucasus, a course bound to exacerbate existing contradictions among the indigenous mountain peoples and release pent-up tensions among regional elites

The entrepreneurs of violence in the Russo-Chechen conflict

What the peace process in Northern Ireland has demonstrated also is that, in order to meet the popular demand for a cessation of violence, what is required is a vision of an alternative future to one plagued by violence, complemented by genuine hope that, over time, peaceful relations (positive peace) will replace a mere cessation of violence (negative peace).[84] In order to transform this aspiration into a reality, the need for leadership at all levels and, preferably, representing all sides of the conflict, is paramount.

In comparison with the situation in Northern Ireland, such leadership has been conspicuous by its absence not only in Russia and Chechnya but, in its response to the Russo-Chechen conflict, by the international community as a whole. Lacking this leadership, such cultural contradictions as the absence of a *Rechsstaat* (law-governed state) in either Russia or Chechnya, combined with extremely weak institutions of civil society operating within an underdeveloped economy inevitably increase the likelihood that entrepreneurs of violence will dominate the political scene, enabling them to perpetuate and intensify the negative attitudes that give rise to violent behaviour.

This is less likely to be the outcome in a democratic state in which civil society has strong foundations rather than in a system in which highly-personalised executive power is exercised virtually unchecked through a vertical structure, be it at national or local level. The danger in the latter system is that the popular yearning for peace is likely to be ignored by those, at all levels, that have a vested interest in prolonging the conflict.

These so-called 'entrepreneurs of violence' may be arms contractors, bureaucrats, businessmen, criminals, military personnel, politicians, religious leaders or warlords. What unites them is that directly or indirectly they profit – politically, economically or socially – from a prolongation of the conflict and are prepared to exploit cultural and structural violence to maintain their privileged position. Should this be threatened by the checks and balances ('right' as represented by a system of justice) designed to prevent or resolve conflict, which tend to be present in any well-functioning society, they are prepared to bypass such structures by resorting to direct violence ('might'). Moreover, as experience from Afghanistan to Colombia to Ulster has shown, the absence of perceived alternative economic opportunities for former combatants increases the likelihood of a reliance on criminality and/or a return to terrorism as a prime source of income;[85] this certainly applies to Chechnya today. Here, as elsewhere, a degree of outside assistance would appear to be essential in countering these trends and remedying such situations.

The entrepreneurs of structural violence

We have already noted in the analysis of cultural contradictions that, in practice, certain Russian principles have given rise to some of the most negative attitudes in the Russo-Chechen confrontation. Thus, colonisation has given rise to Caucasophobia and the demonisation of the Chechens, Orthodoxy to an intolerance of diversity, *derzhavnost'* to (Great) Russian chauvinism, *gosudarstvennost'* to the imposition in Chechnya of a *vertikal'* of power and the tendency to suppress rather than accommodate opposition. That these attitudes weaken rather than strengthen both the territorial integrity of the Russian Federation[86] and her geopolitical interests would be more apparent to all were the Putin administration to be held to account more consistently by other world leaders.

These attitudes, in turn, feed into and give further substance to the Chechen cultural narrative and stiffen such Chechen attitudes as self-determination, articulated as no more than a desire to be free from Russian violence and a longing for what they perceive as 'freedom'. At the same time they consolidate the militarised clans and raise the determination among Chechens to restore their *adat*. Here the clash within Chechen Islam between Sufism and *Wahhabism* comes to the fore, as the former promotes *adat*, whereas the latter advocates the strictest application of *Shari'a*. The growing influence of the *Wahhabites* is manifested both in the failure of an intrinsic component of *adat* – blood vengeance – to deter Chechen killing Chechen and by the militarisation of the *djamaat* (a traditional political entity with a membership drawn usually from neighbouring villages).

These two trends have come together with the recent activisation of 'Shariat' – the Islamic Djamaat of Dagestan – responsible for an increasing number of terrorist attacks – and 'Yarmuk' – its equivalent in Kabardino-Balkaria – which carried out the attack on Nalchik in October 2005.[87] While these trends might be more effective in countering Russian violence than the more traditional forms, they represent a greater obstacle to peace. It remains to be seen whether the new Islamic militancy has been hitherto merely a tactical response to Russian aggression or whether it has already become a part of the broader anti-Western strategy of *jihad*.

For all the importance of specifically Russian and Chechen attitudes and the institutions and laws upon which they are based, it is where attitudes are shared by both sides that most blatant examples of structural violence are to be found. As noted the combination of a weak civil society, a poorly-developed market economy and the absence of a law-governed state combine to produce the triumph of 'might' over 'right', widespread corruption,[88] clientelism rather than market-led relations and impunity for those that break the law. If to this volatile mix is added the xenophobia experienced by both Russians and Chechens as a result of globalisation and extremism emanating from the war on terror and the post-secular discourse of the 'clash of civilisations' then we can see what a fertile ground is provided for the entrepreneurs of violence on both sides.

One of the most disagreeable features of the Russo-Chechen conflict is the abuse directed at those Westerners who genuinely do try to involve themselves in processes of reconciliation. Two of the authors of the Carnegie Policy Brief 35 (February 2005) have fallen foul of this syndrome; on 7 March 2005, Anatol Lieven from the Chechen side, and, on 21 June 2005, Tom de Waal, this time by a Russian website close to the military.[89]

A seemingly ever-present factor of the current conflict has been degree of collusion between warring factions, be it at the level of federal troops selling weapons and ammunition to their opponents or accepting bribes in order to let Chechen fighters through control posts, or Russian officers and Chechen warlords dividing the spoils of the illicit economy in Chechnya.[90] Allowing for the lack of viable economic alternatives in the region, this would appear to be a case of 'greed' (private/criminal power) overriding 'creed' (ethnic/religious power) as the major means of achieving 'need' (economic/political/social power).[91]

Unsurprisingly, the declared motivations of the entrepreneurs of violence are invariably expressed in terms of 'need' and 'creed', rather than 'greed'. Moreover, insofar as competition for economic, political and social power is recognised generally as a legitimate 'need', those effectively excluded from this process are likely to attempt to achieve their goals through means perceived by their opponents, but crucially not by their own supporters, to be illegitimate. The recent rise in popularity among Palestinians of Hamas, despite its advocacy of suicide bombing, is a case in point.[92]

International institutions could assist the peacemakers on both sides by establishing consistent and clear parameters of legitimate 'need' (e.g. allowing albeit some role for factions advocating Chechen independence), thereby exposing the real motives of entrepreneurs of violence on all sides. In the absence of any meaningful role in the peace process for the Chechen resistance, an 'Islamic' outcome – in the form of a *jihad* across the Northern Caucasus – appears to be replacing a 'European' scenario – Chechen national self-determination – as the major objective of the 'irreconcilables'.[93]

While it would appear self-evident that those responsible for perpetuating and exploiting these attitudes need to be held to account, neither the outside world in general nor the West in particular is currently in a particularly strong position so to do. The composite picture that emerges from the war on terror (especially the war in Iraq), globalisation and the post-secular discourse of 'good versus evil', the relative weakness of global civil society vis-à-vis the most powerful states, the absence of a genuinely independent and enforceable international legal framework and the lip service given to notions of equality and fair trade with the less developed world, might lead one to conclude that the present international system, too, has its entrepreneurs of violence who are exploiting these contradictions for their own narrower interests.

The entrepreneurs of direct violence

Insofar as the entrepreneurs of violence exploit attitudes that are manifested in structural violence, it is in the sphere of behaviour (direct violence) that they really come into their own. The ghastly catalogue of brutal violence has been documented sufficiently by respected human rights groups and other NGOs to avoid repeating the detail here.[94] It is worth mentioning, nonetheless, that it is the Chechen terrorist spectaculars (notably Dubrovka in October 2002 and Beslan in September 2004) that grab the world's attention rather than the daily diet of 'disappearances', extra-judicial killings and torture, let alone such 'hidden' violence as the Chechen syndrome, which has affected a considerable proportion of the million plus Russian soldiers who have fought in this discredited and unpopular war.

As noted, the behaviour of both sides might be characterised as constituting differing forms of terrorism. Undoubtedly, war crimes have been committed on both sides by those who continue to profit its continuation. In such circumstances, one can only look to enlightened leaders who are prepared to represent the interests of the many rather than those of the few.

In this respect neither Russia nor Chechnya has been blessed with individuals possessing the qualities needed to achieve peace. In May 1999, a simple majority of the Russian Duma voted to impeach President Boris Yeltsin for launching an illegitimate war on Chechnya in 1994.[95] Although falling short of an admission that the Russian leader had committed war crimes (not least the air and heavy artillery bombardment of Grozny at the beginning of the first war that left up to 25,000 mostly Chechen and Russian civilians dead),[96] this vote did recognise that Yeltsin had blundered into an unnecessarily bloody conflict. He and Chechen President Djokhar Dudaev never met; although most observers noted that a face-to-face meeting would probably have averted or stopped the war.[97] Although, arguably, the inflated ego of each was equally to blame for this (vanity, arguably, being another form of 'greed'), the very asymmetry of the confrontation surely placed more responsibility on the Russian President.[98]

Yeltsin himself has agreed with both his predecessor – Mikhail Gorbachev – and his successor – Vladimir Putin – that the first war was a mistake.[99] Nonetheless, there was no major Western leader at that time prepared to put sufficient pressure on Yeltsin to stop his forces destroying one of their own cities – with a population the size of Edinburgh's! The 'bigger picture' then was the need for Yeltsin to defeat the communists in the Russian presidential elections of 1996 and thus prevent any going back on the privatisation of Russian industry. The cost of the means employed – the lives of thousands of Russian soldiers and tens of thousands of mainly Chechen civilians – to achieve this end appears to have been perceived by many world leaders as regrettable, but unavoidable, collateral damage.[100]

This might be held to represent a triumph in contemporary international politics of the 'consequentialist' (consequences of an action determine whether it is moral) over the 'deontologist' (based on fundamental moral principles) approach.[101] As the insensitive (by Western standards) Russian response to both the Dubrovka and Beslan hostage situations demonstrates, Putin, too, evidently believes firmly that in dealing with Chechnya the ends justify the means. The fact that current Western leaders, and to some extent the civic societies that they represent, since 9/11 have demonstrably shifted significantly towards this viewpoint seriously undermines the chances of success of any values-based approach to the Russo-Chechen conflict.

Conclusion

The paradox of Vladimir Putin is that, although no liberal himself (despite being called a 'flawless democrat' by former German Chancellor Gerhard Schroeder),[102] he is reputedly more of a liberal and a democrat than at least 70 per cent of his population.[103] Insofar as the population of Russia, since the Moscow apartment bombings of 1999, like that of Israel and the USA after their 'Black Septembers', appears to be sufficiently 'traumatised' that a substantial proportion of the voters tend to adopt more hard-line attitudes than their leaders, Putin is faced with a genuine political dilemma.

However, despite being the one leader who could end the violence, he appears reluctant so to do except on terms of total surrender by the entire opposition, reminiscent of the questionable approach adopted towards the Pales-tinians under Yasser Arafat by successive Israeli governments under Ariel Sharon. Putin's failure to engage with any of the Chechen opposition, from Aslan Maskhadov's successor, the late Abdul-Khalim Sadulaev, to the Moscow-based businessman Malik Saidullaev, and his decision to stake instead his entire policy of Chechenisation on a Russian-style *vertikal'* of power represents the single greatest flaw of his Chechen policy.

As has been noted, however, Putin cannot be expected to behave like a demo-crat in the Western sense, because: 'For him, order precedes everything else in the social contract.'[104] This was brought out most forcefully when, on the day after Beslan, Putin declared: 'We showed ourselves to be weak and the weak get beaten.'[105]

Ruslan Khasbulatov claims that Vladimir Putin is personally against the war in Chechnya, but is effectively a 'hostage' to those Russian military leaders, who are growing wealthy from their illicit economic activities in Chechnya.[106] Evidence to support such a viewpoint is provided by the threats issued by such military leaders as Major General Vladimir Shamanov who claimed that if the military was not allowed to continue the war to a victorious end, civil war might erupt in Russia.[107]

The military interest clearly is not just confined to the fighting, as is made clear in the following observation by the British journalist Jonathan Steele:[108]

> The benefits Putin sees in the Chechen war are political, but many less powerful people are making money out of it. Few Russian troops in Chechnya are conscripts: most are there on contract. They are tempted to volunteer by the money they can make there, mainly illegally. At the most basic level are the unofficial 'fees' soldiers charge Chechen drivers and bus passengers at checkpoints.... The Russian human rights organization Memorial has catalogued hundreds of more serious cases of extortion. Chechens are taken in for questioning by Russian troops, and ransomed back to their families. When they are tortured and murdered in custody, as often happens, families sometimes have to pay to get the bodies back.
>
> Senior Russian officers make money from oil. Chechnya is peppered with what the Texans call 'donkeys', those small pumps which nod back and forth as they extract oil. Each donkey is 'owned' by a group of officers, who profit from selling all or part of the oil it produces to black-market tanker drivers, who sell it on in nearby Russian cities. The system relies on collusion with Chechen insurgents and warlords, who get protection money for not attacking the donkeys. Russian forces also sell weapons and information to the insurgents in a reciprocal trade that keeps the war going.[109]

Indeed, as Liz Fuller reported for RFE/RL in 2004:

> Even former Russian troop commander Colonel General Vladimir Moltenskoi has admitted, some Russian officers are making fortunes from the present war by presiding over, and cashing in on, the clandestine export to other Russian regions of Chechen oil and scrap metal.[110]

Set against this context, it is easy to appreciate why the federal forces' response to Maskhadov's final appeal for a ceasefire (and just 30 minutes with the Russian president in order to halt the war)[111] was to assassinate the rebel Chechen leader,[112] an act that even some Russian journalists characterised as a 'political murder'.[113] That Putin exacerbated the fall-out from this killing by insisting that the former president of Chechnya-Ichkeria be buried in an unmarked grave as a terrorist, thus refusing to release Maskhadov's body for a proper Muslim burial demonstrates not only the cultural arrogance and insensitivity of his administration, but also how out of step he was with his own electorate (a poll conducted on 24 March 2005 indicated that 62 per cent of Russians felt that Maskhadov's body should be returned to his relatives).[114]

Given the asymmetry of the conflicting sides, with such Russian leaders, it is hard to imagine what extraordinary qualities would be required by their Chechen equivalents in order for peace to be achieved. Yet even here, there has been a disappointing lack of vision, a lack of realism and an inflated sense of self importance. As with the Viet Cong in Vietnam and the *mujahideen* in Afghanistan, there was inevitable euphoria at the defeat of a superpower, even one in such dire straits as post-Soviet Russia. Yet, far from pulling their country up by the bootstraps as the Vietnamese had done, far too many Chechen leaders took Afghanistan as their example and saw their future in terms of warlordism and criminality, controlling economic resources, territory and even ideology for their own enrichment and political gain. If one adds to this the ideologically-driven impact of the *Wahhabis* on post-war Chechnya then one can see any prospect of a new Islamic state appearing in the Caucasus was regarded, particularly in the West, more with alarm and caution than with open arms.

Thus, even the legitimacy that Aslan Maskhadov gained upon winning the Chechen-Ichkerian presidential election in January 1997 was diluted not only by the refusal of states (except the Taliban in Afghanistan) to recognise the newly independent country, but also by the criminal and anti-Western behaviour of some of the most powerful warlords in Chechnya. We will never know how things would have turned out if (a) Maskhadov had won the support of Western powers (b) if Russia had been less obstructive in the crucial first few years of Chechen independence and (c) had the Chechen factions united behind their newly-elected leader. Whatever his well-documented shortcomings as a political leader, the blame for the failure to negotiate peace in Chechnya, clearly, was not Maskhadov's alone.

It remains to be seen whether a leader can be found in Chechnya or in the Chechen diaspora who could unite these factions and be accepted by the current Russian administration. Tension is obviously rising between Russian officials and Ramzan Kadyrov, who would rather Putin back one of their own *siloviki* – Alu Alkhanov. Alkhanov has called for an end to the power of the clans, identifying the need for 'a merciless struggle against corruption, *klanovost'*, negative phenomena, degrading the moral rectitude of the Chechen people.[115] Moreover, the commander of the pro-Russian *Zapad* forces Kakaev, who is linked to Gantemirov, could have linked up with Alkhanov and the commander of the *Vostok* forces, Sulim Yamadaev, against Kadyrov.

The record thus far indicates that peace is virtually impossible without outside involvement. Instead the Kremlin will insist on imposing a leader on Chechnya through rigged Soviet-style elections. In the absence of any pressure from without, it is difficult to ascertain whether this is simply because the Putin administration knows that any independent candidate would defeat his nominee and that, for regional and domestic geopolitical and economic reasons, this is an outcome to be avoided as long as he is able.

As for Russia, it is not impossible that Putin will have the Constitution amended to allow him to run for a third time in 2008, thus ensuring the continuation in power of the *siloviki* attitudes, institutions and modes of behaviour that have allowed entrepreneurs of violence to flourish in Chechnya.

8 The paths not taken

The Russian failure to reach a political solution in Chechnya

> And yet the war in Chechnya is above all Russia's agony. Leaving aside any moral considerations, it is simply not practical to wish the Russians success in 'winning' this war. Moscow cannot succeed in making Chechnya a normal part of Russia again because the weapon it is using – the Russian armed forces – treats Chechnya as a foreign country, open for marauding and random violence.
>
> (Anna Politkovskaya, *A Dirty War*, 2001)[1]

Russia's determination to 'liberate' Chechnya irrespective of the financial, human or physical cost illustrates how fruitless it is to try and counter 'terrorism' by means of war. As has been noted, a people bent upon freedom being bombed by airplanes from above, lacking an air force of their own, will tend to bomb back from below. It is disingenuous of the Russian authorities to maintain that they are fighting anything other than a guerrilla war in Chechnya. If the Russians are fighting 'international terrorism' in Chechnya, then the international community should be involved. To be sure Basaev and his ilk would have turned their guns on any Western force that might have been sent into Chechnya. The difference is that Western troops would have been considerably less likely than their Russian counterparts to alienate the indigenous population and might well, eventually, have isolated the extremists to such an extent as to make dialogue with more moderate forces possible.[2]

Just as it is obvious that tanks, heavy artillery and warplanes do not represent the best way to fight crime, any objective observer would recognise the dangers of conflating the terms 'terrorist', 'criminal' and 'crazy'. By further demonising 'blacks', 'Caucasians' and 'Muslims', Russia is merely stoking up new conflicts for the future. A political settlement between Russia and Chechnya is essential to both sides. Chechnya has had de facto independence, but its people have not enjoyed freedom. Its future lies in a settlement that would allow the Chechens to claim that they are 'not in Russia, but with Russia'; a relationship which even Basaev had hinted would satisfy him.[3]

The problem lies with Russia's self-identity. Must the Russians have an empire in order to be 'Russian'? And is the only way to keep the multi-confessional Russian Federation together to project a 'great-power' ideology?[4]

Or can Russia resume its transition to a democratic, law-governed state, the borders of which will stretch only as far as to include those who wish to be citizens of the Russian Federation? As the war in Chechnya continues it might be maintained that the warning sounded by Russia's leading human rights activist in 1997 has equal validity for the current Russian regime:

> Such is the nature of the clumsy, unintelligent monster called the traditional Russian state. It is inherently incapable of properly evaluating situations because it feeds off myths alone and in some senses is a myth itself. It cannot live without using force, because its essence is deified, impersonal power, divorced from the power of society. The Russian state does not know how to resolve problems bloodlessly, for blood is its favorite food. Moreover, it doesn't really know how to resolve problems at all. It knows only how to create them.... It was this monster that was defeated in Chechnya.[5]

Although it is primarily for Russia and her citizens to face this dilemma, the West should not stand idly by. It is difficult to disagree with the conclusions of an article published at the turn of the century in *Foreign Affairs*:

> In the Caucasus, as in the rest of the world, the West cannot routinely ignore the force of nationalism movements, which will continue to challenge empires similar to the Russian Federation. All multiethnic societies face nationalism, but not all will collapse – good governance is the key. In future years the West will regularly face the question of how to respond to poorly governed and disintegrating states that do not accommodate minorities.
>
> This is why other vulnerable states, such as China, are watching Chechnya closely. Those seeking independence cannot be dismissed as terrorists or fanatics – although these elements may well be present. Nor can the West simply accept other states' forceful measures against minority populations. Unfortunately, Moscow has made the mistake of pursuing a military solution to an inherently political problem. In doing so, it has jeopardized the country's chances for democracy and reform – and for joining the West by embracing the mores of the 21st century.[6]

The first Chechen War exposed to the world the lack of good governance in Yeltsin's Russia. If Putin genuinely seeks to place national interest above those of his ruling elite, the bleeding wound that is Chechnya must first be healed in the interests of the many, albeit at the expense of the entrepreneurs of violence – the powerful, self-interested few.

Spurred on by the federal forces' initial success, the Russian generals insisted on chasing the rebel formations into the mountains,[7] using many of the tactics (carpet bombing, thermobaric bombs, sweeps and elite force raids)[8] that the Americans have since employed in Afghanistan. Russian commentators have noted ruefully, however, that the Americans have been much more efficient in their campaign, distinguishing between friend and foe among the Afghan population in a way that Russian forces signally have failed to do.[9]

The fact that the Taliban were ousted in little over a month, whereas the Russians have been bogged down in Chechnya for years with still no end in sight, would appear to suggest that the Russian situation is more akin to Israel's than it is to the USA's. The Russian leadership, it would seem, is playing the 'Islamic terrorist' card unashamedly in order to crush the rebellious Chechens, in much the same way as Israeli spokespersons unfailingly refer to Arafat, a Nobel Peace Prize laureate, as a terrorist. Both of these strategies rest upon the assumption that, if the only local alternative – the terrorists – were eliminated from the equation, the Chechens (and Palestinians) would turn to their occupiers for security. There seems little prospect of success in either case. Even as dyed-in-the-wool a Russian nationalist as Eduard Limonov has written:[10]

> Chechnya is not defeated and we can now state with confidence that it will not be defeated. The fighting spirit of the Chechen people has turned out to be stronger than the Russian Army. We need to end the war in Chechnya and give Chechnya its independence. Because the war in Chechnya can be won only by exterminating all Chechens. But this is genocide. The two peoples – the Chechens and the Russians – will not have common cause to live together for some time yet. Perhaps they never will. There is too much blood between us.

These views are strikingly similar to those of the former Chechen-Ichkerian President, Aslan Maskhadov, whose assassination by Russian secret services in March 2005 ended, effectively, any chance of a meaningful dialogue with the Chechen separatist movement. Prior to September 11 this former officer in the Soviet Army wrote:

> This war has opened our eyes. Even for the ordinary Chechen. The ordinary Chechens have seen what Russian occupation means. Even those, who yesterday were loyal to Russia, have now adopted a different stance. After this war Russia has finally lost Chechnya.[11]

However, since September 11, few Chechen commentators, let alone Russian, see complete independence as a solution. The first Russian-backed Head of Administration in Chechnya – Mufti Akhmad Kadyrov – requested temporary dictatorial powers and a dose of 1937 purges to bring his rebellious fellow citizens to order.[12] The former Speaker of the Russian Parliament, Ruslan Khasbulatov, an ethnic Chechen, sought a special status for Chechnya in which the country would be autonomous without destroying the territorial integrity of Russia, with international security guarantees provided by such organs as the Council of Europe and OSCE.[13] The late Djabrail Gakaev, a leading Chechen academic and public figure went even further down the road of compromise, stating that the Chechens must 'realize their national idea ... within the framework of a commonwealth of peoples of Russia'.[14]

Despite hostility from the Putin administration, but in line with preferences indicated in Russian public opinion polls, prominent Chechens, Russians and Americans were meeting, in the summer of 2002 to elaborate a peace plan for Chechnya. This culminated in Maskhadov's envoy, Akhmed Zakaev, attending a major conference in Liechtenstein in August 2002, alongside such Chechen representatives as Ruslan Khasbulatov, who had elaborated his own peace plan for Chechnya, and Aslanbek Aslakhanov, the Russians Ivan Rybkin and the late Yury Shchekochikin, as well as such American public figures as Zbigniew Brzezinski, Alexander Haig and Max Kampelman, who brought their own version of a settlement of the conflict.[15]

The compromise peace plan that emerged would grant Chechnya a degree of autonomy within the Russian territorial space.[16] Although, the World Chechen Congress in Copenhagen was to endorse this plan on 29 October 2002, the fallout from the Dubrovka theatre siege effectively aborted this process.[17]

Alternative plans have been proposed by the shady Chechen 'businessman' Khoj-Ahmed Nukhaev who suggested that Chechnya be divided into two parts; the northern (lowland) Chechnya would remain part of Russia and the mountainous south would become autonomous. He has argued that it is the mountain Chechens who 'are the staunchest bearers of the pre-modern national traditions, refuting any form of statehood whatsoever, be it Russian "constitutional order" or a *Wahhabi* "Islamist state"'. Nonetheless, he warns against kowtowing to the West, urging both Russia and Chechnya to join the anti-Western alliance.[18]

In March 2003, Ilyas Akhmadov, then the Chechnya-Ichkerian Foreign Minister and representative in the United States, also drew up a plan for the future administration of Chechnya that relied upon a UN mandate until free and fair elections could be held in Chechnya.[19] This plan won the support not only of supporters of Chechen self-determination in the USA but also radical members of the European Parliament such as Daniel Cohn-Bendit, Benedetto Della Vedova, Gianfranco Dell'Alba, Olivier Dupuis and José Maria Mendiluce, as well as high-profile human rights activists, such as the French philosopher André Glucksmann.[20]

None of these plans, it would appear, were ever seriously discussed by the Putin administration, who stuck rigidly to the mantra of 'no talks with terrorists or criminals'. This consistent line was still being maintained in the summer of 2006, as is apparent from the Putin administration's response to Zakaev's manifesto sent to participants at the G-8 meeting in St Petersburg in July 2006.[21]

In this approach the Russian president was undoubtedly aided by the fact that, in Chechnya, as in other 'terrorist/national liberation' movements, criminal gangs, indeed, appear to have gained the upper hand and have usurped the traditional *teip* system.[22] There are those who claim that these criminal fraternities are in cahoots with the Russian military commanders and that both sides have a financial interest in prolonging the conflict.[23] The former Soviet dissident and now Russian human rights activist Aleksandr Podrabinek told Radio Free Europe/Radio Liberty in December 2004 that:

The aim is not to defeat the enemy, win the war and end it with a peace treaty. The aim is that this war goes on and on. I believe the main objective of the whole Chechen campaign was to create a state of permanent war in Russia that would allow our Kremlin politicians to rake all sorts of dividends. The most important thing is that this state of war helps maintain tension within society, vote laws that restrict civil liberties, strengthen the army and law enforcement agencies, and – finally – helps army officers make fortunes from the war, as it is now well known.[24]

Certainly, there is a consensus among virtually all those vying for power in a post-war Chechnya that the Chechen field commanders and ideologues of the more militant Islamic orientation, such as Movladi Udugov, have little chance of participating in the post-conflict reconstruction. Neither the Russians nor the Chechens appear to be in the mood for all-inclusive amnesties. While Russia insists that certain leaders of the Chechen resistance will be killed or put on trial, the Chechen deputy to the Russian State Duma, Aslembek Aslakhanov, demands that Russian military commanders be brought before The Hague War Crimes Tribunal.[25]

The Russian policy of pre-emptive assassination of Chechen resistance leaders undoubtedly has borne fruit. Even if one discounts Salman Raduev, who was tried and imprisoned in Russia, where he died in December 2002 in less than fully explained circumstances,[26] the list of victims is impressive. In March 2002, Khattab was killed in Chechnya by federal forces; according to a pro-Chechen website, he was poisoned by Russian agents.[27] Ruslan Gelaev was killed in a skirmish with border guards in Dagestan in February 2004[28] and Zelimkhan Yandarbiev, temporarily President of Chechnya-Ichkeria after Dudaev's assassination, was killed by Russian agents in Qatar earlier in that same month.[29] Although this policy of dubious international legitimacy reached its high point with the assassination of Aslan Maskhadov in March 2005 and drew some heavy criticism from abroad, this did not deter the Russians from successfully eliminating Maskhadov's successor, Sadulaev, in June 2006.

So it transpired that, at the Strasbourg Round Table on Chechnya's future, organised by PACE in the same month that Maskhadov was assassinated, not only were no proponents of Chechen independence invited to participate, but Andreas Gross, PACE's rapporteur for Chechnya insisted that any talk of independence was off the agenda for the next 10–15 years![30] On the face of it, proof positive that the triumph of 'interests' over 'values' had reached even the body charged with upholding those values in Europe. However, PACE has still not entirely ruled out the participation in determining Chechnya's future of such 'pro-western' Chechens seeking a 'European' (i.e. not militant Islamic) solution, such as that formerly represented by Maskhadov and Gelaev and, since their death, by Zakaev.

The golden opportunity missed by Putin occurred when, having won a huge mandate in the presidential election of March 2000, effectively having won militarily the battle for Grozny, and with the Russian electorate sick and tired of the war in Chechnya, he deliberately avoided any engagement with the secessionist leaders of Chechnya, and thus isolated the Islamic fundamentalists. Instead, from June 2000, he announced that the only Chechen with whom he would negotiate would be Akhmad Kadyrov, a former resistance fighter and religious leader, that Putin had appointed his Chief of Administration in Chechnya.

In effect this move defined all Chechen nationalists as terrorists and isolated the Chechen resistance fighters, leaving them with little alternative to abject surrender than sabotage and terrorism. In reality, a long-drawn out guerrilla war continued out of the gaze of an indifferent Russian public and largely excluded Western media. The Russian forces continued to alienate the Chechen population and international human rights agencies, through use of illegal fuel-air and cluster bombs in their air attacks and *zachistki* (sweeps) in their ground operations, in which victims were much more likely to be civilians, rather than Chechen fighters, let alone 'terrorists'.[31]

For both internal and external consumption, Putin and his team continued to use every opportunity to press home that 'the actions of Russia are against extremism ... they are directed entirely against international extremism and terrorism'.[32] For their own different reasons, both Western leaders and the Russian public chose to ignore what was, certainly until 11 September 2001, a grossly distorted representation of the war in Chechnya.

The events of 9/11 did not give Putin a free hand in Chechnya; they merely confirmed retrospectively that, as far as the international community was concerned, he could act as he wished. At the Camp David meeting with the Russian President in the wake of 9/11 President Bush's endorsement of Putin's vision for Russia,'as a country at peace within its borders, with its neighbors, a country in which democracy and freedom and rule of law thrive', seemed to say: 'Stand by my side and proclaim yourself an ally in the war on terror, and all else may be forgiven.'[33]

To exert pressure on the Chechens, Bush insisted that Maskhadov choose between the Islamic militants and Putin, no real choice given the situation.[34] Declarations from other Western leaders followed, epitomised by the then NATO Secretary General, George Robertson's aforementioned comment that 'we have come to see the scourge of terrorism in Chechnya with different eyes'.[35] The then British Foreign Minister, Jack Straw, also voiced his support for Russia.[36] As we have noted, on receiving President Putin at Chequers in December 2001, Tony Blair even went so far as to draw parallels between the September 1999 bombings and the attacks on 9/11.[37]

With such international and domestic support, and with control over the mass media, by 17 April 2002, Putin was able to declare in his state of the union address that the military phase of the conflict over, even though attacks on his forces were continuing as he spoke.[38] Within a month, on 'Victory Day' (9 May 2002), a bomb planted at a military parade in the Dagestan town of Kaspiisk killed 43 soldiers and family members. As pointed out, although Dagestani rather than Chechen militants were blamed, an enraged Russian public was not minded to draw so fine a distinction.[39]

Given the traumatic circumstances of the terror attacks on New York and Washington on 9/11, with their obvious potential for repetition elsewhere, once President Bush had declared that in the global war against terrorism 'you are either with us or against us', every conflict in the world tended to be analysed through the prism of this war. Such concepts as 'pre-emptive defence' and 'illegal combatants', although contrary to international law, were legitimised. For Putin's Russia, embroiled in a stalemate in Chechnya, this came as a blessing. In a world in which media-fuelled stereotypes exert unprecedented power on public perceptions, the complex Chechen cocktail of medieval tradition, nineteenth-century theocratic autonomy and belated twentieth-century nationalism could all to easily be simplified, for both the Russian public and the international community, as anti-Western Islamic terrorism – the so-called scourge of the twenty-first century.

By September 2002, the former Russian Prime Minister, Yevgeny Primakov, published his 'Six Points on Chechnya', calling for negotiations with the Chechen leadership and observing that Russia was losing its civilian control over its military.[40] Something clearly had to be done; but would Primakov's call be heeded, would events work in Putin's favour yet again or did Putin's supporters in the security forces have yet another trick up their sleeve? The Dubrovka hostage-taking crisis of October 2002 was to provide some, but by no means all, of the answers to this question.

The Zakaev extradition case – Russia's Chechnya policy on trial

The Dubrovka siege, occurring in the wake of the Bali terrorist bombing, came at an extremely fortuitous juncture for Putin. Genuine progress was being made throughout the summer of 2002, by Chechen, Russian and Western mediators, to elaborate a peace plan for Chechnya. Akhmed Zakaev attended a major conference in Liechtenstein in August 2002, alongside such high-profile members of the Chechen diaspora as Ruslan Khasbulatov – the former Speaker of Russia's parliament – and Aslanbek Aslakhanov, Duma deputy for Chechnya; prominent Russians such as Ivan Rybkin, another former Speaker of the State Duma and National Security Advisor, and Yury Shchekochikin, a deputy from the Russian parliament; as well as highly-respected American public figures, such as former National Security Advisor to President Carter – Zbigniew Brzezinski, Alexander Haig, former Secretary of State under President Reagan and Max Kampelman, Chair of the American Academy of Diplomacy.

A compromise peace plan was hammered out which would grant Chechnya autonomy within the Russian territorial space. This represented the best peace plan yet tabled for a peaceful resolution of the Chechen conflict and would have satisfied the preferences of the Russian public as expressed in opinion polls. Due to such internal and international pressure, Putin had felt obliged on 24 June 2002, for the first time to draw a clear distinction between the Chechen 'terrorists' and the Chechen people, promising to stop demonising the latter as 'terrorists'.[41]

Clearly, the Chechen resistance, however, was faced with a difficult dilemma in the post-9/11 world order. Whatever the rectitude of their cause, they were seen primarily by the US administration to be backing the wrong side and, like the Palestinians before them, were made to pay a heavy price. This allowed Putin to cut off the exploratory peace talks in Moscow with Maskhadov's envoy, Akhmed Zakaev, and to adopt new, tougher military measures in Chechnya.

In an interview with *Reuters* on 9 September 2002, before the Dubrovka siege, Zakaev accused the Russian authorities of:

> Trying to thrust our movement into the context of international terrorism, in particular after the tragic events in the United States ... but the Russo-Chechen conflict started long before these events, when people did not know of the existence of such terrorism and they did not understand what it meant.

In the wake of the Dubrovka theatre siege, extradition charges were laid retrospectively against Zakaev, generally considered to be the most moderate of all Chechen leaders, for acts of terrorism carried out in the first war.

Following the Dubrovka incident in October 2002, when Chechen fighters seized over 800 hostages in a Moscow theatre, the Russian authorities activated charges of terrorism and murder, which had been filed against Zakaev just after the terrorist attacks in the USA on 11 September 2001. On the basis of these and new charges (including complicity in the hostage crisis and the murder of a Russian priest who was to turn up as a witness in the London hearings) Zakaev's extradition was sought from Denmark, where he had been attending the World Chechen Congress. Despite the political pressure brought to bear on the Danish government by the Putin administration, the court in Copenhagen rejected the application for extradition.[42]

Upon his release Zakaev flew to London on 5 December 2002, where (on the grounds that he was on Interpol's wanted list) he was arrested at Heathrow Airport, but released on bail immediately. On 11 December, the actress and human rights campaigner, Vanessa Redgrave, posted the necessary £50,000 bail to keep Zakaev out of prison and the millionaire Russian businessman, Boris Berezovsky, also about to face extradition proceedings to Russia, arranged for his defence costs to be met.

The leading lawyer, Gareth Peirce, agreed to act as Zakaev's solicitor. This eminent human rights advocate is perhaps best known for her defence of the men convicted of the Guildford bombings (she was played by Emma Thompson in the film *In the Name of the Father*) and, more recently, of the British detainees at Guantanamo Bay. On 14 January 2003, she requested in writing that David Blunkett, then Home Secretary, terminate the extradition procedure. On 30 January 2003 this appeal was rejected and preparations commenced for the hearing at the Bow Street Magistrates Court in London (across the street from the Royal Opera House in Covent Garden).

Mr Timothy Workman was appointed Judge and the Crown Prosecution

Service, acting for the Russian government, appointed to lead the case for the prosecution James Lewis QC, who also acted in this capacity in the Berezovsky case and for General Augusto Pinochet in the former Chilean dictator's extradition hearing.

Edward Fitzgerald QC, who was appointed to lead the defence of Akhmed Zakaev, was the 1998 Times Human Rights Lawyer of the Year, and has figured in some of the UK's most controversial trials, having defended Venables and Thompson (in the Jamie Bulger case), Michael Hickey (in the Bridgewater Three), the families of the Hillsborough stadium tragedy, Mary Bell, Stephen Downing and, posthumously, Derek Bentley. The pre-trial hearing, without the defendant or witnesses was scheduled for 19 May 2003.

In April 2003 I was invited by the defence team to provide an expert report on the case, the final 15-page version of which was submitted on 2 June, just one week before the hearings commenced. The case opened on Monday 9 June and ended on Thursday 13 November 2003 with Judge Workman finding in favour of Zakaev. I was able to attend the hearings on 9 and 10 June (when I was examined by the defence), 30 June, 1, 10 (when I was cross-examined) and 11 July and 13 November 2003 (when the judge's verdict was delivered).[43]

I was asked also to chair the panel debate at the Chechnya film festival on 23 June 2003, at the Institute of Contemporary Arts in the Mall, which was decked out in British and Russian flags for the state visit of President Putin to Buckingham Palace on the following day. The festival was attended by both Akhmed Zakaev and Lord Judd. The panel consisted of two witnesses for the defence in the Zakaev trial – Ivan Rybkin and Tom de Waal, Anna Neistat of Human Rights Watch, Nicola Duckworth from Amnesty International and Aaron Rhodes representing the International Helsinki Federation for Human Rights. A message to the organisers from Yelena Bonner was read out at the beginning of the debate. Although the same Chechen film festival was staged in New York and Washington in 2003, the similar event planned for Moscow in October that year was cancelled by the Russian authorities at the last minute.[44]

The contributions to the Zakaev trial of Tom de Waal and myself were complemented by Russian witnesses for the defence who had been flown in especially for the case. We were followed onto the witness stand by what might best be described as a succession of some of the best representatives of Russian civil society:[45] Yuly Rybakov, Andrei Babitsky and Aleksandr Cherkasov and, on the following day, by Sergei Kovalev and Ivan Rybkin.

Yuly Rybakov's cross-examination (by Mr Lewis QC) was memorable for the dignity with which he explained his position and that of his fellow Russian witnesses:

> I speak to you here with a heavy heart. Not because each of us, citizens of the Russian Federation, who give evidence on behalf of the defence, are putting ourselves in danger upon our return (because we know all too well that they will not forgive us for that) – we are used to such dangers. I speak with a heavy heart because I am obliged to say terrible things about what is

happening in my country. I would be very glad if I could say that in my country the courts are independent, that investigations are conducted properly and impartially but, as an honest man and a patriot, I am bound to tell the truth. I think that I will live, perhaps, until that day when I will be able to speak for the defence in a similar case and say that in my country all is in order, that in my country the death penalty has been abolished, that torture is a thing of the past and that we no longer violate human rights.[46]

Other noted public figures spoke outside of the court in support of Zakaev. Lord Judd, former rapporteur for Chechnya and a member of the Parliamentary Assembly of the Council of Europe (PACE) said of Zakaev after his arrest in London:

Of those associated with the Chechen fighters with whom I have met and spoken, it is with him that I have been able to have some of the most intelligent discussions about the global realities as they affect the people of the Chechen Republic and about the need for a political settlement. His removal at this stage from even tentative steps towards engagement in a political settlement does not seem to me self-evidently to help.[47]

A succession of distinguished visitors attended parts of the trial. For example, Peter Reddaway, Professor of Political Science and International Affairs at the George Washington University, who was visiting the London School of Economics and Political Science, attended some of the hearings and had published during the trial letters in the British press that were critical of Tony Blair and his government's policy towards Chechnya.[48]

Predictably, the delegates to the Liechtenstein conference were among those who spoke out most forcefully against the charges. Ruslan Khasbulatov expressed amazement that Moscow was trying to make a terrorist out of such a person as Akhmed Zakaev. He claimed that: 'it would be funny if it were not so sad'.[49] Ivan Rybkin, who also met Akhmed Zakaev in Zurich in August 2002, confirmed that: 'he is working persistently to achieve peace in Chechnya, not to continue the war. If such negotiators are not good enough for us, then I don't know what comes next.'[50]

Zbigniew Brzezinski, who later briefed President Bush on the case, also spoke out in his defence. On 30 October 2002, the co-chairs of the American Committee for Peace in Chechnya, Brzezinski, Alexander M. Haig Jr and Max M. Kampelman, plus the committee's executive director, Glen E. Howard, had written in connection with the previous extradition trial to the Danish ambassador in Washington, underlining:

We know Mr. Zakaev and have worked with him. His dedicated espousal of a peaceful resolution to the Chechen conflict has made him a crucial interlocutor in efforts to bring an end to the war ... Mr Zakaev's extradition would seriously undermine those crucial endeavours.[51]

The case had a big impact in Russia too, such high-profile journalists as Anna Politkovskaya of *Novaya gazeta* attending the hearings at Bow Street Magistrates' Court throughout the trial. This courageous campaigning journalist, shot dead in Moscow in October 2006, wrote in respect of the Zakaev case, that she: 'welcomes the opportunity to receive, at last, an international judicial appraisal of that which has occurred in Chechnya in the past decade'.[52] The Russian newspaper *Zavtra*, which published an interview in February 2003 with Akhmed Zakaev was accused by the Russian authorities of creating enmity between peoples and warned not to print such material again.[53] The Russian investigative journalist – Andrei Babitsky – who was called by the defence as a witness, publicly expressed doubts on Zakaev's chances of survival, were he to be sent back to a Russian prison.[54] Yelena Bonner, widow of Andrei Sakharov, predicted that Akhmed Zakaev would certainly be tortured in a Russian jail.[55]

Sergei Kovalev, former human rights representative to President Yeltsin and an active human rights activist claimed that the charges relating to the two priests confuse Zakaev with a certain Vakhaev or Makhaev (as he explained personally to me during the case). He concluded: 'at least, when talk is of severed fingers and hostages, insofar as I know Akhmed Zakaev and the overall situation in Chechnya, all of this, it seems to me, is absolute rubbish.'[56]

A favoured explanation for the extradition move advanced by Russian observers (Kovalev, Mil'shtein, Kagarlitsky) is that this case would neutralise Akhmed Zakaev and take him out of the frame as an acceptable negotiating partner for Moscow, which could now go ahead and negotiate a settlement with its own nominated Chechen officials.[57]

This policy deliberately ignored the fact that Chechen representatives had condemned the Dubrovka incident. The World Chechen Congress explicitly stated that: 'it is unacceptable to use terrorist methods to obtain political goals, whether they are committed by groups or by states'.[58]

Akhmed Zakaev himself condemned the hostage-taking incident in its immediate aftermath, saying: 'We said from the beginning, these are not our methods. We cannot come down to the level of our opponents, targeting innocent people and we offer our condolences to the families of people that died in these dramatic events,'[59] adding that 'it brought to naught, for all practical purposes, all the work I had done for a year.'

The messages from the official Russian side were mixed. Whereas Russian Foreign Minister – Igor Ivanov – had likened Akhmed Zakaev to Osama bin Laden, a charge that has generated ridicule among Russian liberal opinion.[60] Sergei Yastrzhembsky, President Putin's aide, had earlier called Akhmed Zakhaev 'a completely normal, sane man with whom one can negotiate'.[61] According to Anna Politkovskaya, the Deputy Prosecutor-General of Russia, Sergei Fridinsky, who attended throughout the trial seated behind the prosecution team, was furious at the attention to minute detail paid by the judge during the proceedings. As she pointed out in a subsequent newspaper article, this is not the way things would have been handled in Moscow.[62]

However, the timing of the case brought against Akhmed Zakaev demonstrates clearly, in my opinion that, since the Dubrovka hostage drama, the Putin administration has sought to exploit what it sees as a new carte blanche to resolve the conflict on its terms without the compromise required to take the Chechen people along with the peace process. Zakaev represents just such a compromise. The case brought against him, against this background, would appear to be one of political expedience as far as the Russian Government is concerned. Given the predominance in Russia today of executive power, there is a very limited hope that its judicial system would afford Akhmed Zakaev or any like-minded supporter of Chechen independence, a fair trial by Western standards.[63] On the political nature of trials involving Chechnya, Yury Samodurov, Director of the Andrei Sakharov Museum in Moscow, wrote at the time of the Budanov case: 'the trial is political not so much for any judgement of Budanov as for the first judgement of the war in Chechnya and the barbaric methods used.'[64]

Some odd characters must have testified over the years, within the hallowed walls of Bow Street Magistrate's Court, but it is unlikely that any evidence quite matched that provided by Ivan Solov'ev – a genuine member of the Russian working class. Small, nervous and suntanned, with dark glasses and a short-sleeved check shirt, Solov'ev must have pinched himself at times to confirm that he really was in London. His evidence revolved around the claim that Zakaev had personally shot off the tips of three of his fingers. I am no expert in firearm injuries but I must say that it looked as though his digits had been lost through an accident with a chainsaw rather than through bullets. 'How,' asked a sceptical Edward Fitzgerald QC, 'did you know it was Zakaev that caused you these injuries if you were facing the wall?' 'Now I remember,' replied Solov'ev, not for the last time, 'he was standing beside me, so I could see him.' So the cross-examination went on, with Solov'ev 'remembering' each time he was caught out. He did not trouble to hide his feelings for Zakaev and his ilk, stating that he had decided to 'help his motherland drag back this thug, because he is feasting here while his countrymen starve'.[65]

Subsequently, Anna Politkovskaya revealed that Solov'ev was actually a habitual drunkard named Viktor Sokolov, who had been set up to give false testimony by the prosecution.[66]

The key moment in the trial came on 24 July when a witness for the prosecution, Duk-Vakha Dashuev – in giving evidence for the defence admitted that his confession to the Russian authorities had been extorted through torture. In his judgement rejecting the extradition claim, Mr Workman found that the Russo-Chechen conflict did represent 'an internal armed conflict. Indeed, many observers would have regarded it as a civil war.' Regarding the delay in bringing these charges and the possibility that they were politically motivated, the judge found 'that it would now be unjust and oppressive to return Mr Zakaev to stand his trial in Russia'. Moreover, in assessing the treatment meted out to Dashuev, Mr Workman came to the 'inevitable conclusion that if the (Russian) authorities are prepared to resort to torturing witnesses there is a substantial risk that Mr Zakaev would himself be subjected to torture'.[67]

Kremlin officials went through the motions of protesting about the 'double standards' of the West in the war on terrorism and pointed to the tendentiousness of the British court,[68] but were at pains to stress that the decision would have little adverse effect on the overall friendly relations between Russia and the UK.[69] The further decision, on 29 November 2003, to grant Akhmed Zakaev political asylum in the UK was greeted in similar fashion.[70]

Whether or not the Russian authorities could have foreseen the humiliation that they were to endure at the hands of the British court is doubtful. Their attempts at damage limitation were assisted not only by a predictable outburst of anger at the decision among sections of the public in Russia and the pro-Russian regime in Chechnya, but also by a pathetically non-committal response to the findings by the British government, which appeared to have been positively embarrassed by the court's decision. As usual it was left to human rights organisations, individual activists and commentators and, most authoritatively in this instance, a British judge, to spell out the significance of this case.

For, in essence, not only Russian justice but also the whole prosecution of the war in Chechnya had been found wanting. The victory belonged not just to Akhmed Zakaev, not just to the Chechen resistance, but also to Russian civil society and their all-too-few supporters in the West. Whether this decision will help or hinder Russia's (let alone Chechnya's) progress towards a democratic society, based on the rule of law, remains to be seen. What one can predict is that, when and if both Russia and Chechnya have truly independent courts, this case will stand out as a milestone along the long road from authoritarianism and injustice. My fear is that independent courts, a strong civil society and a free press are not necessarily consistent with what the Russian President, a large majority of the Russian population and, most worryingly, supporters and allies of Putin in high office in the West, perceive as the 'controlled' or 'sovereign' democracy needed in the conditions currently pertaining in Russia.

Putin's dead end

What is indisputable is that, in the wake of the Dubrovka hostage crisis, Putin not only won back the support of public opinion in Russia for his war, received further backing from the Bush administration, which arranged for Basaev's three fighting units to be added to the list of proscribed terrorist organisations,[71] but also was presented with a window of opportunity to scupper both the Liechtenstein peace process and the World Chechen Congress, which opened in Copenhagen within days of the hostage drama in Moscow. Even before the siege the US Ambassador to Russia had voiced his 'increasing scepticism' towards President Maskhadov as a credible participant in a political solution for Chechnya.[72]

Putin seized the moment to outline a proposed new Constitution for Chechnya and announced a referendum on this and the election of a president of Chechnya within Russia. But as the seasoned Russian political commentator Otto Latsis wrote in *The Russia Journal* (31 January 2003):

The authorities are pursuing one very transparent aim with their idea of a referendum and new presidential elections for Chechnya. They want an argument against those who say they should negotiate with Aslan Maskhadov, the man who was elected Chechen President with Moscow's approval in 1997. The Kremlin doesn't want to talk to Maskhadov, something that is only confirmed by Moscow's insistent campaign to have Akhmed Zakayev, Maskhadov's representative at negotiations, extradited to Russia. The Kremlin's new plan is clear and could be carried out. The idea is to hold a managed referendum followed by a managed election that would elect a new president with whom Moscow would then negotiate. The problem is that the only real way to end any war is to make peace with your adversary and, in the case of the guerrilla war underway in Chechnya, the adversary is the Chechen people, which will only accept negotiations and deals with its own representative – Maskhadov – as legitimate. To ignore this is to let the war continue.

Following the debacle, from the Chechen viewpoint, of the Dubrovka incident, even those moderate Chechens such as Zakaev became fugitives from Russian law,[73] while those intent on carrying on the fight switched their tactics to suicide bombing; from December 2002 until December 2003 over 300 were killed.[74]

Putin, time and again skilfully exploited acts perceived as terror to convince the public that Russia was on the front line against Islamic extremist terror. Typical of this are his comments on the struggle against Islamic fundamentalism in Chechnya in his interview in the *New York Times* on 6 October 2003:

> It is not right to regard members of al Qaeda who are fighting in Chechnya as supporters of independence and democratic development of Chechnya, and to regard those same representatives of al Qaeda who are fighting in Afghanistan and Iraq as criminals. Such a policy will not lead to effective results in joint work on the battle against terrorism.

One may only speculate what influence might have been exerted on public opinion in Russia by the publication of the true figures of Russian losses in the war, put by the Russian Soldiers' Mothers Committee in August 2003 at over 12,000 dead since 1999.[75] A detailed opinion poll, run by VTsIOM for PONARS (Program On New Approaches to Russian Security) just after 9/11 demonstrated how effective Putin's efforts had been in presenting the war as a struggle against terrorism, as fully 93 per cent thought this important in framing their attitude to the war. At the same time only 48 per cent thought human rights issues were important and a mere 9 per cent thought the views of the international community on the war very important.[76]

These views notwithstanding, by the summer of 2002, responsible and formerly high-ranking officials in the United States, Russia and Chechnya were taking the initiative in searching for a political solution. In June 2002, Aslan

Maskhadov offered to cease hostilities by 15 July. Akhmed Zakaev became his roving representative at a series of international gatherings to press forward with this peace process. At this juncture, 61 per cent of Russians polled favoured negotiations with the Chechen leadership, under Maskhadov.[77]

The complexity of Russian perceptions on Chechnya are illustrated by another VTsIOM poll, published in March 2003, which asked Russians to rate Putin's performance over three years as President. This poll indicated that, in the immediate aftermath of the Dubrovka theatre siege, a mere 18 per cent thought he had been successful in defeating the fighters in Chechnya, and just 16 per cent thought his efforts to achieve a political solution there had worked. Nearly three-quarters (74 per cent and 73 per cent, respectively) thought he had been unsuccessful in these two areas. At the same time 71 per cent (against 22 per cent) thought that he had consolidated Russia's position in the world.[78] In January 2004, 80 per cent declared that they intended to vote for him in the presidential elections of April 2004.[79] In the event just over 70 per cent did vote for him, a decisive victory that handed Putin, in effect, the power of a twenty-first century tsar.[80] Since then Putin's popularity has remained high, dipping only in the wake of the cash-for-benefits fiasco in early 2005, but recovering somewhat after the assassination of Maskhadov later that year. His current (as of August 2006) approval rating is 78 per cent, with 76 per cent of Russians polled expressing trust in their President.[81]

From this one might deduce that the Russian people want better results, and thus a higher level of security, than Putin's policies were achieving, given the threat manifested by the Dubrovka and Beslan sieges, but appeared to favour either an intensification of the military effort to finally defeat the 'terrorists', or, if that could not provide security, then a negotiated political settlement that would. Putin, however, is not being held personally to blame for the failure of his policy in Chechnya, even though, to the outsider, he must either feel beholden to his generals to continue the war or is aware that the Russian public is more prepared to tolerate his policies in times of crisis.

As we have seen, Ruslan Khasbulatov, for one, claims that Vladimir Putin is personally against the war, but is effectively a 'hostage' to those Russian military leaders, who are growing wealthy from their illicit economic activities in Chechnya.[82]

Despite the fact that at the time of Dubrovka, only 16.4 per cent of Russians polled advocated storming the building prior to the action, the attack was ordered. All 41 Chechens were killed, many of them as they slept and 129 hostages died from the effects of the poison gas. Although 89 per cent of Russians polled after the event approved of the storming, questions have been raised that still await answers. The State Duma voted against holding an enquiry into the Dubrovka affair. The percentage of Russian voters advocating peace talks over Chechnya fell from 61 per cent to 44 per cent, those for continuing the war rose from 29 per cent to 46 per cent.[83] The hard line had the backing again, albeit temporarily, of the Russian people.

As part of his 'Chechenisation' strategy, Putin also floated the idea of an amnesty that would cover all combatants except those guilty of especially serious crimes. The first Russian amnesty of 12 March 1997 covered member-ship in armed formations and illegal arms trading. However, in the case of a Chechen moderate on trial in 2003 – Said-Magomed Chupalaev, former chief of staff on the eastern front during the first war, a contemporary report indicated that the prosecution was asking for a penalty of 17 years strict regime for pre-cisely these offences. As the author comments: 'if the courts cannot distinguish Chupalayev from Raduyev, or Zakayev from Basayev, the amnesty will be meaningless'.[84]

The well-known Russian political commentator, Boris Kagarlitsky claims the amnesty is forgotten and was only passed in order to stop war crimes trials among Russian generals. There are reports from *Memorial* of Chechen fighters who did surrender under the terms of the amnesty being shot dead on the spot. These same generals are now developing their own criteria for who is a terrorist and who is to be amnestied, with a tendency to label any Chechen male over the age of 12 as a potential terrorist.[85]

Certainly, the 'Putin' Constitution for Chechnya, adopted in March 2003, ostensibly by an overwhelming majority of Chechnya's voters,[86] contains provi-sions that smack of imperialist *diktat*, including the effective banning of political parties advocating Chechen independence.[87]

For their part, the Chechen rebels are caught, nonetheless, between a rock and a hard place. Even if one allows that Maskhadov, Zakaev, Gelaev and other leaders of the secessionist movement did perceive their struggle to be one of national liberation, given the negative memories of the period of de facto independence in 1996–1999 and the general war-weariness of the population of Chechnya, any return to normality, that guaranteed putting an end to arbitrary violence from either side, would be likely to meet with the approval of the Chechens, no matter how far short of independence it fell.[88]

Although, throughout the second war, there appeared to be a division among Chechen leaders of opinion over strategy between the 'nationalist partisans', such as Gelaev, who wished to restrict the fight to Chechnya and its surround-ings and 'religious fundamentalists', such as Basaev, who wished to take the battle to Russia, as long as Russian troops remained in Chechnya, they shared, nonetheless, a common cause.[89] Maskhadov appeared to fluctuate in his support between the two sides, but as he, Gelaev and Basaev were all heroes of the first war, especially the recapture of Grozny in August 1996, the issues that bound them together almost certainly exceeded those that divided them. What the Chechen resistance, as a whole, failed to grasp adequately was that there was no place in the post-9/11 world for such ambiguity.

Conclusion

As long as no compromise is allowed in the war against terrorism, there is little room for moderation in a conflict that one side perceives to be about self-determination and the other about countering terrorism. The rational compromise programme, advanced by those Russians, Chechens and Westerners engaged in the peace process that was interrupted and, eventually, broken off by the Moscow theatre siege of October 2002, would have granted Chechnya a degree of autonomy within Russia with security guaranteed by international bodies. This would have allowed Chechens to reintroduce aspects of *adat* into their socio-political structure, reducing their dependence on *Shari'a* law.[90]

However, although designed to marginalise extremists on both sides and bring a halt to the fighting, at best this plan would have produced weak and untried institutions and would have required decades rather than years to heal the ecological, economic and humanitarian wounds that have accumulated in the ten years of war.[91] The experience of post-war reconstruction in Kosovo, Afghanistan and Iraq does not make one optimistic about a secure and prosperous future anytime soon for the people of Chechnya.

As for Russia, although during, and immediately after, the hostage drama, Russian public opinion temporarily favoured military action in Chechnya over the opening of peace talks, by the beginning of 2003 the approximate 60–30 split in favour of talks had been regained; this two-to-one proportion would appear to reflect more accurately the attitude of ordinary Russians to the war.[92]

Of course, the Chechen wars on occasions have hit the headlines in the Western press. However, this tended to be only when Chechen insurgents launched 'terrorist spectaculars'. In the first war these included the taking of hostages at Budennovsk (June 1995) and Kizlyar (January 1996) and the victorious assault on the capital – Grozny (August 1996) and, in the second, the Dubrovka theatre siege (October 2002), the 'Black Widow' suicide bombings throughout 2003, the assassination of the pro-Kremlin Chechen President, Akhmad Kadyrov, in May 2004 and the Beslan school siege of September 2004. Significantly, the events of the first war were not generally referred to in the Western press as 'terrorist attacks', whereas those in the current war routinely were, especially after 9/11, since when, the Western public has tended to perceive the Chechens, as it were, through Russian eyes.

Although since 11 September 2001, there has been a growing awareness of the danger of giving regimes countering insurgency a carte blanche. For example, a Report of the Policy Working Group on the UN and Terrorism in August 2002 warned that: 'Labelling opponents or adversaries as terrorists offers a time-tested technique to de-legitimize and demonize them.' However, in the post-9/11 world, Maskhadov's apparent closeness to Basaev was never likely to endear him or his supporters to those advocating peaceful solutions to military conflicts.[93] As in the wake of the Dubrovka tragedy, in the public's perception both in Russia and in most of the rest of the world, it was Putin that emerged as the 'peacemaker' and his Chechen opponents as the 'terrorists'.

Taken together, the assassinations on 9 May 2004 in Grozny of Akhmad Kadyrov,[94] Russian President Vladimir Putin's chosen representative in Chechnya, and on 8 March 2005 in Tolstoi-Yurt of Aslan Maskhadov,[95] leader of the Chechen insurgents, appear to have steered Russian policy towards Chechnya into yet another dead end. Since the collapse of the 1996 Khasavyurt Agreement at the end of the first conflict (1994–1996), for which both sides must accept some of the blame, successive attempts by Chechen, Russian and international players to mediate in this dispute have fallen foul of the Putin administration's insistence that the Russo-Chechen confrontation is simply part of the global 'war on terror' and that the only solution is to eradicate all Chechen 'terrorists'.

The support that President Putin received from world leaders, especially President Bush, for his handling of both the Moscow theatre siege and the Beslan school massacre, deflected attention away from the bizarre circumstances of these events, their resolution and aftermath. The primary demand made by the hostage takers on both occasions was an end to the war in Chechnya. This was a course that would have been political suicide for Putin, both domestically and internationally as a leader of the 'anti-terror coalition'. That this was understood by Western leaders has, in effect, let Putin off the hook of having to justify his actions at Dubrovka and Beslan.

It is hard to disagree, nonetheless, with Zbigniew Brzezinski who stated in February 2002:

> The war in Chechnya certainly is not helping the evolution of democracy. It is strengthening the worst remnants of the Soviet system – the apparatus of suppression, the apparatus of coercion. It's not contributing to a healthy political evolution.[96]

The price could be high for the Russian people. Putin's blueprint for Russia as a 'controlled', 'managed' or 'sovereign' democracy appears more likely to end in authoritarianism than in democracy.[97] As Dmitry Trenin concluded prior to Putin's hosting of the G-8 in St Petersburg:

> Until recently, Russia saw itself as Pluto in the Western solar system, very far from the center but fundamentally still a part of it. Now it has left that orbit entirely; Russia's leaders have given up on becoming part of the West and have started creating their own Moscow-centered system.[98]

In such circumstances, Chechnya, whether it likes it or not, looks set to remain within Russia's gravitational pull for the foreseeable future.

9   The international dimension

One must distinguish between terrorism, which is reprehensible in all its forms
and wherever it might be, and crises which genuinely call for the search of a
political solution. This is clearly the case in Chechnya, as we've said for years.
(Dominique de Villepin, then French Foreign Minister, speaking after the
Moscow theatre siege in October 2002)[1]

On the international stage, for reasons which will have become apparent from a
reading of the preceding chapters, both the sympathy and support normally
reserved for nations engaged in such a heroic and at least partly successful
national liberation struggle against overwhelmingly superior odds has, in the
case of Chechnya, been extremely limited from the outset.

The failure of the Russian forces to distinguish between combatants and civilians (both Russian and Chechen) during this war, the widespread abuse by the
Russian troops of alcohol and drugs, and their inability to isolate even the more
extremist of the Chechen leaders made any reconciliation with the Russians
dependent on a radical change in Moscow's attitudes to its rebellious southern
territory. This change was urged upon Russia by human rights organisations in
both Russia and the West and, to a far lesser extent, by certain Western governments. Official Russian responses to such representations were both surly and
dismissive, if not outright threatening.

Unfortunately for the Chechens, the lack of any international recognition for
their cause during the course of the first war, and their subsequent regrettable,
albeit understandable, shift towards more overt manifestations of their adherence
to Islam, was interpreted in the West as a profoundly retrograde step. All that
occurred in the interregnum between the two wars (1996–1999) served to vali-
date in the eyes of the West this interpretation. Western governments clearly did
not want the Chechen separatists to win again, but restricted their criticism of
Russia's conduct of the war to diplomatic attempts to persuade the new Russian
president to seek a political solution. In a rare example of outspoken criticism in
2000, President Clinton's Secretary of State, Madeleine Albright, characterised
the war in Chechnya 'an incredible act of misery'.[2] It is worth pointing out, that
at this time, when still just a presidential hopeful, George W. Bush had

advocated withholding funds from Russia until the Russian government stopped attacking civilians in Chechnya.[3]

To those engaged in studying the conflict in Chechnya, there remains an element of surprise, even frustration, that more public concern has not been raised in the West by one of the bloodiest confrontations on the European continent since the Second World War. Only if one added together the casualties in all of the separate conflicts in the former Yugoslavia, might this figure be approached or even exceeded.[4]

Like the conflicts in Bosnia and Kosovo, reliable statistics of civilian deaths in Chechnya are hard to come by and are prone to be inflated or understated for propaganda purposes by the warring sides. Akhmed Zakaev, the deputy prime minister of the separatist Chechen Republic of Ichkeria claimed in the *International Herald Tribune* on 18 June 2004 that 180,000 civilians had died in the two wars; the figure of over 200,000 dead was admitted in November 2004 even by the pro-Kremlin Chairman of Chechnya's State Council, Taus Djabrailov;[5] an unprecedented high total for those killed in both wars of 250,000 was reported on a pro-separatist website on 20 June 2004,[6] a figure that was raised to 300,000 in June 2005, not as one might assume by a representative of the separatists but by a pro-Moscow Chechen official – Duvakha Aburakhmanov, one of Chechnya's deputy prime ministers![7]

Despite the appalling scale of losses on the Chechen side, the conflict has been a disaster for the Russians too, over and above the desperate fate of those hundreds of thousands of Russian settlers who have fled the fighting in Chechnya and its contiguous territories. Figures for Russian civilian deaths are even harder to come by than those for their Chechen counterparts, one source claiming 21,000 dead and 220,000 driven from Chechnya.[8] Valentina Melnikova, of the Russian Soldiers' Mothers Committee estimated, during an interview on the radio station, *Ekho Moskvy* on 4 May 2004 that 25,000 Russian troops had died in Chechnya.[9] Later that year *RFE/RL*'s Liz Fuller estimated that between 15,000 and 30,000 Russian troops had died in the first decade of the conflict (1994–2004).[10]

By way of comparison, there were 14,751 combat deaths during the Soviet invasion of Afghanistan (1979–1989); the same source citing 8,943 Russian combat deaths in the two Chechen wars up until the end of 2001.[11]

How is it that the two Russo-Chechen wars (1994–1996 and 1999 to date), which have cost the lives of up to one-quarter of the entire Chechen population, as well as those of so many Russian troops, are barely mentioned in any meetings of the G-8, NATO or EU, or even in national parliaments in Western Europe? The pro-separatist Kavkaz Center even accuses Western media and governments of outright hypocrisy in paying more attention to animal rights' issues than to the Chechen War.[12]

Clearly, geography plays a role here. During the NATO campaign in Kosovo, the former Liberal-Democrat leader, Paddy Ashdown, revived memories of Neville Chamberlain's infamous description of the German attack on Czechoslovakia as 'a quarrel in a faraway country between peoples of whom we know nothing'.[13] If people in Western Europe find it so difficult to realign their sense of geography following the collapse of the socialist bloc in the Balkans and Central Europe, how much harder is it for them to comprehend the ethnic and territorial implications of the break-up of the Soviet Union, let alone the constituent parts of the Russian Federation?

Chechnya, which does indeed lie in the south-eastern corner of Europe, remains for most West Europeans a faraway country and the Chechens, a people of whom they know nothing, except for scant details released in the aftermath of the latest 'terrorist spectacular'. Small wonder that those NGOs and individuals that do monitor the conflict and do understand the Chechen people accuse Blair and other Western leaders of 'appeasement' for allowing President Putin a free hand in Russia's crude handling of Chechen self-determination.

By playing the 'Islamic terrorist' card for all it is worth, Putin has effectively given those that still advocate any degree of Chechen separatism a choice between abject surrender and continuing a campaign of sabotage that is perceived in Russia and the West as representing the very Islamic terrorism of which Putin warns. Although this manifestly offers his opponents no real choice, Putin is under little pressure, either domestically or internationally, to acknowledge what is obvious to all who have engaged seriously with the Russo-Chechen conflict: i.e. that the confrontation in Chechnya has much more to do with unresolved conflicts left over from previous eras than it has with international terrorism. Moreover, it would appear blindingly obvious that it is the continuing 'black hole' of lawlessness that exists on all sides in Chechnya that represents the most immediate obstacle to peace.

Perhaps, the debacle in Iraq, a change of administration in the USA or a broader realisation within Russia of the debilitating consequences that the war in Chechnya has on Russian civil society will put pressure on Putin to adopt a more humane and rational approach to settling the Russo-Chechen conflict. For the present, however, the Russian President appears to be firmly in step with the policies introduced by Bush and Sharon, that eradication of terrorism by force is the best way of tackling insurgency, what has been called an 'Israelisation'[14] of the 'war on terror' in Chechnya. Unless this changes then it should come as no surprise that a further 'Palestinisation' of the conflict in Chechnya looks more likely than any 'Good Friday' type of agreement, along the lines of that reached in Northern Ireland, to end military hostilities.

The centuries-long failure of the Russians to accommodate the 'other' represented by the Chechens has turned a minor irritant into a costly fixation. At times, Putin's personal irrationality vis-à-vis Chechnya is all too apparent, as demonstrated most graphically by his outburst in Brussels on 12 November 2002, when he responded angrily to a French journalist who had asked probing but reasonable questions about Chechnya by accusing him of pro-Islamist sympathies and inviting him to Moscow for a circumcision of such effectiveness that nothing would grow![15] Even though Putin has claimed that Chechnya is not for him, personally, a no-go area for discussions, his sensitivity to this subject being brought up in public is well documented.[16]

Opinion polls have shown, however, that ordinary Russians are tired of the war in Chechnya, 68 per cent in August 2006 favouring peace talks, with just 18 per cent for continuing military action.[17] Putin, if he wished, could demonstrate his diplomatic skills and bring an end to the Russo-Chechen conflict. Clearly, however, this is a compromise that he does not appear eager to embrace. He is aware that fear of Chechen terrorism in Russia remains high; prior to the Beslan school siege in 2004, 88 per cent of Russians polled expected a recurrence in the near future.[18]

Even two years after Beslan, the fear in Russia of terrorism remains high, some 74 per cent of Russians polled fearing that they personally or someone close to them was likely to be a victim of a future terrorist act.[19] In continuing to play on these fears, by deliberately confusing Chechen self-determination with Islamic fundamentalist terror, Putin is avoiding having to engage with the complexities of Chechnya.

Like Yeltsin before him, Putin has got a lot of mileage out of demonising the Chechens. In the absence of any pressure from his political allies within the coalition against terror – President Bush, UK Prime Minister Tony Blair and successive Israeli prime ministers still appear to share his uncompromising view that terror can and must be defeated militarily and are all more vulnerable than Putin should their electorate turn against this strategy – it is unlikely that the heroic and concerted efforts of non-governmental organisations to call Russia to account for the tragedy in Chechnya will have the desired effect.

Herein lies the problem. It is vital for Russia, and to some extent its allies, that the true story of Chechnya in all its horror does not attract the full attention of a world community already showing signs of fatigue with the complexity of the conflicts in the Middle East, Afghanistan and Iraq. Therefore, the efforts of those Chechens, Russians and foreign well-wishers who genuinely seek a just and lasting peace in Chechnya are perceived as undesirable, and even dangerous. At the same time, attempts by Chechen 'irreconcilables' to remind the world community of this conflict through spectacular acts of terror like Dubrovka and Beslan merely furnish Putin with further 'proof' that the war that he is waging is solely against terrorism.

Perhaps the unanticipated outcomes that such policies have generated in Afghanistan, Iraq and Palestine eventually will change public opinion around the world. Only then might significant sections of the Russian public be persuaded that the war in Chechnya not only represents a truly shameful 'black page' in the history of post-communist Russia, but also that it remains the biggest single obstacle to the creation in Russia of a genuinely humane, lawful and secure society.

In the winter of 2004–2005, as the current violent stage of the centuries-long Russo-Chechen confrontation entered its second decade, there appeared a significant number of analyses of the causes of the conflict and evaluations of the policies followed thus far by the various parties involved.[20] Less evident were comprehensive assessments of the prospects for a genuine and lasting peace in this region with or without international involvement.[21] Such an examination is now required urgently, not least because a conflict which has exceeded that in the former Yugoslavia in intensity, longevity and civilian casualties and which has produced seemingly never-ending suffering for broad sections of both the Chechen and Russian populations has come to represent a blot on the conscience of concerned citizens as well as an additional source of anger for disaffected Muslims throughout the world.[22] Moreover, the conflict has created a black hole of criminality, impunity and arbitrary violence that threatens to spread far beyond the borders of Russia, let alone Chechnya.

Thus, rather than reassessing why conflict prevention mechanisms failed in 1991–1994 and 1996–1999 to avert the eruption of violence in both December 1994 and October 1999; why peace-enforcement efforts by Russian and both pro- and anti-Russian Chechen factions, as well as attempts at peacekeeping by well-meaning outside organisations, have been so ineffective in halting the violence; and why peacemaking initiatives at local, domestic and international levels have been thwarted at every turn, this chapter seeks to illustrate why a genuine process of peacebuilding cannot be effective unless the attitudes on all sides that beget, condone and encourage the violent behaviour are addressed, preferably with outside assistance.

For, while it might be assumed to be axiomatic that the goal of peace is shared by all interested parties in this conflict, the behaviour and attitudes of certain factions, on all sides, have often been such as to question whether the Russo-Chechen wars have not been instrumentalised to serve the political and economic interests of those identified here as the 'entrepreneurs of violence'. The inaction, indifference, double standards and self interest of the 'democratic' world and the simplistic presentation of the conflict within the parameters of a post-secular discourse of 'good versus evil' combine to distract attention away from the very plain fact that, in a corner of Europe, a continent that aspires to establish in the twenty-first century a society based on shared moral values and principles, thousands of ordinary people are still dying, if not from the violence itself, then from the resulting disease, poverty, ecological degradation and severe psychological trauma.

This plain fact is known well enough to leaders in Russia, the West and throughout the world; at best they dismiss such protestations, urging pragmatism and the need to 'look at the bigger picture', thus emphasising the importance of 'interests' at the expense of 'values'. If one extracts from Table 2.1 a representative selection of factors, one will see how they operate on either side in the context of the Russo-Chechen conflict, (see Table 9.1).

Even this small sample illustrates how these factors, while each being largely characteristic of only one of the parties to the conflict, constitute at the same time something of a mirror image. For example, those perpetrating the sweeps (i.e. the surrounding of a village, followed by house to house searches and reprisals) and the acts of terrorism (e.g. Dubrovka, Beslan) have entirely different perceptions of, and justifications for, their actions from those of their victims, but in either case, the arbitrariness of the violence, the disproportionality of means and ends, and the relative impotency of both the direct and indirect

Table 9.1 Indicative scheme illustrating the application of the Conflict Triangle to Chechnya and type of conflict resolution appropriate to each stage

Behaviour (events)	Attitudes, norms (processes)	Contradictions (invariants)
Direct Violence Peacekeeping	Structural Violence Peacemaking	Cultural Violence Peacebuilding
Selected factors on the Russian side Zachistki (sweeps)	Caucasophobia	Colonisation
Selected factors on the Chechen side Terrorism	Cultural narrative	Asymmetry

victims indicate that the perpetrators of violence have more in common with each other than either do with those on the receiving end.

The prevalence of Caucasophobia (fear of 'persons of Caucasian nationality') – a form of racism – among the Russian population in general, and the federal forces in particular, helps to remove moral obstacles to the inhuman treatment of Chechens and their neighbours. Paradoxically, this confirms the perceptions of the Caucasian peoples within the Russian Federation that they are regarded, nonetheless, as outsiders. This, in turn, fuels anti-Russian sentiments among all Caucasian peoples.[23] The Chechen cultural narrative,[24] of which most Russians are ignorant, but which commemorates both heroic defence against a vastly more numerous foe and the ethnocidal[25] policies adopted against the Chechens by successive Russian and Soviet regimes, justifies, if not legitimises, in the eyes of many Chechens, and, indeed, Western observers, acts that the Russians routinely term 'terrorist'.[26]

As regards the fundamental cultural contradictions, the Russian colonisation of Chechnya in the nineteenth century clearly failed to either co-opt or coerce the Chechens into becoming fully-fledged Russians or even Rossians[27] (non-ethnic Russian citizens of the Empire). It would not be surprising if the average ethnic Russian, influenced, perhaps, by the impressions created in both classical Russian literature and Soviet history books, still regarded the original conquest of the Caucasus as a civilising mission that brought progress to the mountain tribes and, consequently, would perceive manifestations of anti-Russian sentiment as evidence of how ungrateful these peoples were. That such a view is shared neither by Chechens nor their neighbours will be apparent to anyone who has spent any time in the region.

These attitudes notwithstanding, a significant proportion of Russians now wishes the Russian Federation to divest itself of its rebellious southern republic. In a poll published by Moscow's Levada Centre in July 2005, 37 per cent stated that they would either be pleased to be rid of Chechnya (or considered they already were) and a further 17 per cent were indifferent to the prospect of losing it.[28] A poll by the same organisation in August 2005 found that a then all-time low of 19 per cent of Russians favoured continuing military operations in Chechnya against no less than 70 per cent opting for peace negotiations.[29]

A month later, 61 per cent (against 28 per cent) of Russians polled indicated that they thought the war in Chechnya was still going on.[30] By August 2006, only 18 per cent were in favour of continuing the war (with 68 per cent for peace negotiations), but, significantly, in the wake of the death of Shamil Basaev the previous month, only 51 per cent thought the war in Chechnya was continuing as against 37 per cent who considered that the situation, at long last, was stabilising.[31]

Whereas the behaviour on the Russian federal side bears many of the hallmarks of 'state terrorism' and that on the Chechen rebel side those of 'insurgent terrorism',[32] the patterns of behaviour which both sides share might be characterised as a 'rule of terror' by the entrepreneurs of violence. Clearly this represents a dangerous, destabilising situation that could potentially spread well beyond Chechnya.

That the representatives of the warring sides manifestly cannot reach a satisfactory resolution of their differences after more than ten years of the most brutal conflict illustrates the need for a degree of outside involvement if the human rights violations are to end and the present danger of overspill averted. However, there is currently little likelihood either of the Putin administration allowing any outside involvement that might be construed as interference in the internal affairs of the Russian Federation, or of the leaders of democratic societies in the West risking their respective interests (including energy supplies) by taking a values-based stand on the issue of Chechnya.

Here a key role could be played by European, rather than international, institutions, particularly by the Council of Europe and its Parliamentary Assembly (PACE), both of which count Russia as a member. Like the EU, these organisations are based on principles to which most countries and people can aspire: a pluralist liberal democracy with a free market economy and a concern for the rights of all citizens, principles to which the Russian Federation, through its membership, has consented. Other member countries of these institutions not only have extensive experience of dealing with many of the problems that beset the Russians and the Chechens (e.g. the UK and Spain in combating separatist/irredentist movements) but also of mediating successfully in analogous conflict situations (e.g. in the former Yugoslavia).

Of all European countries or institutions, Putin appears to trust Germany most, due in part, no doubt, to his professional experience in the KGB in the former GDR and his fluency in the German language. However, his close personal relationship with Gerhard Schroeder has been replaced with a much more realistic approach by the new Chancellor, Angela Merkel, who initially called for Russia to be treated as a 'partner' (due to common interests) rather than a 'friend' like the USA (with whom values were shared) or a European 'ally' like the UK or France (with whom interests and values coincided).[33] At subsequent meetings, she appears to have adopted a softer approach, although this has not discouraged German academics from calling for the EU to act as a 'third force' in resolving the Russo-Chechen conflict.[34]

Of course, as Bruno Coppetiers *et al.* have demonstrated, the Europeanisation of conflict situations on the 'periphery' of Europe (Cyprus, Georgia, Moldova,

Serbia and Montenegro) is not a recipe for success in itself; for example, the current marked preference for the maintenance of territorial integrity can lead to quite unintended consequences and outcomes.[35]

Such involvement is likely to be most productive if outside agencies, offering experience gained in comparable conflicts, focus on those cultural contradictions that can be resolved without resort to violence. For, if the violence generated by unresolved cultural contradictions creates structural violence in the form of attitudes, institutions, norms and laws, and the latter produces violent behaviour, then it would appear to be putting the cart before the horse to try to prevent direct violence without addressing the attitudes that lay at its roots. By the same token, any attempt to change violent attitudes depends upon a comprehensive understanding of the cultural contradictions that underpin them.

There is a need, therefore, to identify the cultural contradictions in order to see where outside involvement could help construct mechanisms to accommodate and, where necessary, resolve these contradictions. Only then will it be possible to demonstrate how those obstructing this process are, in effect, the entrepreneurs of violence who are responsible for exploiting these contradictions for their own narrow ends, identifying where action, advice or pressure could be brought by internal agencies, assuming that the latter are genuinely interested in a peaceful outcome, to address not only the violent behaviour of these parties, but also the attitudes that legitimise and prolong such violence. Outside involvement, therefore, can be proposed not only in implementing a multi-track approach to monitor the behaviour, address the attitudes and understand the contradictions but also in helping to expose and counter the influence of the entrepreneurs of violence.

Of course, this would rely heavily on a level of media independence and a capability in Russia for civic society to influence politicians that currently are manifestly absent.[36] European involvement, therefore, might be aimed at creating a more transparent and pluralistic political process, improving press freedom and consolidating Russian civic society. Not because Europe seeks to 'interfere' in Russia's internal affairs but because it understands Russia's (and Chechnya's) predicament and genuinely believes that the experience of Council of Europe members shows that the presence of these factors offers the best guarantee of marginalising the entrepreneurs of violence and making it possible to explore ways of resolving conflicts by non-violent means.[37]

Yet in order to resolve the Russo-Chechen conflict, it is precisely in this – the holding to account of those responsible for this state of affairs – that the outside world, at public if not at state level, has a right and a duty to become involved. For example, PACE's recommendation 1479 of 25 January 2006, on the 'Human rights' violations in the Chechen Republic: the Committee of Ministers' responsibility vis-à-vis the Assembly's concerns' opens by reaffirming that: 'the Parliamentary Assembly stresses that the protection of human rights is the core task of all Council of Europe bodies' and closes with the complaint that:

> the Assembly fears that the lack of effective reaction by the Council's executive body in the face of the most serious human rights issue in any of the

Council of Europe's member states undermines the credibility of the Organisation.[38]

Yet, despite these violations, in 2006 Russia was invited not only to be chair
of G-8 in Putin's home city of St Petersburg, but also of the Committee of Ministers of the Council of Europe itself![39]
The 'bigger picture' nowadays is the post-9/11 'war on terror' and the vast
natural energy resources controlled by Russia at a time of uncertainty in areas of
traditional supply. Not only has no major Western leader put any serious pressure on Putin to make peace in Chechnya, but, despite his unsatisfactory handling of the Dubrovka and Beslan hostage sieges and the immoderate attacks of
his spokespersons on both the US and the UK justice systems for granting political asylum to so-called Chechen 'terrorists', he has been feted as being in the
forefront of the battle between 'good' and 'evil' in the post-9/11 world. Such
gestures increase Putin's standing domestically, deflecting the attention of the
Russian public from the shortcomings of his administration.
The scope for international involvement in such circumstances is, therefore,
extremely limited. Although this is due, primarily, to Russian intransigence, the
situation is undoubtedly exacerbated by the passivity of Western governments.
The latter, unlike the former, however, can still be held to account by those that
elect them. There appears to be such a lack of leadership favouring compromise
rather than strength in the international community at present that one could be
forgiven for identifying most current leaders of major powers as entrepreneurs
of violence on a global scale.
Yet the danger presented by the indifference to such a tragedy as that unfold-
ing in Chechnya is that relatively healthy, hitherto secure societies with a law-
governed state, independent media and a strong civil society, appear unwilling
to hold leaders to account for their passivity. The insecurity bred by the war on
terror and discourse of 'good versus evil' seems to have dissuaded the general
public from engaging with the complex processes and unresolved cultural contradictions involved, basing their perceptions exclusively on events – i.e. direct
violence – usually only that perpetrated by the 'other' side.
However, as the war in Iraq has demonstrated, 'violent politics' have a nasty
habit of boomeranging back on the initiators and it might not be until the situation in Chechnya spills over throughout the Northern Caucasus that the world
will sit up and pay attention. The sad truth of the matter is that, in the Russo-
Chechen conflict, too many of the powerful are the immediate beneficiaries of
the continuing conflict, the victims of which have neither the might nor the voice
to counter the power of the entrepreneurs of violence.
For the reasons stated above, therefore, a greater degree of outside involvement than hitherto in the Russo-Chechen conflict would appear to be essential.
Rather than concentrating initially on direct violence alone, a multi-track
approach is required that places the behaviour of all sides involved in the context
of the attitudes, institutions and processes that create structural violence. At the
same time, a clear analysis should be made of how the cultural contradictions that

give rise to these attitudes can so be managed as to avoid or resolve the conflicts contained therein. Some of these may be medium- to long-term initiatives; others may lend themselves to more immediate measures.

As has been stated already, a key role could be played by European institutions. The accession to the EU of Estonia, Latvia and Lithuania has demonstrated clearly that it is possible to move from an authoritarian to a democratic system with outside assistance within a relatively short time frame. It would not be surprising if the people of Georgia and Ukraine were also to see their future increasingly as within the European family of nations.

Russia, meanwhile, appears to be heading in the opposite direction, her traditional emphasis on executive power producing a perception of its national interest that is closer to that of China's; perhaps currently even to that, in foreign policy at least, of the USA, than it is to those of European states. At the institutional level it is within Europe's reach, preferably with American support, to encourage Russia to see that, in terms of stability, prosperity and progress, both her best interests and those of the wider world community are served by rejecting her authoritarian past. If Russia's traditional concerns about following the European path prove too much of an obstacle, Japan might offer an alternative role model. Judging by public pronouncements of leading Russian politicians, such as those by former Minister of Defence, Igor Rodionov, however, it would appear that China's arms-length attitude to European values represents a more attractive example.

Where, then, does this leave the Northern Caucasus in general and Chechnya in particular? On the one hand, the Islamic radicalisation of the Chechen resistance movement has shifted the emphasis away from European standards towards those of the international *jihadists*. On the other hand, Russia's move away from federalism, in effect, seems to torpedo the one immediately possible compromise of an autonomous Chechnya within a genuine Russian Federation. After all, it is hard to imagine the rebellious Chechens being afforded this distinction, while the more compliant Dagestanis, Ossetians and Tatars are not.

Moreover, as has been stated above, the Kremlin is not about to allow, any time soon, a genuinely free and fair election in Chechnya for they are bound to be saddled with a less amenable leader than one they pick for themselves. This in turn is hardly surprising, given that as many as one-fifth of Chechens have been eliminated or displaced by the conflict and that the territory of Chechnya has been transformed into a ruined ecological disaster zone.[40]

However, the Chechens are not the only victims of this conflict; Russian civilians have suffered too, not only in acts of terrorism, nor even due to the aforementioned Chechen syndrome. Instead, under first Yeltsin and then Putin, the Russians have suffered a setback in their dreams of prosperity and progress and appear to have abandoned this for the delusion of great power status and a Russia for the Russians. Although such nationalistic sentiments are understandable in a people traumatised by their recent history, it is worth pointing out to Russian leaders and their public alike that this runs contrary to their own best interests. While painfully slow and imperfect, the moves towards a resolution of such long-running conflicts as those in Northern Ireland and the Middle East do highlight both the central and positive role of outside mediation and the absolute necessity for compromise.

In the final analysis, outside involvement (I have avoided deliberately the use of the word 'intervention') to change attitudes in the Russo-Chechen conflict, can work only if the advisors, donors and mediators are fully aware of the cultural contradictions between Russia, Chechnya and the outside world and are confident that their own attitudes not only reflect a genuine desire to reconcile and assist rather than an attempt to further their self interest, but are perceived as such by the conflicting parties.

The elaboration of a step-by-step programme for the resolution of the conflict in Chechnya could be based therefore on (a) a recognition of the heterogeneity of views on both the Russian and Chechen 'sides' to this conflict against a background of an overwhelming desire for an end to the violence; (b) an identification of those cultural contradictions between Russia and Chechnya, as well as between both and the outside world, which can be resolved without resort to violence; and (c) differentiating between the 'need' and 'greed' of the parties involved and thus recognising that the role of the 'entrepreneurs of violence' is to serve their own private interests rather than those of the people they claim to represent.

For, neither Putin's 'military victory at all costs' nor Basaev's 'freedom or death' is or ever was likely to reconcile the Russian and Chechen peoples, who fate has decreed must live as neighbours. One senses that Putin has realised already that his primary political objective of keeping Chechnya a part of Russian territory can be achieved only by allowing his chosen Chechen entrepreneur of violence, Ramzan Kadyrov, to pacify its recalcitrant population, a decision virtually guaranteed to perpetuate the conflict, prolong the human rights violations and spread resistance throughout the Northern Caucasus. Ironically, even Russian commentators have pointed out that 'one-man-rule' in Chechnya does not fit the traditional power structures of Chechen society and that some form of government that approaches the British parliamentary system would be far more suitable.[41]

Paradoxically, in terms of the triumph of might over right, more of Russia is in danger of becoming like Chechnya, just as, through indifference and excessive caution, civic societies in the West run the risk of becoming as ineffectual as ordinary Russian citizens in restraining their own entrepreneurs of violence. Perhaps, as in Iraq, 'violent' politics needs to be tried and seen to fail in Chechnya before it becomes apparent that a comprehensive internationally-backed programme of peacebuilding really does represent the best way to assist both Russians and Chechens to extricate themselves from the impasse in which they currently find themselves entrenched.

Impact of Chechnya on Russo-British relations: a case study[42]

As the latest British spy scandal[43], in January 2006, to rock Moscow demonstrated, there are some aspects of relations between Russia and the UK that over time barely seem to change at all. The history of mutual mistrust and divergent views between two powers on opposite edges of the European continent was quick to resurface, with the British side claiming that this was a smoke-screen put up by the Kremlin to hide the Putin administration's emasculation of NGOs operating in the capital, and the Russians reacting once more with a heightened degree of sensitivity towards the real intentions of actions within their borders by a Western state.

However, set as it was against the background of Russia flexing its energy muscles in an apparently opportunistic fashion (as much of Europe suffered in the grip of extremely cold weather), this incident did serve to remind both sides of the dynamically-changing nature of other aspects of this relationship. For, rather than employing the traditional 'hard' military threat of the Soviet era, Russia appeared to be revealing for the first time a 'soft', but effective, economic hand. This perception was heightened when, within days, rumours circulated that Russia's state-owned energy giant, Gazprom, was considering a bid for Centrica, Britain's largest provider of gas.[44]

Moreover, the diplomatic spat highlighted the fact that the two areas dominating, currently, the multifaceted and complex network of interests linking the two countries are energy and security. The scale of British investments in the Russian energy sector and the projected dependence in the coming decades of the British economy on Russian energy resources ensure that both sides prioritise this area of cooperation in their bilateral dealings. Similarly, since 9/11 both the Russian Federation and the UK have declared themselves to be allies of the US in the 'war on terror', making cooperation in matters of security the other major priority within this relationship.

Given both the long-term nature of British investments in developing Russia's energy resources and the open-ended nature of the 'War on Terror', maintaining a high degree of political, economic and social stability in Russia would appear to be the main criterion for both sides in order to achieve their respective objectives. It is the interrelated questions of what constitutes this stability and which means might best be employed to secure it that seem to generate serious differences of opinion between the Russian and British sides. Nowhere is this more evident than in the divergent attitudes within and between Russia and the UK to the long-running conflict in Chechnya, the very mention of which in public seems to raise the blood pressure of the Russian president.

To the Putin administration, Chechnya is Russia's front line in the international coalition's 'war on terror', specifically the threat posed by radical Islam, and British complaints over Russia's human rights abuses in the conflict are held to reflect the double standards and lingering Cold War mentality that permeate Western attitudes to post-communist Russia.[45] To members of Russia's embryonic civil society and to its small but active human rights lobby, the federal authorities' Chechen policy represents much that is wrong in post-communist Russian society. The Russian public, except in the aftermath of Chechen terrorist 'spectaculars', would appear to question the efficacy of their President's policies in Chechnya, while approving of Putin's overall performance as President. Thus, in August 2006, although Putin's personal approval rating among Russians remains high, at 78 per cent, more than two-thirds (69 per cent) of those polled would prefer peace talks with the Chechens against 18 per cent favouring Putin's policy of a continuing the war.[46]

Chechen attitudes range from those of Ramzan Kadyrov, who pays lip-service to the Kremlin's authority but, in fact, rules Chechnya through force and terror, to those of the followers of Shamil Basaev, whose irreconcilable armed opposition to Russian rule had branded him an 'international terrorist'. In between we find the vast majority of ordinary Chechens who seek both an end to Russian brutality and survival by whatever means it takes. Thus it was reported by *Interfax* on 2 February 2006, that 86 per cent of Chechens 'link the achievement of peace, stability, justice and order' with the activities of the current (pro-Russian) Chechen authorities.[47] This is hardly surprising, given the circumstances prevailing over the last decade, but should not be taken to mean that these same Chechens necessarily support the policies of the Putin administration. Fully 81 per cent of those recently polled in Chechnya characterised Russia's Chechen policy as 'completely ineffective' or 'not very effective'; 66 per cent indicating that they thought that the Chechens had taken up arms to resist the actions of Russian forces; and only 14 per cent for the struggle for independence.[48]

On the other hand, the British government, while acutely aware of the political and commercial interests invested in good relations with Russia, knows that international inaction over Chechnya, along with conflicts in the Middle East, Iraq and Afghanistan, serves to both anger and radicalise disaffected Muslims within British society and, as such, probably contributed to the London suicide bombings of 7 July 2005. This was highlighted more than once in the correspondence of April–May 2004 between the Cabinet Secretary, Sir Andrew Turnbull, and the Permanent Secretary at the Home Office, Sir John Gieve, on 'Relations with the Muslim Community', leaked to the *Sunday Times*[49] but also by the fact that the Chechen conflict was mentioned in the 'suicide videos' made by Mohammed Sidique Khan[50] and Shehzad Tanweer[51] – two of the 7/7 London bombers.

For most of the British public, the conflict in Chechnya is too complex and distant to register on the radar screen other than following a terrorist 'spectacular'. Thus the tension in Britain tends to between, on the one hand, the government and business circles, which concentrate on Britain's political and commercial 'interests' in Russia and, on the other, what might be broadly termed the 'civil society' or 'human rights lobby'. I acknowledge, of course, that many of those politicians, lawyers, academics and media representatives that speak out on the Chechen issue would not necessarily identify themselves as members of the 'human rights lobby'. Perhaps the 'values community' (i.e. those that insist that 'values' be considered as having at least equal weight to 'interests') might be a more accurate term.

As might be expected, the latter community emphasises the 'values' that are being compromised by inaction over and indifference to both the Chechen's plight and the Russian authorities' apparent impunity. The relative strength vis-à-vis its government of the civil society/human rights lobby in Britain means that the issue of Chechnya is raised at the highest levels more frequently in the UK than it is in Russia. This fact, in itself, becomes an irritant in British–Russian relations to a degree similar to that caused by the underdeveloped system of market regulation on the Russian side.

Of course, the foreign policy of any country is rarely just a zero-sum game between the deontological (based on immutable principles) and consequentialist (the ends justify the means) approaches. Foreign policy may well be both pragmatic and principled, by the same token – it may be neither; usually, it is a mixture of the two, with subtle or, sometimes, not so subtle shifts in one or other direction over time.

Thus, whereas the foreign policy of the United Kingdom under Thatcher and Major, represented by the likes of Douglas Hurd and Malcolm Rifkind, might have had little room for idealism, under the stewardship of Robin Cook, Blair's incoming Labour administration in 1997 might have been predicted to advocate an ethical dimension in foreign policy. Not, it should be stressed, an 'ethical' foreign policy per se, more a belief in the promotion of democracy as being in the interests, in terms of security, prosperity and quality of life, of both Britain and her partners. The subsequent rift in 2003 between Cook and Blair over the war in Iraq, the most divisive repercussion in Britain of the 'war on terror', might be perceived as marking a significant shift in British foreign policy away from principled 'values' and towards pragmatic 'interests'.[52]

The danger for Russia, and for Britain's interests in that country, is that the misguided policies that are claimed to have worked in Chechnya are now being spread throughout the Russian Federation. This tactic, while aimed at creating political stability, which is supported as a key strategy by Britain, actually threatens to harm British economic interests in Russia. As Pavel Erochkine wrote in 2005: 'Russia has a potentially fatal combination of poor property rights, underdeveloped market institutions, a corrupt judicial system and huge resource rents, especially recently,'[53] adding that 'the concentration of power has removed checks and balances on bureaucracy and red tape'.[54] It would be surprising, in the circumstances, if Britain would not prefer to deal with well-regulated countries such as Norway, as a more reliable source of future energy.

Russia's poor performance against international standards in surveys of corruption (Russia was rated 90th worst country out of 146 by Transparency International[55]), civil liberties and political rights (rated 'not free' in both categories by Freedom House[56]) stands in stark contrast to the obligations it has undertaken in international and European organisations.[57] Within Russia this has been achieved by tightening control over the political system and the media.

However, due in no small part to the rapidly rising price of oil, this has been accompanied by economic improvements in the country, although, arguably, corruption and clientelism has prevented this from seeping down sufficiently.

Certainly the mishandling of the cash-for-benefits reform in early 2005 did not inspire confidence that the current Kremlin leadership was on the same wavelength as the majority of ordinary Russians. At the same time the Yukos affair[58] and the murder of US businessman, Paul Klebnikov,[59] give serious pause for thought for anyone contemplating long-term investment in the Russian economy. It is almost as if Putin has privatised political power in Russia and sold it to the highest most loyal bidder. That this should include a region as potentially inflammable as Chechnya might appear to be a derogation of duty to the Russian people on a massive scale.

The dilemmas thus created affect all sides: the Chechens must resign themselves to accommodating Ramzan Kadyrov or seek refuge with the militant rebels – there is little likelihood, in the short term, of the international community doing anything more than cushioning this blow through assistance in reconstruction.[60] The Russian authorities, buoyed by their 'successes' and lack of meaningful criticism in Chechnya and the international arena are likely to carry on with impunity, cracking down hard and indiscriminately on the militants throughout the Northern Caucasus, with predictable results. The remnants of civil society and the human rights lobby in Russia will come under increasing pressure to conform; any form of aid from Britain or her allies in the West may well be perceived as being 'proof' of the existence of a pro-western 'fifth column' in Russian NGOs.

It is in countries like Britain, however, that the tensions are mounting over the wisdom of the government's emphasis on 'interests' rather than 'values' in its relationship with Russia. Although Chechnya may be kept off the main agenda to appease Russian sensitivities,[61] genuine concern is growing over the medium- to long-term effects of policies aimed at short-term political stability in Russia. The sheer scale of British investments into Russian energy means that the British business community is increasingly thinking in terms of policies likely to achieve stability over the next 30 to 40 years. Paradoxically, in this they share the ground already occupied by the civil society/human rights lobby.

If the price for 'pacification' in Chechnya is growing instability across the whole of the Northern Caucasus then it is possible that, sooner or later, the Russian public will tire of the 'Kremlin's paternalistic, Soviet-style rhetoric'[62] and turn, perhaps, to a genuinely populist opponent of Putin, such as Khodorkovsky. The British government might then find itself in the kind of uncomfortable position such as that occupied by the Major administration in 1991, which appeared to be trying to shore up the Soviet system when the Russian people had clearly declared their intention to dispense with it.

The interests of the Russian people are not and certainly do not have to be identical to those of the British or any other European people. However, if one feels that the 'values' (democratic political system, market economy and a free media) that have served most of Europe so well since the end of the Second

World War might, in due course, benefit the Russian people too, then one should not feel constrained to say so. While it may be true that the current Russian leaders are able to pay less attention to their domestic 'values' lobby than most European governments are obliged to do, they are unlikely to jeopardise, in the final analysis, the inward flow of investment from countries such as Britain, by threatening to turn off the oil and gas taps over issues that they manifestly consider are of secondary importance.

Conclusion

The relative impotence of civil society in post-communist Russia[63] makes it very difficult for a reasoned dialogue to take place between those that seek a just and lasting peace and those that seek victory only on their terms. The inability of the Putin administration to 'face down' the latter has restricted severely, hitherto, the opportunities to explore outcomes that are genuinely acceptable to both the Russian and Chechen peoples and lays his Government open to the risk of losing control over a military leadership which has vested economic interests in prolonging the conflict and which, it is generally agreed abroad, has allowed the gross abuse of human rights to occur in Chechnya.

Attempts by some of the most respected representatives of foreign 'civil society' (NGOs, international organisations, etc.) to facilitate such a dialogue have been perceived as unwarranted interference by the Russian side. Thus, such high-profile international figures as former Czech President Vaclav Havel,[64] Mary Robinson (UNHCR), Elizabeth Andersen (Human Rights Watch), Archbishop Desmond Tutu and Frank Judd (PACE) who have criticised Russian actions in Chechnya have been attacked and ridiculed alongside such notable Russian liberals as Grigory Yavlinsky, Sergei Kovalev and Anna Politkovskaya.[65]

Similarly, the Russian side routinely ignores the opinions of highly respected figures from the United States, Russia and Chechnya, who see in such individuals as Zakaev a worthy interlocutor. The tragedy is that, whereas all of the people listed above advocate the development in Russia of a truly democratic, law-governed state as being in the best interests of the Russian people, the current Russian administration has yet to create a normative legal, social or political base that accords with Western notions of democracy. Moreover, this administration tends to react with hostility when such shortcomings are pointed out.

The Russian Government's attempt to 'demonise' any opponent to their disastrous Chechen policies as a 'terrorist', effectively rules out the participation of those Chechens – such as Akhmed Zakaev – who genuinely seek an outcome that is acceptable to both Russian and Chechen sides.[66]

As we have seen, except in the wake of terrorist 'spectaculars', the Russian people, in spite of its Government's policies, overwhelmingly support peace negotiations with the Chechen leadership. In poll after poll Russian respondents have indicated this preference over a continuation of the war. Insofar as Putin has ignored this mandate to bring to a satisfactory end the conflict in Chechnya, much of the blame for the manifestly unsatisfactory state of affairs in the region must be laid at his door.

The Russian Government surely is deluding itself if it thinks that the Chechen people will simply dismiss the loss of over 200,000 or even 300,000 dead, figures admitted, respectively, in November 2004 and June 2005 by the pro-Kremlin Chairman of Chechnya's State Council, Taus Djabrailov,[67] and a deputy prime minister of Chechnya, Duvakha Aburakhmanov,[68] at the hands of the federal forces. Having whipped up anti-Chechen sentiment in Russia, there is unlikely to be any popular support for the substantial investment needed to repair Chechnya's shattered economy, leaving the region unstable and its people resentful. In August 2000, only 17 per cent of Russians polled felt that Russia was obligated to pay war damages to Chechnya, fully 73 per cent being against this.[69] The world community too, suffering already from 'compassion fatigue', is unlikely to prioritise the investment of the billions of dollars required to restore Chechnya's infrastructure.

Having twice failed to establish its own viable institutions and, in the absence of any prospect of an East Timor-type of solution involving substantial outside aid and an interim administration under the auspices of the UN, it would appear that the Chechens are faced with state institutions being imposed from without, by either the Islamic fundamentalist *Wahhabis* or the Russians. Although neither meets the understandable aspirations of the majority of the Chechen people for a normal, prosperous and secure way of life, one can understand why a younger generation, raised with first-hand experience of Russian brutality and Western indifference, might be more tempted, both financially and ideologically, by the allure of a *jihad*, than by what either Russia or US-led globalisation has to offer. This, in turn, will lead the coalition against terror to identify even closer the Chechen with the Palestinian cause – with all too predictable results.

Paradoxically, the one route out of this impasse, in the short term at any rate, appears to be the totality of power invested by President Putin in Ramzan Kadyrov. For his part, Kadyrov holds onto power for his clan in Chechnya by force and terror. However, he has used his position to wrest concessions from the Kremlin that were never offered to Dudaev or Maskhadov, let alone Basaev. The price of paying lip-service to Russian territorial integrity appears to be all the current Chechen administration has to pay for effective self-determination free from brutal Russian interference – the very cause for which Chechens have fought for nearly three centuries.

The problem looming for both Putin and Kadyrov, however, is that separatist aspirations that fall within European parameters appear to have been replaced not just in Chechnya but across the North Caucasus with a more virulent anti-Western *jihad* which threatens to make much of the region an effective no-go zone for ordinary Russians. Putin's 'counter-terrorist operation' has become a self-fulfilling prophecy by creating the very terrorist networks that he purportedly set out to eradicate. Moreover, the style of leadership epitomised by Ramzan Kadyrov and his father before him, which appears to be every bit as brutal as that exercised in Chechnya by the Russians, seems to conform more closely with the style of governance employed by Saddam Hussein than to that advocated by the Council of Europe.

However, in a society ruled by a rigid *vertikal'* of power, with a cowed and muzzled media and lacking either an effective political opposition or a strong independent civil sector, such obvious shortcomings can be camouflaged in a conspiracy of silence. As Andreas Gross of PACE has noted:

> One of the problems of this conflict can be found in the fact that the Chechen conflict is not a decisive problem for the Russian elite at large. While the first Chechen war had been considered a disease, the current situation is generally seen as a nuisance only. Therefore, there is indifference and passivity towards the fights in Chechnya, but no pressure on the Russian authorities to find a solution to the problem. Instead, the Chechen conflict has even been used in Russia's foreign relations, for example with the USA.[70]

Insofar as Russia's core strategy in Chechnya in both wars was the maintenance of control over Chechen territory at all costs, not only to preserve the territorial integrity of the Russian Federation, but also to remain a key player in the Caucasian and Caspian areas, considered strategically vital for political and economic reasons, then Putin's policies may be seen to have been successful, as long as one does not enquire as to the cost. As one sceptical Russian journalist has observed:

> You want loyalty from the Chechens and an end to separatism? Fine. Pay for it by increasing Chechnya's political and economic independence as much as possible.[71]

As the US and the UK were perceived as potential competitors for influence in these very regions, any interference by these powers in Chechnya would be greeted by deep suspicion and resentment, thus narrowing any effective opportunity for involvement.

Indeed, the core strategy for Britain, in common with her Western partners, towards Russia would appear to be the promotion of long-term stability and the development of market relations. Thus, UK governments, be they Conservative or Labour, have harboured the hope that, following the establishment of the post-communist regime in Russia, progress towards a more democratic, law-governed state combined with enhanced prosperity for the bulk of the Russian population (including Chechens) would contribute to the long-term stability of Russia.

In retrospect, it might appear that Britain, in common with the USA and other Western partners, prioritised instead, policies that would ensure that there could be no return to communism, no matter how short term, whereas in Russia, the one-off success in the polls of reformed communist parties in both Lithuania and

Poland might suggest that such a temporary renaissance is to be both anticipated and endured.

The reforms in Russia did indeed prove irreversible but, arguably, only at the cost of undermining Russia's transition to a democratic, law-governed state with a smoothly-functioning market economy: first, in 1993, with Yeltsin's armed assault against the Russian parliament; compounded by the dubious circumstances in which the Russian president was re-elected in 1996 and the devastating economic crisis of 1998; and culminating in the effective takeover of all levers of power in the country from 2000 by Putin's militocracy – the *siloviki*.

10 Conclusion

Could somebody explain to me
for what did we destroy this city,
kill so many people, bury our own!?
This most stupid, most wretched war.
(V. Mironov, 2001)[1]

I have sought in this book to place the current Russo-Chechen confrontation within clear historical and cultural parameters while at the same time taking into account the realities of the post-9/11 world order in the twenty-first century. It is my hope that sufficient evidence has been produced for the reader to understand, if not share, my firm conviction that this conflict is related in many respects much more to longstanding unresolved cultural issues than it is to a worldwide 'war on terror', which has now been discredited in the eyes of so many.

Where possible I have attempted to resist the temptation, alert to the dangers inherent in such an approach, of being seduced by overemphasising what has been termed 'ethnographic romanticism'[2] or 'superficial historicity';[3] in other words attributing virtually all of the causes of the Russo-Chechen conflict to historical and cultural factors. However, while recognising the importance of both the time dynamic and the impact, for good or for ill, of modernity on Russian and Chechen perceptions, it would be unrealistic, it seems to me, to underplay the role of history and cultural narrative in the current conflict, not least because of the sometimes crude manipulation of these issues by those intent on continuing and even exacerbating the war.

In analysing the conflict, I have sought also to avoid where appropriate generalising the parties to the conflict as the 'Russians' or the 'Chechens', acknowledging both the heterogeneity of views and affiliations on either side, and the fact that individuals and groups, be they presidents, generals, warlords or leaders of a broad range of institutions at all levels have presumed to speak and act on behalf of 'people' without seeking either a genuine mandate or troubling to find out what their constituents really want. This caution is all the more necessary as there is disturbing evidence, which, by its nature, is hard to either quantify or verify, of collusion at all levels between Russians and Chechens. Nonetheless, given the significant role played in this conflict by mutual stereotyping and demonisation,[4] I have concluded that the 'imagined communities' of both Russians and Chechens must be given due prominence.

My admittedly pessimistic contention is that, no matter how many well-intenioned peace plans are put forward in order to stop the violence in Chechnya, all will founder as long as the situation is controlled by the entrepreneurs of violence on all sides. However much the UN, the OSCE, PACE, the European Court of Human Rights, NGOs and human rights organisations call for this or that international norm or convention to be observed – in order to stop the manifestations of direct violence occurring – unless real sanctions are threatened, they are likely to be ignored. For as long as sanctions can only be imposed with the agreement of major world powers, then the continued insistence that we 'need to look at the big picture' (the war on terror, globalisation, energy supply and 'good versus evil') will prevail every time.

This brings me to the key question posed in the Introduction: Why a conflict of this scale and intensity has been 'swept under the carpet' and what are the consequences for all of us of such indifference to suffering and violence? It seems to me that the very insecurity engendered by the 'war on terror' has distracted ordinary people in secular societies away from the values that defined Western democratic societies. In terms of Abraham Maslow's hierarchy of needs,[5] much of the population of the Western world post-9/11 appears to have slipped back into focussing on basic issues of security, rather than concentrating on such 'higher' needs as fulfilling their own potential.

This overriding interest in ensuring security from the horrors of terrorism, paradoxically however, has meant that we collectively turn a blind eye to policies elsewhere in the world that manifestly, far from ensuring that security, are almost guaranteed to erode it. Nowhere is this more evident than in the conduct of the so-called 'war on terror', a concept of very questionable coherence from the start. Quite how one wages, let alone wins, a war on a psychological state of mind has never been apparent to me? Although a 'war on terrorism' has more credibility, it is not exactly rational, particularly when the opposing side is labelled 'illegal combatants', and thus, is deprived, it would seem, of any of the legal safeguards afforded to criminals or combatants. However, it is the careless manner in which these two concepts have been used, interchangeably, since the very launch of the 'war' that characterises the 'spin' rather than the substance of the entire undertaking.

Thus, in the immediate aftermath of the attacks on New York and Washington, on 20 September 2001, President George W. Bush referred to a 'war on terror' in his address to the Joint Session of Congress and the American People,[6] while, on the very same day, a letter signed by representatives of the neo-conservative Project for the New American Century endorsed Bush's call for a 'war against terrorism' (advising that a failure to attempt to bring down Saddam Hussein's regime in Iraq would 'constitute an early and perhaps decisive surrender in the war on international terrorism').[7]

What may be safely concluded is that, when such a conflict becomes perceived by its victims as a 'war of terror' directed against them and their co-religionists, the potential consequences not just for their societies, but also for our own, are indeed terrifying.

In both Chechnya and Russia, as has been argued consistently throughout this book, mainstream public opinion has not generally been anything like as extreme as the policies implemented by their respective representatives. The lesson seems to be that, when society allows the entrepreneurs of violence virtually a free hand, such rational notions as moderation, peace and compromise tend to be ignored and forgotten. As a result, it is not only representatives of the 'moderate' Chechen resistance and the international community at large that have been left out of the political process in Chechnya, most importantly, it is the freely-expressed will of the Chechen people themselves that has been deliberately ignored and marginalised.

As has been argued, applying conflict resolution theory to the Russo-Chechen conflict in order to identify optimum strategies for assisting the warring sides to extricate themselves from the present impasse into which their policies and interaction hitherto have led them was never likely in itself to be enough to make genuine progress towards peace. Clearly, unless the manifest widespread desire for peace in Chechnya is translated into a more positive approach from the conflicting parties, including recognition that the ability to compromise is a strength not a weakness, there remains little prospect of constructing a situation in Chechnya in which all sides could count themselves as winners.

This, I have maintained, is more likely to occur with the application of meaningful pressure from leaders of the international community, backed preferably by other influential representatives of world public opinion, who are sufficiently aware of the complexities of this multi-layered conflict. My fear is that, in the absence of such pressure, there is little real hope of doing much more than placing a lid temporarily on the confrontation, leaving out of sight and, thus, out of mind a level of direct violence that could be perceived as 'tolerable' to all except the immediate and helpless victims.

Although the Russians and Chechens, in theory, could out of the four aspects of their conflict solve three (traditional versus modernising society, imperial power versus colonised people and the black hole of lawlessness) bilaterally, in practice, it is quite evident that, at present, they are quite unable to do so. This is due not so much to the exacerbation of the conflict since the declaration of the 'war on terror' after 11 September 2001, as to the exploitation by Putin of his membership of the anti-terrorist coalition to try and impose unilaterally, under the guise of a political settlement, a military solution on Chechnya.

Every time an opportunity for a genuine political solution in Chechnya has appeared, as for example, in the summer/autumn of 2002, events (in this case the Dubrovka theatre siege) have let Putin off the hook. By applying the same yardstick, the assassination of Aslan Maskhadov in March 2005 may be seen to have killed off also the nascent peace talks between the Russian Soldiers' Mothers Committee and representatives of the Maskhadov regime in exile.[8] Literally, as I write these lines, news is breaking of the murder in Moscow of Putin's most consistent critic in Russia, the journalist Anna Politkovskaya. Either Putin is a very lucky politician or there are 'dark forces' in his administration that are working towards achieving, by whatever means, outcomes that are favourable to him.

Given such a situation, the spiral of violence in Chechnya continues. If in May 2004, Basaev's irreconcilables assassinated Kadyrov, in March 2005 the pro-federal forces hit back by murdering Maskhadov, following this up in June 2006 by the assassination of his successor Sadulaev and finally, with the alleged killing of Basaev himself in July 2006. Kadyrov senior was replaced effectively as the Kremlin's choice by his son Ramzan, a strongman with a reputation for thuggish behaviour and torture. It was, after all, as leader of his father's security forces that the younger Kadyrov had finally fulfilled Yermolov's dream of Chechen fighting Chechen, although by no stretch of the imagination as the Pro-consul would have envisaged. Paradoxically, the 'coalition of the willing', having expended so much effort in the 'war on terror' to bring down a strong-arm 'tyrant' like Saddam Hussein, has ensured that among its many unintended consequences has been the establishment and consolidation in Chechnya of a leader who, both in style and rhetoric, appears far closer to the former Iraqi dictator than he is to any pan-European or North American norms of democratic governance.

For the real paradox of the Russo-Chechen conflict is that by failing to achieve the military victory that his advisors such as Patrushev demanded and by opting instead for a policy of 'Chechenisation', Russia appears to have achieved its primary objective of keeping Chechnya as part of the Russian Federation. However, this has arguably been at the cost of losing effective control over Chechen, and potentially, North Caucasian, territory. As things stand today Russia faces losing control not only of Chechnya, but also Ingushetia and Dagestan, as well as facing genuine popular discontent in Karbardino-Balkaria, judging from the fall-out of the *boyeviki* attack on Nalchik in October 2005[9] and North Ossetia, in the wake of the unsatisfactory handling of the Beslan siege and its aftermath.[10]

Russia has also lost its once sizeable ethnic presence in the region. Few right-minded Russians would wish to settle there and Kremlin leverage over Kadyrov and other local leaders seems to wane by the day. The flight from the Caucasus of the once sizeable Russian community has been matched only by a similar flow of immigration to Russia of indigenous peoples of the North Caucasus seeking refuge from the violence that is spreading throughout their home region.[11] Inevitably, both groups will carry with them prejudices reinforced by the terrors they have endured, feeding both 'Caucasophobia' among ethnic Russians and anti-Russians elements of the respective 'cultural narratives' of the Caucasian peoples.

The real and understandable desire of such peoples, including the Chechens – to live according to their Islamic customs and traditions as fully-fledged citizens of their state, be it formally attached to Russia or as a semi-autonomous enclave of Ichkeria, is an option that appears to have been sacrificed at the altar of Russia's, and, even more disturbingly, the West's geopolitical goals.

The danger, as in Palestine, Afghanistan, indeed even in Bradford, is that Muslims, particularly the young and impressionable of fighting age, will perceive this global 'war on terror' as one that is directed by non-Muslims against Muslims, creating heroes and role models of those extremists who are willing to sacrifice themselves by manifesting their strength in the one sphere of modern warfare – faith in the rectitude of their beliefs – in which they appear to be stronger than the West and its secular allies.

I am struck here between the parallels in Chechnya (and Palestine) of the events depicted in Gillo Pontecorvo's classic *The Battle of Algiers*.[12] Although the French military succeed in crushing the wave of Algerian terrorism, it is done by using such means (torture, indiscriminate killings, etc.) that the entire indigenous population, not to mention a good proportion of the French, was alienated and, within a few years, Algeria was liberated. It is rumoured that, during the Iraq War in September 2003, President George W. Bush invited his top military and political advisors to a screening of this film. One can only surmise that either all present left five minutes before the end or, through cognitive consonance and/or dissonance, they just saw what they wanted to see and thus failed signally to grasp the film's object lesson![13]

In Chechnya today, the 'war on terror' has become a self-fulfilling prophecy as the Russians and Americans share a common interest in preventing, by all possible means, the emergence of a radical Islamic state or group of states between the Caspian and Gulf oilfields and Russia's southern borders. Into this volatile mix must be added, however, genuine fears in the Putin administration as to the long-term intentions in this region of the USA, NATO and the EU. The recent belligerent noises emanating from the Kremlin vis-à-vis Georgia would suggest that Russia continues to view its 'Near Abroad' in the same manner as Stalin and his successors in the USSR viewed the peoples' democracies in Eastern Europe. If this is so then Georgia, like Hungary 50 years earlier, would be well advised not to rely on Western assistance to deliver it from its powerful neighbour.

We have noted already the irony of President George W. Bush paraphrasing Stalin's dictum 'he who is not with us, is against us', in the wake of the 9/11 attacks as well as appearing to wave away the collateral damage inflicted in his 'war on terror' with the quintessentially Stalinist formulation; 'you can't make an omelette without breaking eggs'. How ironic, therefore, that more than 50 years after his death, one might reasonably conclude that the Soviet dictator's legacy appears to be alive and well, not just in Russia, but in his rival superpower – the USA! How long, one wonders, before domestic critics of the war in Iraq are routinely called 'enemies of the American people'?

Moreover, but for the whim of Stalin, Chechnya, and perhaps even all of the 'mountain peoples' might have had a status equivalent to that of Estonia, and now be independent. Such concepts, too, as Uzbek and Kazakh nationalism, which have helped to create the very secular Islamic states that Russia and the USA see as both a base and a bastion against Islamic fundamentalism, stem from that same Stalinist policy on ethnic-territorial divisions.

As George Bernard Shaw complained, we learn nothing from history. History, however, as the eminent Russian historian Vassily Klyuchevsky observed over a hundred years ago, has a tendency to make us pay for the lessons that we do not learn! For Russia, the cost has been much more than just two bloody, unwinnable wars, but arguably, the chance of creating, at long last, a state based on a normal, democratic and law-governed existence.

For the West there is a real danger that the very success of counter-terrorist operations in Afghanistan, Palestine and Chechnya will persuade both public and decision-makers alike to widen the spectrum of problems that can be solved by such forceful application of military might, with fairly predictable consequences beyond the short term. Once democracies lose the power to question the 'right' of the application of 'might' on each and every occasion, a slide away from democracy into authoritarianism cannot be ruled out. When 'moderate' voices are ignored and, as a consequence, more 'radical' forms of opposition emerge, the labelling of such legitimate opponents as 'terrorists' is clearly both opportunistic and counter-productive. On the evidence produced here, it would be difficult not to come to the conclusion that this is precisely what is occurring in Russia and that, perhaps, the process has already been, in the main, completed.

The problem is not per se that the current Russian administration (and a significant proportion of the Russian population) thinks that such a policy serves its best interests, so much as the impression given by Western powers that this does not really constitute a problem at all. One could forgive the government of the United Kingdom, for example, for identifying the Russian Federation, like China, as an important commercial partner. The 'war on terror' notwithstanding, one is considerably less comfortable, however, in recognising Russia as a strategic ally, let alone as a 'friend', thus promoting the status of our relationship with this authoritarian regime to an importance comparable to that occupied by France, Germany or the USA. I cannot be alone in feeling uneasy about being counted as a friend of a state which allows its best journalists and oppositionist politicians to be killed, seemingly with impunity, and those of its businessmen who dare to speak out against such crimes to be incarcerated in Siberia.

This policy of averting our collective gaze from the tragedy that is Chechnya undoubtedly has contributed directly to the loss of life of hundreds of thousands of innocent people, including such shining beacons of the values in which we in the West purport to believe as Anna Politkovskaya. Moreover, it has poisoned, figuratively, as well as literally, the economic, physical, political and social environment of much of the North Caucasus in particular, and the rest of Russia in general. The only way to avoid accepting our responsibility in this humanitarian disaster is to ignore it and pretend that it has not happened, a truly shameful and cowardly response. The consequences of so doing, I fear, are all too predictable for all concerned. In this sense the Russo-Chechen conflict should serve as a timely warning to each and every one of us.

At the very beginning of my involvement with the Zakaev extradition hearings in June 2003, I arrived in London without a pair of cufflinks. Walking from my hotel in Russell Square to the Bow Street Magistrates' Court in Covent Garden I passed a traditional gentleman's outfitting store and bought a pair of links shaped liked old computer keys – one bore the word 'Delete', the other 'Escape'. Struck by the serendipity of this purchase, upon meeting Zakaev at the court, I showed him the links, explaining that each represented his possible fate. I promised him, nonetheless, that were he to win his case, I would present them to him, which in November of that year I duly did. Zakaev, thankfully and to my great personal satisfaction, did escape; the future that fate had, and still has in store, for far too many of his people, however, to my deep dismay, remains 'Delete'.

It is high time, perhaps, for all of us who are genuinely concerned at the ongoing trauma that is Chechnya, to roll up our sleeves and do something constructive towards bringing it to an end. This will not only, I believe, serve the interests of the Chechen and Russian peoples, but also reaffirm and consolidate the values which have created the relatively humane societies in which we in the West still are fortunate enough to live.

Notes

Preface

1 Translation in Laurence Kelly, *Tragedy in the Caucasus*, London: Constable, 1977, p. 207.
2 For five different versions of his death, see Ruslan Zhadaev, 'Taina smerti Basaeva' (The secret of Basaev's death) in *Chechenskoe obshchestvo*, 16:81, 25 July 2006, www.chechensociety.net (last accessed 1 August 2006).
3 The current leader of the 'irreconcilable' Chechen forces, Doku Umarov, has already stated that Shamil Basaev 'will undoubtedly occupy the most honourable position in the constellation of Chechen popular heroes; legends and songs will be composed, and books written about him', see Sergei Markedonov, 'An Imperfect Amnesty', posted on *Johnson's Russia List*, #194, 27 August 2006.
4 This e-book is available via www.kavkazcenter.com/eng/help/ebook.shtml (last accessed 1 August 2006).
5 Che Guevara, *Guerrilla Warfare*, New York: Vintage, 1969.
6 Régis Debray, *Revolution in the Revolution*, Pelican Latin American Library, Harmondsworth: Penguin, 1967.
7 Carlos Marighella, 'Mini-Manual of the Urban Guerrilla', in *For the Liberation of Brazil*, Pelican Latin American Library, Harmondsworth: Penguin, 1971.

1 Introduction

1 André Glucksmann, 'If Putin has an Ally, it is Basaev', *The Chechen Society Newspaper*, 13, 4 July 2005.
2 Moshe Gammer, *The Lone Wolf and the Bear: Three Centuries of Russian Defiance of Russian Rule*, London: Hurst, 2006, p. 219.
3 There exists a substantial literature in English on the run up to and conduct of the first Russo-Chechen War. Among the most valuable sources are, in alphabetical order, Vanora Bennett, *Crying Wolf: The Return of War to Chechnya*, London: Pan, 2001; John B. Dunlop, *Russia Confronts Chechnya: Roots of a Separatist Conflict*, Cambridge: Cambridge University Press, 1998; Carlotta Gall and Tom de Waal, *Chechnya: A Small, Victorious War*, London: Pan, 1997; Tracey German, *Russia's Chechen War*, London: RoutledgeCurzon, 2003; Anatol Lieven, *Chechnya: Tombstone of Russian Power*, New Haven: Yale University Press, 1999. Anne Nivat, *Chienne de Guerre: A Woman Reporter Behind the Lines of the War in Chechnya*, translated by Susan Darnton, New York: Public Affairs, 2001; Robert Seely, *Russo-Chechen Conflict, 1800–2000: A Deadly Embrace*, London: Frank Cass, 2001; Sebastian Smith, *Allah's Mountains: Politics and War in the Russian Caucasus*, New York: I.B. Tauris, 1998. For Russian perspectives, in English, that covers both wars, see Dmitri V. Trenin and Aleksei Malashenko with Anatol Lieven, *Russia's Restless Frontier:*

The Chechnya Factor in Post-Soviet Russia, Washington, DC: Carnegie Endowment, 2004 and Anna Politkovskaya, *A Dirty War: A Russian Reporter in Chechnya*, translated by John Crowfoot, London: Harvill Press, 2001.

4 John B. Dunlop, *The 2002 Dubrovka and 2004 Beslan Hostage Crises: A Critique of Russian Counter-Terrorism*, Stuttgart: ibidem-Verlag, 2006.

5 For example by Svante E. Cornell in his 'International reactions to massive human rights violations: the case of Chechnya', *Europe-Asia Studies*, 51:1, January 1999, pp. 85–100.

6 Ibid., p. 97.

7 See I. William Zartman's analysis of these categories in the conference report 'The Economics of War: The Intersection of Need, Creed and Greed', organised on 10 September 2001 (!) at the Woodrow Wilson International Center for Scholars in Washington, DC. www.ipacademy.org/PDF_Reports/econofwar.pdf (last accessed 25 September 2006). I have elected to follow this line of analysis rather than the alternative 'greed' and 'grievance' approach to civil wars advocated by Collier and Hoeffler, see Paul Collier and Anke Hoeffler, 'Greed and grievance in civil war', *Oxford Economic Papers*, 56:4, 2004, pp. 563–595, oep.oxfordjournals.org/cgi/content/full/56/4/563 (last accessed 25 September 2006). A recent critique of this approach may be found in Anthony Vinci, 'Greed-grievance reconsidered: the role of power and survival in the motivation of armed groups', *Civil Wars*, 8:1, March 2006, pp. 25–45.

8 In employing this concept I acknowledge the groundbreaking work of Christoph Zürcher, see Christoph Zürcher and Jan Koehler, 'Institutions and organized violence in post-socialist societies', *Berliner Osteuropa Info*, 17, 2001, p. 49. The term 'violent entrepreneurs' appears to have been used first, although in the context of Russia rather than Chechnya, by Vadim Volkov in his 'Violent entrepreneurship in post-Communist Russia', *Europe-Asia Studies*, 51:5, 1999, pp. 741–754; and was subsequently employed by Georgi M. Derlugian in his 'Che Guevaras in turbans: the twisted lineage of Islamic fundamentalism in Chechnya and Dagestan', *New Left Review*, 237, 1999, pp. 3–27; James Hughes prefers the term 'conflict entrepreneurs' in his 'Chechnya: the causes of a protracted post-Soviet conflict', *Civil Wars*, 4:4, Winter 2001, p. 40. A similar concept – that of 'greedy spoilers' was proposed as far back as 1997 by Stephen J. Stedman, see his 'Spoiler problems in peace processes', *International Security*, 22:2 (1997), pp. 5–53.

9 I have used these terms as understood in the UN lexicon, in which counter-terrorism is seen specifically as a security task while anti-terrorism is viewed as the use of a broad range of political, legal, economic and other instruments, rather than the definitions used in US military doctrine (in which anti-terrorism represents defensive measures to reduce the threat of terrorism), see Ekaterina Stepanova, *Anti-terrorism and Peace-building During and After Conflict*, Stockholm: SIPRI, June 2003, p. 8. For further definitions of these two terms, see Patrick Hayden, 'The war on terrorism and the just use of military force', in Patrick Hayden, Tom Lansford and Robert P. Watson (eds), *America's War on Terror*, Aldershot: Ashgate, 2003, pp. 105–121.

10 For a detailed analysis of the layers of conflict, see John Russell, 'A war by any other name: Chechnya, 11 September and the war on terrorism', in Richard Sakwa (ed.) *Chechnya: From the Past to the Future*, London: Anthem, 2005, pp. 239–264.

11 For a Russian description of 'empire', see Emil Pain, 'V Rossii ogromnyi resurs etnicheskoi nenavisti' (In Russia there are huge reserves of ethnic hatred), *Izvestiya*, 23 March 2004.

12 I do not claim, of course, to have invented this description, it being in common currency by the beginning of the second war, see Sergei Kovalev, 'Putin's war', in *The New York Review of Books*, 10 February 2000. Among the colourful alternative descriptions employed by Russian observers to describe the situation in Chechnya, I might pick out 'pirate kingdom' (*piratskoye korolevstvo*), used by Leonid Radzikhovsky in his interview with Ol'ga Shlyakhtina, 'Chechnya ostayotsya

piratskim korolevstvom' (Chechnya remains a pirate kingdom), www.kavkaz-forum.ru/politic/14153.html (last accessed 25 September 2006).

13 See John Russell, 'Death à la carte', *The World Today*, 61:4, April 2005, pp. 24–25.

14 Mark Franchetti, 'Death of the woman who shamed Moscow', *Sunday Times*, 8 October 2006, p. 6.

15 In Tanya Lokshina in collaboration with Ray Thomas and Mary Mayer (eds), *The Imposition of a Fake Political Settlement in the Northern Caucasus: The 2003 Chechen Presidential Election*, Stuttgart: ibidem-Verlag, 2005, pp. 264–271.

16 Ibid., p. 266.

17 Ibid., p. 265.

18 Stephen Blank, 'Russia's Ulster: the Chechen war and its consequences', *Demokratizatsiya: The Journal of Post-Soviet Democratization*, Winter 2001.

19 W. Joseph Stroube, 'Russia spins global energy spider's web', *Asia Times*, 25 August 2006, accessed on *Johnson's Russia List*, #194, 27 August 2006.

20 Gammer (2006), op. cit., p. 219.

2 The roots of violence in the Russo-Chechen conflict: identifying Galtung's Conflict Triangle

1 Andrei Piontkovsky, 'Russia has lost the war in Chechnya', *Chechnya Weekly*, 4: 37, 16 October 2003.

2 J. Galtung, 'Three approaches to peace: peacekeeping, peacemaking and peacebuilding' in J. Galtung (ed.), *Peace, War and Defense: Essays in Peace Research*, Vol. II, Copenhagen: Christian Ejlers, 1976, pp. 282–304.

3 See, for example, Hugh Miall, Oliver Ramsbotham, Tom Woodhouse, *Contemporary Conflict Resolution*, Cambridge: Polity, 1999, p. 22.

4 United Nations Association of Great Britain and Northern Ireland Briefing (revised 17 February 2004), www.una-uk.org/UN&C/peacemaking.html (accessed 24 February 2004).

5 John Paul Lederach, *Building Peace*, Washington, DC: United States Institute of Peace, 1997.

6 Hugh Miall *et al.*, op. cit., p. 16. Lederach's own triangle is based on a system of bottom-up grass-roots, middle-level and top leaders, ibid., p. 18.

7 J. Galtung, *Peace by Peaceful Means: Peace and Conflict, Development and Civilization*, London: Sage, 1996, p. 112.

8 An earlier version of this table first published in John Russell, 'Obstacles to peace in Chechnya: the scope for international involvement', *Europe-Asia Studies*, 58: 6, September 2006, p. 948.

9 For aspects of the 'Chechen syndrome', see Yuri Zarakhovich, 'Chechnya's walking wounded' *Time Europe*, 28 September 2003, www.time.com/time/europe/html/031006/syndrome.html (last accessed 25 September 2006).

10 This figure is given by Emil Pain in Nairi Hovsepyan and Lyubov Tsukanova, 'Chechnya and Russia. War and peace', *New Times,* December 2003, www.newtimes.ru/ewng/detail.asp?art_id=535, (accessed 23 January 2004).

11 For a good description of this phenomenon, see Stephen L. Webber, 'Introduction: the society-military interface in Russia', in Stephen L. Webber and Jennifer G. Mathers (eds), *Military and Society in Post-Soviet Russia*, Manchester: Manchester University Press, 2006, note 12, pp. 28–29.

12 In March 2005 Human Rights Watch published a briefing paper entitled 'Worse than a war: "disappearances" in Chechnya – a crime against humanity', hrw.org/backgrounder/eca/chechnya0305/ (last accessed 25 September 2006).

13 See UN Commission for Human Rights (UNCHR) report 2001/24 on 'The situation in the Republic of Chechnya in the Russian Federation', expressing 'grave concern' at 'reports indicating disproportionate and indiscriminate use of Russian military

force' and 'strongly condemning' such actions, www.unhchr.ch/huridocda/huri-doca.nsf/(Symbol)/E.CN.4.RES.2001.24.En?Opendocument   (last   accessed   18 August 2006).

14 For a detailed examination of this concept in the Chechen context, see Richard Sakwa, 'Chechnya: a just war fought unjustly?' in Bruno Coppieters and Richard Sakwa (eds), *Contextualising Secession: Normative Studies in Comparative Perspective*. Oxford: Oxford University Press, 2003, pp. 156–186.

15 Steven T. Katz, 'Mass death under communist rule and the limits of "otherness"', in Robert S. Wistrich (ed.), *Demonizing the Other: Antisemitism, Racism and Xeno-phobia*, Amsterdam: Harwood Academic Publishers, 1999, p. 280.

16 See UNCHR report 2001/24, op. cit.

17 See Human Rights Center *Memorial* (Moscow) Appeal to the UN Commission for Human Rights in March 2003, www.memo.ru/eng/memhrc/texts/uno2003b.shtml (last accessed 18 August 2006); part of one of these sweeps is shown in Paul Mitchell's film *Hot Spots: Chechnya*, screened on BBC 4, 4 July 2004.

18 John Reuter, 'Chechnya's suicide bombers: desperate, devout, or deceived?' 16 September 2004, peaceinchechnya.org/reports/SuicideReport/ (last accessed 9 March 2005).

19 This concept is discussed in a number of histories of the Chechen conflict published in Russia; see, for example, Nikolai Grodnensky, *Neokonchennaya voina: istoriya vooruzhennogo konflikta v Chechne* (Unfinished War: the History of the Armed Conflict in Chechnya), Minsk: Kharvest, 2004, p. 5.

20 See Yury Botyakov, 'Abrechestvo – real'nost' i predrassudki' (The Abrek way of life – reality and prejudices), in *Nezavisimaya gazeta,* 29 August 2003; for a good source in English, see Gammer (2006), p. 114.

21 See Coppetiers and Sakwa, op. cit., p. 164.

22 Apart from the titles listed by Guevara, Debray and Marighela (notes 5–7), see John Lee Anderson, *Guerrillas*, London: HarperCollins, 1993; and Walter Laqueur, *Guerrilla: A Historical and Critical Study,* London: Wiedenfeld & Nicholson, 1977.

23 C.W. Blandy, *Chechnya: Normalisation, Conflict Studies Research Centre, Report 40*, June 2003, p. 35.

24 See 'Open Letter to President Bush', dated 10 March 2003, from Vladimir Bukovsky   and   Elena   Bonner,   published   in   FrontPageMagazine.com, www.hrvc.net/west/10–03–2003.htm (last accessed 18 August 2006).

25 For the first Palestinian *intifada*, see Zeev Schiff, *Intifada: The Palestinian Uprising*, New York: Simon & Schuster, 1990; for the second (al-Aqsah) *intifada*, see Roane Carey (ed.), *The New Intifada: Resisting Israel's Apartheid*, New York: Verso, 2001.

26 See Timothy Furnish, 'Ritual beheading in the name of Islam', *Middle East Quarterly*, Spring 2005, accessed on www.meforum.org/article/713 (last accessed 17 August 2006).

27 Among the extensive contemporary literature on this highly-relevant topic, I would pick out the following for a good introduction: Walter Laqueur, *A History of Terrorism*, London: Transaction, 2002; Gus Martin, *Understanding Terrorism: Challenges, Perspectives, and Issues*, London: Sage, 2003; Jonathan White, *Terrorism and Homeland Security: An Introduction*, 5th edn, Belmont, CA: Wadsworth, 2005; Paul Wilkinson, *Terrorism versus Democracy*, 2nd edn, London: Cass, 2006.

28 For an analysis of 'warlordism' (*caudillismo*), see Georgi Derlugian, 'The structures of Chechnya's quagmire', *PONARS Policy Memo*, 309, November 2003, pp. 3–4.

29 Physicians for Human Rights' report of May 2001, 'Endless brutality: war crimes in Chechnya', see www.phrusa.org/research/pdf/chech_report_final.pdf (last accessed 25 September 2006).

30 *My War Gone By, I Miss it So* London: Transworld Publishers, 2000, p. 236, quoted in Cerwyn Moore, 'Reading the hermeneutics of violence: the literary turn and Chechnya', *Global Society*, 20: 2, April 2006, p. 189.

31 See report of 4 August 2004 by the International Helsinki Federation for Human Rights, 'Chechnya: enforced "disappearances", extrajudicial killings and unlawful detentions – an update', www.ihf-hr.org/viewbinary/viewdocument.php?doc_id= 6069 (last accessed 18 August 2006).

32 For the Kremlin's indifference to the ruling by the European Court of Human Rights in favour of the mother of a young Chechen ordered killed by a Russian general, see Anna Politkovskaya, 'Za narushenie prava na zhizn'' (For violating the right to life), *Novaya gazeta*, 57, 31 July 2006. For the Court's ruling, on 27 July 2006, see European Court of Human Rights, 'Russia held responsible for Chechen disappearance', Russian Justice Initiative's, *News*, www.srji.org/en/news/2006/07/10/ (accessed 30 August 2006).

33 See Tom Parfitt, 'The Republic of Fear', *Sunday Times*, 20 August 2006.

34 Aleksandr Solzhenitsyn, *The Gulag Archipelago 1918–1956*, translated by H.T. Willetts, London: Collins and Harvill Press, vols. V–VII, p. 405.

35 Anna Politkovskaya, 'Karatel'nyi sgovor' (Punishment pact), *Novaya gazeta*, 74, 28 September 2006.

36 Ibid. For Dubrovka and Beslan, see Dunlop (2006), op. cit.

37 Sonia Oxley (Reuters), 'Russian troops carry out 10 percent of Chechen kidnaps', published in *Johnson's Russia List*, #9170, 6 June 2005.

38 See, for example, Ruslan Zhadaev, 'One year without Kadyrov, *Chechen Society newspaper*, 9:47, 11 May 2005.

39 Cerwyn Moore, 'Counter-insurgency and counter hostage-taking in the North Caucasus', *Central Asia-Caucasus Analyst*, 23 August 2006.

40 Lawrence A. Uzzell, 'The refugees: "a pattern of intimidation"', The Jamestown Foundation's *Chechnya Weekly*, 4:4, 13 February 2003, www.cdi.org/russia/ 244–14.cfm (last accessed 18 August 2006).

41 For the Russian side, see Open Letter to President Bush, dated 10 March 2003, from long-term Russian dissidents and human rights activists Vladimir Bukovsky and Yelena Bonner, accusing the FSB of being behind many of the protection rackets in Chechnya, published in FrontPageMagazine.com, www.hrvc.net/west/10–03–2003. htm (last accessed 18 August 2006); for the Chechen side, see Jonathan Steele, 'Doing well out of the war: reflections on the stand-off between Russia and Chechnya', *London Review of Books*, 26:20 19 October 2004, on www. selvesandothers.org/ article5936.html (last accessed 25 September 2006).

42 For an interesting discussion on both the ineffectiveness and immorality of torture, see Amos N. Guiora and Erin M. Page, 'The unholy trinity: intelligence, interrogation and torture' (July 2005). Case Legal Studies Research Paper No. 05–13 Available at SSRN: ssrn.com/abstract=758444 (last accessed 18 August 2006).

43 See the Human Rights Watch report of October 2000, entitled '"Welcome to Hell": arbitrary detention, torture and extortion in Chechnya – the Chernokozovo Detention Center', www.hrw.org/reports/2000/russia_chechnya4/detention-center.htm (last accessed 18 August 2006).

44 See Tom Parfitt, 'Putin is silent as fiercest critic is murdered', *Guardian*, 9 October 2006. The article was published posthumously as 'Naznachaem tebya terroristom: antiterroristicheskaya politika pytok na Severnom Kavkaze' (We appoint you as terrorist: the anti-terrorist policy of torture in the North Caucasus), *Novaya gazeta, 78*, 12 October 2006.

45 I.e. the 'fear of persons of Caucasian nationality', see Z. Sikevich, 'The Caucasus and "Caucasus phobia"', translated by Robin Jones for Rosbalt News Agency, 18 December 2002 at www.rosbaltnews.com/2003/02/07/60777.html. (Last accessed 25 September 2006). The term in Russian is 'kavkazofobia', see Zinaida Sikevich, 'Etnichesaya nepriyazn' v massovoi sosnanii rossiyan' (Ethnic hostility in the mass consciousness of Russians), in G. Vitkovskaya and A. Malashenko (eds), *Neterpimost' v Rossii: stariye i noviye fobii* (Intolerance in Russia: Old and New Phobias),

Moscow: Carnegie, 1999, pp. 99–112, subsequently published in English as A. Malashenko and G. Vitkovskaya (eds), *Intolerance in Russia: Old and New Phobias*, Moscow: Carnegie, 1999.

46 www.levada.ru/press/2006091302.html (accessed 15 September 2006).

47 In July 2005, 58 per cent of Russians polled were moderately or decisively for the concept of 'Russia for the Russians', with just 32 per cent against, www.levada.ru/press/2005070410.html (last accessed 22 July 2006).

48 Lev Gudkov and Boris Dubin, 'Svoeobraziye russkogo nationalizma' (Russia's distinctive brand of nationalism), *Pro et Contra*, September–October 2005, p. 9.

49 For a comprehensive account of this phenomenon, see Michael Bhatia (Guest Editor), 'The politics of naming', *Third World Quarterly*, Special Issue, 26:1, 2005.

50 See A. Malashenko and G. Vitkovskaya (eds), *Intolerance in Russia: Old and New Phobias*, Moscow: Carnegie, 1999.

51 See Sergei Kovalev, 'After Chechnya', *The New York Review of Books*, 17 July 1997.

52 Putin asserted in his first state of the union address as president in July 2000 that authority 'should rely on the law and a single, vertical line of executive power'. See 'Mr Putin's two faces, Russia's likely future is growing clearer', the *Guardian*, 12 July 2000.

53 For the importance of cultural narrative in the Armenian case, see Khachig Tololyan, 'Cultural narrative and the motivation of the terrorist', *The Journal of Strategic Studies*, Special Issue: Inside Terrorist Organizations, edited by David C. Rapoport, 10:4, December 1987, pp. 218–233.

54 See V.A. Dmitriev (ed.), *Adat: traditsii i sovremennost'* (*Adat:* Traditions and the Present Day), Moscow-Tbilisi: MNIINK, 2003.

55 For an explanation of *nokhchallah*, see Gammer (2006), pp. 3, 5, 7; and www.chechnyafree.ru/index.php?lng=rus&section=nohrus&row=0 (last accessed 25 September 2006).

56 The role of the concept 'freedom' in the Chechen psyche, it is argued, is as central as it is to the Roma. See Emil Pain and Arkady Popov, 'Vlast' i obshchestvo na barrikadakh' (Power and society at the barricades), *Izvestiya,* 10 February 1995. The traditional Chechen greeting is 'Be Free!' ('Marsha woghiyla' in the masculine form); see also Gammer (2006), op. cit., pp. 5–6.

57 'Russia is digging itself a grave in Chechnya'. Interview by Alan Tskhurbaev in *Chechen Society*, 14 (52), 19 July 2005.

58 See Y. Chesnov, 'Byt' chechentsem: lichnost' i etnicheskiye identifikatsii naroda' (To be a Chechen: individuality and ethnic identification of a nation), www.sakharov-center.ru/chs/chrus04_4.htm. (Last accessed 25 September 2006).

59 See Mayrbek Vachagaev, 'Evolution of the Chechen Jamaat', The Jamestown Foundation's *Chechnya Weekly*, 6:14, 6 April 2005. For activities of the djamaat in, respectively, Dagestan and Kabardino-Balkaria, see 'Djamaat "Shariat": "The Territory of Jihad Extends!"', 2 July 2005, www.kavkazcenter.com/eng/content/2005/07/02/3918.shtml (last accessed 25 September 2006); and 'Napadeniye na Nal'chik' (The attack on Nalchik), www.rian.ru/actual/nalchik_attack_131005/ (last accessed 25 September 2006). See also Andrew McGregor, 'Military Jama'ats in the North Caucasus: A Continuing Threat', The Jamestown Foundation Conference 'The Future of the North Caucasus', 14 September 2006, www.jamestown.org/nccp-91406.php (accessed 27 September 2006).

60 See the report, dated March 1996, for the United States Institute of Peace by Patricia Carley, 'Self Determination: Sovereignty, Territorial Integrity, and the Right to Secession', Peaceworks 7, www.usip.org/pubs/peaceworks/pwks7.html (last accessed 19 August 2006).

61 See his *Modernity at Large: Cultural Dimensions of Globalization*, Minneapolis, MN: University of Minnesota Press, 1996, p. 166, quoted in Harsha Ram, 'Prisoners of the Caucasus: literary myths and media representations of the Chechen conflict',

Berkeley Program in Soviet and Post-Soviet Studies – Working Paper Series, Summer 1999, p. 17, note 37. socrates.berkeley.edu/~bsp/publications/1999_01-ram.pdf (last accessed 25 September 2006).

62 Ol'ga Shlyakhtina in conversation with Sergei Markedonov, 'V Chechne ne postkonfliktnoye uregulirovaniye, a smena pokolenii separatistov (In Chechnya we do not have post-conflict stabilisation, but a change of generations amongst the separatists), www.kavkaz-forum.ru/reconstruction/11702.html?print=on (accessed 5 October 2005).

63 For the Chechen 'rebel' perception of the role of Shari'a in Chechen society, see Movladi Udugov, 'Security in Exchange for Independence', www.kavkazcenter.com/eng/islam/conception/security_for_freedom.shtml (last accessed 19 August 2006).

64 See Simona Piattoni, *Clientelism, Interests, and Democratic Representation: The European Experience in Historical and Comparative Perspective*, Cambridge: Cambridge University Press, 2001; Boris Sokolov characterises Chechnya, Ingushetia, Dagestan and Kabardino-Balkariya as being dominated by 'feudal-type patron–client relations', in 'Kavkaz "otdadut vragam"' (They will hand over the Caucasus to their enemies), www.prognosis.ru/news/secure/2006/2/15/ke.html.

65 Liz Fuller, 'Dmitrii Kozak: troubleshooter or scapegoat?' *RFE/RL Reports, North Caucasus*, 5:25, 27 June 2005.

66 ww1.transparency.org/cpi/2005/cpi2005_infocus.html (last accessed 19 August 2006).

67 www.freedomhouse.org/template.cfm?page=47&nit=366&year=2005 (last accessed 19 August 2006).

68 Ol'ga Shlyakhtina in conversation with Sergei Markedonov, 'V Chechne ne postkonfliktnoye uregulirovaniye, a smena pokolenii separatistov (In Chechnya we do not have post-conflict stabilisation, but a change of generations amongst the separatists), www.kavkaz-forum.ru/reconstruction/11702.html?print=on (accessed 5 October 2005).

69 See the Council of Europe's European Commission Against Racism and Intolerance Third Report on the Russian Federation, adopted on 16 December 2005, www.coe.int/t/e/human_rights/ecri/1-ECRI/2-Country-by-country_approach/Russian_Federation/Russian_Federation_CBC_3.asp (last accessed 19 August 2006).

70 Human Rights Center *Memorial* (Moscow) report, 2 March 2006, 'The Chechen Republic; Consequences of "Chechenization" of the Conflict', www.memo.ru/eng/memhrc/texts/6chechen.shtml (last accessed 18 August 2006).

71 See Russian Justice Initiative's report on Chechnya, *Impunity*, www.srji.org/en/Chechnya/impunity (last accessed 30 August 2006);

72 Asiyet Vazaeva, 'Chechnya tribunal proposed', *Caucasus Reporting Service*, 174, 11 April 2003.

73 For a brief discussion of this concept in the context of the Chechen wars, see John Russell, 'On the side of might', *The World Today*, 56:12, December 2002, pp. 17–18.

74 See 'The New Jews', in *The Economist*, 17 February, 2005, www.economist.com/printedition/displayStory.cfm?Story_ID=3672697 (last accessed 25 September 2006).

75 The literature on this topic is well-known and copious enough to require listing here; suffice to say that political writers at least since Machiavelli have pointed out the 'double-edged sword' that colonialism represents. Jean-Paul Sartre's *Colonialism and Neocolonialism*, London: Routledge, 2001, still represents a good critique of the topic. Perhaps Gillo Pontecorvo's film *The Battle for Algiers* (Italy/Algeria 1965) remains the most accessible and clear exposure of modern colonialism and its role in the development of terrorism.

76 See Sergei Gradirovsky, 'Harvesting new peoples', *Russia in Global Affairs*, 1, January–March 2006.

77 In Maura Reynolds, 'Moscow has Chechnya back – now what?', *Los Angeles Times*, 19 June 2000.

78 For a good introduction to this topic, see Boris Kagarlitsky, 'Nostalgia for Soviet period', *Moscow Times*, 16 September 2000, accessed on www.cdi.org/russia/johnson/4517.html (last accessed 17 August 2006)

79 Susan B. Glasser and Peter Baker, 'Chechnya war a deepening trap for Putin', *Washington Post*, 13 September 2004, p. A01.

80 One of the first articles to note the importance of this factor in post-communist Russian foreign policy was David Kerr's, 'The New Eurasianism: the rise of geopolitics in Russia's foreign policy', *Europe-Asia Studies*, 47:6, September 1995, pp. 977–988.

81 John Squier, 'Civil society and the challenge of Russian gosudarstvennost', *Demokratizatsiya: The Journal of Post-Soviet Democratization*, Spring 2002, pp. 166–183.

82 David Remnick, 'Letter from Moscow: post-imperial blues: billionaire oligarchs, Chechen suicide bombers, generals nostalgic for empire – and the reign of Vladimir Putin', in *The New Yorker*, 13 October 2003, accessed on *Johnson's Russia List*, #7367, 14 October 2003.

83 See Pavel Felgenhauer, 'After the theatre, the drama continues', *The New Statesman*, 4 November 2002, accessed on *Johnson's Russia List*, # 6533, 5 November 2002.

84 See Peter J.S. Duncan, *Russian Messianism: Third Rome, Holy Revolution, Communism and After*, London, Routledge, 2000.

85 See Patricia Carley, op. cit.

86 Quoted in Dov Lynch, '"The enemy is at the gate": Russia after Beslan', *International Affairs*, 81:1, 2005, p. 158.

87 For a discussion of these concepts vis-à-vis Chechnya, see Mike Bowker, 'Russia and Chechnya: the issue of secession', *Nations and Nationalism*, 10:4, 2004, pp. 461–478.

88 A thought-provoking introduction to the concept of 'moral asymmetry' in conflict situations is provided by the Oxford Leverhulme Programme on the Changing Character of War, under Professor Hew Strachan, see ccw.politics.ox.ac.uk/index.asp (last accessed 19 August 2006).

89 A trans-disciplinary research programme on 'Diasporas, Migration and Identities' has been established in the UK. For details, see www.diasporas.ac.uk/ (last accessed 19 August 2006).

90 Although now somewhat overtaken by events, the best reference books on this topic remain Alexandre Bennigsen and S. Enders Wimbush, *Muslims of the Soviet Empire: A Guide*, London: Hurst, 1985; and Yaacov Ro'i, *Islam in the Soviet Union: From World War II to Gorbachev*, London: Hurst, 2000. These have been supplemented more recently by Galina Yemelianova, *Russia and Islam: A Historical Survey*, Basingstoke: Palgrave, 2002.

91 For Sufism, see Mayrbek Vachagaev, 'The role of Sufism in the Chechen resistance', The Jamestown Foundation's *Chechnya Weekly*, 6:16, 28 April 2005; for an historical view, see Anna Zelkina, *In Quest of God and Freedom: Sufi Response to the Russian Advances in the North Caucasus (Chechenya and Daghestan)*, London: Hurst, 2000.

92 See www.globalsecurity.org/military/world/gulf/wahhabi.htm (last accessed 25 September 2006).

93 See Mikhail Delyagin, 'Russia after Putin', quoted in Victor Yasmann, 'Slavic converts to radical Islam pose new threat', *RFE/RL*, 25 August 2006.

94 Yo'av Karny, *Highlanders: A Journey to the Caucasus in Quest of Memory*, New York, Farrar, Straus & Giroux, 2000. See also Ram, op. cit., p. 4.

95 www.mountainman.com.au/un_ddri.html (last accessed 19 August 2006).

96 For the Palestinian precedent, see their 'Declaration of Independence', 15 November 1988, www.palestine-net.com/politics/indep.html (last accessed 19 August 2006).

97 For a Chechen view on this, in English, see Udugov, op. cit. For A Russian view, see Al'fred Kokh, 'Kak ya ponimayu chechentsev. Chetyre vzlgyada' (How I understand the Chechens. Four viewpoints), 3 September 2005, www.polit.ru/analytics/2005/09/03/4vzglyada.html (accessed on 19 October 2005).

98 Anna Politkovskaya, 'Vsya Chechnya v krugu sem'i' (All of Chechnya surrounded by the family), *Novaya gazeta*, 41, 9 June 2005

99 Verse 4 of the National Anthem of Chechnya-Ichkeria contains the words: 'Never will we appear submissive before anyone, Death or Freedom – we can choose only one way', www.amina.com/article/anthem.html (last accessed 30 November 2002).

100 The economist, Professor Adam Albekov, speaking at the Strasbourg Round Table organised by PACE in March 2005, see 'Nekrugly krugly stol' (The Unrounded Round Table), *Chechenskoye obshchestvo*, 6:44, 29 March 2005.

101 For a good discussion of the implications of the absence of aspects of modern society in Russia, including a law-governed state, see Alexander M. Domrin, 'Ten years later: society "civil society," and the Russian state', *The Russian Review*, 62:2, pp. 193–211.

102 'The Political Situation in the Chechen Republic: measures to increase democratic stability in accordance with Council of Europe standards', Doc. 10276, 17 September 2004, assembly.coe.int/Documents/Working/Docs/doc04/EDOC10276.htm (last accessed 5 May 2005).

103 See John Baylis and Steve Smith (eds), *The Globalization of World Politics: An Introduction to International Relations*, 2nd edn, Oxford: Oxford University Press, 2001; in the context of terrorism, see Mary Kaldor, 'Terrorism as regressive globalisation', 25 September 2003, www.opendemocracy.net/debates/article-3–77–1501.jsp (last accessed 25 September 2006).

104 Best exemplified, of course, by Samuel P. Huntington's seminal article, 'The clash of civilizations', published in *Foreign Affairs*, 72:3, Summer 1993, pp. 22–49; The theme was picked by Russian journalists covering the Chechen war, see Igor Rotar', 'Konflikt tsivilizatsii na Severnom Kavkaze' (The clash of civilisations in the North Caucasus), *Nezavisimaya gazeta*, 23 May 1998.

105 'Terror na Kavkaze: druz'ya i vragi' (Terror in the Caucasus: Friends and Foes), *Izvestiya*, 10 June 2005.

106 Links between poor economic performance and the establishment of the rule of law in transition countries such as Russia are explored in Ksenia Yudaeva, Maria Gorban, Vladimir Popov and Natalia Volchkova, 'Down and Up the Stairs: Paradoxes of Russian economic growth', www.gdnet.org/pdf/draft_country_studies/Russia_final.pdf (last accessed 19 August 2006)

107 See M. Howard, 'Mistake to declare this a "war"', *RUSI Journal*, 146:6, December 2001, pp. 1–4.; see also Paul Rogers, *A War on Terror: Afghanistan and After*, London: Pluto, 2004.

108 See his 'The wrong war', *Foreign Affairs*, 81:4, July/August 2002, p. 34.

109 See Domrin, op. cit.; Marcia A. Weigle, 'On the road to the Civic Forum: state and civil society from Yeltsin to Putin', *Demokratizatsiya: The Journal of Post-Soviet Democratization*, Spring 2002, pp. 117–146.

110 www.levada.ru/press/2006091302.html (accessed 15 September 2006).

111 See 'Grigoryants comments on Civic Forum', The Jamestown Foundation's *Chechnya Weekly*, 2:44, 11 September 2001.

112 Ram, op. cit., p. 4.

113 'Russia 2005: the Logic of Backsliding', *New Europe Review*, 2:3, 2005, accessed on *Johnson's Russia List*, #9172, 8 June 2005.

114 For an account of the main pro-Russian Chechen forces, see Aleksei Makarkin, 'Alu

Alkhanov – novy chechensky vybor Kremlya' (Alu Alkhanov – the Kremlin's new Chechen choice), www.politcom.ru/2004/analit139.php (last accessed 25 September 2006).

115 See Musa Muradov, 'Navstrechu referendumu: Ogranichenny izbytochny kontingent' (Towards the referendum: the limited surplus contingent), *Kommersant''*, 4 March 2003. The Russian journalist, Vadim Rechkalov, claims that "in the many times I have been to Chechnya over the past several years I have never met a single Russian soldier or FSB official who knew the Chechen language", 'Budet lokal'nye stychki s zhertvami do 100 chelovek, a voiny ne budet' (There will be local skirmishes with up to 100 victims, but there will be no war), *Izvestiya*, 2 August 2004.

116 See Yaroslava Tan'kova, 'Pochemy russkie stanovyatsya islamskimi terroristami' (Why Russians become Islamic terrorists), *Komsomol'skaya pravda*, 16 August 2006, www.kp.ru/daily/23756/56219/ (last accessed on 30 August 2006).

117 The title of an article by Tom de Waal in the *Guardian*, 30 August 2004 (just two days *before* the beginning of the Beslan siege).

3 A tragic history: unresolved contradictions in the Russo-Chechen relationship

1 See 'Chechen Resistance; myth and reality', published in *Accord* 16, www.c-r.org/accord/engage/accord16/06.shtml (accessed 23 June 2006).

2 See Justin Marozzi, *Tamerlane: Sword of Islam, Conqueror of the World,* London, HarperCollins, 2004, pp. 194–197.

3 Ibid., p. 170.

4 Alexander Cherkasov, 'The Chechen maze: looking for a way out', in Tanya Lokshina, Ray Thomas and Mary Mayer (eds), *The Imposition of a Fake Political Settlement in the Northern Caucasus: the 2003 Chechen Presidential Election,* Stuttgart: ibidem-Verlag, 2006, p. 31.

5 For an analysis of the layers of conflict, see John Russell, 'A war by any other name: Chechnya, 11 September and the war on terrorism', in Richard Sakwa (ed.) *Chechnya: From the Past to the Future,* London: Anthem, 2005, pp. 239–264.

6 Gammer (2006), op. cit., p. 16. For a detailed account of the Russian conquest of the Caucasus, see John F. Baddeley, *The Russian Conquest of the Caucasus*, London: Longmans, Green and Co., 1908 (reprinted by Elibron Classics, 2004); and Gammer (2006) op. cit.; see also the latter's 'Russian strategies in the conquests of Chechnia and Dagestan, 1825–1859' in Marie Broxup (ed.), *The North Caucasus Barrier: The Russian Advance Towards the Muslim World*, New York: St. Martin's, 1992, pp. 45–61.

7 Ivan Rybkin, *Consent in Chechnya, Consent in Russia,* London: Lytten Trading, 1998, p. 157.

8 Gammer (2006), op. cit., p. 35.

9 Gammer (2006), op. cit., p. 170.

10 For Deir Yassin (9 April 1948) see Benny Morris, 'The Arab-Israeli War', www.crimesofwar.org/thebook/arab-israeli-war.html (last accessed 25 September 2006); for Wounded Knee (29 December 1890), see Dee Brown, *Bury My Heart at Wounded Knee: An Indian History of the American West*, New York: Owl Books, 1970.

11 For Yermolov's own account of his early career (and a striking portrait of the General on the cover), see Alexey Yermolov (edited by Alexander Mikaberidze), *The Czar's General: The Memoirs of a Russian General During the Napoleonic Wars*, Welwyn Garden City: Ravenhall Books, 2005.

12 Gammer (2006), op. cit., p. 37.

13 Gammer (2006), op. cit., p. 35.

14 Marie Bennigsen, 'Chechnia: political developments and strategic implications for

the North Caucasus', *Central Asian Survey*, 18:4, December 1999, p. 536; Also reported in Ilyas Akhmadov, *The Russian-Chechen Tragedy: The Way to Peace and Democracy: Conditional Independence Under an International Administration*, accessed on peaceinchechnya.org/peace/peace_akhmadov2.htm.

15 Gammer (2006), op. cit., p. 39.

16 Anna Politkovskaya, 'Ramzan Kadyrov – krasa Chechni' (Ramzan Kadyrov – the beautiful face of Chechnya), *Novaya gazeta*, 42, 5 June 2006.

17 Gammer (2006), op. cit., p. 10.

18 In Jean-Christophe Peuch, 'Chechnya: ten years after – the logic behind the first Chechen war', *RFE/RL Features,* 10 December 2004.

19 Gammer (2006), op. cit., p. 58.

20 Sergei Kovalev, 'After Chechnya', *The New York Review of Books*, 17 July 1997.

21 Susan B. Glasser and Peter Baker, 'Chechnya war a deepening trap for Putin', *Washington Post*, 13 September 2004, p. A01.

22 Boris Sokolov, 'Kavkaz "otdadut vragam"' (They will hand over the Caucasus to their enemies), www.prognosis.ru/news/secure/2006/2/15/ke.html (last accessed 15 February 2006).

23 Valentina Melnikova, of the Russian Soldiers' Mothers Committee released the figure of 25,000 on 4 May 2004, during an interview on the radio station, Ekho Moskvy. See Charles Gurin, 'Group claims 25,000 Russian soldiers have died in Chechnya', The Jamestown Foundation's *Eurasia Daily Monitor*, 1: 3, 5 May 2004. For the activities of the SMC, see Valerie Zawilskie, 'Saving Russia's sons: the soldiers' mothers and the Russian Chechen wars', in Stephen L. Webber and Jennifer G. Mathers (eds) *Military and Society in Post-Soviet Russia*, Manchester: Manchester University Press, 2006, pp. 228–229, note 12.

24 Paul F. Kisak, 'Recently declassified Soviet war and U.S. covert casualties', www.geocities.com/echomoscow/warcasualties.html (last accessed 25 September 2006).

25 Gammer (2006), op. cit., p. 114.

26 Ibid.

27 Gammer (2006), op. cit., p. 38.

28 Gammer (2006), op. cit., p. 158. The harsh treatment of the Chechens by the Soviets followed in spite of the support lent by Chechen fighters to the Red Army against Denikin's White forces in the region during the Russian Civil War, see Abdurrahman Avtorkhanov, 'The Chechens and Ingush during the Soviet period and its antecedents', in Marie Bennigsen Broxup (ed.) *The North Caucasus Barrier*, New York: St Martin's, 1992, p. 155.

29 www.chechnya-mfa.info/legal/1.htm (last accessed 25 September 2006).

30 Dunlop (2006), op. cit., p. 142.

31 Gammer (2006), op. cit., pp. 214–218.

32 *Time*, 4 March 1996.

33 For an account of the deportations, see: Robert Conquest, *The Nation Killers: The Soviet Deportation of Nationalities,* New York: Macmillan, 1970; and Aleksandr M. Nekrich, *The Punished Peoples: The Deportation and Fate of Soviet Minorities at the End of the Second World War*, New York: Norton, 1978.

34 The title given in Russian ('Malen'kaya pobedonosnaya voina') to an article by Yury Shchekochikin in *Literaturnaya gazeta,* 2 August 1995, in an ironic reference to the quick victory over Japan predicted incorrectly by Tsar Nicholas II in 1904. It was also adopted as a subtitle of an account of the Russo-Chechen war by two Moscow-based Western journalists; see Carlotta Gall and Thomas de Waal, *Chechnya: A Small Victorious War*, London: Pan, 1997.

35 *Izvestiya,* 29 November 1994.

36 For a survey of this clash, see Richard Sakwa, 'Chechnya: the pre-politics of partition', *London Centre of International Relations, Working Paper*, no. 4, 2001.

37　A Russian interpretation of this may be found in Yury Mironov 'Oslepleniye nenavist'yu' (Blinded by hate), pravda.ru/hotspots/2001/12/18/34908.html.

38　In an attempt to render the difference in English between 'russkie' (ethnic Russians) and 'rossiyane' (citizens of the Russian Federation), Bill Bowring has suggested that the latter be termed 'Rossians', see his 'Austro-Marxism's last laugh? The struggle for recognition of national-cultural autonomy for Rossians and Russians', *Europe-Asia Studies*, 54:2, 2002, pp. 229–250.

39　See Andrei Cherkizov, 'Snyatoye obvineniye – islamofobiya ne pomekha' (The accusation is withdrawn – Islamophobia is no obstacle), in ntvru.com/chas/15Nov2001/fobia.html (last accessed 25 September 2006).

40　*Segodnya*, 17 December 1994.

41　'Doku Umarov: "Russkaya armiya v Chechnye vydokhlas"' (Doku Umarov: 'The Russian army in Chechnya has exhausted itself'), *Radio Svoboda*, 15 July 2005, www.chechenpress.com (last accessed 15 July 2005).

42　David Remnick, *Resurrection: The Struggle for a New Russia*, New York: Random House, 1997, p. 266.

43　*Novoye vremya*, 52, 2000, p. 21.

44　Gammer (2006), op. cit., pp. 5–6; see also Lyoma Usmanov, 'The Chechen nation; a portrait of ethnical features', 9 January 1999, www.truth-and-justice.info/chechnat.html (last accessed 25 September 2006).

45　Gammer (2006), op. cit., p. 7.

46　www.international-alert.org/simple/projects/fsu/chechen2.htm, p. 3. Russian popular opposition to the first war has been well documented, see, for example, Anatol Lieven, *Chechnya: Tombstone of Russian Power*, New Haven: Yale University Press, 1999, pp. 196–197.

47　John Russell, 'On the side of might', *The World Today*, 56:12, December 2002, pp. 17–18.

48　Mary Kaldor, 'Terrorism as regressive globalisation', Open Democracy website, 25 September 2003, www.opendemocracy.net/debates/article-3-77-1501.jsp (last accessed 25 September 2006).

49　For details of the 'information war', see T.L. Thomas, 'Manipulating the mass Consciousness: Russian and Chechen "Information War" Tactics in the Second Chechen-Russian Conflict', in Mrs A.C. Aldis (ed.) 'The Second Chechen War', *Conflict Studies Research Centre, Report P31*, June 2000, pp. 112–129.

50　James Hughes, 'Chechnya: the causes of a protracted post-Soviet conflict', *Civil Wars*, 4:4, Winter 2001, pp. 11–48; Ruslan Khasbulatov, 'Gosudarstvo, politika i separtizm' (State, politics and separatism), *Nezavisimaya gazeta*, 14 December 2000; and Valeriy Tishkov, *Ethnicity, Nationalism and Conflict In and After the Soviet Union*, London: Sage, 1997, p. 186 have warned against romanticising 'ethnic' components in the Russo-Chechen conflict. However, these components clearly remain a factor in the unresolved confrontation.

51　See John Russell, 'Mujahedeen, mafia, madmen: Russian perceptions of Chechens during the wars in Chechnya, 1994–96 and 1999–2001', *Journal of Communist Studies and Transition Politics*, 18:1, March 2002, pp. 73–96.

52　An account of the early years of this transition may be found in Robert Clyde, *From Rebel to Hero: the image of the Highlander, 1745–1830*, East Linton: Tuckwell Press, 1998.

53　Matt Bivens, 'An American fighter's war in Chechnya', www.themoscowtimes.com/stories/2003/07/21 (accessed 25 July 2003).

54　Harsha Ram, 'Prisoners of the Caucasus: literary myths and media representations of the Chechen conflict', *Berkeley Program in Soviet and Post-Soviet Studies – Working Paper Series*, Summer 1999, p. 6.

55　Lev Tolstoi, *Hadji-Murat*, Moscow, Khudozhestvennaya literatura, 1965.

56　'Cossack Lullaby' by Mikhail Lermontov, translated in Laurence Kelly, *Tragedy in the Caucasus,* London: Constable, 1977, p. 207. A documentary film about the current conflict, called 'Chechen Lullaby' (Nino Kirtadze, France, 2000) commences with a reading in Russian from this poem.

57 See, for example, www.abrek.vov.ru/ (accessed 19 November 2002).

58 The word *razboinik* (robber) can also be used in an affectionate, jocular sense, particular when addressing children, to mean a 'scamp' or a 'scallywag'.

59 Yury Botyakov, 'Abrechestvo – real'nost' i predrassudki' (The Abrek way of life – reality and prejudices), in *Nezavisimaya gazeta,* 29 August 2003.

60 See Khachig Tololyan, op. cit., pp. 218–233.

61 See the report on Chechnya in 1992 of the International Alert fact-finding commission, p. 3, www.international-alert.org/simple/projects/fsu/chechen2.htm (accessed 15 November 2002).

62 Charles King poses this question in his 'Crisis in the Caucasus: a new look at Russia's Chechen impasse', *Foreign Affairs,* 82:2, March/April, 2003, pp. 134–138.

63 Al'fred Koch 'Kak ya ponimayu chechentsev. Chetyre vzglyada' (How I understand the Chechens. Four viewpoints), Polit.ru website, 3 September 2005, www.polit.ru/analtics/2005/09/03/4vzglyada_print.html (accessed 19 October 2005).

64 Ol'ga Shlyakhtina in conversation with Sergei Markedonov, 'V Chechne ne postkonfliktnoye uregulirovaniye, a smena pokolenii separatistov (In Chechnya we do not have post-conflict stabilisation, but a change of generations amongst the separatists), www.kavkaz-forum.ru/reconstruction/11702.html?print=on (accessed 5 October 2005).

65 For a later account of this theme see his interview, published on 18 December 2003, with Peter Lavelle, United Press International's Moscow-based analyst, untimely-thoughts.com/?art=268, (last accessed 25 September 2006).

66 From 'Eurasia Insight', 14 September 2001, www.reliefweb.int/w/R (accessed 11 December 2001).

67 'Chechenskaya voina mozhet prodlit'sya do 2020 goda' (The Chechen war could last until 2020), zakaev.ru/turnover/comment/15042.html (last accessed 25 September 2006).

68 Emil Pain (2004), op. cit.

69 Ariel Cohen, 'Chechnya: New Dimensions of the Old Crisis', *Russian Outlook: AEI Online,* 1 February 2003, www.aei.org/include/pub_print.asp?pubID=15848 (last accessed 25 September 2006). Putin's *polpred* in the North Caucasus, Dmitry Kozak, is said to have discussed the building of a wall with Israeli ministers, see 'Is Moscow planning to wall off Chechnya?', The Jamestown Foundation's *Eurasia Daily Monitor,* 6:42, 10 November 2005.

70 See Nairi Hovsepyan and Lyubov Tsukanova, 'Chechnya and Russia. War and peace', *New Times,* December 2003, www.newtimes.ru/eng/detail.asp?art_id=535 (last accessed 25 September 2006); For an American viewpoint, see David Remnick, *Resurrection: The Struggle for a New Russia,* New York, Random House, 1997, p. 266; For an earlier Russian view, see Sergei Kovalev, 'After Chechnya', *The New York Review of Books,* 17 July 1997.

71 A feature of the administration of Putin (himself, of course, a former head of the FSB) is the extremely high proportion of former security chiefs in key positions. See Gregory Feifer, 'Russia: President boosts power of security services', *Centre for Defense Information Weekly,* no. 248, www.cdi.org/russia/248–16.cfm (last accessed 25 September 2006).

72 For an overview of the SVR, see Gordon Bennett, 'The SVR: Russia's intelligence Service, March 2000, www.fas.org/irp/world/russia/svr/c103-gb.ht

73 Interview with Andrei Uglanov, 'Pobeda vlasti; zhertva prinyata (Victory for the regime; the sacrifice is accepted), *Argumenty i fakty,* no. 50, 10 December 2003.

74 Ol'ga Kryshtanovskaya, 'Rezhim Putina: liberal'naya militokratiya?' (Putin's regime: a liberal militocracy?), *Pro et Contra,* 7:4, Autumn 2002, p. 162. Ivan

Rybkin provides very similar figures for 2002, estimating that 26 per cent of Putin's administration is drawn from the security services, compared to 3.6 per cent of Gorbachev's, see 'Towards Peace in Chechnya', Carnegie Endowment for International Peace, Russian and Eurasian Program, 23 October 2002, www.ceip.org/files/events/events.asp?pr=2&EventID=525 (15 November 2002).

75 'Mr Putin's two faces: Russia's likely future is growing clearer', Leader in the *Guardian*, 12 July 2000.

76 As noted by Moscow University professor, Leonid Smirnyagin, an expert on federalism, and quoted by Paul Goble, 'Eye on Eurasia: Putin's failing federalism', UPI, 2 March 2003, www.interestalert.com/brand/siteia.shtml?Story=st/sn/03020004aaa012e8.upi&Sys=p (accessed 3 March 2005).

77 Anatol Lieven, 'Nightmare in the Caucasus', *The Washington Quarterly*, Winter, 2000, p. 149.

78 The connection between 'failed' states and the rise of terrorism, although not specifically directed at Chechnya, is forcefully argued in Robert I. Rotberg, 'Failed states in a world of terror', *Foreign Affairs*, 81:4, July/August 2002, pp. 127–140; for a quite different view on what constitutes a 'rogue state' in the contemporary world, see Noam Chomsky, *Rogue States: The Rule of Force in World Affairs,* London: Pluto, 2000.

79 Federation of American Scientists, *The Chechen Chronicles 1999*, www.fas.org/man/dod-101/ops/war/2000/01/chechen/185.htm (last accessed 11 December 2001).

80 A useful Russian perspective on this dilemma is provided by Zinaida Sikevich, 'Process of National Self-Determination', a special for the Rosbalt News Agency on 18 February 2003, translated by Robin Jones, www.rosbaltnews.com/2003/02/19/61421.html (last accessed 3 March 2003).

81 Ravil Zaripov, 'Interv'yu s generalem Aleksandrom Lebedym' (Interview with General Aleksandr Lebed), *Komsomol'skaya pravda*, 19 March, 1996

82 *The Russia Journal*, 22–28 March 1999.

83 Yuri N. Maltsev, 'Russia's war on Chechnya', 28 October 2002, www.mises.org/fullstory.aspx?control=1080 (accessed 7 March 2005).

84 Article 8, point 4, forbids the creation and functioning of social organisations that aim to violate the territorial integrity of the Russian Federation. The Russian president is also given the right to remove the elected president of Chechnya (Article 72d). See www.chechnya.gov.ru/republic/const/ (last accessed 25 September 2006).

85 Among the numerous sources on this topic I would recommend an excellent article by a Chechen still living in the war zone, that covers many of the wide range of abuses committed in Chechnya, see Imran Ismailov, 'Paradoxes of the war in Chechnya', *Prague Watchdog*, 31 October 2002, watchdog.cz/index.php?show=000000–000005–000001–000119&lang=1 (Last accessed 25 September 2006); Among good articles by Russians to appear on this topic are Pavel Felgenhauer, 'The Russian army in Chechnya', Crimes of War Project, 18 April 2003, crimesofwar.org/print/chechnya/chech-felgenhauer-print.html (last accessed 25 September 2006); Anna Politkovsaya, 'S kem vesti peregovory v Chechnye (With whom we should negotiate with in Chechnya), *Novaya gazeta*, 71, 1 October 2001; for hostage taking by the Chechen side, see Valery Zhuravel' and Viktor Velichkovsky, 'Pokhishcheniya prodolzhayutsya' (The abductions continue), *Nezavisimoye voennoye obozreniye*, 23 August 2002, nvo.ng.ru/printed/wars/2002–08–23/2_help.html (last accessed 25 September 2006); for Western viewpoints, see Jeremy Putley, 'Crime without punishment: Russian Policy in Chechnya', 28 July 2003, www.opendemocracy.net/debates/article-2-95-1388.jsp (last accessed 25 September 2006); and Anne Nivat, 'Chechnya: brutality and indifference', Crimes of War Project, 6 January 2003, www.crimesofwar.org/print/onnews/chechnya-print.html (last accessed 25 September 2006).

86 For the experience of the Chechens in exile, see Michaela Pohl, '"It cannot be that

our graves will be here": the survival of Chechen and Ingush deportees in Kaza-khstan, 1944–1957', *Journal of Genocide Research*, 4:3, September 2002, pp. 401–430.

87 Timur Aliev, 'Chechen heroes of the Soviet war', *Chechen Society Newspaper*, 9:47, 11 May 2005, trans. Susan Sly.

88 See www.chechnyafree.ru/index.php?lng=eng&section=fwareng&row=4 (Last accessed 25 September 2006).

89 Steven T. Katz, 'Mass death under Communist rule and the limits of "otherness"', in Robert S. Wistrich (ed.) *Demonizing the Other: Antisemitism, Racism and Xeno-phobia*, Amsterdam: Harwood Academic Publishers, 1999, p. 280.

90 See Yan Chesnov, 'Byt' chechentsem: lichnost' i etnicheskiye identifikatsii naroda' (To be a Chechen: individuality and ethnic identification of a nation), www.sakharov-center.ru/chs/chrus04_4.htm (last accessed 25 September 2006).

91 For adat, see V.A. Dmitriev (ed.), *Adat: traditsii i sovremennost'* (*Adat*: Traditions and the Present Day), Moscow-Tbilisi: MNIINK, 2003; for *nokhchallah*, see www.chechnyafree.ru/index.php?lng=rus&section=nohrus&row=0 (last accessed 25 September 2006).

92 Stephen Handelman, *Comrade Criminal: The Theft of the Second Russian Revolution*, London: Michael Joseph, 1994, p. 39.

93 Martin McCauley, *Bandits, Gangsters and the Mafia: Russia, the Baltic States and the CIS Since 1992*, London: Pearson Education, 2001.

94 Handelman, op. cit., p. 223.

95 The Amnesty International report on Chechnya, dated 23 June 2004, is entitled 'Normalization in whose eyes?', web.amnesty.org/library/print/ENGEUR 460272004 (last accessed 25 September 2006).

96 Mayrbek Vachagaev, 'The role of Sufism in the Chechen resistance', The Jamestown Foundation's *Chechnya Weekly*, 6:16, 28 April 2005.

97 See Julie Wilhelmsen, 'Between a rock and a hard place: the Islamisation of the Chechen separatist movement', *Europe-Asia Studies*, 57:1, January 2005, pp. 35–39.

98 John Russell, 'Exploitation of the "Islamic Factor" in the Russo-Chechen conflict before and after 11 September 2001', *European Security*, 11:4, Winter 2002, pp. 96–109.

99 In the Freedom House 'Nations in Transit' Democracy Scores for 2005, Russia (5.61) was sandwiched between Kosovo (5.32) and Kyrgyzstan (5.64). 1 represents the highest and 7 the lowest level of democracy. www.freedomhouse.org/research/ nitransit/2005/addendum2005.pdf (accessed 30 March 2005).

100 Poll conducted by the Levada organisation on 24 March 2005, see www.levada/ru/press/2005032402.html (accessed 31 March 2005).

101 See Fiona Hill, 'Kremlin Stage-Managing Chechen Parliamentary Elections', inter-view on 22 November 2005 with the US Council of Foreign Relations, www.cfr.org/publication/9268/hill.html?breadcrumb=default (last accessed 25 Sep-tember 2006).

102 See Moscow News, 4 February 2005, 'UK broadcasts Basayev interview despite Russian protests', www.mosnews.com/news/2005/02/04/channel4ignore.shtml (last accessed 25 September 2006).

103 See David Gollust, 'US says network had legal right to carry interview with Chechen rebel leader', 29 July 2005, www.voanews.com/english/archive/ 2005–07/2005–07–29-voa63.cfm?CFID=13056619&CFTOKEN=34271962 (last accessed 25 September 2006).

104 www.levada.ru/chechnya.html (last accessed 25 September 2006)

105 www.levada.ru/chechnya.html (last accessed 25 September 2006)

106 On 3 March 2006, the Levada Centre reported that 64 per cent of Russians polled were for peace negotiations and just 21 per cent for continuing military operations in Chechnya, www.levada.ru/press/2006030303.html (last accessed 8 March 2006).

107 www.levada.ru/press/2006020708.html (last accessed 25 September 2006).

108 www.levada.ru/press/2006083102.html (last accessed 15 September 2006).
109 Dmitri Trenin, Carnegie Endowment for International Peace Policy Brief, 28, November 2003, *The Forgotten War: Chechnya and Russia's Future*, p. 4.
110 3 March 2006, www.levada.ru/press/2006030303.html (last accessed 8 March 2006).
111 Ironically, Solzhenitsyn has become an outspoken supporter of Putin's Chechen policy; see Nick Paton Walsh, 'Comrades fall out in Russia's battle of the dissidents', *Guardian*, 6 July, 2002.
112 See the monitoring accounts of the 2003 Chechen presidential election by the Moscow Helsinki Group. For example, Ruslan Umarov, 'Otvety Akhmata Kadyrova na voprosy Internet-SMI "Kavkazsky Uzel"' (Akhmat Kadyrov's answers to questions of the "Caucasus Junction" internet site), www.mhg.ru/24957D5/26E7F5C (last accessed 25 September 2006). These accounts have been gathered together and translated into English in Tanya Lokshina, Ray Thomas and Mary Mayer (eds), *The Imposition of a Fake Political Settlement in the Northern Caucasus: The 2003 Chechen Presidential Election*, Stuttgart: ibidem-Verlag, 2006. For Umarov's interview with Kadyrov, see pp. 60–64.

4 Of wolves and werewolves: demonisation in the Russo-Chechen confrontation

1 Quoted in Gammer (2006), op. cit., p. v.
2 Guest Editor: Michael Bhatia, 'The politics of naming', *Third World Quarterly*, Special Issue, 26:1, 2005.
3 At time of Dubrovka, www.greatestjeneration.com/archives/000552.php (last accessed 25 September 2006).
4 See Vyacheslav Mironov, *Ya byl na etoi voine* (I was in that war), original was published in 1995 online, www.artofwar.spb.ru:8101/mironov/index_tale_mironov.html. The English translation (by Alex Dokin), 'Assault on Grozny Downtown' was published in 2001 online, lib.ru/MEMUARY/CHECHNYA/chechen_war.txt (last accessed 25 September 2006)
5 As seen in the Channel 4 documentary film *The Betrayed* (directed by Clive Gordon), 1995.
6 See, for example, his admission that he organised the Beslan operation, published on the pro-independence Chechen website *Daymohk* on 17 September 2004, www.daymohk.info/cgi-bin/orsi3/index.cgi?id=8428;idt=17200409;section=1 (accessed 7 October 2004).
7 Johanna Nichols and Arbi Vagapov, *Chechen–English and English–Chechen Dictionary*, London: RoutledgeCurzon, 2004, p. 465.
8 Gammer (2006), op. cit., p. 20.
9 For an updated analysis of Russian demonisation of the Chechens, see John Russell, 'Terrorists, bandits, spooks and thieves: Russian demonisation of the Chechens prior to and since 9/11', *Third World Quarterly*, 26:1, 2005, pp. 101–116.
10 This was claimed by Maskhadov's successor, Abdul-Khalim Sadulaev in an interview given to the *Kavkaz-Tsentr* website on 8 March 2006 (the first anniversary of Maskhadov's death), www.kavkaz.org.uk/russ/2006/03/08/42656.shtml (accessed 8 March 2006).
11 John Russell, 'Mujahedeen, mafia, madmen: Russian perceptions of Chechens during the wars in Chechnya, 1994–96 and 1999–2001' *Journal of Communist Studies and Transition Politics*, 18:1, March 2002, pp. 73–96.
12 Frederick J. Hacker, *Crusaders, Criminals, Crazies: Terror and Terrorism in Our Time*, New York: Norton, 1976.
13 Jonathan R. White, *Terrorism: An Introduction*, 2nd edn, Belmont, CA: Wadsworth, 1998, p. 24.

14 Johan Galtung introduced this with his concept of 'topdogs versus underdogs', see his *Peace. Research. Education. Action: Essays in Peace Research*, Vol. 1, Copenhagen: Christian Ejlers, 1975, pp. 23–24.
15 *Washington Post*, 10 September 1995.
16 Gammer (2006), op. cit., p. 166.
17 *Time*, 4 March 1996.
18 *Argumenty i fakty*, 38, September 2000, p. 6.
19 *Argumenty i fakty*, 44, October 2000, p. 23.
20 *Memorial*, along with the Russian Soldiers' Mothers Committee and the Moscow branch of the Helsinki Monitoring Group are among Russian NGOs singled out for praise for their work on monitoring human rights violations in Chechnya in reports by PACE. See Document 10276, dated 17 September 2004, 'The political situation in the Chechen Republic: measures to increase democratic stability in accordance with Council of Europe standards', assembly.coe.int/Documents/WorkingDocs/doc04/EDOC10276.htm (accessed 7 March 2005).
21 See www.memo.ru (last accessed 25 September 2006).
22 Its website is www.coe.int/ (last accessed 25 September 2006).
23 *Novoye vremya*, 40, 1999, p. 9.
24 *The Economist*, 24 October 1994, p. 48.
25 Michael Haney, 'Russia's first televised war: public opinion on the crisis', *Transition*, 1:5, 1995, pp. 6–8.
26 *Novoye vremya*, 44, 1999, p. 20.
27 For a Western view, see Ellen Mickiewicz, *Changing Channels: Television and the Struggle for Power in Russia*, New York: Oxford University Press, 1997, p. 247 and, for a Russian, *Informatsionnaya voina v Chechne: Fakty, Dokumenty, Svidetel'stva. Noyabr' 1994–sentyabr' 1996* (The Information War in Chechnya: Facts, Documents, Evidence. November 1994–September 1996), p. 371.
28 Galina Zvereva, 'Chechenskaya voina v diskursakh massovoi kyl'tury Rossii: formy reprezentatsii vraga' (The Chechen War in the discourse of Russia's mass culture: forms of representation of the enemy), Polit.ru website, 7 December 2002, www.polit.ru/country/2002/12/07/479426.html (accessed on 23 February, 2005).
29 For example, the demonisation of Saddam Hussein at the time of the first Gulf War, see Norman Fairclough, *Media Discourse*, London: Edward Arnold, 1995, pp. 94–102.
30 See Simon Dixon, 'The Russians and the Russian question', in Graham Smith (ed.), *The Nationalities Question in the Post-Soviet States*, Harlow: Longman, 1996, pp. 47–74.
31 See Valery Tishkov, 'Geopolitika chechenskoi voiny: "natsional'nyi interes" kak sopernichestvo biurokratii i elit' (Geopolitics of the Chechen War: 'National interest' as rivalry between bureaucracies and elites), *Svobodnaya mysl'*, 4, 1997, p. 68.
32 Chapter 1 of Charles W. Kegley Jr (ed.), *International Terrorism: Characteristics, Causes, Controls*, Basingstoke: Macmillan, 1990, pp. 11–26.
33 In November 1995, Maskhadov explicitly informed the Russian media 'Never will I descend to terrorism. We are warriors, not assassins', see *Transition*, 19 April 1996, p. 2. Khattab was commonly portrayed as a 'military fanatic'; see *Izvestiya*, 3 December 1999.
34 *Novoye vremya*, 38, 1999, p. 10.
35 *NTV*, 23 April 2000.
36 'Dzhinn na zhipe' (Genie in a jeep) was the title of an article on Khattab, *Novoye vremya*, 43, pp. 12–14.
37 *Time*, 6 December 1999.
38 See Aleksandr Iskandaryan, 'Chernofobia' (Fear of the 'Blacks'), *Novoye vremya*, 32, 1996, pp. 12–14. For an example of use of the word 'Chechenofobia', see *Argumenty i fakty*, 38, September 1999, p. 9.

39 See Yan Chesnov, 'Chechentsem byt' trudno' (It is not easy to be a Chechen), in *Nezavisimaya gazeta*, 22 September 1994.

40 Yuri N. Maltsev, 'Russia's war on Chechnya', 28 October 2002, www.mises.org/ fullstory.aspx?control=1080 (accessed 7 March 2005).

41 BBC film in 'Assignment' series by Angus Roxburgh, *Chechnya: A Russian Nightmare*. For an assessment of Dudaev's sanity, see Anatol Lieven, *Chechnya: Tombstone of Russian Power*, New Haven: Yale University Press, 1999, p. 67.

42 *Segodnya*, 16 January 1996.

43 *Moscow News*, no. 17–18, 15–21 May 1997, p. 3.

44 *Trud*, 10 September 1997.

45 www.mosnews.com/mn-files/chechnyaelections.shtml (last accessed 25 September 2006).

46 Interview with Shamil Basaev, www.chechnya.xnet.is/texts/basayev2.html.

47 Yuri N. Maltsev, 'Russia's war on Chechnya', 28 October 2002, www.mises.org/ fullstory.aspx?control=1080 (accessed 7 March 2005).

48 *Argumenty i fakty*, 51, 1994, p. 2.

49 Moshe Gammer claims that it was this division that invented 'Russian roulette'. Gammer (2006), op. cit., p. 108.

50 Timur Aliev, 'Chechen heroes of the Soviet War', *Chechen Society newspaper*, 9:47, 11 May 2005.

51 *Argumenty i fakty*, 52, 1994, p. 2.

52 *Novoye vremya*, 38, 1996, p. 8.

53 www.chechnya.org/anthem.html.

54 www.chechnyafree.ru/html/Slova_gimna_rus.htm (last accessed 9 October 2006).

55 See cover of *Novoye vremya*, 38, September 1996.

56 *Moskovskiye novosti*, 18–25 June 1995, p. 4.

57 *Moscow News*, 15–21 May 1997, p. 1.

58 L. Tolstoi, *Hadji-Murat*, Moscow: Khudozhestvennaya literatura, 1965, p. 110 (my translation).

59 Channel 4 documentary film *The Betrayed*.

60 John Sweeney, 'Revealed: Russia's worst war crime in Chechnya', *Observer*, 5 March 2000.

61 A British Officer, *The Powers of Europe and Fall of Sebastopol*, Boston: Higgins & Bradley, 1856, p. 296.

62 Ibid., p. 284.

63 David Remnick, *Resurrection: The Struggle for a New Russia*, New York: Random House, 1997, pp. 266–267.

64 'Dve voiny' (Two Wars), *Novoye vremya*, 47, 1999, pp. 12–14.

65 'Pochemu voyuet Kavkaz...' (Why the Caucasus is howling...), *Ogonyok*, 26, 20 September 1999.

66 *Argumenty i fakty*, 38, September 2000, p. 6.

67 20 January, 2006, www.levada.ru/press/2006012001.html (last accessed 8 March 2006).

68 *Novoye vremya*, 52, 2000, pp. 20–21.

69 This alienation is portrayed in Aleksandr Rogozhkin's film *Blokpost*, ORT video, 1998.

70 *Novoye vremya*, 52, 2000, p. 21.

71 Michael Haney, 'Russia's first televised war: public opinion on the crisis', *Transition*, 1:5 (1995), pp. 6–8.

72 *Izvestiya*, 11 September 1999.

73 *Argumenty i fakty*, 38, 1999.

74 'Survivor of Chechnya's Chernokozovo camp a broken man', AFP report posted 17 April 2000 on *Johnson's Russia List*, #4253, www.cdi.org/russia/johnson/4253.html (last accessed 25 September 2006).

75 www.rian.ru/rian/chechnya/en/02/06.html.

76 Dmitry Linchevsky, *Mayatnik* (Pendulum), zhurnal.lib.ru/l/linchewskij_d_i/dixon. shtml (accessed on 30 September 2006).

77 Avraam Shmulevich, 'Mest za prezidenta (Revenge for the President), *APN Publikatsii*, 27 June 2006, www.apn.ru/publications/article9916.htm (accessed 17 September 2006).

78 N.S. Astashkin, *Po vol'chemu sledu: khroniki chechenskikh voin* (Following wolf tracks: chronicles of the Chechen wars), Moscow: Veche, 2005.

79 See Vyacheslav Mironov, 'Ya byl na etoi voine' (I was in that war), original published in 1995 online, www.artofwar.spb.ru:8101/mironov/index_tale_mironov. html. The English translation (by Alex Dokin), 'Assault on Grozny Downtown' was published in 2001 online, lib.ru/MEMUARY/CHECHNYA/chechen_war.txt (last accessed 25 September 2006)

80 See Igor Mariyukin, 'Tri nochi, chetyre dnya' (Three nights, four days), www.artofwar.ru/mariukin/tale_mariukin_3.html (last accessed 25 September 2006).

81 *Chekhi* (which means Czech in Russian) appears to have derived from a combination *chechentsy* and *dukhi*, see Vadim Rechkalov, 'Razboi na Ploshchadi Trekh Durakov' (Robbery on Three Fools' Square), main.Izvestiya.ru/print/?id=26227.

82 See bestbooks.ru/Child/Chukovsky/0101.shtml.

83 *Time*, 6 December 1999.

84 Galina Zvereva, 'Chechenskaya voina v diskursakh massovoi kyl'tury Rossii: formy reprezentatsii vraga' (The Chechen War in the discourse of Russia's mass culture: forms of representation of the enemy), Polit.ru website, 7 December 2002, www.polit.ru/country/2002/12/07/479426.html (accessed on 23 February, 2005).

85 See his 'Our own and strangers', english.mn.ru/english/issue.php?2002–5–15 (last accessed 25 September 2006).

86 *Chistilishche* ('Purgatory') directed by Aleksandr Nevzorov, ORT Video, 1998.

87 www.salon.com/travel/feature/1999/10/02/moscow.index.html.   Jeffrey   Taylor, 'Russia on the edge'. The Russian government sent a video 'nasty' containing this footage to the Council of Europe in April 2000.

88 See the video 'Oborotni' online, www.compromat.ru/main/chechya/video1.htm (last accessed 25 September 2006).

89 Andrew Osborn, 'How a young conscript became a Russian saint', *Independent*, 24 November 2004.

90 Thus, of those polled recently in Chechnya, 66 per cent thought that Chechen men and women had taken up arms to resist the violent actions of Russian forces, against only 14 per cent who identified the struggle for independence, see Musa Basnukhaev and Magomed Iriskhanov, 'Obshchestvennoye mneniye Chechni o situatsii v chechenskoi respublike' (Chechen public opinion on the situation in the Chechen Republic),   *Vestnik   obshchestvennogo   mneniya*,   4,   July–August,   2004, www.levada.ru/vestnik78.html (last accessed 25 September 2006).

91 www.rferl.org/newsline/2002/06/1-RUS/rus-250602.asp (last accessed 25 September 2006).

92 www.kavkaz.org.uk/eng/print.php?id=3090.

93 See Jamal Ginazov and Aslanbek Dadaev, 'Chechens march on Europe – with a ball', *Caucasus Reporting Service*, 236, 3 June 2004.

94 Steve Rosenberg, 'Chechen football stars cry foul' 13 September 2005, news.bbc.co.uk/1/hi/world/europe/4242926.stm (accessed 17 September 2006).

95 www.eurosport.com/home/pages/v4/l0/s22/e9815/event_lng0_spo22_evt9815.shtml (accessed 17 September 2006).

96 See www.levada.ru/press/2005070410.html (last accessed 25 September 2006).

97 See report of 22 July 2005 for the *Memorial* organisation's 'Migration and Law' network by S.A. Gannushkina (ed.), 'Polozheniye zhitelei Chechni v Rossiiskoi

Federatsii, iyun' 2004g–iyun' 2005g' (The situation of residents of Chechnya in the Russian Federation, June 2004–June 2005), p. 8, www.memo.ru/hr/news/5gannush7. htm (last accessed 25 September 2006).

98 'The New Jews', *The Economist*, 17 February 2005.

99 Aleksei Malashenko and Dmitry Trenin, *Vremya Yuga: Rossiya v Chechne, Chechnya v Rossii* (The Time of the South: Russia in Chechnya, Chechnya in Russia), Moscow: Gendal'f, 2002, p. 173.

100 Stephen Badsey, 'Media Interaction in the Kosovo Conflict, March-June 1999', paper at the Political Studies Association Conference, London, 2000, www.psa.ac. uk/cps/2000/Badseyper cent20Stephen.pdf.

101 'No end in sight to the war in Chechnya', *The Russia Journal*, 16 September 2002.

102 See, for example, Aleksei Meshkov, '2003: crucial year for fighting terrorism', *International Affairs, (Moscow),* 49:2, 2003, pp. 6–10.

103 Catherine Belton, 'Putin facing his biggest challenge', *Moscow Times*, 9 September 2004.

104 Yuri N. Maltsev, 'Russia's war on Chechnya', 28 October 2002, www.mises.org/ fullstory.aspx?control=1080 (accessed 7 March 2005).

105 Zinaida Sikevich, 'The Caucasus and "Caucasus phobia"', translated by Robin Jones for Rosbalt News Agency, 18 December 2002, www.rosbaltnews.com/2003/ 02/07/60777.html; for Alekseyeva, see www.csce.gov/pdf/101502CSCEbriefing.pdf.

106 Andrei Piontkovsky, 'Russia has lost the war in Chechnya', *Chechnya Weekly*, IV:37, 16 October 2003.

5 Wars by any other name: Yeltsin's 'restoration of constitutional order' and Putin's 'counter-terrorist operation'

1 Galina Zvereva, 'Chechenskaya voina v diskursakh massovoi kyl'tury Rossii: formy reprezentatsii vraga' (The Chechen War in the discourse of Russia's mass culture: forms of representation of the enemy), Polit.ru website, 7 December 2002, www.polit.ru/country/2002/12/07/479426.html (accessed on 23 February, 2005).

2 For first conflict, see Michael McFaul, 'Eurasia letter: Russian politics after Chechnya', in *Foreign Policy*, 99, Summer 1995, p. 164; for second, see Yelena Bonner's speech in March 2000, warning of a 'new Stalinism' in Putin's Russia. See www.bbc.co.uk, 9 March 2000.

3 Hostilities largely ceased in the month before the second round, see Yitzhak M. Brudny, 'In pursuit of the Russian presidency: why Yeltsin won the 1996 Russian presidential election, *Communist and Post-Communist Studies*, 30:3, 1997, pp. 255–275.

4 By bringing forward the elections from June to March, Putin was able to get them out of the way before spring and the anticipated consolidation of the Chechen forces could dampen public support for his war.

5 See McFaul, op. cit., p. 152.

6 See V. Aleksin and A. Shaburkin, 'Voina bez vykhodnikh' (War without days off), *Nezavisimaya gazeta*, 25 September 1999.

7 In a survey of 'Man of the Year' in Russia for the year 2000, Putin garnered 48 per cent of the votes, *Segodnya*, 20 January 2001.

8 'Putins War', *The New York Review of Books*, 47:2, 10 February 2000, www.nybooks.com/articles/225 (last accessed 5 May 2005).

9 See Vadim Dubnov, in *Novoye vremya*, 52, 2000, p. 19.

10 *Time*, 17 July 2000.

11 See *Novoye vremya*, 47, 1999, p. 13.

12 Graeme P. Herd, 'The "counter-terrorist operation" in Chechnya: "information warfare" aspects', *The Journal of Slavic Military Studies*, 13:4, December 2000, pp. 57–83.

13 This had been a feature of the first war, see *Novoye vremya*, 1997, 5, pp. 10–11; in

the second war, such sites as *Kavkaz-Tsentr* carried material in support of the Chechens, a good example being the open letter dated 22 August 2000 from Shamil Basaev to Vladimir Putin calling the Russian president "terrorist Number One", www.kavkaz.org/news/2000/8/22/news1.htm.

14 Shannon Peters Talbott, 'Early Chechen coverage tests print journalists' independence', *Transition*, 2:16, 1996, pp. 48–51.

15 Channel 4 documentary film *Babitsky's War*, broadcast on 4 September 2000. His employers Radio Free Europe/Radio Liberty gave a chronology of the affair on its website, see www.referl.org/nca/special/babitsky/chronology.html.

16 See 'Postscript' by John Crowfoot in Anna Politkovskaya, *A Dirty War: A Russian Reporter in Chechnya*, London: The Harvill Press, 2001, pp. 316–323.

17 See her 'Poisoned by Putin', *Guardian*, 9 September, 2004.

18 It was hinted that Masyuk's abduction by a rival warlord might have been a snub to Basaev, see *Argumenty i fakty*, 27, July 1997, p. 3; 29, July 1997, p. 3.

19 Vyacheslav Izmailov, 'Den'gi na porokhovuyu bochku' (Money for a powder keg), *Novaya gazeta*, 23, 30 March 2006.

20 For a good account of this, see Boris Kagarlitsky, 'Russia chooses – and loses' in the October 1996 edition of *Current History*, www.currenthistory.com/archiveoct96/Kagarlitsky.html (last accessed on 25 September 2006).

21 See Fedor Burlatsky, 'Yeltsin: a turning point', *Transition*, 1:3, 1995, p. 8.

22 See his 'Killing Chechnya', *The New York Review of Books*, 6 April 1995, p. 15.

23 It is estimated that 25,000 Russians and Chechens (mostly civilians) died in this onslaught.

24 Figures for Northern Ireland provided by the Northern Ireland Office website, www.nio.gov.uk/secstats0498.htm; the higher figure is quoted by Russian human rights activist, Sergei Kovalev, in his 'Russia after Chechnya', *New York Review of Books*, 17 July 1997, p. 27; John Dunlop suggests a figure of 46,500 in his 'The Forgotten War', *Hoover Digest*, 2002, no. 1, www-hoover.stanford.edu/publications/digest/021/dunlop.html. BBC Monitoring reported Anatoly Kulikov, deputy chairman of the Russian State Duma committee on security, as revealing on TV that 45,000 had died in the conflict since 1994, see *Johnson's Russia List*, #216, 28 September 2006.

25 See his *After the USSR: Ethnicity, Nationalism, and Politics in the Commonwealth of Independent States*, Madison, WI: University of Wisconsin, 1995, p. 221.

26 A group of these 'boy soldiers' taken captive by the Chechens is pictured on the front cover of Anatol Lieven (1999), op. cit.

27 'Dudayev's regime: the handover of Soviet military hardware', in Robert Seely, op. cit., ch. 5, pp. 114–141.

28 Interview by Yevgeny Shchekochikin in *Literaturnaya gazeta*, 2 August 1995, p. 12.

29 Daniel S. Treisman, 'Russia's "ethnic revival": the separatist activism of regional leaders in a postcommunist order', *World Politics*, 49, January 1997, pp. 212–249.

30 Displayed on Russian screens by such films as *Chistilishche* ('Purgatory').

31 Channel 4 film *The Betrayed.*

32 Arkady Chereshnya, 'Bumerang terrorizma vozvrashchaetsya v Rossiyu' (The boomerang of terrorism returns to Russia), *Literaturnaya gazeta*, .42, 18 October 1995, p. 11.

33 Gall and de Waal (1997), op. cit., p. 11; Stasys Kriezys and Romanas Sedlickas, *The War in Chechnya*, College Station, TX: A & M University Press, 1999, p. 103, state 'over five hundred' died in this initial assault.

34 Scott Parrish, 'A turning point in the Chechen conflict', *Transition*, 1:13, 1995, pp. 42–46.

35 *Novoye vremya*, 3, 1996.

36 Pavel Felgenhauer, 'After the theatre, the drama continues', *The New Statesman*, 4 November 2002.

37 The irony is brought out fully, through montage, in Paul Mitchell's film *Hot Spots: Chechnya*, screened on BBC 4, 4 July 2004.

38 Anders Aslund, 'Go long on Russia – Russian economic conditions', *The International Economy*, July–August 2000, pp. 38–39.

39 www.chechnya.org/current/truce.html (last accessed 30 November 2001).

40 For a detailed examination of these concepts in the Chechen context, see Richard Sakwa, 'Chechnya: a just war fought unjustly?' in Bruno Coppieters and Richard Sakwa (2003) *Contextualising Secession: Normative Studies in Comparative Perspective*, Oxford: Oxford University Press, 2003, pp. 156–186.

41 Sergei Stepashin, then Rushailo's predecessor as Minister of the Interior, had called for this on NTV's *Itogi* programme on 7 March 1999 after the abduction by Chechen rebels at Grozny airport of MVD General Gennady Shpigun, see his interview on NTV's *Geroi dnya* (Hero of the Day), 5 October 1999, www.yabloko.ru/Engl/TV/step-ntvr-geroy-1.html (last accessed 25 September 2006).

42 Quoted in 'Chechnya: Impotent Fury', *The Russia Journal*, 22–28 March 1999.

43 Report of Interior Minister, Vladimir Rushailo, to the Federation Council on 3 July 1999, see Yelena Loria in *Novye izvestiya*, 7 July 1999, calling for the application of Russia's counter-terrorism laws to deal with Chechen banditry.

44 Svante E. Cornell, 'The war against terrorism and the conflict in Chechnya: a case for distinction', in *The Fletcher Forum of World Affairs*, 27:2, Summer/Fall 2002, p. 171.

45 Dr Mark A. Smith, 'Russian perspectives on terrorism', *Conflict Studies Research Centre, Report C110*, Defence Academy of the United Kingdom, January 2004, p. 3.

46 Ibid., pp. 3–4.

47 This aspect of the conflict has tended to be overlooked by Western observers, although it is implicit in Putin's warning about the 'arc of instability extending from the Philippines to Kosovo', see interview with *Paris Match*, 6 July 2000. See also, Aleksei Malashenko and Dmitry Trenin (2002), op. cit., pp. 186–188.

48 See, for example, Fiona Hill of the Brooking Institute in Washington, in Catherine Belton's 'Putin is facing his biggest challenge', *Moscow News*, 9 September 2004.

49 The sources pointing to a 'conspiracy' are numerous, the most widely-reviewed being Yuri Felshtinsky and Alexander Litvinenko, *Blowing Up Russia*, New York: Liberty, 2002 and David Satter, *Darkness at Dawn: The Rise of the Russian Criminal State*, New Haven: Yale University Press, 2003, as well as the documentary film *Assassination of Russia*, Charles Gazelle Transparences Productions, France, 2002, financed by Boris Berezovsky.

50 See Channel 4 *Dispatches* programme 'Dying for the President', screened on 9 March 2000.

51 For Basaev's denial of the apartment bombs in Moscow, see 'Chechen warlord denies connection to Moscow explosion', report by Associated Press on 12 September 1999, posted on the Chechen website, www.amina.com/news/99/99.9.12.html; For his admission that he masterminded the Dubrovka hostage-taking incident, see 'Chechen warlord claims theatre attack', on the BBC website, 1 November 2002, news.bbc.co.uk/1/hi/world/europe/2388857.stm (last accessed 25 September 2006); for Beslan, see *Daymohk* on 17 September 2004, www.daymohk.info/cgi-bin/orsi3/index.cgi?id=8428;idt=17200409;section=1.

52 See Anatoly Medetsky, 'Two get life in prison for '99 bombings', *Moscow Times*, 13 January 2004.

53 *RFE/RL Newsline*, 2 May 2002.

54 See Bronwen Maddox, 'An unwinnable war, but Russia cannot quit', *The Times*, 13 May 2003, but assessing the total strength of the opposition at only 1,500 men, as reported by a pro-Moscow Chechen website, www.chechnyafree.ru (accessed on 22 January 2004).

55 'Forgiven, but not forgotten', Crisis in Chechnya: Special Report, *Guardian*, 17 February 2000.

56 The deputy general procurator of the Russian federation, Vladimir Kolesnikov, claimed in an interview that Boris Berezovsky paid for their release, Vyacheslav Izmailov, 'Den'gi na porokhovuyu bochku' (Money for a powder keg), *Novaya gazeta*, 30 March 2006.

57 'International horror at beheadings', BBC website, 9 December 1998, news.bbc.co.uk/1/hi/world/europe/231318.stm (last accessed 25 September 2006).

58 'Second Chechnya War, 1999–????' www.globalsecurity.org/military/world/war/chechnya2.htm (last accessed 25 September 2006).

59 *Izvestiya*, 13 November 1999.

60 *The Russia Journal*, 1–7 November 1999.

61 *Izvestiya*, 4 November 1999.

62 The most publicised was the kidnapping of British aid workers Camilla Carr and Jon James, who were released with the assistance of Berezovsky and Raduev in September 1998. See *Sunday Times*, 11 October 1998. It was estimated that kidnappings throughout the region in 1997 earned the Chechen bands $20 million, *Argumenty i fakty*, 48, November 1998, p. 11.

63 In December 1996, six Red Cross workers were killed and in December 1998, the severed heads of four engineers working for a British telecommunications company were discovered. www.russiatoday.com/rtoday/news/01.html (accessed on 8 December 1998).

64 I witnessed the first of these on ORT on 4 September 1997.

65 *Segodnya*, 14 September 1999.

66 The impact of the precedents set by the West's campaign in Kosovo should not be underestimated. Emil Pain notes that 'The Russian military argued: if NATO can shell civilian objects in a sovereign country for the sake of political aims we can do the same in our own country'. Pain (2004), op. cit.

67 See *Novoye vremya*, 4, 2000, p. 4.

68 My thanks to Stephen White and Martin Dewhirst, from the University of Glasgow, for their useful comments on these articles.

69 Emil Pain, 'The second Chechen War: possible scenarios', in *Central Asia and the Caucasus: Database*, ca-c.org/dataeng/bk02.04.pain.shtml (last accessed 25 September 2006).

70 The American TV station CNN describes '*Wahhabism*' as 'a fundamentalist form of Islam founded in Saudi Arabia in the 18th century by Mohammad Ibn Abdul-Wahhab and the ruling Saudi dynasty, which felt that the local practice of Islam needed to return to its original purity. An offshoot of the Sunni Hanbali legal school, it is based on a literal translation of the Koran and rejects mysticism in any form' … adding that 'Osama bin Laden represents a militant extremist form of Wahhabism', see edition.cnn.com/SPECIALS/2001/trade.center/islam/wahhabism.html (last accessed 25 September 2006).

71 *Nezavisimaya gazeta*, 14 January 2000.

72 *Time*, 19 February 1996, p. 22.

73 *Novoye vremya*, 7, 2000, p. 20.

74 *Tribuna*, 14 September 1999

75 *Tribuna*, 16 September 1999.

76 From an interview published in *Novaya gazeta*, 19–25 June 2000. Shamanov was later elected Governor of the Ulyanovsk Region, see Boris Kagarlitsky, 'Insane "Heroes" of our Time', *Moscow Times*, 25 June 2002.

77 www.cnn.com/2001/WORLD/europe/06/04/russia.execution/ (last accessed 25 September 2006). Troshev was finally dismissed in December 2002 in the wake of the furore over a Russian court's decision to find Colonel Yury Budanov to be not responsible for his actions, when accused of raping and murdering a Chechen teenage girl, see the *Guardian*, 19 December 2002.

78 Chechen political scientist, Zaindi Choltaev quoted this number in December 2003,

see Nairi Hovsepyan and Lyubov Tsukanova, 'Chechnya and Russia. War and peace', (2003), op. cit.

79 'The Russian ultimatum to Chechnya: a humanitarian outrage', *Relief International*, 7 December 1999,

80 John Sweeney, 'Revealed: Russia's worst war crime in Chechnya', *Observer*, 5 March 2000.

81 'The Chernokozovo Detention Center', Human Rights Watch Report, '"Welcome to Hell": arbitrary detention, torture and extortion in Chechnya', see hrw.org/reports/2000/russia_chechnya4/.

82 www.glasnostonline.org/rus/pollBooth.php?op=results&pollID=1.

83 See George Bush's message to Maskhadov, reported in *Novaya gazeta*, 75, 15 October 2001.

84 See Lev Lurie, 'The Russian media turns', *Institute for War and Peace Reporting: Caucasus*, 14, 14 January 2000.

85 www.levada.ru/chechnya.html (last accessed 25 September 2006).

86 C.W. Blandy, 'Chechnya: dynamics of war, brutality and stress', *Conflict Studies Research Centre, Report P35*, July 2001, p. 10.

87 See Ilya Maksakov and Dmitry Chernogorsky, 'Vykhod boevikov iz Groznogo byl operatsiei rossiiskikh voisk' (The withdrawal of fighters from Chechnya was an operation by federal Russian troops), *Komsomol'skaya pravda*, 3 February 2000.

88 See *Izvestiya*, 9 August 2000.

89 *Kommersant''*, 6 October 2000.

90 Glasnost Foundation, www.russiatoday.com/glasnost. In June 2001, Baraev was shot dead by federal troops in Chechnya.

91 For a comprehensive account of the restructuring of relations between Putin and the oligarchs, see William Tompson, 'Putin and the "oligarchs": a two-sided commitment problem', *Chatham House Briefing Note*, August 2004, www.riia.org/pdf/research/rep/BNAug04.pdf.

92 See Oleg Panfilov, *Putin and the Press: The Revival of Soviet-style Propaganda*, London: Foreign Policy Centre, 2005, p. 26.

93 See Dunlop (2006), op. cit.

94 Dunlop (2006), op. cit.

95 www.peaceinthecaucasus.org/reports/Beslan.pdf (last accessed 31 August 2006).

96 'The October 2002 Moscow hostage-taking incident', *RFE/RL Organized Crime and Terrorism Watch*, 18 December 2003 and 8 and 15 January 2004.

97 Dunlop (2006), op. cit., pp. 79–87; for evidence suggesting that the security forces had pre-planned the storming of the school, see Valery Dzutsev and Alan Tskhurbaev, 'Beslan siege unravels, slowly and bloodily', *Caucasus Reporting Service*, 250, 3 September 2004. Other witnesses have claimed that it was armed Ossetians that commenced firing, see Ruslan Aushev, former president of Ingushetia, quoted in 'Could the Beslan tragedy have been avoided?', The Jamestown Foundation's *Chechnya Weekly*, 5:34, 8 September 2004.

98 Dunlop (2006), op. cit., pp. 88–96; the use of flamethrowers was confirmed by Ruslan Tebiev, whose wife was among the casualties at Beslan, see 'Incredible Dialogue for the Truth on Beslan', *Liberation* (France), 9 June 2005; for use of both forms of weapons, see Valery Dzutsev, 'Uncomfortable truths from Beslan probe', *Caucasus Reporting Service*, 317:2, 6 December 2005. See also Pavel Fel'gengauer, 'Kak shturmovali shkolu' (How the School was stormed), *Novaya gazeta*, 74, 7 October 2004.

99 Dunlop (2006), op. cit., pp. 106–114. See also the article by Anna Politkovskaya, 'Spasat' ne prikazali' (There were no orders to save people), *Novaya gazeta*, 84, 15 November 2004.

100 Foreword to Greg Austin, *Political Change in Russia: Implications for Britain*, London: Foreign Policy Centre, 2004, p. v.

101 For the impact of 9/11 on the 'Islamic factor' in the war in Chechnya, see John Russell, 'Exploitation of the "Islamic factor" in the Russo-Chechen conflict before and after 11 September 2001', *European Security*, 11:4, Winter 2002, pp. 96–109.

102 *Tribuna*, 14 and 16 September 1999.

103 *Guardian*, 14 November 2003.

104 milprob.narod.ru/17.05.02gazeta86.htm (last accessed 25 September 2006).

105 Quoted in Mark Kramer, 'The perils of counterinsurgency: Russia's war in Chechnya', *International Security*, 29:3, Winter 2004/5, p. 17.

106 In August 2004, Vadim Rechkalov admitted that bloody skirmishes would continue but that there would be no war, see his 'Budut lokal'nye stychki s zhertvami do 100 chelovek, a voiny ne budet' (There will be local skirmishes with up to 100 victims, but there will be no war), *Izvestiya*, 2 August 2004.

107 Otto Latsis claims that around one million Russians had gone through the Chechen conflict by October 2002, see his 'Another short, victorious war?', *The Russia Journal*, 27 September–3 October 2002. Official Russian sources had earlier put the figure at just under 400,000, see *Argumenty i fakty*, 12 June 2002. As noted, other Russian experts, such as Emil Pain, put the figure at 1.5 million.

108 Liz Fuller (2004), op. cit., reports that the concept was first proposed by Emil Pain in January 1995.

109 PACE Document 10276, dated 17 September 2004, 'The political situation in the Chechen Republic: measures to increase democratic stability in accordance with Council of Europe standards', assembly.coe.int/Documents/WorkingDocs/doc04/EDOC10276.htm (accessed 7 March 2005).

110 Announced by the Russian minister for Chechnya, Stanislav Ilyasov, see RFE/RL's Valentinas Mite, 'Russia: plans for referendum in Chechnya may be a hollow gesture', accessed on *Johnson's Russia List*, #6574, 27 November 2002.

111 Article 8, point 4, forbids the creation and functioning of social organisations ... that aim to ... violate the territory integrity of ... the Russian Federation. The Russian President is also given the right to remove the elected President of Chechnya (Article 72d). See www.chechnya.gov.ru/republic/const/ (last accessed 25 September 2006).

112 The death of Maskhadov produced a wealth of literature and comment, well documented and reproduced by *Johnson's Russia List*, #9082, 9 March 2005 *passim.*

113 Although the speculation and analysis following Sadulaev's death was understandably much less than that following Maskhadov's assassination, it too can be accessed via *Johnson's Russia List*, #140, 19 June 2006.

114 www.gazeta.ru/print/2003/03/25/Chechenvoter.shtml (last accessed 25 September 2006).

115 www.osce-ngo.net/030328.pdf.

116 See Andrei Riskin, 'Kak "izbirali" Kadyrova' (How Kadyrov was "elected"), *Nezavisimaya gazeta*, 6 October 2003.

117 Lokshina (2006), op. cit., p. 44.

118 Ibid., p. 16.

119 Ibid., p. 80.

120 John Russell, 'Primed to explode', *The World Today*, 60:6, June 2004, pp. 20–21.

121 See interview given to Chechen press website on 1 August 2004, www.chechenpress.info/news/2004/08/01/07.shtml (last accessed 25 September 2006).

122 Aleksei Malashenko, 'Chechnya: vybory posredi terrora' (Chechnya: elections amidst terror), Moscow Carnegie Centre *Brifing* (Briefing), 6:8–9, August–September 2004.

123 PACE Document 10276, dated 17 September 2004, 'The political situation in the Chechen Republic: measures to increase democratic stability in accordance with Council of Europe standards', assembly.coe.int/Documents/WorkingDocs/doc04/EDOC10276.htm (accessed 7 March 2005).

124 Ibid.
125 Ruslan Zhadaev, 'Parliamentskie vybory: byl li vybor? (Parliamentary elections: Was there a choice?), *Chechenskoe obshchestvo*, 26, 7 December 2005.
126 See 'Analysts say Kadyrov viewed as future Chechen leader, consolidates power', *Itar-Tass*, 7 February 2006.
127 *Itar-Tass*, 7 February 2006
128 See Timur Aliev, 'Kremlin's pick to replace Kadyrov', *The Moscow Times*, 18 June 2004; for a list of Chechen *teips*, see C.W. Blandy, 'Chechnya: normalisation', op. cit., p. 40.
129 See Timur Aliev, 'Idushchie na tretii srok' (Going for the third term), *Chechenskoe obshchestvo*, 17, 8 August 2006.
130 Kaz de Jong, S. van der Kam, N. Ford, S. Hargreaves, R. van Oosten, D. Cunningham and G. Boots (2004), *The Trauma of the Ongoing War in Chechnya*, quoted in Dov Lynch, '"The enemy is at the gate": Russia after Beslan', *International Affairs*, 81:1, p. 146.
131 See John Reuter, 'Chechnya's suicide bombers: desperate, devout or deceived?', Report for The American Committee for Peace in Chechnya, 16 September 2004, peaceinchechnya.org/reports/SuicideReport/ (last accessed 9 March 2005); Anne Speckhard and Khapta Akhmedova, 'The making of a martyr: Chechen suicide terrorism', *The Journal of Studies in Conflict and Terrorism*, 29:5, July–August 2006, pp. 429–492.
132 Johan Galtung, 'Crafting Peace; on the Psychology of the TRANSCEND Approach', www.transcend.org/t_database/articles.php?ida=221.
133 Makarkin, A., 'Alu Alkhanov – novy chechensky vybor Kremlya' (Alu Alkhanov – the Kremlin's new Chechen choice), www.politcom.ru/2004/analit139.php (last accessed 25 September 2006). Alkhanov duly won this election in August 2004.
134 This point is made even by a Western observer who is among those least sympathetic to independence for Chechnya. See Ware, R.B., 'Can Moscow engineer a political solution in Chechnya?', www.rferl.org/newsline/2004/06/5-NOT/not-080604.asp (last accessed 25 September 2006).
135 Musa Basnukhaev and Magomed Iriskhanov, 'Obshchestvennoye mneniye Chechni o situatsii v chechenskoi respublike' (Chechen public opinion on the situation in the Chechen Republic), *Vestnik obshchestvennogo mneniya*, 4, July–August 2004, www.levada.ru/vestnik78.html (last accessed 25 September 2006).
136 C.W. Blandy, 'Chechnya; the search for a strong successor', *Conflict Studies Research Centre, Caucasus Series*, 04/19, July 2004, p. 3.
137 Sergei Markedonov, 'Effektivnee borot'sya za nezavisimuyu Ichkeriyu pod rossiiskim flagom' (It's more effective to fight for Ichkerian independence under the Russian flag), *Natsional'niye interesy* (National Interests) website, 11 October 2006, www.niros.ru/comments/158.html (accessed 11 October 2006).
138 The phrase is used by Sergei Markedonov in his 'Chechnya: ugroza sistemnogo separatizma' (Chechnya: the threat of system separatism), *APN Proyekt* instituta natsional'nogo strategii, 24 January 2005.
139 Ivan Sukhov, 'Chechensky ochag' (Chechen hearth), *APN Proyekt* instituta natsional'noi strategii, 16 August 2005. www.apn.ru/publications/article1519.htm (accessed 17 September 2006).
140 Ibid.
141 Emil Souleimanov, *Central Asia–Caucasus Analyst*, 31 May 2006.
142 'Pochti polovina sotrudnikov militsii Chechnyi byvshiye boyeviki: 7 tysyach chelovek' (Almost half of those serving in Chechnya's police force are former fighters: seven thousand persons), www.newsru.com/russia/21oct2005/chechnya.html (last accessed 25 September 2006).
143 Anna Politkovskaya, 'Vsya Chechnya v krugu sem'i' (All of Chechnya surrounded by the family), *Novaya gazeta*, 41, 9 June 2005.

144 See interview with the president of APN's Institute of National Strategy, Mikhail Remizov, 'Chechenskuyu vitrinu "razvitogo feodalizma" pora zakryvat'' (It is time to close the Chechen shop window of 'developed feudalism'), 15 September 2006, *APN Kommentarii*, 51, www.apn.ru/news/article10390.htm (accessed 17 September 2006).
145 Boris Sokolov, 'Kavkaz "otdadut vragam"' (The Caucasus will be handed to the enemy), www.prognosis.ru/print.html?id=6687 (accessed 15 February 2006).
146 Anna Politkovskaya, 'Vsya Chechnya...', op. cit.

6 9/11, Chechnya and the war on terror

1 news.bbc.co.uk/1/hi/world/middle_east/2455845.stm (last accessed 25 September 2006).
2 reliefweb.int (accessed on 8 October 2001.
3 Vladimir Rushailo pinned the blame on Basaev and Khattab, *NTV*, 13 September 1999.
4 The Dagestanis were obvious candidates, given the heavy fighting in Dagestan in August and September 1999.
5 Khattab is generally thought to have been a Jordanian, see *Novoye vremya*, 42, 2000, p. 21, although some sources claim that he was a Saudi citizen, see *Novoye vremya*, 37, 1999, p. 6.
6 A number of Western observers, including Anne Appelbaum, Helen Womack (*Independent*, 27 January 2000) and John Sweeney (*Observer*, 12 March 2000) reported the prevalence of such rumours, citing the Tret'yakov article *Nezavisimaya gazeta*, 12 October 1999, an article in *Moskovskaya pravda* on 25 August 1999 entitled 'Opasnye igry v kremlevskikh zastenkakh' (Dangerous games in the Kremlin prisons) and the strange case of the FSB agents caught planting a bomb in Ryazan. See www.intellectualcapital.com/issues/issue318/item7167.asp. Aleksandr Lebed' also hinted that the Kremlin was behind the Moscow bombings, see *Izvestiya*, 30 September 1999.
7 According to the BBC (19 November 1999), the Kremlin insisted that all Russian media must refer to the Chechens as 'terrorists'. On 17 August 1999, ORT had banned all interviews with Islamist leaders in Dagestan and Chechnya.
8 For the 'arc of Islamic fundamentalism', see Vadim Belotserkovsky, 'Kakaya "duga" ugrozhaet miry?', (Which 'arc' threatens the world?), *Novaya gazeta*, 31, 20 July 2000.
9 For an example of these parallels being drawn, see the article by Aleksandr Pikaev of Moscow's Carnegie Institute, 'Islamsky fundamentalism – obshchy vrag Rossii i SShA (Islamic fundamentalism – the common enemy of Russia and the USA), www.inosmi.ru, (accessed on 2 October 2001).
10 *Guardian*, 26 September 2001.
11 *Guardian*, 29 November 2001.
12 See Eric Margolis, 'The evil empire lives ... with U.S. support', *Toronto Sun*, 10 October 1999.
13 Gordon M. Hahn, 'Putin's Muslim challenge', *The Russia Journal*, 5:2, 25–31 January 2002.
14 This figure is confirmed by the Levada Centre, www.levada.ru/chechnya.html (last accessed 25 September 2006).
15 www.wciom.ru/vciom/new/public/020325_putin.htm.
16 www.levada.ru/press/2005031800.html (last accessed 25 September 2006).
17 www.levada.ru/press/2006100301.html (last accessed 3 October 2006).
18 www.levada.ru/chechnya.html (last accessed 25 September 2006).
19 Dunlop (2006), op. cit., pp. 108–109.
20 An impressive account of the Russo-Chechen conflict, published in Moscow, devotes

an entire chapter to the 'Islamic factor'. See chapter 3 in Aleksei Malashenko and Dmitry Trenin, *Vremya yuga: Rossiya v Chechnye, Chechnya v Rossii* (The Time of the South; Russia in Chechnya, Chechnya in Russia), Moscow: Gendal'f, 2002; this volume was subsequently published in English as *Russia's Restless Frontier: The Chechnya Factor in Post-Soviet Russia,* Washington, DC: Carnegie, 2004.

21 John Russell, 'Mujahedeen, mafia, madmen ...: Russian perceptions of Chechens during the wars in Chechnya, 1994–1996 and 1999–to date', *Journal of Communist Studies and Transition Politics*, 18:1, March 2002, pp.73–96.

22 *Argumenty i fakty*, 48, November 1998, p. 11.

23 www.russiatoday.com/rtoday/news/01.html (accessed 8 December 1998).

24 *Segodnya*, 14 September 1999.

25 A good account of the Chechen attitude to '*Wahhabism*' is that provided by the French journalist Anne Nivat, in her *Chienne de Guerre: A Woman Reporter Behind the Lines of the War in Chechnya,* New York: Public Affairs, 2001. See especially ch. 1, pp. 1–30.

26 Boris Berezovsky had been accused by Basaev of financing the invasion of Dagestan in August 1999, see *Izvestiya*, 17 September 1999.

27 See 'Berezovsky: vzryvy v Moskve i Volgodonske organizovali rossiiskie spetss-luzhby', www.ntvru.com/russia14Dec2001/bb.html.

28 *Moscow Times*, 16 July 1998.

29 For example, the article by Georgy Bovt and Svetlana Babaeva, 'Bush prinyal Putina kak otsa rodnogo' (Bush greeted Putin like his own father), izvestiya.ru, 15 November 2001.

30 See M. Howard, 'Mistake to declare this a "war"', *RUSI Journal*, 146:6, December 2001, pp. 1–4; Grenville Byford, 'The wrong war', *Foreign Affairs*, 81:4, July/August 2002, p. 34.

31 Short legal definition proposed by A.P. Schmid to United Nations Crime Branch (1992), see www.unodc.org/unodc/terrorism_definitions.html (last accessed 25 September 2006).

32 Thus, an opinion poll in July 2003 indicated that at the same time as 61 per cent of Russians polled favoured flushing out the Chechen fighters by means of *zachistki* (sweeps), 67 per cent acknowledged that a partisan war was going on in Chechnya. www.vciom-a.ru/press/2003081100.html.

33 *Transition*, 19 April 1996, p. 2.

34 *Voina* (War) by Aleksei Balabanov (2002) CTB Film Company. For a full review of what the critic labels 'this piece of nationalist, warmongering propaganda', see Andrew James Horton, '*War*, what is it good for?' www.kinoeye.org/02/18/horton18_no3.php (last accessed 25 September 2006).

35 One would anticipate that Ministry of Interior (MVD) and Federal Security Service (FSB) troops, rather than those of the Russian Ministry of Defence, should be employed in such an operation, see Dr J.S. Main, '"Counter-terrorist operation" in Chechnya: on the legality of the current conflict', ibid., pp. 19–37.

36 Reliable casualty figures for the conflict are extremely hard to find, there being some agreement that the second war has been just as bloody as the first, see John Dunlop, 'The Forgotten War', *Hoover Digest*, 1, 2002, www.hoover.stanford.edu/publications/digest/021/dunlop.html (last accessed 20 June 2004).

37 Eventually, in August 2003, the Central Institute of Public Opinion Polling (VTsIOM) was taken over by the state after it had published a poll showing that only 28 per cent of those Russians polled supported the war, with 57 per cent advocating peace talks with the rebels, www.vciom-a.ru/press/2003081100.html. The independent spirit of the polling organisation was continued, however, by the erstwhile VTsIOM director, Yury Levada, in the Centre that now bears his name.

38 A considerable literature has been built up on this phenomenon, one of the most informative works being that by Scott Atran, 'The Genesis and future of suicide

terrorism', www.interdisciplines.org/terrorism/papers/1/22/ (last accessed 25 September 2006). Subsequently, works have appeared which are concerned specifically with this phenomenon in Chechnya, see Anne Speckhard and Khapta Akhmedova, 'The making of a martyr: Chechen suicide terrorism', *The Journal of Studies in Conflict and Terrorism* 29:5, July–August 2006, pp. 429–492; John Reuter, 'Chechnya's suicide bombers: desperate, devout, or deceived?', peaceinchechnya.org/reports/SuicideReport/.

39 Gal Luft, 'The Palestinian H-bomb', *Foreign Affairs*, 81:4, July/August 2002, pp. 6–7.

40 The Russian rationale for this is given concisely in Yury Fedorov, 'A global web of terror', *International Affairs (Moscow)*, 49:2, 2003, pp. 93–101.

41 Derived from the concept in politics of 'compassion fatigue', see Susan D. Mieller, *Compassion Fatigue: How the Media Sells Disease, Famine, War and Death*, New York: Routledge, 1999.

42 From a conversation with the author held at the 'Chechnya Today' conference, School of Oriental and African Studies, London, 22 November 2002.

43 Ruslan Isakov, of the Kavkaz-Tsentr News Agency, 'Moscow's propaganda tricks', reported in *Johnson's Russia List*, #9716, 13 June 2006.

44 See, 'Maskhadov pokazal arabskim zhurnalistam zhivogo Basaeva' (Maskhadov shows Arab journalists a live Basaev), lenta.ru, 22 July 2002, www.46info.ru/html/lenta/2002–6/22/a317.html (last accessed 25 September 2006); Pavel Felgenhauer, 'Bloody Chechen Deadlock', *Moscow Times*, 26 September 2002.

45 Murad Batal Al-Shashani, 'The Killing of Abu Al-Walid and the Russian policy in Chechnya', *Central Asia–Caucasus Analyst*, 5 May 2004.

46 Brian Williams, 'Unravelling the links between the Middle East and Islamic militants in Chechnya', *Central Asia–Caucasus Analyst*, 12 February 2003.

47 Andrew McGregor, 'Amir Abu Al-Walid and the Islamic component of the Chechen War', *Central Asia–Caucasus Analyst*, 26 February 2003.

48 www.terrorismanswers.com/groups/chechens.html.

49 www.wciom.ru/?pt=48&article=341.

50 *The Jamestown Monitor*, 7:197, 11 October 2001.

51 Brian Williams, 'Unravelling the Links between the Middle East and Islamic Militants in Chechnya', *Central Asia–Caucasus Analyst*, 12 February 2003 estimates 200–300.

52 news.bbc.co.uk/1/hi/world/europe/1936998.stm (last accessed 25 September 2006).

53 'Vzryv v Kaspiiske, 9 maya 2002 goda' (Explosion in Kaspiisk, 9 May 2002), *Novaya gazeta* special investigation, www.novayagazeta.ru/rassled2/vzrivi/karta-kaspiysk.shtml (last accessed 25 September 2006).

54 www.rferl.org/newsline/2002/06/1-RUS/rus-250602.asp (last accessed 25 September 2006).

55 www.rferl.org/newsline/2002/12/161202.asp (last accessed 25 September 2006).

56 www.rferl.org/newsline/2002/04/260402.asp (last accessed 25 September 2006).

57 See Vadim Dubnov, 'Lyudi-bomby' (Human bombs), *Novoye vremya*, 25, 2003, p. 15.

58 Anne Speckhard and Khapta Akhmedova, 'The making of a martyr: Chechen suicide terrorism', *The Journal of Studies in Conflict and Terrorism*, 29:5, July–August 2006, pp. 429–492.

59 Ibid.

60 Ibid.

61 Yuri N. Maltsev, 'Russia's war on Chechnya', 28 October 2002, www.mises.org/fullstory.aspx?control=1080 (accessed 7 March 2005).

62 Ibid.

63 See articles by Bobo Lo, 'No compromises', Jack Thompson, 'Telling lies' and John Russell, 'On the side of might', *The World Today*, 56:12, December 2002, pp. 13–18.

64 news.bbc.co.uk/1/low/world/europe/3020231.stm (last accessed 25 September 2006).

65 Late US President Ronald Reagan resurrected this concept in world politics, not least through his characterisation of the Soviet Union as the 'evil empire'.

66 For Russia, the apartment bombings of 1999; for Israel, the start of the Al-Aqsah intifada in 2000; and for the US, the suicide attacks of 11 September 2001.

67 In Russia, this is best exemplified by Putin's infamous promise to 'waste (the terrorists) even in the shithouse'. See V. Aleksin and A. Shaburkin, 'Voina bez vykhodnikh' (War without days off), *Nezavisimaya gazeta*, 25 September 1999.

68 Immortalised in US General Tommy Franks' admission in 2003 that, in Iraq, 'we don't do body counts', 'Counting the civilian cost in Iraq', BBC website, 6 June 2005, news.bbc.co.uk/2/hi/middle_east/3672298.stm (last accessed 30 September 2006).

69 High-ranking officers in the Israeli Defense Forces are beginning to question this strategy. See G. Luft, 'The Palestinian H-bomb' (2002), op. cit., pp. 6–7.

70 Although there are no official figures for either of the Russo-Chechen wars, most impartial observers put total casualty figures at between 100,000 and 300,000 for both conflicts. For the first war, Russian human rights activist Sergei Kovalev quotes a figure of 100,000 in 'Russia after Chechnya', *New York Review of Books,* 17 July 1997, p. 27. The American political scientist John Dunlop suggests a figure of 46,500 in 'The Forgotten War'.

71 Artur Arkhipov, 'What the war in Chechnya costs Russia', *Zhurnalist*, 7, July 2005, accessed on *Johnson's Russia List*, #9205, 19 July 2005; Ilyas Akhmadov gives a figure of between $2 and $3 billion dollars a year; reported in Ilyas Akhmadov, *The Russian-Chechen Tragedy: The Way to Peace and Democracy: Conditional Independence Under an International Administration*, peaceinchechnya.org/peace/peace_akhmadov2.htm.

72 Ibid.

73 Andrei Lebedev, *Izvestiya*, 9 September 2004.

74 See A. Nivat, 'Chechnya: brutality and indifference', Crimes of War Project, 6 January 2003, www.crimesofwar.org/print/onnews/chechnya-print.html (last accessed 25 September 2006).

75 Nick Paton Walsh, 'Russia's man in reign of terror in Chechnya', *Guardian*, 13 January 2004.

76 See Ilona Vinogradova, 'Chechensky konflikt vykhodit za predely respubliki' (The Chechen conflict is spreading beyond the borders of the republic), *Izvestiya*, 24 June 2004.

77 Speckhard and Akhmedova (2006), op. cit.

78 See A. Yurkovsky, 'Mirror of a war', World Press Review, 30 January 2002, www.worldpress.org/Europe/921.cfm (last accessed 25 September 2006).

79 Sergei Reznik, 'Alu Alkhanov: davleniye so storony federal'nogo tsentra ya ne ispytyvayu' (Alu Alkhanov: I feel no pressure from the central federal authorities), *Yuzhny Federal'nyi*, 18 July 2006, u-f.ru/ru/Archive/2006/7/27/Article/ID_1980 (accessed on 30 September 2006).

80 'Containment' here is understood as George Kennan's celebrated interpretation of the concept in X, 'The sources of Soviet conduct', *Foreign Affairs*, 26:2, July 1947, pp. 566–82.

81 Originally published in Alex P. Schmid, *Political Terrorism*, Amsterdam: North-Holland 1988, pp.58–59, reproduced in his 'Frameworks for conceptualising terrorism', *Terrorism and Political Violence*, 16:2, Summer 2004, p. 201.

82 Ekaterina Stepanova, *Anti-terrorism and Peace-building During and After Conflict*, Stockholm: Stockholm International Peace Research Institute, 2003, p. 4.

83 C.W. Blandy, 'Chechnya: the search for a strong successor', *Conflict Studies Research Centre: Caucasus Series,* 04/19, July 2004, p. 4. In October 2005, Alu Alkhanov admitted that 7,000 former *boyeviki* made up almost half of the forces of law and order in Chechnya, 'Pochti polovina sotrudnikov militsii Chechnyi byvshiye

boyeviki: 7 tysyach chelovek' (Almost half of those serving in Chechnya's police force are former fighters: seven thousand persons), www.newsru.com/russia/21oct2005/chechnya.html (last accessed 25 September 2006).

84 See John Russell, 'Exploitation of the "Islamic factor" in the Russo-Chechen conflict before and after 11 September 2001', *European Security*, 11:4, Winter 2002, pp. 96–109.

85 Mary Kaldor, 'Terrorism as regressive globalisation', Open Democracy website, 25 September 2003, www.opendemocracy.net/debates/article-3–77–1501.jsp (last accessed 25 September 2006).

86 Sergei Markedonov, 'Terror zakonchilsya. Zabud'te' (The terror is over. Forget it), APN, www.apn.ru/?chapter_name=print_impres&data_id=586&do=view_single (last accessed 25 September 2006).

87 On 2 February 2006, Zakaev was removed from his post as Deputy Chair for Foreign Affairs of the Ichkerian cabinet in a move by Sadulaev to concentrate political power within the borders of Chechnya, see chechenpress.co.uk/english/news/2006/02/06/01.shtml.

88 'Russia angered by Zakayev statement on Nalchik crisis, urges London to act', *Moscow News*, 17 October 2005.

89 On 27 May 2006, Zakaev was promoted to the post of Chechnya-Ichkeria's Foreign Minister, see 'Zakaev gets a promotion', The Jamestown Foundation's *Chechnya Weekly*, 7:22, 1 June 2006 (last accessed 25 September 2006).

90 See www.russialink.org.uk/kursk/events.htm (last accessed 25 September 2006).

91 :www.wciom.ru/vciom/new/public/030325_putin.htm.

92 www.chechenpress.com/news/06_2002/25_06.shtml.

93 *Guardian*, 29 November 2001. Within a fortnight of 9/11, the then German Chancellor – Gerhard Schroeder, had stated that "As regards Chechnya, there will be and must be a more differentiated evaluation in world opinion," *Guardian*, 26 September 2001.

94 *Guardian*, 22 December 2001.

95 Aleksandr Iskandryan, quoted in Tom de Waal, 'A War of Unintended Consequences, 18 November 2004, www.indexonline.org.

7 Entrepreneurs of violence

1 Title of an article devoted to an interview with Basaev by the Polish journalist Witold St Michalowski, published by Kavkaz-Center on 19 August 2006, www.kavkazcenter.com/russ/content/2006/07/18/45973.shmtl (accessed 19 August 2006).

2 Epitomised, during the first war by President Clinton's appearance at the Victory Day Parade in Moscow on 9 May 1995, *Novoye vremya*, 15, 1995, p. 25; and during the second by the Queen's reception of Putin at Windsor in April 2000, *Independent on Sunday*, 18 April 2000.

3 'Chechnya: predvaritel'nie itogi' (Chechnya: provisional results), *Svobodnaya mysl'*, 1, 1997, p. 38.

4 'A war Russia cannot afford to lose', *Transition*, 2: 11, 1996, p. 31.

5 For reports on the bombings, see *Segodnya*, 1, 6, 10, 14 September, 1999.

6 *Argumenty i fakty*, 4, 2001.

7 *Novoye vremya*, 5, 1997, p. 8.

8 Nikolai V. Grammatikov, 'The Russian intervention in Chechnya in November 1994: issues and decision-making', *The Journal of Slavic Military Studies*, 11:4, 1998, pp. 128–129.

9 *Moskovskiye novosti*, 35, 14–20 September 1999, p. 7.

10 In the first war he is credited with masterminding, on 16 April 1996, the ambush at Yarysh-Mardy of the 245th regiment, which lost 76 dead. *Novoye vremya*, 43, 1999, p. 12.

11 *Izvestiya*, 28 September 1999. Elizabeth Fuller, to whom I am grateful for providing me with a copy of her unpublished article on the demonisation of the Chechens by the Russian media during the early phase of the first war, has traced the growing involvement of Russian government officials with Chechen 'oppositionists' throughout 1994, see 'Chechen politics: a murky prospect', *Transition*, 1:3, 1995, pp. 11–13.

12 *Izvestiya*, 17 September 1999.

13 *Segodnya*, 14 March 2000.

14 *Izvestiya*, 1 October 1999.

15 *Izvestiya*, 27 October 1999.

16 *Argumenty i fakty*, 38, September 1999, p. 9.

17 Valery Tishkov, 'Geopolitika chechenskoi voiny: "natsional'nyi interes" kak sopernichestvo biurokratii i elit' (The geopolitics of the Chechen war: "national interest" as rivalry between bureaucracies and elites), *Svobodnaya mysl'*, 4, 1997, pp. 65–74.

18 *Komsomol'skaya pravda*, 19 March 1996.

19 This act is attributed to Khattab on the FSB website, see www.fsb.ru/foto/hattab/hattab.html (accessed 30 September 2006).

20 In a thought-provoking address delivered at a Guardian/RUSI conference on the 'War against terrorism' in the wake of September 11, Malise Ruthven made the point that 'every step towards Bin Laden's demonisation raises his stature among his supporters', *Guardian*, 30 October 2001.

21 For example, the BBC's Malcolm Haslett's analysis 'Jihad or Russian conspiracy?', 11 August 1999, news.bbc.co.uk/1/hi/world/europe/417797.stm (last accessed 25 September 2006).

22 Of the many reports compiled by human rights organisations on war crimes committed in Chechnya, one of the most detailed is that produced by the Physicians for Human Rights in May 2001, 'Endless brutality: war crimes in Chechnya', see www.phrusa.org/research/pdf/chech_report_final.pdf (last accessed 25 September 2006).

23 In April 2003, the Council of Europe threatened to set up an international war crimes tribunal on Chechnya, if the situation did not improve, *Agence France Presse*, 2 April 2003; see also the report of the Council of Europe's Committee for the Prevention of Torture and Inhuman or Degrading Treatment or Punishment, concerning the Chechen Republic of the Russian Federation, 10 July 2003, www.cpt.coe.int/documents/rus/2003–33-inf-eng.htm (last accessed 25 September 2006).

24 For example when UN war crimes prosecutor Carla del Ponte met Akhmed Zakaev in March 2002, see *Agence France Presse* 11 March 2002.

25 See Robert Wielaard, 'Chechnya query incenses Putin', *Washington Post*, 13 November 2002.

26 Andrei Piontkovsky, 'Russia has lost the war in Chechnya', *Chechnya Weekly*, 4:37, 16 October 2003.

27 For a good account of Akhmad Kadyrov's position, see Ilya Milshtein, 'Simply Kadyrov', www.newtimes.ru/eng/detail.asp?art_id=865. (last accessed 25 September 2006).

28 Interview with *Ekho* radio, published in *Komsomol'skaya pravda*, 19 January 2004, www.kp.ru/online/news/8202/. The same interview notes Kadyrov Senior's call for Vladimir Putin to be made President for life!

29 A translation of an article published in January 2004 by *Die Welt* alleged that Kadyrov's son, Ramzan, has a prison in his house for torturing captured Chechens, who were beginning to fear his so-called 'death battalions', even more than the Russian forces. www.inopressa.ru/print/welt/2004/01/23/11:20:42/Chechnia (last accessed 25 September 2006). For more allegations of Ramzan Kadyrov's brutality against fellow Chechens as well as the description of his father being 'reviled by Chechens as a traitor', see Nick Paton Walsh, 'Russia's man in reign of terror in Chechnya', *Guardian*, 13 January 2004.

30 *The Economist*, 11–17 October 2003.

31 Ahmed Rashid, 'The Mess in Afghanistan', *The New York Review of Books*, 12 February 2004, p. 26.

32 Ibid., p. 27.

33 Much of this section has been based on my contribution, entitled 'Basayev: the beast of Beslan?' to Stephen D. Shenfield's Research Report *'Chechnya and Russia: A Post-Beslan Symposium*, 29, January 2005, published online as *JRL Research and Analytical Supplement* by *Johnson's Russia List*, #9024, www.cdi.org/russia/johnson/9024.cfm (last accessed 12 October 2006).

34 In his televised address to the nation on 4 September, the day after the conclusion of the Beslan siege, President Putin did not mention Chechnya once; see 'Could the Beslan tragedy have been avoided?', The Jamestown Foundation's *Chechnya Weekly*, 5:34, 8 September 2004.

35 The declaration was published in full, without alterations or editing, by the pro-independence Chechen website *Daymohk* on 17 September 2004, see www.daymohk.info/cgi-bin/orsi3/index.cgi?id=8428;idt=17200409;section=1.

36 Best exemplified by his 'Book of a Mujahideen', see www.kavkazcenter.com/eng/help/ebook.shtml (last accessed 1 August 2006).

37 See Tom de Waal, 'Basayev and Maskhadov under pressure', *Caucasus Reporting Service* 252, 8 September 2004.

38 Quoted in Valery Dzutsev and Alan Tskhurbaev, 'Beslan siege unravels, slowly and bloodily', *Caucasus Reporting Service* 250, 3 September, 2004.

39 For the aims and targets of terrorism, see Alex Schmid, 'Goals and objectives of international terrorism', in Robert O. Slater and Michael Stohl (eds), *Current Perspectives on International Terrorism*, Basingstoke: Macmillan 1988, pp. 47–87.

40 Walter Laqueur, *The Age of Terrorism*, Boston: Little, Brown and Company, 1987, p. 121.

41 Basaev states quite explicitly in his message that the suicide attacks on aircraft and the metro in Moscow in the run-up to Alu Alkhanov's victory were 'our vote ahead of time' in the presidential elections in Chechnya.

42 Throughout his message, Basaev refers to Russia as *Rusnya*, a term intended, perhaps, to be both derogatory and to establish, albeit phonetically, an equivalence between Chechnya and Russia.

43 Originally published in Alex P. Schmid, *Political Terrorism*, Amsterdam: North-Holland 1988, pp. 58–59, reproduced in his 'Frameworks for conceptualising terror-ism', *Terrorism and Political Violence*, 16:2 (Summer 2004), p. 201.

44 Robert Pape, 'The strategic logic of suicide terrorism', *American Political Science Review*, 97:3, August 2003, p. 355.

45 Max Abrahms, 'Are terrorists really rational? The Palestinian example', *Orbis*, Summer 2004, p. 549.

46 Chris Hedges, 'On war', *The New York Review of Books*, 51:20, 16 December 2004, p. 14.

47 Mikhail A. Alexseev, 'Back to Hell: civilian-military "audience costs" and Russia's wars in Chechnia', in Stephen L. Webber and Jennifer G. Mathers, *Military and Society in Post-Soviet Russia*, Manchester: Manchester University Press, 2006, pp. 106–107.

48 *Izvestiya*, 6 December 2004.

49 *Izvestiya*, 7 December 2004.

50 *Izvestiya*, 8 December 2004.

51 See another article by Vadim Rechkalov called 'Gori v zakone' (Mountains in law) [a play on the Russian of *vory v zakone*, meaning a 'brotherhood of thieves' JR], *Moskovsky komsomolets*, 14 February 2005, www.compromat.ru/main/chechnya/vzakone.htm (accessed 18 August 2005).

52 *Izvestiya*, 9 December 2004.

53 Svetlana Meteleva, 'Ubit' Basayeva mozhno. No nikomu ne nuzhno' (Basaev could be killed. But nobody needs this), *Moskovsky komsomolets*, 21 March 2005.

54 *Izvestiya*, 10 December 2004.

55 Stephen Blank, 'Russia's Ulster: the Chechen War and its consequences', *Demokratizatsiya*, Winter 2001.

56 See, for example, V. Mironov, *Ya byl na etoi voine. Chechnya. Year 1995* (I fought in this war. Chechnya. Year 1995), Moscow, 2001, pp. 413–414.

57 Avraam Shmulevich, 'Mest' za prezidenta' (Revenge for the President), *APN Publikatsii*, 27 June 2006, www.apn.ru/publications/article9916.htm (accessed 17 September 2006).

58 Valentinas Mite, 'Basayev appointment sends signal to Russia and beyond', *RFE/RL*, 28 June 2006.

59 12 July 2006, news.bbc.co.uk/1/hi/world/europe/5168984.stm (accessed 17 September 2006).

60 See picture of Kadyrov and Putin in *Novaya gazeta*, 9 June 2005. Interview with Aleksei Malashenko by Vladlen Maksimov, 'Lyudi ne rozhdayutsya fanatikami i terroristami' (People are not born fanatics and terrorists), 1 October 2004, www.carnegie.ru/ru/print/7124-print.htm (last accessed 15 November 2004).

61 This claim was made by Yulia Latynina on *Ekho Moskvy* on 15 July 2006, and reported by John Dunlop, 'Putin, Kozak and Russian policy toward the North Caucasus', The Jamestown Foundation Conference on 14 September 2006 'The Future of the North Caucasus', www.jamestown.org/nccp-91406.php (accessed on 28 September 2006).

62 www.inopressa.ru/print/welt/2004/01/23/11:20:42/Chechnia.

63 PACE Document 10276, dated 17 September 2004, 'The political situation in the Chechen Republic: measures to increase democratic stability in accordance with Council of Europe standards', assembly.coe.int/Documents/WorkingDocs/doc04/EDOC10276.htm (accessed 7 March 2005).

64 'Chechnya's Deputy Prime Minister intends to kill Basayev before 9 May', *Caucasian Knot News*, 29 April 2005.

65 See Nick Paton Walsh, 'Russia's man in reign of terror in Chechnya', *Guardian*, 13 January 2004.

66 Nick Paton Walsh, 'Land of the Warlords', *Guardian*, 13 June 2006.

67 Mark Franchetti, 'In the torture cell of Chechnya's tyrant', *Sunday Times*, 30 April 2006, p. 1:21.

68 BBC Radio Four, broadcast 26 November 2005.

69 Artyom Liss, 'Chechnya's gun-toting strongman', 26 November 2006, news.bbc.co.uk/1/hi/world/europe/4470784.stm (accessed 17 September 2006).

70 Anna Politkovskaya, 'Ramzan Kadyrov – krasa Chechni' (Ramzan Kadyrov – the beautiful face of Chechnya), *Novaya gazeta*, 42, 5 June 2006.

71 Valeriya Novodvorskaya, 'Boisya chekistov, prinosyashchikh dary (Beware Chekists, bearing gifts), *Novoye vremya*, 11, 20 March 2005, p. 13.

72 *Itar-Tass*, 7 February 2006.

73 Emil Souleimanov, *Central Asia–Caucasus Institute Analyst*, 31 May 2006.

74 Malashenko (2004), op. cit.

75 Ivan Sukhov, 'Chechensky ochag' (Chechen hearth), *APN Proyekt* institute natsional'noi strategii, 16 August 2005, www.apn.ru/publications/article1519.htm (accessed 17 September 2006).

76 'Boxer Tyson welcomed in Chechnya', BBC, 15 September 2005, news.bbc.co.uk/1/hi/world/europe/4250126.stm (accessed 30 September 2006).

77 'First beauty queen named in Chechnya', *Moscow News*, 28 May 2006.

78 Liz Fuller, 'Chechnya: premier seeks to change his image', *RFE/RL Features*, 19 May 2006.

79 Kevin Daniel Leahy, 'Kadyrov's bluff: why Chechnya's strongman continues to test his political boundaries', *Central Asia–Caucasus Analyst*, 17 May 2006.

80 Nick Paton Walsh, 'Land of the warlords', *Guardian*, 13 June 2006.

81 Vadim Rechkalov, www.compromat.ru/main/chechnya/vzakone.htm (18 August 2005).

82 'Aleksei Makarkin: zadacha Kremlya – ogranichit' klanovuyu sistemu' (Aleksei Makarkin: the task of the Kremlin is to limit the clan system), on Kavkaz-Forum's 'Rekonstruktsiya Chechni' (Reconstruction of Chechnya) website 19 July 2005, www.kavkaz-forum.ru/politic/11389.html?print=on (accessed 5 October 2005).

83 17 March 2006, as reported by the *Central Asia-Caucasus Analyst*, www.caciana-lyst.org/view_article.php?articleid=4125 (30 September 2006).

84 For an explanation of these concepts, see Johan Galtung, 'Violence, peace, and peace research', *Journal of Peace Research*, 6:3, 1969, pp. 167–191.

85 For case studies in Northern Ireland, the Philippines and the Middle East, see Kim Cragin and Peter Chalk, *Terrorism and Development: Using Social and Economic Development to Inhibit a Resurgence of Terrorism*, Santa Monica, CA: RAND, 2003; for links between narcotics and insurgency in Afghanistan, Burma, Colombia and Peru, see Svante Cornell, 'The interaction of narcotics and conflict', *Journal of Peace Research*, 42:6, 2005, pp. 751–760.

86 The illusory nature of Russian territorial integrity is examined by Sergei Marke-donov in his 'Chechnya: ugroza sistemnogo separatizma' (Chechnya: the threat of system separatism), *APN Proyekt* instituta natsional'noi strategii, 24 January 2005.

87 For Dagestan, 'Djamaat "Shariat": "The Territory of Jihad Extends!"', 2 July 2005, www.kavkazcenter.com/eng/content/2005/07/02/3918.shtml (last accessed 25 September 2006); for Kabardino-Balkaria, 'Napadeniye na Nal'chik' (The attack on Nalchik) in www.rian.ru/actual/nalchik_attack_131005/ (last accessed 25 September 2006).

88 In 2005, Russia was rated 90th worst out of 146 countries for levels of corruption by Transparency International, see Jennifer Moll and Richard Gowan (eds), *Losing Ground: Russia's European Commitments to Human Rights*, London: Foreign Policy Centre, 2005, p. 24.

89 For Anatol Lieven, see 'Tsirkulyar po pravil'nomy osveshcheniyu sobytii v Chechne' (Circular on the correct illumination of events in Chechnya), www.kavkaz.org.uk/russ/article.php?id=31149 (last accessed 25 September 2006); for Tom de Waal, see 'Tomas de Vaal i biznes na krovi' (Thomas de Waal and busi-ness in blood), www.chechnya.ru/view_all.php?part=pub.

90 See, for example, Mikhail A. Alexseev, 'Security Sell-out in the North Caucasus 2004: How Government Centralization Backfires', *PONARS Policy Memo*, 344, November 2004.

91 See 'The economics of war: the intersection of need, creed and greed', organised on 10 September 2001 at the Woodrow Wilson International Center for Scholars in Washington, DC. www.ipacademy.org/PDF_Reports/econofwar.pdf (last accessed 25 September 2006). I have elected to follow this line of analysis rather than the 'greed' and 'grievance' approach of Paul Collier and Anke Hoeffler, see their 'Greed and grievance in civil war', *Oxford Economic Papers Advance Access*, 20 August 2004, oep. oxfordjournals.org/cgi/content/abstract/56/4/563 (last accessed 25 September 2006)

92 For Kremlin recognition of the political wing of Hamas, while refusing to acknow-ledge the political legitimacy of any of the Chechen resistance, see Andrew McGre-gor, 'Distant relations: Hamas and the Mujahideen of Chechnya', The Jamestown Foundation's *Chechnya Weekly*, 7:8, 23 February 2006.

93 This interpretation has been strongly rejected by Akhmed Zakaev, whose role in the Chechen resistance was first downgraded and then restored in recent reshuffles, see his 'Zapad dal sanktsiyu na dolguyu voinu v Chechne' (The West has sanctioned a long war in Chechnya), an interview on 6 February 2006 with Radio Svoboda's

Andrei Babitsky, published by Chechen Press, www.chechenpress.info/events/
2006/02/09/01.shtml17936; for an account of the reshuffle, see Andrei Smirnov,
'Sadulaev's new decrees reveal divisions within the separatist movement', The
Jamestown Foundation's *Chechnya Weekly*, 7:6, 9 February 2006.

94 See, for example, The Norwegian Helsinki Committee, *Report III/2002*, 'The ethnic
war: persecution of Chechens in the Russian Federation', Oslo, 2002, Amnesty
International's report of 23 June 2004 '"Normalization" in whose eyes?',
web.amnesty.org/library/print/ENGEUR460272004 (last accessed 25 September
2006); in March 2005, Human Rights Watch published a briefing paper entitled
'Worse than a war: "disappearances" in Chechnya – a crime against humanity',
hrw.org/backgrounder/eca/chechnya0305/ (last accessed 25 September 2006); the
Parliamentary Assembly of the Council of Europe (PACE) also reported in 2004 on
'The political situation in the Chechen Republic: measures to increase democratic
stability in accordance with Council of Europe Standards', assembly.coe.int/docu-
ments/WorkingDocs/doc04/EDOC10276.htm (last accessed 25 September 2006).

95 The vote fell just 17 short of the two-thirds majority (300) needed to impeach the
President, see 16 May 1999, news.bbc.co.uk/1/hi/world/europe/344805.stm (last
accessed 25 September 2006).

96 Sergei Kovalev, 'Nekotoriye itogi chechenskoi kampanii' (Some results of the
Chechen campaign), *Nezavisimaya gazeta*, 22 February 1995.

97 Sergei Stepashin, Yeltsin's FSB chief in 1994, is one of the few to reject this
scenario, placing the blame for the impasse squarely on Dudayev's intransigence.
See his interview of 11 May 2002, in Lyudmila Telen, 'Last but one
hero', english.mn.ru/english/issue.php?2002-50–11 (last accessed 25 September
2006).

98 Articulated, for example, by Robert Parsons, the former BBC correspondent covering the Chechen conflict, in the film *Chechen Lullaby* by Nino Kirtadze, Arte, Paris,
2000.

99 Maria Eismont, 'Chechnya – "samoe silnoe razocharovaniye" prezidenta Yeltsina'
(Chechnya is President Yeltsin's 'greatest disappointment'), *Segodnya*, 20 October
1995.

100 For the lack of idealism in the search for peace in either the UN or the EU, see John
Lloyd, 'Broken dream', *FTmagazine*, 8–9 October 2005, p. 8; for Western leaders,
see André Glucksmann, 'Le noveau tsar vous dit merci', (The new tsar thanks you),
Le Monde, 10 March 2005.

101 For an application of this debate to the Iraq War, see Keith Burgess-Jackson,
'Bush's critics as repeat offenders', *TCS Daily*, 3 July 2003, www.tcsdaily.com/
article.aspx?id=070303A (last accessed 25 September 2006).

102 See Spiegel Online, 1 December 2004, 'Moscow mon amour: Gerhard Schroeder's
dangerous liaison', service.spiegel.de/cache/international/0,1518,330461,00.html
(last accessed 25 September 2006). In December 2005, the former German Chancellor was appointed Chairman of Gazprom's Baltic pipeline subsidary, see
www.mosnews.com/news/2005/12/10/gerschr.shtml (last accessed 25 September
2006).

103 This claim was made by Mikhail Khodorkovsky in his article 'Crisis of Russian lib-
eralism', 29 March 2004, see www.mosnews.com/column/2004/03/29/khodor-
kovsky.shtml (last accessed 25 September 2006).

104 Aleksei Venediktov, chief editor of *Ekho Moskvy* radio station, in David Remnick
(2003).

105 Susan B. Glasser and Peter Baker, 'Chechnya War a deepening trap for Putin',
Washington Post, 13 September 2004, p. A01.

106 Interview in *Le Monde*, 4 November 2002, reported in *Johnson's Russia List* (*JRL*),
6 November 2002, #6536.

107 See Vladimir Gutnov, 'Rossiya ne dolzhna opravdyvatsya za svoe stremlenie pokon-

chit' s terrorizmom' (Russia doesn't have to justify its efforts to put an end to terrorism), *Nezavisimaya gazeta*, 4 November 1999.

108 Jonathan Steele is a very experienced observer of the Soviet and Russian scene; as far back as 1974, when an exchange student at Moscow State University, I smuggled Jonathan past the watchful eyes of the *dezhurniye* (hostel wardens) so that he could see for himself the delights of life in Stalin's 'wedding cake' skyscraper set atop the Lenin Hills.

109 Jonathan Steele, 'Doing well out of the war: reflections on the stand-off between Russia and Chechnya', *London Review of Books*, 19 October 2004, www.selvesandothers.org/article5936.html (last accessed 25 September 2006).

110 Liz Fuller (2004), op. cit.

111 See Channel 4 Dispatches *Chechnya: The Dirty War*, screened 25 July 2005.

112 See edition of *Novoye vremya*, 11, 20 March 2005, entitled 'Bez Maskhadova' (Without Maskhadov), pp. 6–13.

113 Vadim Dubnov, 'Vera i beznadezhnost': kak pogib chelovek, u kotorogo davno ne bylo vykhoda'' (Faith and hopelessness: how perished a man, for whom there had long since been no way out), *Novoe vremya*, 11, 20 March 2005, pp. 6–10; for Maskhadov's last interview, published on the day before his death – see Liz Fuller, 'Chechen leader gives exclusive interview to *RFE/RL*', www.rferl.org/featuresarticle/2005/03/C8BF5CC0-D91F-4DAC-9185-A451B1124B1D.html (last accessed 25 September 2006).

114 See www.levada/ru/press/2005032402.html (last accessed 25 September 2006).

115 newsru.com/russia/29may2006/klan_print.html (last accessed 23 August 2006).

8 The paths not taken: the Russian failure to reach a political solution in Chechnya

1 *A Dirty War: A Russian Reporter in Chechnya*, London: Harvill Press, p. xxxii.

2 This argument developed by Sergei Kovalev in his 'Sny politicheskogo idealista' (Dreams of a political idealist), *Novoye vremya*, 9, 2000, pp. 10–15.

3 See *Novoye vremya*, 7, 1997, p. 10.

4 Questions posed by Marina Koldobskaya in *Novoye vremya*, 28, 2000, p. 5.

5 Sergei Kovalev, 'After Chechnya', *The New York Review of Books*, 17 July 1997.

6 Rajan Menon and Graham E. Fuller, 'Russia's ruinous Chechen War', *Foreign Affairs*, 79:2, March/April 2000, pp. 43–44.

7 A strategy questioned by Putin's predecessor as Prime Minister, Sergei Stepashin, in his celebrated article claiming that the attack on Chechnya had been planned from the spring of 1999, see *Nezavisimaya gazeta*, 14 January 2000.

8 See 'Chechenskaya voina v voprosakh i otvetakh: Analiticheskoye issledovanie (The Chechen War in questions and answers: an analytical inquiry), www.chechenpress. com/news/2004/08/20/06.shmtl (last accessed 18 January 2005).

9 'V chem bandity v Chechne luchshe talibov?' (In what way are the bandits in Chechnya better than the Taliban?), *Novaya gazeta*, 15 November 2001.

10 In Boris Kagarlitsky, 'Topor proigrannoi voiny' (The hatchet of a lost war), *Novaya gazeta*, 2, 14 January 2002.

11 Aslan Maskhadov, 'Posle etoi voiny Rossiya okonchatel'no poteryala Chechnyu' (After this war Russia has finally lost Chechnya), *Novoye vremya*, 26, 2001, p. 8.

12 Interview with Anna Politkovskaya, 'Esli by diktatorom v Chechne byl ya...' (If I were to be dictator in Chechnya...), *Novaya gazeta*, 20, 21 March 2002.

13 Ruslan Khasbulatov, 'Zachem Rossii nuzhna Chechnya? (Why does Russia need Chechnya?), *Novaya gazeta*, 6, 26 January 2002.

14 See his article 'Chechnya okazalas' na ostrie bor'by raznykh geostrategii' (Chechnya has found itself on the spike of the battle of different geostrategies), *Yabloko Rossii*, 45, 30 October 1999, p. 4.

15 See their 'An opening on Chechnya', *Washington Post*, 4 July 2001.
16 Sanobar Shermatova, 'Chechen plan hammered out', *IWPR*, 30 August 2002, www.peaceinthecaucasus.org/peace/peacenews_shermatova.htm (accessed on 25 September 2006).
17 www.peaceinchechnya.org/peace/peace_liechtenstein.htm.
18 From *Eurasia Insight*, 14 September 2001, www.reliefweb.int/w/R.
19 Reported in Ilyas Akhmadov, *The Russian-Chechen Tragedy: The Way to Peace and Democracy: Conditional Independence Under an International Administration*, peaceinchechnya.org/peace/peace_akhmadov2.htm.
20 See Transnational Radical Party Press Release, 1 May 2003, coranet.radicalparty.org/pressreleases/press_release.php?func=detail&par=4423# (accessed 30 September 2006).
21 Liz Fuller, 'Chechnya: resistance leadership affirms readiness for peace talks', *RFE/RL*, 14 July 2006, www.rferl.org/featuresarticle/2006/07/61768e74-f83c-49b6-ac10-908755cace88.html (last accessed 20 July 2006).
22 Ruslan Khasbulatov has noted the demise in the influence of the *teip*, see 'Gosudarstvo, politika i separtizm' (State, politics and separatism), *Nezavisimaya gazeta*, 14 December 2000. Sergei Kovalev remarks on the criminalisation of the Chechen gangs, see his 'Dve voiny' (Two wars), *Novoye vremya*, 47, 1999, pp. 12–14.
23 Anna Politkovskaya, 'S kem vesti peregovory v Chechnye' (With whom we should negotiate in Chechnya), *Novaya gazeta*, 71, 1 October 2001.
24 Jean-Christophe Peuch, 'Chechnya: ten years after – the logic behind the first Chechen war', *RFE/RL Features*, 10 December 2004.
25 Interview with *Frankfurter Allgemeine Zeitung*, 1 February 2002.
26 15 December 2002, news.bbc.co.uk/1/hi/world/europe/2577065.stm (last accessed 17 September 2006).
27 See 'Amir Khattab stal shakhidom' (Emir Khattab has become a martyr), www.kavkaz.org/russ/article, (accessed on 28 April 2002).
28 2 March 2004, news.bbc.co.uk/1/hi/world/europe/3525717.stm (last accessed 17 September 2006).
29 13 February 2004, news.bbc.co.uk/1/hi/world/europe/3486179.stm (last accessed 17 September 2006).
30 Andreas Gross, 'O nezavisimosti mozhno budet govorit' cherez let 10–15' (One may talk of independence in about 10–15 years), *Chechenskoye obshchestvo*, 6: 44, 29 March 2005.
31 See Pavel Felgenhauer, 'The Russian Army in Chechnya', op. cit.
32 Reuters report in *Russia Today*, 18 April 2000. On 2 March 2000, *Agence France Presse* quoted Presidential advisor, Sergei Yastrzhembsky, as saying: 'The West does not understand the circumstances of terrorism in Russia. No country in the world has confronted terrorism on such a grand scale.'
33 Fred Hiatt, 'Democracy on Hold', *Washington Post*, 6 October 2001.
34 *Novaya gazeta*, 15 October 2001.
35 *Guardian*, 29 November 2001.
36 'Straw backs Russia over Chechnya', *The Times*, 1 November 2001.
37 *Guardian*, 22 December 2001.
38 news.bbc.co.uk/1/hi/world/europe/1936998.stm (last accessed 25 September 2006).
39 www.grani.ru/blast.
40 *Rossiiskaya gazeta*, 10 September 2002.
41 *RFE/RL*, 26 June 2002.
42 For the full text of the Danish Ministry of Justice's decision not to extradite Zakaev, see www.tjetjenien.dk/congress/extradition.html (last accessed 25 September 2006).
43 Judge Workman's findings are presented in full, in English, courtesy of the zakaev.ru

website, zakaev.ru/turnover/papers/50592.html (last accessed 25 September 2006); and on www.hrvc.net/west/15–11–03.html (last accessed 25 September 2006).

44 www.chechnyafilmfestival.org/mosc.htm (accessed 25 October 2003).

45 For an interesting article on the concept of civil society, see Jürgen Kocka, 'Civil society from a historical perspective', *European Review*, 12:1, February 2004, pp. 65–79.

46 zakaev.ru/turnover/quotes (last accessed 25 September 2006).

47 The Jamestown Foundation's *Chechnya Weekly*, 4:3, 6 February 2003.

48 'Chechnya – an apology', *Guardian*, 30 June 2003; 'Linking Chechnya to Iraq was wrong', *The Times*, 28 July 2003.

49 In an interview granted to *Gazeta wyborcza*, 12 November 2002.

50 Steven Lee Myers, 'Chechen in extradition dispute: criminal or peacemaker?', *New York Times*, 9 December 2002.

51 ACPC, 30 October in The Jamestown Foundation's *Chechnya Weekly*, 3:3, 4 November 2002.

52 *Novaya gazeta*, 3 March 2003.

53 www.gazeta.ru/print/2003/02/27/Communistsdai.shtml.

54 www.amnesty.org/russia/zakayev_case.html (last accessed 25 September 2006).

55 www.chechnya.nl/news.php?id=371&lang=eng.

56 zakaev.ru/turnover/comment/19105.html (last accessed 25 September 2006).

57 Boris Kagarlitsky, 'Zakaev out of the game', *Moscow Times*, 10 December 2002.

58 tcehtchenieparis.free.fr/text/Copenhagen-reso-29–10–02.htm.

59 news.bbc.co.uk/1/hi/world/europe/2364271.stm (last accessed 25 September 2006).

60 www.gazeta.ru/print/2002/12/07/zakaevdvames.shtml (last accessed 25 September 2006).

61 The Jamestown Foundation's *Chechnya Weekly*, 2:36, 9 October 2001.

62 *Novaya gazeta*, 14 July 2003.

63 The Freedom House rating for 'rule of law' in Russia was 5.13 in 2003, see www.freedomhouse.org/pdf_docs/research/nitransit/2003/nitrussia2003.pdf.

64 See Ian Traynor, 'Chechen murder trial limps to an end', *Guardian*, 28 June 2002.

65 *Novaya gazeta*, 14 July 2003.

66 *Novaya gazeta*, 4 August 2003.

67 See Judge Timothy Workman's summing up, zakaev.ru/turnover/papers/50592.html (last accessed 25 September 2006); and www.hrvc.net/west/15–11–03.html (last accessed 25 September 2006).

68 See, for example, Presidential aide Sergei Yastrzhembsky's comments after the court's decision was announced, newsfromrussia.com/main/2003/11/13/51210.html (last accessed 25 September 2006).

69 For Yastrzhembsky's comment on this, see Peter Graff's article for Reuters 'Britain refuses to extradite Zakayev', www.rusnet.nl/news/2003/11/14/breakingnews01.shtml (last accessed 25 September 2006).

70 zakaev.ru/news/52359.html (last accessed 25 September 2006).

71 The three banned groups are the Islamic International Brigade, the Special Purpose Islamic Regiment and the Riyadus–Salikhin Reconnaissance and Sabotage Battalion of Chechen Martyrs, see news.bbc.co.uk/1/hi/world/europe/2810153.stm (last accessed 25 September 2006).

72 *Agence France Presse*, 9 September 2002; Ambassador Vershbow had been more circumspect when, in March 2002, he had claimed: 'The issue of Chechnya is certainly a difficult item in our relations. International terrorism is part of the Chechen problem. Some Chechen separatists, indeed, have participated in terrorist acts.' www.wps.ru/chitalka/terror/en/archives.php3?d=20&m=3.

73 The prospects for any alleged or convicted Chechen 'terrorist' surviving long in Russian jails are grim if one studies the fate of Turpal-Ali Atgeriev and Salman Raduev, both of whom were arrested, tried and convicted in Dagestan. Both died in

mysterious circumstances in Russian jails, officially the former of a heart attack and the latter through internal bleeding.

74 news.bbc.co.uk/1/low/world/europe/3020231.stm (last accessed 25 September 2006).

75 *Agence France Presse*, 11 August 2003.

76 Theodore P. Gerber and Sarah E. Mendelson, 'The disconnect in how Russians think about human rights and Chechnya: a consequence of media manipulation', *PONARS Policy Memo*, 244, January, 2002.

77 www.wciom.ru/vciom/new/press/press020731_17.htm.

78 'Tri   goda   Prezidentstva   (Three   years   of   presidency),   www.vciom-a.ru/press/2003032601.html.

79 www.vciom-a.ru/press/2004012800.html.

80 The phrase is from the BBC's Stephen Dalziel, 15 March 2004, news.bbc.co.uk/1/hi/world/europe/3511164.stm (last accessed 17 September 2006).

81 www.levada.ru/press/2006091302.html (accessed 16 September 2006).

82 Interview in *Le Monde*, 4 November 2002, reported in *Johnson's Russia List*, #6536, 6 November 2002.

83 www.wciom.ru/vciom/new/press/021029_terror.htm. Within a month the proportion approving the storming had dropped to 78 per cent, see www.wciom.ru/vciom/new/press/press221204_28.htm.

84 zakaev.ru/turnover/comment/14903.html (last accessed 25 September 2006).

85 Boris Kagarlitsky, 'Zakaev out of the game', *Moscow Times*, 10 December 2002.

86 Officially, the turnout was 89.48 per cent, with 95.97 per cent approving the Constitution. For a sceptical account of the vote, see International Helsinki Federation for Human Rights Report, 'The Constitutional referendum in Chechnya was neither free nor fair', www.osce-ngo.net/030328.pdf.

87 Article 8, point 4, forbids the creation and functioning of social organisations ... that aim to ... violate the territory integrity of ... the Russian Federation. The Russian President is also given the right to remove the elected President of Chechnya (Article 72d). See www.chechnya.gov.ru/republic/const/.

88 Chechnya received the lowest rating of 7 for both level of political rights and civil liberties in the Freedom House country ratings for 2003, see www.freedomhouse.org/ratings/index.htm.

89 See Umalt Dudayev, 'Chechnya: the fighting goes on', *Caucasus Reporting Service*, 214, 15 January 2004.

90 Islam represents arguably the easiest way for Chechens to distinguish themselves from the Russians, an important requirement in a civil war. Were they able to live, as they would prefer, according to their own customs, they would not require imported elements of Islam to make this distinction.

91 To his credit, the former Speaker of the Russian Parliament, Ruslan Khasbulatov, has persisted in advocating this peace plan, despite no encouragement whatsoever from the Putin administration. For a round-table discussion of this plan, see Nairi Hovsepyan and Lyubov Tsukanova, 'Chechnya and Russia. War and peace', *New Times*, December 2003, www.newtimes.ru/eng/detail.asp?art_id=535 (last accessed 25 September 2006).

92 www.vciom-a.ru/press/2003032601.html; by the end of 2003, this had hardened to 67 per cent in favour of peace negotiations and only 20 per cent for continuing the war, vciom-a.ru/press/2003121301.html

93 Paragraph 14, see www.un.org/terrorism/a57273.htm (last accessed 25 September 2006).

94 John Russell, 'Primed to explode', *The World Today*, 60:6, June 2004, pp. 20–21.

95 'How Maskhadov was killed: yet another Russian mystery', The Jamestown Foundation's *Chechnya Weekly*, 16:11, 16 March 2005.

96 www.rferl.org/nca/features/2002/02/01022002102012.asp.

97 Vitaly Tret'yakov drew attention to this phenomenon in his article 'Diagnoz: upravlyayemaya demokratiya' (The diagnosis is a managed democracy), *Nezavisimaya gazeta*, 13 January 2000.

98 Dmitri Trenin, 'Russia leaves the West', *Foreign Affairs*, 85:4, July/August 2006, p. 87.

9 The international dimension

1 In a radio interview on 26 October 2002 to Europe One, reported in the *Irish Examiner*, 28 October 2002.

2 See www.cbsnews.com/stories/2000/01/31/world/main155042.shtml (last accessed 25 September 2006).

3 GeorgeWBush.com: 'Issues: policy points overview', 2 April 2000.

4 Vanessa Pupavac, 'Disputes over war casualties in former Yugoslavia', *Radical Statistics*, 69, Autumn 1998, www.radstats.org.uk/no069/article3.htm (last accessed 25 September 2006).

5 'Over 200,000 killed in Chechnya since 1994 – pro-Moscow official', *Moscow News*, 19 November 2004 www.mosnews.com/news/2004/11/19/civiliandeath.shtml (last accessed 25 September 2006).

6 www.kavkazcenter.com/eng/article.php?id=2899.

7 '300,000 killed in Chechen wars – pro-Moscow official', *Moscow News*, 27 June 2005.

8 Ol'ga Shlyakhtina in conversation with Sergei Markedonov, 'V Chechne ne postkonfliktnoye uregulirovaniye, a smena pokolenii separatistov' (In Chechnya we do not have post-conflict stabilisation, but a change of generations among the separatists), www.kavkaz-forum.ru/reconstruction/11702.html?print=on (accessed 5 October 2005).

9 See Charles Gurin, 'Group claims 25,000 Russian soldiers have died in Chechnya', The Jamestown Foundation's *Eurasia Daily Monitor*, 1:3, 5 May 2004.

10 Liz Fuller, 'Look back in anger – ten years of war in Chechnya', *RFE/RL Features*, 11 December 2004.

11 See Paul F. Kisak, 'Recently declassified Soviet War and U.S. covert casualties', www.geocities.com/echomoscow/warcasualties.html (last accessed 25 September 2006). The same source cites 8,943 Russian combat deaths in the two Chechen wars up until the end of 2001. Liz Fuller gives the total Soviet troop losses in Afghanistan as 14,453 (see note 591).

12 See Sirajdin Sattaev, 'Litsemeriye i nenavist'' (Hypocrisy and hate), www.kavkaz.org.uk/russ/article.php?id=23998.

13 Paddy Ashdown, 'We must aim for a Kosovan protectorate', *Observer*, 28 March 1999. If one takes Iceland as the western, and the Urals as the eastern, extreme of Europe then the midway line would run through Priština, placing the capital of Kosovo firmly in the centre of Europe!

14 This development was noted by Tony Wood, 'The case for Chechnya', *New Left Review*, 30, November–December 2004, pp. 5–36.

15 See Robert Wielaard, 'Chechnya query incenses Putin', *Washington Post*, 13 November 2002.

16 See, for example, Committee to Protect Journalists Report 'Attacks on the press in 2005', www.cpj.org/attacks05/europe05/russia_05.html.

17 www.levada.ru/chechnya.html (last accessed 25 September 2006).

18 www.levada.ru/takoemnenie.html (last accessed 25 September 2006).

19 www.levada.ru/press/2006091302.html (accessed 15 September 2006).

20 For a comprehensive coverage of such articles, see *Johnson's Russia List*, especially #8492–8504, 10–17 December 2004.

21 Exceptions to this rule were the Carnegie Endowment for International Peace Policy

Brief, 35, *A Spreading Danger: Time for a New Policy Towards Chechnya*, by Fiona Hill, Anatol Lieven and Thomas de Waal, 23 February 2005; and a series of articles published by Radio Free Europe/Radio Liberty, see, for example, Liz Fuller (2004), op. cit.

22 See www.timesonline.co.uk/article/0,,2087–1688261,00.html (last accessed 25 September 2006).

23 Yury Soshin, 'Papakha s ushami' (*Papapkha* – the traditional Caucasian headwear – with ear-flaps), 12 July 2005, www.globalrus.ru/opinions/778113/ (last accessed 25 September 2006).

24 Khachig Tololyan, 'Cultural narrative and the motivation of the terrorist', *The Journal of Strategic Studies*, Special Issue: Inside Terrorist Organizations, edited by David C. Rapoport, 10:4, December 1987, pp. 218–233

25 In distinguishing 'ethnocide' from 'genocide', Steven T. Katz, citing the Stalinist deportations of the Second World War, claims that the 'intent was to destroy a variety of minority cultures and ambitions built on them, rather than to murder all the members of a specific people', see S.T. Katz, 'Mass death under communist rule and the limits of "otherness"', in Robert S. Wistrich (ed.), *Demonizing the Other: Antisemitism, Racism and Xenophobia*, Amsterdam: Harwood Academic, 1999, p. 280.

26 See Svetlana Pankratova, 'Rossiya i PACE po-raznomu smotryat na bor'bu s terroriz-mom' (Russia and PACE do not see eye-to-eye on the battle against terrorism), www.Izvestiya.ru/politic/490012, 7 October 2004.

27 For an explanation of this term, see Bill Bowring, 'Austro-Marxism's last laugh? The struggle for recognition of national-cultural autonomy for Rossians and Russians', *Europe-Asia Studies*, 54:2, 2002, pp. 229–250.

28 levada.ru/press/2005070410.html (last accessed 25 September 2006).

29 www.levada.ru/chechnya.html (last accessed 25 September 2006).

30 www.levada.ru/press/2005100506.html (last accessed 25 September 2006); See also Marina Volkova, 'Myatezhnaya respublika glazami Putina' (The rebellious republic through Putin's eyes), *Nezavisimaya gazeta*, 12 October 2004.

31 www.levada.ru/press/2006091302.html (accessed 15 September 2006).

32 I am using these terms as generally understood in the literature on terrorism. For a good analysis of both, see Paul Wilkinson, *Terrorism Versus Democracy: The Liberal State Response*, London: Cass, 2001, especially ch. 1 'Insurgency and terrorism', pp. 1–18 and 'State terror', pp. 40–45.

33 Ralf Beste, Ralf Neukirch and Gabor Steingart 'Merkel pushes Russian diplomatic role', *Spiegel Online International*, 23 January 2006, www.spiegel.de/international/spiegel/0,1518,396756,00.html (last accessed 25 September 2006).

34 Uwe Hallbach, 'An escalation of violence in the Caucasus, hardening in Russia', *SWP Comments*, Stiftung Wissenschaft und Politik (German Institute for International and Security Affairs), 30, October 2004, pp. 6–8.

35 Bruno Coppetiers, M. Emerson, M. Huysseune, T. Kovziridze, G. Noutcheva, N. Tocci and M. Vahl, (eds) *Europeanization and Conflict Resolution: Case Studies from the European Periphery*, Gent: Academia Press, 2004, pp. 237–242.

36 For an up-to-date insight into levels of press and NGO freedom in Russia, see Mischa Gabowitsch, 'Inside the looking glass: a reply to Nicolai N. Petro', 17 February 2006, www.opendemocracy.net/debates/article.jsp?id=6&debateId=28&articleId=3259 (last accessed 25 September 2006).

37 Dmitri V. Trenin, Carnegie Endowment for International Peace Policy Brief, 42, *Reading Russia Right*, October 2005, pp. 1–11.

38 assembly.coe.int/Main.asp?link=/Documents/AdoptedText/ta06/ERES1479.htm (last accessed 25 September 2006).

39 See Andrew Kuchins, 'Russian democracy and civil society: back to the future', Testimony Prepared for US Commission on Security and Cooperation in Europe, 8

February 2006, www.carnegieendowment.org/publications/index.cfm?fa=view&id=18007&prog=zru (last accessed 25 September 2006).

40 For example, an estimated 500,000 landmines have been deployed in Chechnya, see Mark Kramer, 'The perils of counterinsurgency: Russia's war in Chechnya', *International Security*, 29:3, Winter 2004/5, p. 26.

41 See interview by Ol'ga Shlyakhtina with Sergei Markov, 'Dlya Putina Chechnya bol'she ne vopros No. 1' (For Putin Chechnya is no longer the number 1 question), 5 October 2005, www.kavkaz-forum.ru/politic/11596.html (last accessed 5 October 2005).

42 Published in its original form as 'The impact of Chechnya and the "War on Terror" on British–Russian relations', Hanna Smith (ed.), *The Two-Level Game: Russia's Relations with Great Britain, Finland and the European Union*, Helsinki: Aleksanteri Institute, 2006, pp. 67–85.

43 'UK diplomats in spying row', BBC website, 23 January 2006, news.bbc.co.uk/1/hi/world/europe/4638136.stm (last accessed 25 September 2006).

44 'Russia's Gazprom considers bid for British Gas owner Centrica', *Guardian*, 3 February 2006.

45 One has only to read the verbatim reports of the Parliamentary Assembly of the Council of Europe (PACE) debate on human rights in Chechnya, on 25 January 2006, to realise how sensitive Russian delegates remain to international debate on this topic, see assembly.coe.int/Main.asp?link=/Documents/Records/2006–1/E/0601251000E.htm (last accessed 25 September 2006).

46 www.levada.ru/chechnya.html (last accessed 25 September 2006).

47 *Johnson's Russia List*, #33, 2006, 3 February 2006.

48 Musa Basnukhaev and Magomed Iriskhanov, 'Obshchestvennoye mneniye Chechni o situatsii v chechenskoi respublike' (Chechen public opinion on the situation in the Chechen Republic), *Vestnik obshchestvennogo mneniya*, 4, July–August, 2004, www.levada.ru/vestnik78.html (last accessed 25 September 2006).

49 The full text of the correspondence may be found on www.timesonline.co.uk/article/0,,2087–1688261,00.html (last accessed 25 September 2006).

50 BBC website, 17 November 2005, news.bbc.co.uk/1/hi/uk/4444358.stm.

51 See, for example, Sandra Laville and Vikram Dodd, 'One year on, a London bomber issues a threat from the dead', *Guardian*, 7 July 2006.

52 Even after his sudden death in August 2005, there were detractors who criticised Robin Cook for hypocrisy and inaction. See, for example, 'The dark heart of Robin Cook's "ethical" foreign policy', www.medialens.org/alerts/05/050822_the_dark_heart_of_robin_cook.php (last accessed 25 September 2006). *Moscow News*, 17 October 2005.

53 Pavel Erochkine, 'Russia and its oil: friends and foes', Jennifer Moll (ed.), *Blueprint for Russia*, London: Foreign Policy Centre 2005, p. 23.

54 Ibid., p. 26.

55 See Jennifer Moll and Richard Gowan (eds), *Losing Ground: Russia's European Commitments to Human Rights*, London: Foreign Policy Centre 2005, p. 24.

56 In the Freedom in the World 2006 report, see 65.110.85.181/uploads/pdf/Charts2006.pdf; Russia was also ranked 138th (out of 167 countries) in the reporters Without Borders' Worldwide Press Freedom Index of 2005, see www.rsf.org/rubrique.php3?id_rubrique=554 (last accessed 25 September 2006).

57 For a good recent overview of Russia's record in the Council of Europe and OSCE, see Moll and Gowan (eds), op. cit.

58 For the Yukos affair, see BBC, 23 December 2004, 'Q&A: the battle for Yukos', news.bbc.co.uk/1/hi/business/4097967.stm (last accessed 25 September 2006);

59 For Klebnikov's murder, see his obituary in *The Economist*, 15 July 2004.

60 On 18 January 2006, Benita Ferrero-Waldner, the EU external relations commissioner, promised a social rehabilitation scheme for the North Caucasus worth 20

million euros, www.rferl.org/featuresarticle/2006/01/d3a3debb-4431–4a15–9add-88b24ccbe015.html (last accessed 25 September 2006).

61 A good example of this was George W. Bush's State of the Nation Address on 31 January 2006, which managed to mention Beslan without reference to Chechnya, news.bbc.co.uk/1/hi/world/americas/4668628.stm (last accessed 25 September 2006).

62 Maria Lipman, 'Increasing authoritarianism and the causes of public discontent', Moll (ed.), op. cit., p. 46.

63 The Freedom House rating for Russia in this sphere for 2003 was 4.25 on a scale from 1 (high) to 7 (low). Chechnya, unsurprisingly, was rated at 7 for both political rights and civil liberties; see www.freedomhouse.org/pdf_docs/research/nitransit/2003/nitrussia2003.pdf.

64 See, for example, Havel's open letter on the eve of Putin's visit to Prague in March 2006, 'Havel and Tutu condemn Chechnya abuses', The Jamestown Foundation's *Chechnya Weekly*, 7:9, 6 March 2006.

65 For Anatoly Chubais' attack on Grigory Yavlinsky, for example, see 'Is it treason to question war aims?', *Moscow Times*, 16 November, 1999.

66 'Despite Moscow's demonisation of him, perhaps because of it, Mr Zakaev has prominent supporters.' Steven Lee Myers, 'Chechen in extradition dispute: criminal or peacemaker?', *New York Times*, 9 December 2002.

67 'Over 200,000 killed in Chechnya since 1994 – pro-Moscow official', *Moscow News*, 19 November 2004 www.mosnews.com/news/2004/11/19/civiliandeath.shtml (last accessed 25 September 2006).

68 '300,000 killed in Chechen wars – pro-Moscow official', *Moscow News*, 27 June 2005.

69 Yury Levada, 'Rossiyane ustali ot voiny' (Russians are tired of the war), *Obshchaya gazeta*, 17–23 August 2000, quoted in Lilia Shevtsova, *Putin's Russia*, translated by Antonina W. Bouis, Washington, DC: Carnegie, p. 286 n. 2.

70 PACE, Document 10276, dated 17 September 2004, 'The political situation in the Chechen Republic: measures to increase democratic stability in accordance with Council of Europe standards', assembly.coe.int/Documents/WorkingDocs/doc04/EDOC10276.htm (accessed 7 March 2005).

71 Valery Vyzhutovich, 'Great status', *Rossiiskaya gazeta*, 14 June 2005, translated and reported in *Johnson's Russia List*, #9177, 15 June 2005.

10 Conclusion

1 V. Mironov, *Ya byl na etoi voine. Chechnya. 1995* (I Fought in this War. Chechnya. Year 1995), Moscow, 2001, pp. 413–414.

2 Valeriy Tishkov, *Ethnicity, Nationalism and Conflict In and After the Soviet Union*, London: Sage, 1997, p. 186.

3 Also a term employed by Tishkov, see Hughes (2001), op. cit., p. 20.

4 See John Russell, 'Terrorists, bandits, spooks and thieves: Russian demonisation of the Chechens before and since 9/11', *Third World Quarterly*, 26:1, 2005, pp. 101–116.

5 See Abraham H. Maslow, *Motivation and Personality*, 3rd edn, New York: Harper-Collins, 1987.

6 See www.whitehouse.gov/news/releases/2001/09/20010920–8.html (last accessed 25 September 2006).

7 www.newamericancentury.org/Bushletter.htm (last accessed 25 September 2006).

8 Anna Politkovskaya, 'Soldatskiye materi uyekhali dumat' nad predlozheniyenami chechenskoi storony. Ostanovit li eto terakty? (Soldiers' mothers have departed to consider the proposals from the Chechen side. Will this halt the acts of terror?), *Novaya gazeta*, 15, 28 February 2005.

9 See 'Boi v gorode' (Battle in the town), *Novoye vremya*, 42, 23 October 2005, pp. 6–13.

10 See, for example, the detailed specialist coverage of Beslan in *Novaya gazeta*; see www.novayagazeta.ru/rassled2/beslan/karta.shtml (last accessed 25 September 2006).

11 Maksim Glikin,'Velikhoye pereseleniye kavkaztsev' (The great resettlement of the Caucasians), *Nezavisimaya gazeta*, 27 November 2002.

12 By a strange twist of fate, Gillo Pontecorvo died on 12 October 2006, the very day that this manuscript was completed.

13 See Michael Kaufman, 'What does the Pentagon see in *Battle of Algiers*?', *New York Times*, 4, 7 September 2003, p. 3.

Select bibliography

Books

A British Officer (1856) *The Powers of Europe and Fall of Sebastopol*, Boston: Higgins & Bradley.

Anderson, J. (1993) *Guerrillas,* London: HarperCollins.

Appadurai, A. (1996) *Modernity at Large: Cultural Dimensions of Globalization*, Minneapolis, MN: University of Minnesota Press.

Astashkin, N.S. (2005) *Po vol'chemu sledu: khroniki chechenskikh voin* (Following Wolf Tracks: Chronicles of the Chechen Wars), Moscow: Veche.

Baddeley, J. (1908) *The Russian Conquest of the Caucasus*, London: Longmans, Green and Co. (reprinted by Elibron Classics, 2004).

Baylis, J. and Smith, S. (eds) (2001) *The Globalization of World Politics: An Introduction to International Relations*, 2nd edn, Oxford: Oxford University Press.

Bennett, V. (2001) *Crying Wolf: The Return of War to Chechnya*, London: Pan.

Bennigsen, A. and Wimbush, S.E. (1985) *Muslims of the Soviet Empire: A Guide*, London: Hurst.

Bird, C. (2003) *To Catch a Tartar: Notes from the Caucasus*, London: John Murray.

Brown, D. (1970) *Bury My Heart at Wounded Knee: An Indian History of the American West*, New York: Owl Books.

Broxup, M.B. (ed.) (1992) *The North Caucasus Barrier: The Russian Advance Towards the Muslim World*, New York: St. Martin's Press.

Carey, R. (ed.) (2001) *The New Intifada: Resisting Israel's Apartheid*, New York: Verso.

Chomsky, N. (2000) *Rogue States: The Rule of Force in World Affairs*, London: Pluto.

Clyde, R. (1998) *From Rebel to Hero: The Image of the Highlander, 1745–1830*, East Linton: Tuckwell Press.

Conquest, R. (1970) *The Nation Killers: The Soviet Deportation of Nationalities*, New York: Macmillan.

Coppieters B. and Sakwa, R. (2003) *Contextualising Secession: Normative Studies in Comparative Perspective*, Oxford: Oxford University Press.

Coppetiers, B., Emerson, M., Huysseune, M., Kovziridze, T., Noutcheva, G., Tocci, N. and Vahl, M. (eds) (2004) *Europeanization and Conflict Resolution: Case Studies from the European Periphery*, Gent: Academia Press.

Cragin, K. and Chalk, P. (2003) *Terrorism and Development: Using Social and Economic Development to Inhibit a Resurgence of Terrorism*, Santa Monica, CA: RAND.

Debray, R. (1967) *Revolution in the Revolution*, Pelican Latin American Library, Harmondsworth: Penguin.

Dmitriev, V.A. (ed.) (2003) *Adat: traditsii i sovremennost'* (Adat: Traditions and the Present Day), Moscow-Tbilisi: MNIINK.

Dobaev, I.P. (2003) *Islamskii radikalism: genesis, evolyutsiya, praktika* (Islamic Radicalism: Genesis, Evolution, Practice), Rostov-On-Don: SKNTs VSh.

Duncan, P. (2000) *Russian Messianism: Third Rome, Holy Revolution, Communism and After*, London: Routledge.

Dunlop, J.B. (1998) *Russia Confronts Chechnya: Roots of a Separatist Conflict*, Cambridge: Cambridge University Press.

Dunlop, J.B. (2006) *The 2002 Dubrovka and 2004 Beslan Hostage Crises: A Critique of Russian Counter-Terrorism*, Stuttgart: ibidem-Verlag.

Evangelista, M. (2002) *The Chechen Wars: Will Russia Go the Way of the Soviet Union?* Washington, DC: Brookings Institution Press.

Fadeev, R. (2005) *Kavkazskaya voina* (The Caucasus War), Moscow: Algoritm.

Fairclough, N. (1995) *Media Discourse*, London: Edward Arnold.

Fawn, R. (ed.) (2003) *Realignments in Russian Foreign Policy*, London: Frank Cass.

Fawn, R. and White, S. (eds) (2002) *Russia after Communism*, London: Frank Cass.

Felshtinsky, Y. and Litvinenko, A. (2002) *Blowing Up Russia*, New York: Liberty.

Fowkes, B. (ed.) (1998) *Russia and Chechnia: The Permanent Crisis. Essays on Russo-Chechen Relations*, Basingstoke: Macmillan.

Gall, C. and de Waal, T. (1997) *Chechnya: A Small, Victorious War*, London: Pan.

Galtung, J. (ed.) (1976) *Peace, War and Defense: Essays in Peace Research*, Vol. II, Copenhagen: Christian Ejlers.

Galtung, J. (1996) *Peace by Peaceful Means: Peace and Conflict, Development and Civilization*, London: Sage.

Gammer, M. (2006) *The Lone Wolf and the Bear: Three Centuries of Russian Defiance of Russian Rule*, London: Hurst.

German, T. (2003) *Russia's Chechen War*, London: RoutledgeCurzon.

Griffin, N. (2001) *Caucasus: In the Wake of Warriors*, London: Review.

Grodnensky, N. (2004) *Neokonchennaya voina: istoriya vooruzhennogo konflikta v Chechne* (Unfinished War: the History of the Armed Conflict in Chechnya), Minsk: Kharvest.

Guevara, C. (1969) *Guerrilla Warfare*, Vintage: New York.

Hacker, F. (1976) *Crusaders, Criminals, Crazies: Terror and Terrorism in Our Time*, New York: Norton.

Handelman, S. (1994) *Comrade Criminal: The Theft of the Second Russian Revolution*, London: Michael Joseph.

Hayden, P., Lansford, T. and Watson, R.P. (eds) (2003), *America's War on Terror*, Aldershot: Ashgate.

Karny, Y. (2000) *Highlanders: A Journey to the Caucasus in Quest of Memory*, New York: Farrar, Straus and Giroux.

Kavtaradze, S.D. (2005) *Ethnopoliticheskie konflikty na postsovietskom prostranstve* (Ethnopolitical Conflicts in the Post-Soviet Space), Moscow: Ekzamen.

Kegley, C. (ed.) (1990) *International Terrorism: Characteristics, Causes, Controls*, Basingstoke: Macmillan.

Kelly, L. (1977) *Tragedy in the Caucasus*, London: Constable.

Khazanov, A. (1995) *After the USSR: Ethnicity, Nationalism, and Politics in the Commonwealth of Independent States*, Madison, WI: University of Wisconsin.

Kriezys, S. and Sedlickas, R. (1999) *The War in Chechnya*, College Station,TX: A & M University Press.

Laqueur, W. (1977) *Guerrilla: A Historical and Critical Study*, London: Wiedenfeld & Nicholson.

Laqueur, W. (2002) *A History of Terrorism*, London: Transaction.

Latynina, Y. (2005), *Djakhannam, ili Do vstrechi b Adu* (Djakhannam, or See you in Hell), Moscow: Eksmo.

Lederach, J.P. (1997) *Building Peace*, Washington, DC: United States Institute of Peace.

Lieven, A. (1999) *Chechnya: Tombstone of Russian Power*, New Haven: Yale University Press.

Lloyd, A. (2000) *My War Gone By, I Miss It So*, London: Transworld Publishers.

Lokshina, T. with Thomas, R. and Mayer, M. (eds) (2005), *The Imposition of a Fake Political Settlement in the Northern Caucasus: The 2003 Chechen Presidential Election*, Stuttgart: ibidem-Verlag.

McCauley, M. (2001) *Bandits, Gangsters and the Mafia: Russia, the Baltic States and the CIS Since 1992*, London: Pearson Education.

Malashenko, A. and Vitkovskaya, G. (eds) (1999) *Intolerance in Russia: Old and New Phobias*, Moscow: Carnegie.

Marighela, C. (1971) '*Mini-Manual of the Urban Guerrilla*', in *For the Liberation of Brazil, Pelican Latin American Library*, Harmondsworth: Penguin.

Marozzi, J. (2004) *Tamerlane: Sword of Islam, Conqueror of the World*, London: Harper-Collins.

Martin, G. (2003) *Understanding Terrorism: Challenges, Perspectives, and Issues*, London: Sage.

Maslow, A.H. (1987) *Motivation and Personality*, 3rd edn, New York: HarperCollins.

Miall, H., Ramsbotham, O. and Woodhouse, T. (1999) *Contemporary Conflict Resolution*, Cambridge: Polity.

Mickiewicz, E. (1997) *Changing Channels: Television and the Struggle forPower in Russia*, New York: Oxford University Press.

Mieller, S. (1999) *Compassion Fatigue: How the Media Sells Disease, Famine, War and Death*, New York: Routledge.

Mironov, V. (2001) *Ya byl na etoi voine. Chechnya. 1995* (I Fought in this War. Chechnya. Year 1995), Moscow: Biblion-Russkaya Kniga.

Murphy, P. (2004) *The Wolves of Islam: Russia and the Faces of Chechen Terror*, Dulles: Brassey's.

Nekrich, A. (1978) *The Punished Peoples: The Deportation and Fate of Soviet Minorities at the End of the Second World War*, New York: Norton.

Nichols, J. and Vagapov, A. (2004) *Chechen–English and English–Chechen Dictionary*, London: RoutledgeCurzon.

Nivat, A. (2001) *Chienne de Guerre: A Woman Reporter Behind the Lines of the War in Chechnya*, translated by Susan Darnton, New York: Public Affairs.

Piattoni, S. (2001) *Clientelism, Interests, and Democratic Representation: The European Experience in Historical and Comparative Perspective*, Cambridge: Cambridge University Press.

Politkovskaya, A. (2001a) *A Dirty War: A Russian Reporter in Chechnya*, translated by John Crowfoot, London: Harvill Press.

Remnick, D. (1997) *Resurrection: The Struggle for a New Russia*, New York: Random House.

Rogers, P. (2004) *A War on Terror: Afghanistan and After*, London: Pluto.

Ro'i, Y. (2000) *Islam in the Soviet Union: From World War II to Gorbachev*, London: Hurst.

Rybkin, I. (1998) *Consent in Chechnya, Consent in Russia*, London: Lytten Trading.

Sakwa, R. (ed.) (2005) *Chechnya: From the Past to the Future*, London: Anthem.

Sartre, J.-P. (2001) *Colonialism and Neocolonialism*, London: Routledge.

Satter, D. (2003) *Darkness at Dawn: The Rise of the Russian Criminal State*, New Haven: Yale University Press.

Schiff, Z. (1990) *Intifada: The Palestinian Uprising*, New York: Simon & Schuster.

Schmid, A.P. (1988) *Political Terrorism*, Amsterdam: North-Holland.

Seely, R. (2001) *Russo-Chechen Conflict, 1800–2000: A Deadly Embrace*, London: Frank Cass.

Shevtsova, L. (2003) *Putin's Russia*, translated by Antonina W. Bouis, Washington, DC: Carnegie.

Slater, R.O. and Stohl, M. (eds) (1998) *Current Perspectives on International Terrorism*, Basingstoke: Macmillan.

Smith, G. (ed.) (1996) *The Nationalities Question in the Post-Soviet States*, Harlow: Longman.

Smith, H. (ed) (2006) *The Two-Level Game: Russia's Relations with Great Britain, Finland and the European Union*, Helsinki: Aleksanteri Institute.

Smith, S. (1998) *Allah's Mountains: Politics and War in the Russian Caucasus*, New York: I.B. Tauris.

Solzhenitsyn, A. (1975) *The Gulag Archipelago 1918–1956*, translated by H.T. Willetts, London: Collins and Harvill Press.

Stepanova, Ekaterina (2003) *Anti-terrorism and Peace-building During and After Conflict*, Stockholm: Stockholm International Peace Research Institute (SIPRI).

Tishkov, V. (1997) *Ethnicity, Nationalism and Conflict In and After the Soviet Union*, London: Sage.

Tolstoi, L. (1965) *Hadji-Murat*, Moscow: Khudozhestvennaya literatura.

Trenin D. and Malashenko, A., with A. Lieven (2004) *Russia's Restless Frontier: The Chechnya Factor in Post-Soviet Russia*, Washington, DC: Carnegie Endowment.

Webber, S.L. and Mathers, J.G. (2006) *Military and Society in Post-Soviet Russia*, Manchester: Manchester University Press.

White, J. (2005) *Terrorism and Homeland Security: An Introduction*, 5th edn, Belmont, CA: Wadsworth.

Wilkinson, P. (2006) *Terrorism Versus Democracy*, 2nd edn, London: Frank Cass.

Wistrich, R.S. (ed.) (1999), *Demonizing the Other: Antisemitism, Racism and Xenophobia*, Amsterdam: Harwood Academic Publishers.

Yemelianova, G. (2002) *Russia and Islam: A Historical Survey*, Basingstoke: Palgrave.

Yermolov, A. (edited by Mikaberidze, A.) (2005) *The Czar's General: The Memoirs of a Russian General During the Napoleonic Wars*, Welwyn Garden City: Ravenhall Books.

Zelkina, A. (2000) *In Quest of God and Freedom: Sufi Response to the Russian Advances in the North Caucasus* (Chechenya and Daghestan), London: Hurst.

Chapters in books

Alexseev, M.A. (2006) 'Back to Hell: civilian–military "audience costs" and Russia's wars in Chechnia', in Webber, S.L. and Mathers, J.G. (eds), *Military and Society in Post-Soviet Russia*, Manchester: Manchester University Press, pp. 97–113.

Avtorkhanov, A. (1992) 'The Chechens and Ingush during the Soviet period and its antecedents', in Broxup M.B. (ed.), *The North Caucasus Barrier*, New York: St. Martin's Press, pp. 146–194.

Baev, P. (2005) 'Chechnya and the Russian military: a war too far?', in Sakwa, R. (ed.), *Chechnya: From the Past to the Future*, London: Anthem, pp. 117–130.

Cherkasov, A. (2006) 'The Chechen maze: looking for a way out', in Lokshina, T., Thomas, R. and Mayer, M. (eds), *The Imposition of a Fake Political Settlement in the Northern Caucasus: The 2003 Chechen Presidential Election,* Stuttgart: ibidem-Verlag.

Dixon, S. (1996) 'The Russians and the Russian Question', in Smith, G. (ed), *The Nationalities Question in the Post-Soviet States*, Harlow: Longman, 1996, pp. 47–74.

Gakaev, D. (2005) 'Chechnya in Russia and Russia in Chechnya', in Sakwa R. (ed.) *Chechnya: From the Past to the Future*, London: Anthem, pp. 21–42.

Gammer, M. (1992) 'Russian strategies in the conquests of Chechnia and Dagestan, 1825–1859' in Broxup, M.B. (ed.), *The North Caucasus Barrier: The Russian Advance Towards the Muslim World*, New York: St. Martin's Press, pp. 45–61.

Galtung, J. (1976b) 'Three approaches to peace: peacekeeping, peacemaking and peace-building' in Galtung, J. (ed.), *Peace, War and Defense: Essays in Peace Research*, Vol. II, Copenhagen: Christian Ejlers, pp. 282–304.

Hayden, P. (2003) 'The war on terrorism and the just use of military force', in Hayden, P., Lansford, T. and Watson, R.P. (eds), *America's War on Terror*, Aldershot: Ashgate, pp. 105–121.

Katz, S.T. (1999) 'Mass death under communist rule and the limits of "otherness"', in Wistrich, R.S. (ed.) *Demonizing the Other: Antisemitism, Racism and Xenophobia*, Amsterdam: Harwood Academic Publishers, pp. 266–292.

Pain, E. (2005) 'The Chechen War in the context of contemporary Russian politics', in Sakwa R. (ed.), *Chechnya: From the Past to the Future*, London: Anthem, pp. 67–78.

Russell, J. (2005a) 'A war by any other name: Chechnya, 11 September and the War on Terrorism', in Sakwa, R. (ed.), *Chechnya: From the Past to the Future*, London: Anthem, pp. 239–264.

Russell, J. (2006a) 'The Impact of Chechnya and the "War on Terror" on British–Russian Relations', in Smith, H. (ed.), *The Two-Level Game: Russia's Relations with Great Britain, Finland and the European Union*, Helsinki, Aleksanteri Institute, pp. 67–85.

Sakwa, R. (2003) 'Chechnya: a just war fought unjustly?', in Coppieters, B. and Sakwa, R. (eds), *Contextualising Secession: Normative Studies in Comparative Perspective*, Oxford: Oxford University Press, pp. 156–186.

Schmid, A.P. (1998) 'Goals and Objectives of International Terrorism', in Slater, R.O. and Stohl, M. (eds), *Current Perspectives on International Terrorism*, Basingstoke: Macmillan, pp. 47–87.

Shearman, P. and Sussex, M. 'Globalisation, "New Wars" and the War in Chechnya', in Sakwa, R. (ed.) (2005) *Chechnya: From the Past to the Future*, London: Anthem, pp. 199–222.

Sikevich, Z. (1999) 'Etnichesaya nepriyazn' v massovoi sosnanii rossiyan' (Ethnic hostility in the mass consciousness of Russians), in Vitkovskaya, G. and Malashenko, A. (eds), *Neterpimost' v Rossii: stariye i noviye fobii* (Intolerance in Russia: Old and New Phobias), Moscow: Carnegie, pp. 99–112.

Tishkov, V. (2005) 'Dynamics of a society at war: ethnographical aspects', in Sakwa, R. (ed.) *Chechnya: From the Past to the Future*, London: Anthem, pp. 157–180.

Ware, R.B. (2005) 'A Multitude of Evils: Mythology and Political Failure in Chechnya', in Sakwa, R. (ed.), *Chechnya: From the Past to the Future*, London: Anthem, pp. 79–116.

Webber, S.L. (2006) 'Introduction: the society-military interface in Russia', in Webber,

S.L. and Mathers, J.G. (eds), *Military and Society in Post-Soviet Russia*, Manchester: Manchester University Press, pp. 1–36.

Zawilskie, V. (2006) 'Saving Russia's sons: the soldiers' mothers and the Russian Chechen wars', in Webber, S.L. and Mathers, J.G. (eds), *Military and Society in Post-Soviet Russia*, Manchester: Manchester University Press, pp. 228–240.

Articles in academic journals

Abrahms, M. (2004) 'Are terrorists really rational? The Palestinian example', *Orbis*, 48:3, Summer, pp. 533–549.

Aslund, A. (2000) 'Go long on Russia – Russian economic conditions', *The International Economy*, July–August, pp. 38–39.

Bhatia, M. (Guest editor) (2005) 'The politics of naming', *Third World Quarterly*, 26:1, Special Issue.

Blank, S. (2001) 'Russia's Ulster: the Chechen War and its consequences', *Demokratizatsiya: The Journal of Post-Soviet Democratization*, Winter.

Bowker, M. (2004) 'Russia and Chechnya: the issue of secession', *Nations and Nationalism*, 10:4, pp. 461–478.

Bowring, B. (2002) 'Austro-Marxism's last laugh? The struggle for recognition of national-cultural autonomy for Rossians and Russians', *Europe—Asia Studies*, 54:2, pp. 229–250.

Brudny, Y. (1997) 'In pursuit of the Russian presidency: Why Yeltsin won the 1996 Russian presidential election', *Communist and Post-Communist Studies*, 30:3, pp. 255–275.

Byford, G. (2002) 'The wrong war', *Foreign Affairs*, 81:4, July/August, pp. 34–43.

Collier, P. and Hoeffler, A. (2004) 'Greed and grievance in civil war', *Oxford Economic Papers*, 56:4, pp. 563–595.

Cornell, S.E. (1999) 'International reactions to massive human rights violations: the case of Chechnya', *Europe—Asia Studies*, 51:1, January, pp. 85–100.

Cornell, S.E. (2002) 'The war against terrorism and the conflict in Chechnya: a case for distinction', *The Fletcher Forum of World Affairs*, 27:2, Summer/Fall, pp. 167–184.

Cornell, S. (2005) 'The interaction of narcotics and conflict', *Journal of Peace Research*, 42:6, pp. 751–760.

Derlugian, G.M. (1999) 'Che Guevaras in turbans: the twisted lineage of Islamic fundamentalism in Chechnya and Dagestan', *New Left Review*, 237, pp. 3–27.

Domrin, A.M. (2003) 'Ten years later: society, "civil society," and the Russian state', *The Russian Review*, 62:2, pp. 193–211.

Fedorov, Y. (2003) 'A global web of terror', *International Affairs (Moscow)*, 49:2, pp. 93–101.

Furnish, T. (2005) 'Ritual beheading in the name of Islam', *Middle East Quarterly*, Spring, pp. 51–57.

Gradirovsky, S. (2006) 'Harvesting new peoples', *Russia in Global Affairs*, 1, January–March.

Grammatikov, N.V. (1998) 'The Russian intervention in Chechnya in November 1994: issues and decision-making, *The Journal of Slavic Military Studies*, 11:4, pp. 111–132.

Gudkov, L. and Dubin, B. (2005) 'Svoeobraziye russkogo nationalizma' (Russia's distinctive brand of nationalism), *Pro et Contra*, September–October.

Guiora, A.N. and Page, E.M. (2005) 'The unholy trinity: intelligence, interrogation and torture', July, Case Legal Studies Research Paper No. 05–13.

Herd, G.P. (2000) 'The "counter-terrorist operation" in Chechnya: "information warfare" aspects', *The Journal of Slavic Military Studies*, 13:4, December, pp. 57–83.

Hewitt, G. (Guest Editor), Special issue on Chechnya, *Central Asian Survey,* 22:4, December 2003.

Howard, M. (2001) 'Mistake to declare this a "war"', *RUSI Journal,* 146:6, December, pp. 1–4.

Hughes, J. (2001) 'Chechnya: the causes of a protracted post-Soviet conflict', *Civil Wars,* 4:4, Winter, pp. 11–48.

Huntington, S. (1993) 'The clash of civilizations', *Foreign Affairs*, 72:3, Summer, pp. 22–49.

Kagarlitsky, B. (1996) 'Russia chooses – and loses' *Current History*, October, www.currenthistory.com/archiveoct96/Kagarlitsky.html.

Kagarlitsky, B. (1997) 'Chechnya: predvaritel'nie itogi' (Chechnya: provisional results), *Svobodnaya mysl'*, 1, pp. 33–44.

Kerr, D. (1995) 'The new Eurasianism: the rise of geopolitics in Russia's foreign policy', *Europe–Asia Studies*, 47:6 September, pp. 977–988.

King, C. (2003) 'Crisis in the Caucasus: a new look at Russia's Chechen impasse', *Foreign Affairs*, 82:2, March/April, pp. 134–138.

Kramer, M. (2004/5) 'The perils of counterinsurgency: Russia's war in Chechnya', *International Security*, 29:3, Winter, pp. 5–63.

Kryshtanovskaya, O. (2002) 'Rezhim Putina: liberal'naya militokratiya? (Putin's regime: a liberal militocracy?), *Pro et Contra*, 7:4, Autumn.

Kryshtanovskaya, O. and White, S. (2003) 'Putin's militocracy', *Post-Soviet Affairs*, 19:4, October–December, pp. 289–306.

Lapidus, G. (2002) 'Putin's War on Terrorism: Lessons from Chechnya', in *Post-Soviet Affairs*, 18:1, January–March, pp. 41–48.

Lieven, A. (2000) 'Nightmare in the Caucasus', *The Washington Quarterly*, Winter, pp. 145–159.

Luft, G. (2002) 'The Palestinian H-bomb', *Foreign Affairs*, 81:4, July/August, pp. 2–7.

Lynch, D. (2005) '"The enemy is at the gate": Russia after Beslan', *International Affairs*, 81:1, pp. 141–161.

McFaul, M. (1995) 'Eurasia letter: Russian politics after Chechnya', *Foreign Policy*, 99, Summer, pp. 149–165.

Menon, R. and Fuller, G. (2000) 'Russia's ruinous Chechen War', in *Foreign Affairs*, 79:2, March/April, pp. 32–44.

Moore, C. (2006a) 'Reading the hermeneutics of violence: the literary turn and Chechnya', *Global Society*, 20:2, April, pp. 179–198.

Pape, R. (2003) 'The strategic logic of suicide terrorism', *American Political Science Review*, 97:3, August, pp. 343–361.

Pohl, M. (2002) '"It cannot be that our graves will be here": the survival of Chechen and Ingush deportees in Kazakhstan, 1944–1957', *Journal of Genocide Research*, 4:3, September, pp. 401–430.

Ram, H. (1999) 'Prisoners of the Caucasus: literary myths and media representations of the Chechen conflict', *Berkeley Program in Soviet and Post-Soviet Studies – Working Paper Series*, Summer.

Rotberg, R.I. (2002) 'Failed states in a world of terror', *Foreign Affairs,* 81:4, July/August, pp. 127–140.

Russell, J. (2002a) 'Mujahedeen, mafia, madmen…: Russian perceptions of Chechens during the wars in Chechnya, 1994–1996 and 1999–to date', *Journal of Communist Studies and Transition Politics*, 18:1, March, pp. 73–96.

Russell, J. (2002b) 'Exploitation of the "Islamic factor" in the Russo-Chechen conflict before and after 11 September 2001', *European Security*, 11:4, Winter, pp. 96–109.

Russell, J. (2005b) 'Terrorists, bandits, spooks and thieves: Russian demonisation of the Chechens before and since 9/11', *Third World Quarterly*, 26:1, pp. 101–116.

Russell, J. (2006b) 'Obstacles to peace in Chechnya: the scope for international involvement', *Europe-Asia Studies*, 58:6, September, pp. 941–964.

Shevtsova, L. (2005) 'Russia 2005: the logic of backsliding', *New Europe Review*, 2:3.

Speckhard, A. and Akhmedova, K. (2006) 'The making of a martyr: Chechen suicide terrorism', *The Journal of Studies in Conflict and Terrorism*, 29:5, July–August, pp. 429–492.

Squier, J. (2002) 'Civil society and the challenge of Russian gosudarstvennost', *Demokratizatsiya: The Journal of Post-Soviet Democratization*, Spring, pp. 166–183.

Stedman, S.J. (1997) 'Spoiler problems in peace processes', *International Security*, 22:2, pp. 5–53.

Tishkov, V. (1997) 'Geopolitika chechenskoi voiny: "natsional'nyi interes" kak sopernichestvo biurokratii i elit' (The geopolitics of the Chechen war: 'national interest' as rivalry between bureaucracies and elites), *Svobodnaya mysl'*, 4, pp. 65–74.

Tololyan, K. (1987) 'Cultural narrative and the motivation of the terrorist', *The Journal of Strategic Studies*, Special Issue: Inside Terrorist Organizations, 10:4, December, pp. 218–233.

Treisman, D. (1997) 'Russia's "ethnic revival": the separatist activism of regional leaders in a postcommunist order', *World Politics*, 49, January, pp. 212–249.

Trenin, D. (2006) 'Russia leaves the West', *Foreign Affairs*, 85:4, July/August, pp. 87–96.

Vinci, A. (2006) 'Greed-grievance reconsidered: the role of power and survival in the motivation of armed groups', *Civil Wars*, 8:1, March, pp. 25–45.

Volkov, V. (1999) 'Violent entrepreneurship in post-Communist Russia', *Europe-Asia Studies*, 51:5, pp. 741–754.

Weigle, M. (2002) 'On the road to the Civic Forum: state and civil society from Yeltsin to Putin', *Demokratizatsiya: The Journal of Post-Soviet Democratization*, Spring, pp. 117–146.

Wilhelmsen, J. (2005) 'Between a rock and a hard place: the Islamisation of the Chechen separatist movement', *Europe-Asia Studies*, 57:1, pp. 35–59.

Wood, T. (2004) 'The case for Chechnya', *New Left Review*, 30, November–December, pp. 5–36.

X, (1947) 'The sources of Soviet conduct', *Foreign Affairs*, 26:2, July, pp. 566–582.

Zürcher, C. and Koehler, J. (2001) 'Institutions and organized violence in post-socialist societies', *Berliner Osteuropa Info*, 17, pp. 48–53.

Articles in periodicals and newspapers

Aleksin, V. and Shaburkin, A. (1999) 'Voina bez vykhodnikh' (War without days off), *Nezavisimaya gazeta*, 25 September.

Aliev, T. (2004) 'Kremlin's pick to replace Kadyrov', *Moscow Times*, 18 June.

Aliev, T. (2005a) 'Chechen heroes of the Soviet War', *Chechen Society newspaper*, 9:47, 11 May.

Aliev, T. (2005b) 'Terror na Kavkaze: druz'ya i vragi' (Terror in the Caucasus: friends and foes), *Izvestiya*, 10 June.

Aliev, T. (2006) 'Idushchie na tretii srok' (Going for the third term), *Chechenskoe obshchestvo*, 17, 8 August.

Al-Shashani, M.B. (2004) 'The killing of Abu Al-Walid and the Russian policy in Chechnya', *Central Asia—Caucasus Analyst*, 5 May.

Anonymous, (2005) 'The New Jews', *The Economist*, 17 February.

Belotserkovsky, V. (2000) 'Kakaya "duga" ugrozhaet miry?' (Which 'arc' threatens the world?), *Novaya gazeta*, 31, 20 July.

Belton, C. (2004) 'Putin is facing his biggest challenge', *Moscow News*, 9 September.

Bovt, G. and Babaeva, S. (2001) 'Bush prinyal Putina kak otsa rodnogo' (Bush greeted Putin like his own father), *Izvestiya*, 15 November.

Botyakov, Y. (2003) 'Abrechestvo – real'nost' i predrassudki' (The Abrek way of life – reality and prejudices), *Nezavisimaya gazeta*, 29 August.

Burlatsky, F. (1995) 'Yeltsin: a turning point', *Transition*, 1:3, p. 8.

Chereshnya, A. (1995) 'Bumerang terrorizma vozvrashchaetsya v Rossiyu' (The boomerang of terrorism returns to Russia), *Literaturnaya gazeta*, 42, 18 October, p. 11.

Chesnov, Y. (1994) 'Chechentsem byt' trudno' (It is not easy to be a Chechen), *Nezavisimaya gazeta*, 22 September.

Cuny, F.C. (1995) 'Killing Chechnya', *The New York Review of Books*, 6 April, pp. 15–17.

de Waal, T. (2004a) 'Europe's darkest corner', *Guardian*, 30 August.

de Waal, T. (2004b) 'Basayev and Maskhadov Under Pressure', *Caucasus Reporting Service*, 252, 8 September.

Dubnov, V. (2003) 'Mest': Nechelovechesky factor (Revenge: the inhuman factor), *Novoye vremya*, 25, 22 June, pp. 12–16.

Dubnov, V. (2005) 'Vera i beznadezhnost': kak pogib chelovek, u kotorogo davno ne bylo vykhoda'' (Faith and hopelessness: how perished a man, for whom there had long since been no way out), *Novoe vremya*, 11, 20 March, pp. 6–10.

Dudayev, U. (2004) 'Chechnya: the fighting goes on', *Caucasus Reporting Service*, 214, 15 January.

Dzutsev, V. and Tskhurbayev, A. (2004) 'Beslan siege unravels, slowly and bloodily' *Caucasus Reporting Service*, 250, 3 September.

Eismont, M. (1995) 'Chechnya – "samoe silnoe razocharovaniye" prezidenta Yeltsina' (Chechnya is President Yeltsin's 'greatest disappointment'), *Segodnya*, 20 October.

Felgenhauer, P. (1996) 'A war Russia cannot afford to lose', *Transition*, 2: 11, pp. 30–35.

Felgenhauer, P. (2002a) 'Bloody Chechen deadlock', *Moscow Times*, 26 September.

Felgenhauer, P. (2002b) 'After the theatre, the drama continues', *The New Statesman*, 4 November, pp. 25–26.

Felgenhauer, P. (2004) 'Kak shturmovali shkolu' (How the school was stormed), *Novaya gazeta*, 74, 7 October.

Franchetti, M. (2006a) 'In the torture cell of Chechnya's tyrant', *Sunday Times*, 30 April.

Franchetti, M. (2006b) 'Death of the woman who shamed Moscow', *Sunday Times*, 8 October.

Fuller, L. (1995) 'Chechen politics: a murky prospect', *Transition*, 1:3, pp. 11–13.

Fuller, L. (2004) 'Look back in anger – ten years of war in Chechnya', *RFE/RL Features*, 11 December.

Fuller, L. (2005) 'Dmitrii Kozak: troubleshooter or scapegoat?', *RFE/RL Reports*, North Caucasus, 5:25, 27 June.

Gakaev, D. (1999) 'Chechnya okazalas' na ostrie bor'by raznykh geostrategii' (Chechnya has found itself on the spike of the battle of different geostrategies), *Yabloko Rossii*, 45, 30 October.

Glasser, S. and Baker, P. (2004) 'Chechnya War a deepening trap for Putin', *Washington Post*, 13 September, p. A01.

Glikin, M. (2002) 'Velikhoye pereseleniye kavkaztsev' (The great resettlement of the Caucasians), *Nezavisimaya gazeta*, 27 November.

Glucksmann, A. (2005a) 'Le noveau tsar vous dit merci' (The new Tsar thanks you), *Le Monde*, 10 March.

Glucksmann, A. (2005b) 'If Putin has an ally, it is Basaev', *The Chechen Society Newspaper*, 13:51, 4 July.

Glucksmann, A. (2005c) 'Russia is digging itself a grave in Chechnya', interview by Alan Tskhurbaev, *The Chechen Society Newspaper*, 14:52, 19 July.

Gross, A. (2005) 'O nezavisimosti mozhno budet govorit' cherez let 10–15' (One may talk of independence in about 10–15 years), *Chechenskoye obshchestvo*, 6:44, 29 March.

Gurin, C. (2004) 'Group claims 25,000 Russian soldiers have died in Chechnya', The Jamestown Foundation's *Eurasia Daily Monitor*, 1:3, 5 May.

Gutnov, V. (1999) 'Rossiya ne dolzhna opravdyvatsya za svoe stremlenie pokonchit' s terrorizmom' (Russia does not have to justify its efforts to put an end to terrorism), *Nezavisimaya gazeta*, 4 November .

Hahn, G.M. (2002) 'Putin's Muslim challenge', *The Russia Journal,* 5:2, January, pp. 25–31.

Hedges, C. (2004) 'On war', *The New York Review of Books*, 51:20, 16 December.

Hiatt, F. (2001) 'Democracy on hold', *Washington Post*, 6 October.

Hovsepyan, N. and Tsukanova, L. (2003) 'Chechnya and Russia. War and peace', *New Times*, December.

Iskandaryan, A. (1996) 'Chernofobia' (Fear of the 'Blacks'), *Novoye vremya*, 32, August, pp. 12–13.

Iskander, F. (1999) 'Pochemu voyuet Kavkaz...' (Why the Caucasus is howling...), *Ogonyok*, 26, 20 September.

Izmailov, V. (2006) 'Den'gi na porokhovuyu bochku' (Money for a powder keg), in *Novaya gazeta,* 23, 30 March.

Kagarlitsky, B. (2000) 'Nostalgia for Soviet period', *Moscow Times*, 16 September.

Kagarlitsky, B. (2002a) 'Topor proigrannoi voiny' (The hatchet of a lost war), *Novaya gazeta*, 2, 14 January.

Kagarlitsky, B. (2002b) 'Insane "heroes" of our time', *Moscow Times*, 25 June.

Kagarlitsky, B (2002c) 'Zakaev out of the game', *Moscow Times*, 10 December.

Kaufman, M. (2003) 'What does the Pentagon see in "Battle of Algiers"?', *New York Times*, 7 September, 4, p. 3.

Khasbulatov, R. (2000) 'Gosudarstvo, politika i separatizm' (State, politics and separatism), *Nezavisimaya gazeta*, 14 December.

Khasbulatov, R. (2002) 'Zachem Rossii nuzhna Chechnya? (Why does Russia need Chechnya?), *Novaya gazeta*, 6, 26 January.

Kovalev, S. (1995) 'Nekotoriye itogi chechenskoi kampanii' (Some results of the Chechen campaign), *Nezavisimaya gazeta*, 22 February.

Kovalev, S. (1997) 'After Chechnya', *The New York Review of Books*, 17 July.

Kovalev, S. (1999) 'Dve voiny' (Two wars), *Novoye vremya*, 47, November, pp. 12–14.

Kovalev, S. (2000a) 'Putin's war', *The New York Review of Books*, 10 February.

Kovalev, S. (2000b) 'Sny politicheskogo idealista' (Dreams of a political idealist), *Novoye vremya*, 9, 2000, pp. 10–15.

Latsis, O. (2002) 'Another short, victorious war?', *The Russia Journal*, 27 September–3 October.

Laville, S. and Dodd, V. (2006) 'One year on, a London bomber issues a threat from the dead', *Guardian*, 7 July.

Leahy, K.D. (2006) 'Kadyrov's bluff: why Chechnya's strongman continues to test his political boundaries', *Central Asia-Caucasus Analyst*, 17 May.

Lloyd, J. (2005) 'Broken Dream', *FTmagazine*, 8–9 October.

McGregor, A. (2003) 'Amir Abu Al-Walid and the Islamic component of the Chechen War', *Central Asia-Caucasus Analyst*, 26 February.

McGregor, A. (2006) 'Distant relations: Hamas and the Mujahideen of Chechnya', The Jamestown Foundation's *Chechnya Weekly*, 7:8, 23 February.

Maddox, B. (2004) 'An unwinnable war, but Russia cannot quit', *The Times*, 13 May.

Maksakov, I. and Chernogorsky, D. (2000) 'Vykhod boevikov iz Groznogo byl operatsiei rossiiskikh voisk' (The withdrawal of fighters from Chechnya was an operation by federal Russian troops), *Komsomol'skaya pravda*, 3 February.

Margolis, E. (1999) 'The evil empire lives … with U.S. support', *Toronto Sun*, 10 October.

Maskhadov, A. (2001) 'Posle etoi voiny Rossiya okonchatel'no poteryala Chechnyu' (After this war Russia has finally lost Chechnya), *Novoye vremya*, 26, 1 July, pp. 6–8.

Medetsky, A. (2004) 'Two get life in prison for '99 bombings', *Moscow Times*, 13 January.

Moore, C. (2006b) 'Counter-insurgency and counter hostage-taking in the North Caucasus', *Central Asia—Caucasus Analyst*, 23 August.

Muradov, M. (2003) 'Navstrechu referendumu: Ogranichenny izbytochny kontingent' (Towards the referendum: the limited surplus contingent), *Kommersant''*, 4 March.

Myers, S.L. (2002) 'Chechen in extradition dispute: criminal or peacemaker?', *New York Times*, 9 December.

Novodvorskaya, V. (2005) 'Boisya chekistov, prinosyashchikh dary (Beware Chekists, bearing gifts), *Novoye vremya*, 11, 20 March.

Osborn, A. (2004) 'How a young conscript became a Russian saint', *Independent*, 24 November.

Pain, E. (2004) 'V Rossii ogromnyi resurs etnicheskoi nenavisti' (In Russia there are huge reserves of ethnic hatred), *Izvestiya*, 23 March.

Pain, E. and Popov, A. (1995) 'Vlast' i obshchestvo na barrikadakh (Power and society at the barricades), *Izvestiya*, 10 February.

Parfitt, T. (2006a) 'The republic of fear', *Sunday Times*, 20 August.

Parfitt, T. (2006b) 'Putin is silent as fiercest critic is murdered', *Guardian*, 9 October.

Parrish, S. (1995) 'A turning point in the Chechen conflict', *Transition*, 1:13, pp. 42–46.

Piontkovsky, A. (2003) 'Russia has lost the war in Chechnya', *Chechnya Weekly*, 4:37, 16 October.

Politkovskaya, A. (2001b) 'S kem vesti peregovory v Chechnye' (With whom we should negotiate in Chechnya), *Novaya gazeta*, 71, 1 October.

Politkovskaya, A. (2002) 'Esli by diktatorom v Chechne byl ya…' (If I were to be dictator in Chechnya…), *Novaya gazeta*, 20, 21 March.

Politkovskaya, A. (2004a) 'Poisoned by Putin', *Guardian*, 9 September.

Politkovskaya, A. (2004b) 'Spasat' ne prikazali' (There were no orders to save people), *Novaya gazeta*, 84, 15 November.

Politkovskaya, A. (2005a) 'Soldatskiye materi uyekhali dumat' nad predlozheniyenami chechenskoi storony. Ostanovit li eto terakty? (Soldiers' mothers have departed to consider the proposals from the Chechen side. Will this halt the acts of terror?), *Novaya gazeta*, 15, 28 February.

Politkovskaya, A. (2005b) 'Vsya Chechnya v krugu sem'i' (All of Chechnya Surrounded by the Family), *Novaya gazeta*, 41, 9 June.

Politkovskaya, A. (2006a) 'Ramzan Kadyrov – krasa Chechni' (Ramzan Kadyrov – the beautiful face of Chechnya), *Novaya gazeta*, 42, 5 June 2006.

Politkovskaya, A. (2006b) 'Za narushenie prava na zhizn'' (For violating the right to life), *Novaya gazeta*, 57, 31 July.

Politkovskaya, A. (2006c) 'Karatel'nyi sgovor' (Punishment pact), *Novaya gazeta*, 74, 28 September.

Politkovskaya, A. (2006d) 'Naznachaem tebya terroristom: antiterroristicheskaya politika pytok na Severnom Kavkaze' (We appoint you as terrorist: the anti-terrorist policy of torture in the North Caucasus), *Novaya gazeta*, 78, 12 October.

Rashid, A. (2004) 'The Mess in Afghanistan', *The New York Review of Books*, 12 February, pp. 24–27.

Rechkalov, V. (2004a) 'Budet lokal'nye stychki s zhertvami do 100 chelovek, a voiny ne budet' (There will be local skirmishes with up to 100 victims, but there will be no war), *Izvestiya*, 2 August.

Rechkalov, V. (2004b) 'Armiya Basaeva' (Basaev's army), *Izvestiya*, 6 December.

Rechkalov, V. (2004c) 'Bazy Basaeva' (Basaev's bases), *Izvestiya*, 7 December.

Rechkalov, V. (2004d) 'Den'gi Basaeva' (Basaev's money), *Izvestiya*, 8 December.

Rechkalov, V. (2004e) 'Marshruty Basaeva' (Basaev's routes), *Izvestiya*, 9 December.

Rechkalov, V. (2004f) 'Ideologiya Basaeva' (Basaev's ideology), *Izvestiya*, 10 December.

Rechkalov, V. (2005) 'Gori v zakone' (Mountains in law) *Moskovsky komsomolets*, 14 February.

Reddaway, P. (2003a) 'Chechnya – an apology', *Guardian*, 30 June.

Reddaway, P. (2003b) 'Linking Chechnya to Iraq was wrong', *The Times*, 28 July.

Remnick, D. (2003) 'Letter from Moscow: post-imperial blues: billionaire oligarchs, Chechen suicide bombers, generals nostalgic for empire – and the reign of Vladimir Putin', *The New Yorker*, 13 October.

Reynolds, M. (2000) 'Moscow has Chechnya back – now what?', *Los Angeles Times*, 19 June.

Reznik, Y. (2006) 'Alu Alkhanov: davleniye so storony federal'nogo tsentra ya ne ispytyvayu' (Alu Alkhanov: I feel no pressure from the central federal authorities), *Yuzhny Federal'ny*, 18 July.

Riskin, A. (2003) 'Kak "izbirali" Kadyrova' (How Kadyrov was "elected"), *Nezavisimaya gazeta*, 6 October.

Rotar', I. (1998) 'Konflikt tsivilizatsii na Severnom Kavkaze' (The clash of civilisations in the North Caucasus), *Nezavisimaya gazeta*, 23 May.

Russell, J. (2002c) 'On the side of might', *The World Today*, 56:12, December, pp. 17–18.

Russell, J. (2004) 'Primed to explode', *The World Today*, 60:6, June, pp. 20–21.

Russell, J. (2005c) 'Death à la Carte', *The World Today*, 61:4, April, pp. 24–25.

Shchekochikin, Y. (1995) 'Malen'kaya pobedonosnaya voina' (A small, victorious war), *Literaturnaya gazeta*, 2 August.

Smirnov, A. (2006) 'Sadulaev's new decrees reveal divisions within the separatist movement', The Jamestown Foundation's *Chechnya Weekly*, 7:6, 9 February.

Sossinsky, S. (2002) 'Our own and strangers', *Moscow News*, 15 May.

Steele, J. (2004) 'Doing well out of the war: reflections on the stand-off between Russia and Chechnya', *London Review of Books*, 26:20 19 October.

Stroube, W.J. (2006) 'Russia spins global energy spider's web', *Asia Times*, 25 August.

Sweeney, J. (2000) 'Revealed: Russia's worst war crime in Chechnya', *Observer*, 5 March.

Talbott, S.P. (1996) 'Early Chechen coverage tests print journalists' independence', *Transition*, 2:16, pp. 48–51.

Tan'kova, Y. (2006) 'Pochemy russkie stanovyatsya islamskimi terroristami' (Why Russians become Islamic terrorists), *Komsomol'skaya pravda*, 16 August.

Traynor, I. (2002) 'Chechen murder trial limps to an end', *Guardian*, 28 June.

Tret'yakov, V. (2000) 'Diagnoz: upravlyayemaya demokratiya' (The diagnosis is a managed democracy), *Nezavisimaya gazeta,* 13 January.

Uglanov, A. (2003) 'Pobeda vlasti: zhertva prinyata (Victory for the regime: the sacrifice is accepted), *Argumenty i fakty*, 50, 10 December.

Uzzell, L.A. (2003) 'The refugees: "a pattern of intimidation"', The Jamestown Foundation's *Chechnya Weekly*, 4:4, 13 February.

Vachagaev, M. (2005a) 'Evolution of the Chechen Jamaat', The Jamestown Foundation's *Chechnya Weekly*, 6:14, 6 April.

Vachagaev, M. (2005b) 'The Role of Sufism in the Chechen Resistance', The Jamestown Foundation's *Chechnya Weekly*, 6:16, 28 April.

Vazaeva, A. (2003) 'Chechnya tribunal proposed', *Caucasus Reporting Service*, 174, 11 April.

Vinogradova, I. (2004) 'Chechensky konflikt vykhodit za predely respubliki' (The Chechen conflict is spreading beyond the borders of the republic), *Izvestiya*, 24 June.

Walsh, N.P. (2002), 'Comrades fall out in Russia's battle of the dissidents', *Guardian*, 6 July.

Walsh, N.P. (2004) 'Russia's man in reign of terror in Chechnya', *Guardian*, 13 January.

Walsh, N.P. (2006) 'Land of the warlords', *Guardian*, 13 June.

Wielaard, R. (2002) 'Chechnya query incenses Putin', *Washington Post*, 13 November 2002.

Williams, B. (2003) 'Unravelling the links between the Middle East and Islamic militants in Chechnya', *Central Asia—Caucasus Analyst*, 12 February.

Zarakhovich, Yuri (2003) 'Chechnya's walking wounded', *Time Europe*, 28 September.

Zaripov, R. (1996) 'Interv'yu s generalem Aleksandrom Lebedym' (Interview with General Aleksandr Lebed), *Komsomol'skaya pravda,* 19 March.

Zhadaev, R. (2005a) 'One year without Kadyrov', *Chechen Society Newspaper*, 9:47, 11 May.

Zhadaev, R. (2005b) 'Parliamentskie vybory: byl li vybor? (Parliamentary elections: was there a choice?), *Chechenskoe obshchestvo*, 26, 7 December.

Zhadaev, R. (2006) 'Taina smerti Basaeva' (The secret of Basaev's death), *Chechenskoe obshchestvo*, 16:81, 25 July.

Zhuravel', V. and Velichkovsky, V. (2002) 'Pokhishcheniya prodolzhayutsya' (The abductions continue), *Nezavisimoye voennoye obozreniye*, 23 August.

Official documents, reports, conferences, etc.

American Committee for Peace in Chechnya Report (2004) 'Chechnya's suicide bombers: desperate, devout, or deceived?', by J. Reuter, 16 September, peaceinchechnya.org/reports/SuicideReport/.

Amnesty International Report (2004) '"Normalization" in whose eyes?', 23 June web.amnesty.org/library/print/ENGEUR460272004.

Carnegie Endowment for International Peace Policy Brief (2003), *The Forgotten War: Chechnya and Russia's Future*, by D. Trenin, 28, November.

Carnegie Endowment for International Peace Policy Brief (2005) *A Spreading Danger: Time for a New Policy Towards Chechnya*, by Fiona Hill, Anatol Lieven and Thomas de Waal, 35, 23 February.

Carnegie Endowment for International Peace Policy Brief (2005) *Reading Russia Right*, by D. Trenin, 42, October.

Conflict Studies Research Centre Report (2000) *The Second Chechen War*, by A.C. Aldis, (ed.), P31, June.

Conflict Studies Research Centre Report (2003) *Chechnya: Normalisation*, by C.W. Blandy, P40, June.

Conflict Studies Research Centre Report (2003) *Chechnya: Dynamics of War, Brutality and Stress*, by C.W. Blandy, P35, July.

Conflict Studies Research Centre Report (2004) *Russian Perspectives on Terrorism*, by M.A. Smith, C110, January.

Conflict Studies Research Centre Caucasus Series (2004) *Chechnya: The Search for a Strong Successor*, by C.W. Blandy, 04/19, July.

Conflict Studies Research Centre Caucasus Series (2004) *Chechnya after Beslan*, by C.W. Blandy, 04/27, October.

Conflict Studies Research Centre Caucasus Series (2005) *The End of Ichkeria?*, by C.W. Blandy, 05/17, April.

Conflict Studies Research Centre Caucasus Series (2005) *North Caucasus: On the Brink of Far-Reaching Destabilisation*, by C.W. Blandy, 05/36, August.

Conflict Studies Research Centre Caucasus Series (2006) *Whither Ingushetia?*, by C.W. Blandy, 06/03, January 2006.

Council of Europe's Committee for the Prevention of Torture and Inhuman or Degrading Treatment or Punishment (2003) 'Concerning the Chechen Republic of the Russian Federation', 10 July, www.cpt.coe.int/documents/rus/2003–33-inf-eng.htm.

Council of Europe's European Commission Against Racism and Intolerance Third Report (2005) 'The Russian Federation', www.coe.int/t/e/human_rights/ecri/1-ECRI/2-Country-by-country_approach/Russian_Federation/Russian_Federation_CBC_3.asp.

Federation of American Scientists (2000) *The Chechen Chronicles 1999*, www.fas.org/man/dod-101/ops/war/2000/01/chechen/185.htm.

Foreign Policy Centre, London (2004) *Political Change in Russia: Implications for Britain*, by G. Austin.

Foreign Policy Centre, London (2005) *Blueprint for Russia*, J. Moll (ed.).

Foreign Policy Centre, London (2005) *Losing Ground: Russia's European Commitments to Human Rights*, J. Moll and R. Gowan (eds).

Foreign Policy Centre, London (2005) *Putin and the Press: The Revival of Soviet-style Propaganda*, by O. Panfilov.

Freedom House Country Report: Russia (2005), www.freedomhouse.org/template.cfm?page=47&nit=366&year=2005.

Human Rights Watch (2000) '"Welcome to Hell": arbitrary detention, torture and extortion in Chechnya – the Chernokozovo Detention Center', www.hrw.org/reports/2000/russia_chechnya4/detention-center.htm.

Human Rights Watch (2005) 'Worse than a war: "disappearances" in Chechnya – a crime against humanity', March, hrw.org/backgrounder/eca/chechnya0305/.

International Helsinki Federation for Human Rights (2003) 'The Constitutional referendum in Chechnya was neither free nor fair', 28 March, www.osce-ngo.net/030328.pdf.

International Helsinki Federation for Human Rights (2004) 'Chechnya: enforced "disappearances", extrajudicial killings and unlawful detentions – an update', 4 August, www.ihf-hr.org/viewbinary/viewdocument.php?doc_id=6069.

The Jamestown Foundation Conference (2006) 'The future of the North Caucasus', 14 September: A. McGregor, 'Military Jama'ats in the North Caucasus: a continuing threat'; J.B. Dunlop, 'Putin, Kozak and Russian policy toward the North Caucasus'; M. Vachagaev, 'The Chechen resistance: yesterday, today and tomorrow'; M. al-Shishani, 'The rise and fall of Arab fighters in Chechnya'.

Médecins Sans Frontières (2002) 'Report on Chechnya-Ingushetia: a deliberate strategy of non-assistance to people in crisis', www.msf.org/msfinternational/invoke. cfm?component=report&objectid=A50E954B-EA6A-4582-A7B6937099F518C2&method=full_html.

Memorial (2003) Appeal to the UN Commission for Human Rights, March. www.memo. ru/eng/memhrc/texts/uno2003b.shtml.

Memorial Report (2005) 'Polozheniye zhitelei Chechni v Rossiiskoi Federatsii, iyun' 2004g – iyun' 2005g' (The situation of residents of Chechnya in the Russian Federation, June 2004–June 2005), S. Gannushkina (ed.), 22 July, www.memo.ru/hr/news/ 5gannush7.htm.

Memorial Report, (2006) 'The Chechen Republic: consequences of "Chechenization" of the conflict', 2 March, www.memo.ru/eng/memhrc/texts/6chechen.shtml.

Norwegian Helsinki Committee Report (2002) 'The ethnic war: persecution of Chechens in the Russian Federation', Oslo, III/2002.

Parliamentary Assembly of the Council of Europe, (2004) 'The political situation in the Chechen Republic: measures to increase democratic stability in accordance with Council of Europe standards', Doc. 10276, 17 September, assembly.coe.int/Documents/Working/Docs/doc04/EDOC10276.htm.

Physicians for Human Rights Report (2001) 'Endless brutality: war crimes in Chechnya', May, www.phrusa.org/research/pdf/chech_report_final.pdf.

PONARS Policy Memo (2002) 'The Disconnect in How Russians Think About Human Rights and Chechnya: A Consequence of Media Manipulation', by T.P. Gerber and S.E. Mendelson, 244 January.

PONARS Policy Memo (2003) 'The structures of Chechnya's quagmire', by G. Derlugian, 309, November.

PONARS Policy Memo (2004) 'Security sell-out in the North Caucasus 2004: how government centralization backfires', by M.A. Alexseev, 344, November.

Relief International (1999) 'The Russian ultimatum to Chechnya: a humanitarian outrage', 7 December.

Russian Justice Initiative Report on Chechnya (2005) 'Impunity', www.srji.org/en/ Chechnya/impunity.

Transparency International (2005) 'Corruption Perceptions Index for 2005', ww1.transparency.org/cpi/2005/cpi2005_infocus.html.

UN Commission for Human Rights (2001) 'The situation in the Republic of Chechnya in the Russian Federation', 2001/24, www.unhchr.ch/huridocda/huridoca.nsf/(Symbol)/ E.CN.4.RES.2001.24.En?Opendocument.

Woodrow Wilson International Center for Scholars in Washington, DC Conference Report (2001) 'The economics of war: the intersection of need, creed and greed', organised on 10 September, www.ipacademy.org/PDF_Reports/econofwar.pdf.

Online material

Websites

American Enterprise Institute, www.aei.org.

Amina, www.amina.com.

APN, www.apn.ru.

Art of War, www.artofwar.ru.

BBC, news.bbc.co.uk.

Beslan (*Novaya gazeta*), beslan-2004.narod.ru.

Carnegie Endowment for International Peace, www.ceip.org.

Centre for Defense Information, www.cdi.org.

Changing Character of War, ccw.politics.ox.ac.uk.

Chechen Press, www.chechenpress.com.

Chechen Republic, www.chechnya.gov.ru.

Chechnya Free, www.chechnyafree.ru.

Chechnya, Ministry of Foreign Affairs, www.chechnya-mfa.info.

CNN, edition.cnn.com.

Compromat, www.compromat.ru.

Conciliation Resources, www.c-r.org.

Crimes of War Project, crimesofwar.org.

Daymohk, www.daymohk.info.

Diasporas, Migration and Identities, www.diasporas.ac.uk.

Federation of American Scientists, www.fas.org.

Freedom House, www.freedomhouse.org.

Geocities, www.geocities.com.

Global Development Network, www.gdnet.org.

Global Security, www.globalsecurity.org.

Human Rights Violations in Chechnya, www.hrvc.net.

Institute for War and Peace Reporting, www.iwpr.net.

International Alert, www.international-alert.org.

Johnson's Russia List, www.cdi.org/russia/johnson.

Kavkaz-Forum, www.kavkaz-forum.ru/.

Kavkaz-Tsentr, www.kavkazcenter.com.

Levada Centre, www.levada.ru.

Mises Institute, www.mises.org.

Moscow Helsinki Group, www.mhg.ru.

Moscow News, www.mosnews.com.

New American Century, www.newamericancentury.org.

New Times, www.newtimes.ru.

'Nord-Ost' (*Novaya gazeta*), www.novayagazeta.ru/rassled2/nord-ost/karta.shtml.

Northern Ireland Office, www.nio.gov.uk.

Novosti, www.rian.ru.

NTV, ntvru.com.

Okhota na Zakaeva (The hunt for Zakaev), zakaev.ru.

Open Democracy, www.opendemocracy.net.

Palestine Ministry of Information, www.palestine-net.com.

Peace in Chechnya, peaceinchechnya.org.

Polit.ru, www.polit.ru.

Politcom.ru, www.politcom.ru.
Political Studies Association, www.psa.ac.uk.
Prague Watchdog, watchdog.cz.
Pravda, pravda.ru.
Prognosis, www.prognosis.ru.
Reporters without Borders, www.rsf.org.
RFE/RL, www.rferl.org.
Rosbalt, www.rosbaltnews.com.
Royal Institute for International Affairs, www.riia.org.
Russia Today, www.russiatoday.com.
Sakharov Centre, www.sakharov-center.ru.
The Times/Sunday Times, www.timesonline.co.uk.
Truth and Justice Publications, www.truth-and-justice.info.
Untimely Thoughts, untimely-thoughts.com.
US Council for Foreign Relations, www.cfr.org.
Voice of America, www.voanews.com.
VTsIOM, www.wciom.ru.
Vzryvy v Rossii (Explosions in Russia) (*Novaya gazeta*), www.novayagazeta.ru/rassled2/
   vzrivi/karta.shtml.
White House, www.whitehouse.gov.
Yabloko, www.yabloko.ru.

Online books and articles

Basaev, S. 'Book of a Mujahiddeen' (e-book), www.kavkazcenter.com/eng/help/
   ebook.shtml.
Shenfield, S.D. (2005) 'Chechnya and Russia: a post-Beslan symposium', Research
   Report, 29, January, published online as *JRL Research and Analytical Supplement*,
   www.cdi.org/russia/johnson/9024.cfm.

Index

245th motorized rifle regiment 97
9/11 (11 September 2001) xii, 4, 8, 11–16, 18–20, 23–7, 36–8, 41, 47, 54, 67, 89–92, 94–5, 97–8, 102, 106–9, 133, 136, 138, 144, 146–7, 157, 160, 168–70, 172

Abrahms, Max 117
abrek xvii, 13, 32, 39, 46, 60, 178n20
Aburakhmanov, Duvakha 150, 165
adat xvii, 11, 18, 20, 33, 39, 46, 50, 86, 119, 125, 147, 180n54
Afghanistan 7, 14, 23, 41, 51, 54, 98, 103, 113–14, 125, 130, 144, 147, 152, 172–3; Afghan War 12, 32, 35, 54, 60, 98, 150
Akhmadov, Ilyas 29, 48, 108, 114, 134
Akhmedova, Khapta 100
Albright, Madeleine 149
Aleksandr I, Tsar 31
Alekseyeva, Lyudmilla 68
Alexeev, Mikhail 119
Algeria 43, 172
Aliev, Timur 24
Alkhanov, Alu 15, 48, 84–6, 88, 104, 106, 117, 121, 123, 130
al-Qaeda 75, 98, 101, 106–8, 144
Al-Walid, Abu 97
American Committee for Peace in Chechnya 140
Ammar, Abu 75
Amnesty International 82, 139
Andersen, Elizabeth 164
anti-terrorism 3, 5, 74, 83, 148, 170, 176n9; containment 5, 104; root causes 5, 90, 105–6
apartheid 21, 55, 89
APN xvi, 88; Institute of National Strategy 85, 88
Appadurai, Arjun 18

Arab fighters xi, 58, 75, 90, 97–9, 111–12; Arabic script 55, 97
Arafat, Yasser 22, 57, 128, 133
Argumenty i fakty 55, 63
Arutyunov, Sergei 40
Ashdown, Paddy 150
Aslakhanov, Aslambek 84, 134–5, 137
Astashkin, Nikolai 63
asymmetry 11, 12, 14, 18, 22, 27–30, 50, 52, 54, 65, 105, 127, 130, 154, 182n88
Atgeriev, Turpal-Ali 99, 213n73
aul xvii, 60
Aum Shinrikyo 112

Babitsky, Andrei 34, 70, 139, 141, 195n15
Baltic 18, 35, 45, 65–6; Estonia 34, 44, 109, 158; Latvia 158; Lithuania 158, 166
Baluyevsky, Yury 103
Baraev, Arbi 41, 65, 80, 99, 198n90
Baraev, Movsar 100
Baraeva, Khaba 99–100
Basaev, Shamil x–xiii, 6, 14, 39, 48, 53, 58, 65, 70, 72, 82, 97, 99, 105–6, 108, 110–12, 131, 146–7, 159, 161, 165, 171, 207n35; assassination of Kadyrov 84, 171; Beslan x, xii, 74, 89, 106–7, 114–21, 196n51; Budennovsk 73, 112, 116; charisma 39, 58, 111, 120, 146; Dagestan xii, 73, 77, 111, 119; death x–xiii, 48, 107, 120–1, 155, 171; Dubrovka 74, 99, 115–16, 196n51; entrepreneur of violence 6, 114–21; field commander 58, 80, 112; international terrorist 39, 48, 58, 86, 99, 108, 112, 121, 143, 161; Islamist 105, 111–12, 114, 146; lone wolf 60; loses foot 79, 111; Moscow bombs 74, 196n51; Vedeno x, 41; warlord 41, 114

238   *Index*

BASEES 78
Batako-yurt 116
Battle of Algiers 172, 181n75
Belkovsky, Stanislav 85
Berezovsky, Boris 48, 71, 75, 93, 111,
138–9, 197n62
Beslan x, xii, 1, 7, 15, 21–2, 24, 48–9,
66–8, 70, 74, 80–1, 84, 89, 92, 97, 100,
103–4, 106–7, 114–17, 120–1, 127–8,
145, 147–8, 152–3, 157, 171, 198n98,
218n10
bin Laden, Osama 76, 89, 93, 98, 107, 112,
141
'Black Septembers' 63, 89, 97, 102, 128,
204n66
'Black Widows' 99–101, 147
Blair, Tony 91, 94, 98, 109, 136, 140,
151–2, 162
Blunkett, David 138
bombs: apartment block bombings (1999)
xii, 59, 62–3, 74, 76–8, 80–1, 83, 89–90,
93, 95, 97, 99, 109, 111, 128, 136; Bali
97, 137; carpet bombing 35, 43, 60, 70,
106, 132; Grozny Stadium 84; Grozny
truck bomb 97, 100–1; Hiroshima 94,
115; Kaspiisk 99, 136; London 7/7 161;
Pushkin Square 79; Ryazan' 74, 80, 93;
suicide 13, 24, 63, 67, 86, 89, 93, 96–7,
99–101, 109, 113, 117, 126, 144, 147;
thermobaric (fuel-air) 78, 132, 136;
Znamenskoye 101
Bonner, Yelena 90, 139, 141, 178n24,
179n41
Book of a Mujahideen xi, 207n36
Borovoi, Konstantin 76
boyeviki xvii, 19, 32, 63, 88, 106, 116,
120, 171
Bradford 172
Brandt, Willy 68
Braveheart 38
Brezhnev, Leonid 46
Brzezinski, Zbigniew 134, 137, 140, 148
Budanov, Yury 104, 106, 142, 197n77
Budennovsk 62, 73, 89, 95, 112, 116, 147
Buinaksk 74, 95, 111
Burlatsky, Fedor 71
Bush, George W. 2, 13, 41, 44, 79, 91, 94,
98, 107–8, 136–7, 140, 143, 148–9,
151–2, 169, 172, 218n61
Byford, Grenville 25, 94, 183n108

Carnegie Institute (Centre) 21, 27, 67, 126
Carr, Camilla 75, 197n62
Carter, President James E. 137

Caucasus 2, 8, 18, 30–1, 39, 45, 52, 64, 68,
82, 88, 102, 111, 130, 132, 154, 166,
171; Abkhazia 42, 51, 61, 72, 120;
Caucasian character 61; Caucasians 17,
39, 64–5, 67, 90, 131, 171;
'Caucasophobia' 11, 16, 20, 27, 65,
67–8, 107, 125, 154, 171, 179n45;
Cherkess 38–9; Cossacks 17; Great
Caucasian War xi, 33, 38–9, 43, 59–60;
Kabardinians 38; Kabardino-Balkaria
126, 171; Nogays 33; North Caucasus
xii, 6, 17, 19–21, 32, 34, 51, 64–5, 69,
80, 86, 88, 107–8, 120–4, 126, 157–9,
163, 165, 171, 173; North Ossetia 116,
120, 158, 171
Chamberlain, Neville 150
Chechen: beauty competition 123; blood
feud 14, 18, 34, 37, 119, 125;
charismatic leaders 39, 54; Chechen vs.
Chechen 31, 85–6, 113, 171; cultural
narrative x, 11, 17, 20, 23, 39, 43, 45,
67, 87, 125, 154, 168, 171, 180n53;
diaspora 11, 22–3, 39, 66, 124, 130,
137; field commanders 23, 41, 45, 57–9,
72, 79–80, 111–12, 121, 135; 'freedom'
cult 11, 18, 20, 24, 26, 35, 40, 49–50,
86, 90, 120, 125, 131; gangs 18, 46, 56,
61, 79, 134; language 1, 35, 38, 53;
nationalism 18, 35, 41, 137; 'noble
robbers' 39; refugees 15, 94, 108;
religiosity 34, 92–3; resistance xi, 22,
34–5, 43–4, 63, 65, 70, 87, 97, 108, 121,
135–6, 138, 143, 158, 170; Russian
perceptions of 4, 35, 39, 44, 54, 57–62,
98, 100, 137, 154–5, 165; separatism 5,
24, 47, 85–6, 92, 97, 107–8, 133, 149,
151, 166; survival 11, 23–4, 30, 47, 52,
161; traditions xi, 33, 35, 37, 40, 85,
134, 137, 159, 171; warlords 11, 14, 16,
19, 23, 37, 41, 50, 61, 64, 66, 71, 73, 75,
99, 113–14, 122, 125–6, 129–30, 168;
'wolf' identification viii, 33, 39, 53,
60–1, 63, 97
'Chechen syndrome' 11–12, 16, 82, 113,
127, 158, 177n9
'Chechen trail' 80
Chechenisation i, 5–6, 15–16, 27–8, 33,
59, 80–8, 92, 103–4, 108, 113–14, 122,
128, 145, 171
Chechnya: autonomy 22–3, 27, 44, 48–9,
87, 133–4, 137, 147, 158, 171;
beheadings 7, 11, 14, 16, 37, 64–5, 76,
93; British telecom engineers 75, 93;
budget 124; coat-of-arms 60;

constitution 84, 109, 121, 146; economy 23, 28, 46–7, 123, 147, 165–6, 173; elections 7, 48, 51, 84–6, 116, 144, 158; environment 23, 28, 147, 153, 158, 173; film festival 139; flag 60–1, 97, 112; independence 41, 43, 46, 56, 62, 64, 74–5, 85, 87, 93, 100, 120, 131, 133, 135, 142, 146, 161; inter-war period 64, 70, 75, 93, 146, 149, 153; national anthem 60, 183n99; *Nokchiin mokhk* 53; occupied homeland 11, 23, 30, 50, 100, 107, 114, 121, 133; opinion polls 49, 84, 86, 123, 161; parliament 85, 124; president 64, 84–5, 92, 104, 127, 144, 147; referendum 83–4, 143–4; Russian-speaking population xii, 36, 80, 107, 150, 171; secession 42, 74, 113, 182n87; self-determination 4, 11, 13, 18, 20, 23, 26, 30, 35, 42–4, 52, 89–90, 104, 109, 117–18, 125, 127, 151–2, 165; 'separatism-lite' 87; society 19, 28, 37, 86, 159, 173; state formation 37, 41, 46, 165; 'systemic' separatism 87, 200n138; unemployment 123; wall 40
Chechnya-Ichkeria 6, 30, 33, 41–2, 48, 59–60, 64–5, 67, 74–5, 83, 95, 103, 105, 121, 129–30, 133–5, 150, 171, 183n99, 205n89
Chekist xvii, 76
Cherkasov, Aleksandr 8, 29, 139
Chernokozovo 15, 63, 78
Chernomyrdin, Viktor 59, 73
Chernyshev, Prince 32
China 43, 132, 158, 173; Taiwan 52; Tibet 18, 52; Uighurs 42
Chistilishche 64
Christian Science Monitor 39
Chukovsky, Kornei 64
Chupalaev, Said-Magomed 146
Churchill, Winston 8
CIS xvi; Armenia 43–4, 66; Black Sea 35, 45; Caspian Sea 51, 75, 166, 172; Central Asia 34, 36, 43–4; Georgia 22, 30, 34–5, 42, 57, 155, 158, 172; Kazakhstan 33, 43, 45; Moldova 22, 155; 'Near Abroad' 8, 51, 67, 172; Tajikistan 98; Turkmenistan 34; Ukraine 51, 158; Uzbekistan 29
civil society 5, 11–12, 14, 16, 19, 25–6, 47, 108, 124, 126–7, 139, 143, 151, 156–7, 161–4, 183n101
clash of civilisations 18, 24, 26, 37, 67, 91, 107, 126, 183n104
clientelism 11, 19–20, 25, 126, 181n64

Clinton, President William J. 149, 205n2
coalition ('of the willing') 5, 15, 90, 92, 94, 98, 101–2, 105, 109, 148, 152, 160, 165, 170–1
cognitive consonance 86, 172
cognitive dissonance 86, 172
Cohn-Bendit, Daniel 134
Cold War 17, 35, 37, 52, 98, 106–7, 160
Colombia 125
colonisation 4, 11, 21, 25, 27, 36, 43–4, 50, 125, 154, 170
Committee of Soldiers' Mothers (CSM) xvi, 32, 57, 72, 144, 150, 170, 185n23, 191n20
'complexity fatigue' 5, 96, 98
conflict resolution 2, 4, 10–12, 21, 54, 154, 170
conspiracy theories 74, 77, 80, 112, 116, 120, 196n49
Cook, Robin 80, 162, 217n52
Cooper, James Fennimore 38
Copenhagen 134, 138, 143
Coppetiers, Bruno 155
corruption 11, 19–20, 25, 45, 57, 88, 113–14, 124, 126, 130, 162–3
Cossack Lullaby (poem) x, xii, 38, 54
Council of Europe 83, 114, 122, 127, 133, 135, 150, 155–7, 166
counter-terrorism i, 3, 8, 63, 90, 92, 94–5, 101, 173; combating 5, 103; eradication 5, 101–4, 148, 151; insurgency 47, 63, 101–4, 108
'counter-terrorism operation' *see* Second Chechen War
'Creed', 'Greed', 'Need' xi, 3, 126–7, 159, 209n91
Cuny, Frederick C. 71
Czechoslovakia 14, 64, 150, 164; Ruthenians 42; Slovakia 42

Dadi Yurt 30
Dagestan/Dagestani xii, 39–40, 44, 59, 62, 65, 74, 76–8, 93, 99, 111–12, 119, 122, 125, 136, 158, 171
Dashuev, Duk-Vakha 142
Debray, Régis xi
dedovshchina (hazing) xvii, 12, 177n11
Dell'Alba, Gianfranco 134
Della Vedova, Benedetto 134
demonisation 3, 4, 11, 17, 24, 33, 53–5, 57–8, 60, 63, 67, 125, 152, 164, 169; banditry 11, 13, 16–17, 31–2, 37, 40, 46–7, 55, 58–9, 63, 66, 78–9, 92; *barany* (sheep) 53; Chechenophobia 58;

demonisation *continued*
  chechevitsa (lentil) 55; *chekhi* 64,
    193n81; *cherniye* (blacks) 16, 64, 131;
    chernozhopy (black arses) 17, 64; *chichi*
    64; criminals 18, 26, 32–3, 37, 41, 43,
    45–6, 55, 58–9, 63, 66, 71, 92, 101,
    125–6, 130–1, 134, 144; *dukhi* (spooks)
    64; 'madmen' 54–6, 58–9, 63, 92, 115,
    131; LKN 64; *mafia/mafiosi* 17, 23, 43,
    54, 58, 66, 69, 72, 112; *modjakhedy*
    (mujahideen) 64; *obezyany* (monkeys)
    58, 64; *Rusnya* 53, 207n42; *sobaki*
    (dogs) 53, 61; *svinya* (pigs) 53; terrorists
    37, 58–9, 66, 97, 99, 101, 109, 114, 131,
    134, 136–7, 140, 146–7, 153, 164; *vor*
    (thief) 46; werewolves (*oborotni*) 53,
    63, 65; 'wicked' Chechen x, xii, 38, 54;
    wolf 53, 60–1, 63–5; *zhurnalyugi*
    (journalist scumbags) xviii, 57
Denmark 101, 123, 138, 140
deportation (1944) 18, 30, 33, 35–6, 38–9,
    43, 45–6, 55; Kazakhstan 33, 43, 45;
    Siberia 33, 43, 45
deported peoples 45, 185n33; Balkars 45;
    Bulgarians 45; Crimean Tatars 45;
    Greeks 45; Kalmyks 45; Karachai 45,
    74; Koreans 45; Meskhetian Turks 45;
    Poles 45; Volga Germans 45; *see also*
    Ingush
derzhavnost' xvii, 11, 21–2, 25, 40, 51, 125
Dewhirst, Martin 197n68
Die Welt 122, 206–7n29
Djabrailov, Taus 85, 150, 165
djamaat xvii, 18, 125, 180n59
djigit xvii, 38, 59, 92
Doktor Aibolit 64
Dubnov, Vadim 35, 62
Dubrovka (Nord-Ost) xii, 1, 7, 15, 33, 41,
    49, 67–8, 73–4, 80–1, 83, 91–2, 97–8,
    100–1, 107, 134, 138, 143, 145, 147–9,
    152–3, 157, 170
Duckworth, Nicola 139
Dudaev, Djokhar 33, 41, 43, 55, 57,
    59–60, 63, 70–2, 93, 109, 111, 127, 135,
    165
Dudaev, Lechi 79
Dunlop, John B. 80, 92, 195n24, 198n98
Dupuis, Olivier 134
Dying for the President 93
Dzasokov, Aleksandr 116

East Timor 42, 44, 52, 165; *Falantil* 42
Economist, The 56, 67, 113
Eisenstein, Sergei 59

Ekazhovo x
Enderi 31
energy 8, 21, 26, 51, 155, 157, 160, 162–3,
    169; Centrica 160; Gazprom 160
entrepreneurs of violence 3, 5–6, 14, 16,
    19, 26–7, 70, 110–30, 132, 153, 155–7,
    159, 169–70
Erochkine, Pavel 161
ethnocide 11–12, 45, 216n25
Eurasia 29, 34, 40, 182n80
Europe i, 2–3, 5, 14, 18–19, 21, 24, 28, 51,
    71, 87, 107, 113, 153, 155, 158, 160,
    162–3, 215n13
European Court of Human Rights 14, 110,
    169, 179n32
European Union 114, 150, 155, 158, 172

Felgenhauer, Pavel 22, 34, 110
filtration camps *see* Chernokozovo
First Chechen War (1994–1996) i, 1–2, 5,
    18, 36, 43, 61–5, 67, 69–80, 82, 86,
    89–90, 95, 99, 110–12, 127–8, 132,
    146–8, 150, 166; restoration of
    constitutional order 5, 43, 62, 69, 72–4,
    82, 134
Fitzgerald, Edward QC 138, 142
France x, 43, 149, 151, 172; Corsica 42;
    French resistance 94
Franchetti, Mark 122
Freedom House 19, 162, 189n99, 214n88,
    218n63
Fridinsky, Sergei 141
From Our Own Correspondent 122
FSB xvi, 7, 74, 80–1, 90, 93, 99, 115, 123;
    'dirty tricks' 5, 7, 80–1, 92–3, 171
Fuller, Liz 129, 150, 206n11

G-8 xi, 91, 134, 148, 150, 157
Gakaev, Djabrail 133
Galtung, Johan 3, 10–11, 27, 89; Galtung's
    Conflict Triangle 3, 10–11, 154
Gammer, Moshe 32–3, 35, 54
Gantamirov, Beslan 58
gazavat xvii, 32–3, 59
Gelaev, Ruslan 58, 72, 111, 135, 146
genocide 12, 50, 106, 133, 216n25
geopolitics 11, 21, 26, 125, 171
Germany 25, 71, 81, 91, 128, 150, 155,
    173; GDR 155
Gieve, Sir John 161
globalisation 4, 11, 24, 26, 36–7, 47, 105,
    107, 126–7, 165, 169, 183n103;
    regressive globalisation 36, 107,
    183n103

Glucksmann, André 1, 18, 134
Gorbachev, Mikhail 35, 127
Gosudarstvennost' xvii, 11, 21–2, 40, 51, 125
Grachev, Pavel 33, 72
Grabbe, General 32
Great Patriotic War *see* Second World War
Greetings from Grozny 96
Gross, Andreas 24, 83, 85, 122, 135, 166
Grozny 15, 29, 33, 58–9, 62–3, 66, 70–3, 78–80, 84, 95–7, 101, 110–11, 115, 121, 127, 135, 146–7
GRU xvi, 72, 120
Guardian 122
guerrilla warfare 11, 13, 16, 77, 79, 95, 106, 113, 131, 136, 144
Guevara, Che xi, 58, 120

Hacker, Frederick J. 54–5; 'Crazies', 'Criminals', 'Crusaders' 54–5, 58–9
Hadji-Murat 38, 60
Haig, Alexander 134, 137, 140
Handelman, Stephen 46
Havel, Vaclav 164
Hedges, Chris 119
Hoover Institution (Stanford) 91
hostage taking xi–xii, 7, 11, 15, 21, 24, 33, 37, 45, 62, 64, 71, 75, 89, 92, 95, 97, 99–100, 112–17, 121, 128, 137–8, 141–3, 145, 147–8, 157
Howard, Glen E. 140
Howard, Sir Michael 25, 94, 183n107
human rights 7–8, 12, 14, 19–20, 23, 39, 47, 57, 61, 63, 71, 80–2, 84, 90, 94–5, 98, 106, 109, 132, 134, 136, 138–41, 143–4, 149, 156, 160–3
Human Rights Watch 82, 113, 139, 164
Hungary 172
Hurd, Douglas 162
Hussein, Saddam 86, 119, 166, 169, 171
Hussein, Uday 66

Ichkeria *see* Chechnya-Ichkeria
Ilyukhin, Viktor 76
Imam 33
indigenous peoples 23, 36, 50, 52; Aborigines 36, 52; Inuit 23; Lapps 23; 'small' peoples (Russian Far North) 36; Zulus 36
information war 4, 54–7, 67, 111, 186n49, 194n12; Internet 37, 70
Ingush/Ingushetia x, 38–9, 45, 59, 62, 65, 104, 106, 116, 171
Institute for War and Peace Reporting 115

Institute of Contemporary Arts 139
International Alert 36
International Helsinki Federation for Human Rights 84, 139
International Herald Tribune 150
intifada 11, 13, 16, 95; Al-Aqsah 96
Iraq 2, 7, 14, 23, 47, 54, 66, 103, 107, 110, 119, 121, 127, 144, 147, 151–2, 157, 159, 169, 171–2; Fallujah 115
Ireland: Good Friday Agreement 48; IRA 42, 109, 119, 123; Irish 18, 23, 123; Northern Ireland 48, 71–2, 96, 104–5, 118–19, 124, 151, 159
Iskander, Fazil' 61
Islam xi, 7, 11, 23, 26, 28–9, 33–5, 47, 55, 88–91, 93–4, 97, 105, 109, 111, 117, 119–20, 122, 125–6, 130, 134, 149, 151, 171, 214n90; 'arc of instability' 81, 90, 97, 108; 'Islamic factor' 5, 12, 16, 20, 34, 47, 92, 202n20; Islamic fundamentalism 6, 21, 26, 36, 44, 55, 57, 59, 64, 79, 81, 86, 88, 90, 92–3, 97–8, 105, 107–9, 111–12, 117, 126, 135–6, 144, 151–2, 158, 165; Koran 34, 111, 115
Ismailov, Aslanbek 79
Israel 7, 13, 23, 40, 89, 93–4, 96–7, 101–2, 107, 119, 128, 133; Deir Yassin 31
Israpilov, Khunkarpasha 79
Ivanov, Igor 141
Ivanov, Viktor 92
Izvestiya 68, 112, 119

James, Jon 75, 197n62
Jamestown Foundation 80
Japan 112, 158
Jews 18, 23, 57, 64, 115
jihad xi, 14, 75, 83, 89, 100, 115, 118, 126, 158, 165
Judd, Lord 84, 139–40, 164
jus ad bellum 74; *jus in bello* 12–13, 25, 74

Kadyrov, Akhmad 31, 33, 48, 59–60, 65, 83–4, 86, 92, 99, 103, 113, 122, 133, 136, 171; death 65, 84, 108, 147, 171
Kadyrov, Ramzan 6, 14–16, 27, 31, 66, 85, 87–8, 103, 106–8, 113–14, 120–4, 130, 159, 161, 163, 171, 206–7n29; entrepreneur of violence 121–4, 159
Kadyrova, Zulai 122
'Kadyrovisation' 88, 124
Kadyrovtsy xvii, 88, 103, 106, 120, 122
Kagarlitsky, Boris 110, 141, 146

Kakiev, Said-Magomed 124, 130
Kaldor, Mary 36
Kampelman, Max 134, 137, 140
Karny, Yo'av 55
Kashmir 2, 42, 96
Kaspiisk 99, 136
Katyr Yurt 61, 79
Katz, Steven T. 45, 216n25
Kavkaz-Tsentr 150
Kazantsev, Viktor 33
KGB xvi, 7, 155
Khan, Mohammed Sidique 161
Khasavyurt 73, 112, 122, 147
Khasbulatov, Ruslan 41, 84, 105, 128,
   133–4, 145, 214n91
Khattab 58, 73, 75, 77, 79, 80, 82, 97, 99,
   111–12, 135
Khaybakh 30
Khazanov, Anatoly 72
Khodorkovsky, Mikhail 163, 210n103
Khrushchev, Nikita 17
Khudovich, General 30
kinzhal xvii, 37, 53
Kiriyenko, Sergei 76
Kizlyar/Pervomaiskoye 73, 89, 95, 112,
   147
klanovost' xvii, 130
Klebnikov, Paul 163
Klyuchevsky, Vassily 21, 173
Koch, Al'fred 39
Konakov, Air Force Chief 78
kontraktnik xvii, 12
Kosovo 52, 67, 77, 81, 90, 96, 98, 108,
   147, 150, 197n66; KLA 42; Kosovars
   18, 42
Kovalev, Sergei 32, 61, 70, 90, 139, 141,
   164
Kozak, Dmitry 19, 123–4; *polpred* xvii, 19
Kryshtanovskaya, Ol'ga 40
Kulikov, Viktor 82
Kurdistan 52; Kurds 18, 42, 112; PKK 42
Kurilovo 65
Kursk affair 108

Last of the Mohicans 38
Latsis, Otto 143–4, 199n107
Lavrov, Sergei 22
Le Monde 91, 110
Lebed', Aleksandr 43, 73, 112
Lederach, Jean Paul 10
Lefortovo 58
Lermontov, Mikhail x, xii, 38–9, 54, 59
Levada Centre 154, 202n37
Lewis, James, QC 139

Liechtenstein 134, 137, 140, 143
Lieven, Anatol 126
Limonov, Eduard 133
Liss, Artyom 122
List'ev, Vladislav 62
Lloyd, Anthony 14
London 69, 82, 138, 140, 142, 173

Magomadova, Luisa 100
Major, John 162–3
Malashenko, Aleksei 21, 67
Maltsev, Yuri 44, 59
Mandela, Nelson 57
Mansur, Sheikh 33, 54
Marighela, Carlos xi
Markedonov, Sergei 18–19, 200n138,
   209n86
marsho (freedom) xvii, 35, 180n56
Maskhadov, Aslan 5–6, 32–3, 41, 48, 54,
   58, 60, 64–5, 70, 72, 75, 79, 82–4, 86,
   97, 108, 111–12, 114, 118, 121, 128–30,
   134, 136, 138, 143–7, 165, 170; Beslan
   107, 114; death 33, 48, 65, 83, 107,
   122–3, 129, 133, 135, 147, 170–1,
   199n112
Maslow, Abraham 169
Masyuk, Yelena 70, 195n18
Médecins sans Frontières 82, 85–6, 111
media 9, 56–7, 59, 63, 65, 67–8, 70–2, 76,
   78–80, 87, 90, 93–4, 101, 106–8,
   111–12, 114, 124, 150, 156–7, 161–3,
   166; ABC 48; *Agence France Presse*
   90; bias 39; BBC 122; Channel 2
   (Russian) 64; Channel 4 (UK) 48, 93;
   CNN 37; *Ekho Moskvy* xvii, 32;
   Glasnost' Media 78; *Interfax* 49, 91,
   124; *Interfax-Vremya* 41; ITAR-TASS
   80; NTV xvi, 58, 70; ORT xvi, 71;
   Reuters 138
Melnikova, Valentina 32, 150
Memorial 7, 29, 56, 82, 84, 129, 146,
   191n20
Mendeluce, José Maria 134
Merkel, Angela 155
Mi-26 military helicopter 97
MID xvi, 40
Middle East 4, 22, 45, 96–8, 119, 152,
   159; Egypt 75; Jordan 75; Kuwait 52;
   Lebanon 41, 66, 110; Qatar 103, 135;
   Saudi Arabia 8, 97
'might' over 'right' 11, 14–15, 19–20, 25,
   47, 125–6
Mikhailov, General 58, 64
Mironov, Oleg 84

Mironov, Vyacheslav 168, 190n4
Mises Institute 44, 59, 100
Mitchell, Paul 96, 196n37
MOD (Russian) xvi, 202n35
'modernising' society 4, 33, 37–8, 40–1,
    43, 50, 52, 105, 170
Mogutin, Yury 58
Moltenskoi, Vladimir, Col.-Gen. 129
Moscow 33, 40–2, 46, 48, 54, 58, 70,
    73–4, 76–9, 89–90, 93, 98, 101, 131,
    132, 138–42, 144, 148–51, 153, 160,
    171; apartment bombings 74, 76–7, 93,
    95, 98–9, 111; theatre siege *see*
    Dubrovka
Moscow Helsinki Group 68
Moscow News 64
mountain people 8, 11, 14, 23, 26, 30, 39,
    43, 52, 59–61, 82, 134, 154
Moussaoui, Zacarias 98
Mufti xvii, 33, 83, 133
mujahideen xvii, 54, 64, 116, 121, 130;
    'mujahideen, mafia, madmen' 54, 58
mukhadjirstvo xvii, 22, 38, 43
Muslims x–xi, 2, 19, 23, 27, 34, 48, 59, 75,
    77, 88, 91, 107, 115, 129, 131, 153, 161,
    172
Mutsuraev, Timur 63
MVD xvi, 40

Nalchik 108, 126, 136, 171
Naqshbandiya xvii
Narodnost' (national principle) xvii, 50–1,
    66–7
Native American Indians 30, 38, 50;
    Removal Acts 38; Wounded Knee 31
NATO 35, 51–2, 67, 77, 98, 136, 150, 172,
    197n66
Nazis 39, 55, 60; *Untermenschen* 50
Nazran 115
Neistat, Anna 139
Nevzorov, Aleksandr 64
New York Times 144
Nezavisimaya gazeta 77
Nikishin, Yury 46
'noble savage' 38
nokhchallah 18, 46, 180n55
'Nord-Ost' *see* Dubrovka
Novaya gazeta 70, 113, 218n10
Novocherkassk 17
Novoye Ogarevo 74
Novy Vzglyad 58
Nukhaev, Khozh-Akhmed 40, 134

Ocalan Abdullah 112

oil 8, 44, 46, 72, 75, 113, 120, 129, 163–4
Oktyabr' 59
oligarchs 51, 71
OMON xvi, 100
OSCE xvi, 56, 87, 133, 169

PACE xvi, 19, 24, 56, 83–5, 110, 122,
    135, 140, 155–6, 164, 166, 169, 217n45;
    Strasbourg Round Table 135
Pain, Emil 31, 40, 83, 197n66
Palestine 2, 7, 13, 18, 23, 52, 89, 93, 96,
    99, 101–2, 107, 109, 126, 133, 138,
    151–2, 165, 172–3; Hamas 126
Pape, Robert 117
Paris Match 98
Patrushev, Nikolai 92, 171
peace: 'negative' 124; peacebuilding 3, 6,
    10–11, 153; peacekeeping 3, 10–11,
    153; peacemaking 3, 6, 10–11; peace
    plans 99, 101, 104, 134, 137, 147;
    'positive' 124
Peirce, Gareth 138
Perevezentsev, Roman 71
Peter the Great 31
Petrosyan, Yevgeny 96
Philippines 81, 90, 98, 108
Physicians for Human Rights 206n22
Piontkovsky, Andrei 10, 93
Podrabinek, Aleksandr 134
Poland 167
'politics of naming' *see* demonisation
Politkovskaya, Anna vii, 7, 14–15, 24,
    69–70, 88, 113, 122, 131, 141–2, 164,
    173; death 14–15, 70, 141, 171, 173,
    179n44
PONARS xvi, 144
Pontecorvo, Gillo 172, 181n75, 219n13
Porshnev, Igor 41
post-secular discourse 11, 19, 22, 24–6,
    47, 127
post-Soviet space 8
Potemkin, Pavel, Lt-Gen. 30
Prague Watchdog 82
Primakov, Yevgeny 74, 137
Project for the New American Century 169
Pskovsk paratroopers 111
Pushkin, Aleksandr 38, 59
Putin, Vladimir xi, 2–8, 10, 15–17, 19–22,
    25, 27, 33, 37, 40, 47–51, 59, 63, 66,
    68–70, 73, 76, 78–82, 85, 90–1, 93,
    94–5, 97–9, 101, 104, 107–9, 111, 123,
    128–30, 132, 135–8, 143–5, 148, 151–2,
    155, 157, 159, 161, 163, 170–1;
    accession to power 20, 69–70, 80, 111;

Putin, Vladimir *continued*
  acting president 81; administration 3, 5,
    21, 24, 27, 30, 47, 66–8, 82, 88, 92,
    98–9, 106–7, 114, 116, 121, 125, 130,
    134, 138, 142, 148, 155, 157, 160–1,
    164–5, 167, 172; authoritarian 81, 87,
    128, 143; Chechen policy 48, 59, 74, 77,
    79, 82–7, 101, 104, 113, 117–18, 120–1,
    128–9, 136, 146–7, 151, 157, 159, 161,
    166; constitution 44, 130; democrat 74,
    81, 128; entrepreneur of violence 47;
    head of FSB 74; intemperate language
    69, 76, 113, 151, 157; president i, 7, 21,
    51, 66, 78–9, 91, 102, 113, 121, 136,
    138, 141, 143, 145, 151, 161, 165;
    prime minister 73–4, 76, 79–80, 123;
    statist 22; third term 85, 130; *vertikal'* of
    power 40, 80
Pyatigorsk 66

Qadiriya xviii

Radio Liberty *see* RFE/RL
Raduev, Salman 59–60, 73, 99, 111–12,
  146, 212–13n73
Ram, Harsha 26, 38
Rechkalov, Vadim 82, 120, 124
Rechsstaat (law-governed state) 11, 24, 26,
  34, 157; absence of 45, 47, 124, 126
Reddaway, Peter 140
Redgrave, Vanessa 138
Remizov, Mikhail 88
Remnick, David 22, 35
'Restoration of constitutional order' *see*
  First Chechen War (1994–1996)
RFE/RL xvi, 70, 80, 134, 150
Rhodes, Aaron 139
Rifkind, Malcolm 162
Rob Roy 38
Robertson, George 91, 109, 136
Robinson, Mary 164
Rodionov, Igor 158
Rodionov, Yevgeny 65
Roma 18, 35, 50
Rosenberg, Steve 122
Rostov-on-Don 1
Rudakov, A.L. 69; *The Chechen Mafia* 69
Rushailo, Vladimir 74
Russell-Johnston, Lord 110
Russia, Russian Federation xii–xiii, xvi,
  1–9; autocracy 50–1; chauvinism 11, 17,
  20, 67, 125; Civic Forum 25;
  Constitution 10, 130; Duma 57, 76, 127,
  135, 137, 145; ethnic Russians 28, 34,

57, 67–8, 77, 171; federalism 17, 40, 52;
  federal forces 15, 45–7, 63, 66–7, 70,
  72–3, 83, 87, 95, 103, 112–13, 126–7,
  129, 131–3, 136; generals 31, 45, 57,
  67–8, 72, 76–9, 95, 128, 132, 134–5,
  145–6; General Staff 103; imperial
  power 4, 17, 21, 30–1, 35–6, 44, 50, 54,
  56, 59, 66, 119, 131, 146, 170;
  intolerance of diversity 11, 17, 20, 22,
  40, 50–1; Kremlin xi–xii, 1, 6, 14–15,
  27, 41, 48, 51, 55–7, 59, 65–6, 68, 72,
  74, 83–7, 90, 92, 106, 108, 112–14, 121,
  130, 135, 143–4, 147, 150, 158, 160–1,
  163, 165, 171–2; language 2; military
  losses 32, 67, 80, 144, 150; *mission
  civilatrice* 30, 36, 50, 154; nationalism
  17; non-ethnic Russians (Rossians) 34,
  57, 67, 77, 154, 186n38; obsession with
  Chechnya 35, 40, 151; opinion polls 25,
  48–9, 56–7, 62–3, 66–7, 76–9, 86, 91–2,
  98–9, 108, 129, 134, 137, 145, 152, 154,
  161, 164–5; orthodoxy 11, 22, 50–1,
  125; Presidency 51, 69–70, 111;
  presidential elections 69, 71, 76, 77–8,
  128, 135, 144, 194n4; relations with UK
  6, 80, 159–64; RSFSR xvi; 'Russia for
  the Russians' 17, 66, 158; security
  services 41, 51, 80; 'small, victorious
  war' 5, 33, 35, 70, 93, 185n34; society
  1, 19–20, 24, 41, 68; Southern Federal
  District 19, 123; Supreme Soviet 71, 84;
  special forces (*spetsnaz*) x, xviii, 33, 63,
  99, 111; suppression 11, 15, 17, 22, 31,
  38–40, 49–51, 65, 87, 125
Russia Journal, The 43, 143
Russian roulette 192n49
Russo-Chechen conflict: alcohol 12, 59,
  123, 149; amnesties 88, 95, 99, 135,
  146; arbitrary brutality 11, 14, 16, 36,
  38, 45, 50, 59–61, 65, 67, 80, 82, 87,
  103, 110, 112, 114, 146, 153; 'black
  hole of lawlessness' 4, 7, 30, 36, 44–5,
  67, 93, 103, 113, 151, 153, 170; cost
  102, 204n71; cultural contradictions 4,
  124–5, 154, 157, 159; death squads 14,
  106, 122; disappearances 11, 12, 82,
  106, 127; disproportionate force xiii,
  11–12, 16, 43, 45, 78, 103, 105, 153;
  extrajudicial killings 7, 11, 14, 27, 82,
  93, 127, 129; extremism 11, 19, 20, 126,
  136, 147, 149; fatalities 72, 95, 102,
  104, 112, 117, 127, 150, 165, 173,
  204n70; human rights abuses 39–40, 56,
  71, 82, 155–6, 159–60, 164; impunity

11, 14, 25, 27, 45, 105, 110, 153; illicit economy 46, 129–30, 134–5; indiscriminate force/violence xiii, 11–12, 16, 43, 45, 78, 103, 105, 149, 163; intimidation 11, 15, 27, 122; kidnapping 15, 27, 30, 45, 70–1, 76, 94; massacres 30–1, 106; narcotics 12, 15, 45, 58, 110, 149; 'normalisation' i, 85, 104; peace treaties 33, 73, 95, 147; political solution 30, 82–3, 96–7, 99, 101, 105, 107, 109, 131–2, 140, 143–5, 149, 165–6, 170; protection rackets 11, 15; underdevelopment 11, 24, 124, 126, 162; war crimes 5, 78, 80, 86, 88, 94, 104–5, 118, 127, 135
Ryazan' 74, 80, 93
Rybakov, Yuly 139–40
Rybkin, Ivan 134, 137, 139–40

Sadulaev, Abdul-Khalim 83, 105, 120, 128, 135, 199n113
Saidullaev, Malik 32, 84, 105, 128
St Petersburg xi, 54, 91, 123, 134, 148, 157
Sakharov, Andrei 90, 141; Museum 142
Sakwa, Richard 13
Samashki 61
Samodurov, Yury 142
Savage Division 59
Schmid, Alex 106, 118
Schroeder, Gerhard 91, 128
Scotland 2, 37, 44, 50, 60; Edinburgh 128; Highland clearances 38; Highlanders 37–8, 44, 59; St Andrews 2
Scott, Walter 37–8
Sechin, Igor 92
Second Chechen War (1999–2006) i, 1–2, 5, 30, 36, 43, 55–9, 64–7, 69–72, 74–86, 89, 91, 95, 98–9, 112–19, 146, 150; counter-terrorist operation 5, 30, 36, 43, 46, 69, 76–7, 81, 87, 90, 92, 95, 112, 165
Second World War 2, 4, 33, 35, 39, 43, 45, 60, 71, 94, 150, 163–4; Brest fortress 45; Stalingrad 71
Shakirov, Raf 68
Shamanov, Vladimir, Gen. 78, 197n76
Shamil, Imam xi, 39, 43
Shaposhnikov, Yevgeny 72
Shari'a xviii, 11, 18, 20, 27, 33, 59, 64, 76, 86, 93, 147
Shariat 125
Sharon, Ariel 128, 151
Shaw, George Bernard 173

Shchekochikin, Yury 134, 185n34
Shevardnadze, Eduard 35
Shevtsova, Lilia 27
Shpigun, Gennady 77
siloviki xviii, 7, 17, 20, 40, 49, 68, 73, 76, 80, 121, 130, 167
slavery 21, 30, 53, 55, 89
soccer x–xi, 66; CSKA Moscow 66; Terek Grozny 66, 121
Sokolov, Boris 88, 181n64
Solov'ev (Sokolov), Ivan 142
Solov'ev, Vadim 82
Solzhenitsyn, Aleksandr 14, 111
Sossinsky, Sergei 64
Soviet Union (USSR) 7–8, 17, 22–3, 28–9, 31–3, 36–9, 41, 44–6, 50–1, 54, 84, 91, 98, 130, 134, 148, 163; Armed Forces 54, 60, 72, 109, 133; Bolsheviks 32, 39; Chechen-Ingush Autonomous Republic 46; collapse 34–5, 42, 46, 72, 151; CPSU xvi, 50; Friendship of the Peoples 66; Marxism-Leninism 22–3, 50; patriotism 34, 50; Red Army 98; Soviet 'Empire' 29, 35–6, 44, 50

Spain 119, 155; Civil War 71; ETA 42, 109, 118; Franco 71; Guernica 71
Speckhard, Anne 100
Sri Lanka 43
Stalin, Iosif 7, 18, 30, 33, 36, 39, 42, 44–5, 50, 94, 172
Starovoitova, Galina 90
state terrorism *see* terrorism
Steele, Jonathan 129, 211n108
Stepanova, Ekaterina 106
Stepashin, Sergei 74, 77, 123, 210n97
Straus, Ira 39
Straw, Jack 136
structural violence *see* violence
Strukova, Marina 63
Sudan 14, 109
Sufism xviii, 47, 125, 182n91
Sunday Times 161
SVR xvi, 40
Sysoev, General 30–1

Taliban 54, 114, 130, 133
Tamerlane 29, 39
Tamils 42
Tanweer, Shehzad 161
tariqat xviii, 18,
Tatarstan 34, 42–4, 57, 158
teip (clan) xviii, 11, 18, 20, 37, 46, 50–1, 58, 125, 134; *Benoi* 85, 121

Terek River x, 13, 29
territorial integrity 4, 11, 17, 20, 22, 26,
    28, 34, 36, 42–3, 51–2, 67, 74, 87, 118,
    120, 125, 133, 165, 209n86
terrorism i, 2, 11, 13–14, 22, 24–5, 37, 41,
    43, 55, 67, 73–4, 89–91, 95–7, 108, 131,
    136, 141, 144, 147, 149, 152–4, 169;
    'conflict-related' 106; 'failed states' 41;
    insurgent 12, 14, 22, 155; international
    48, 58, 89, 93–4, 108–9, 131, 136, 138,
    151, 161, 169; Islamic 77, 90–1, 98,
    102–4, 106, 114, 137, 144, 151–2, 158,
    165; 'mega-terrorism' 106;
    'spectaculars' i, xii, 1, 7, 49, 67, 107,
    112, 114, 127, 147, 151–2, 161, 164;
    state 14, 22, 25, 106, 155;
    state-sponsored 14; strategy 118; suicide
    terrorism 94, 98, 118, 161, 202–3n38
    see also bombs; 'super-terrorism' 106;
    tactic 117–18; terrorists and freedom
    fighters 13, 54, 89
Thatcher, Margaret 162
Third World Quarterly 53
Tibelius, Vyacheslav 71
Tokhtamish 29
Tolstoi, Lev 38, 59–60
Tolstoi-Yurt 147
torture 7, 11, 14–16, 18, 27, 64, 82, 106,
    127, 129, 142, 179n42
'traditional' society 4, 33, 37–8, 50–2,
    105, 170
Transparency International 19, 162,
    209n88
traumatised democracies 5, 90, 96–7, 105,
    107, 128
Trenin, Dmitry 67, 148
Tret'yakov, Vitaly 77
Troshev, Gennady, Gen. 58, 78, 197n77
Turkey 22, 42, 112
Turnbull, Sir Andrew 161
Tutu, Archbishop Desmond 164
Tyson, Mike 123

Udugov, Movladi 111, 135
Ullmann, Eduard 104, 106
Umarov, Doku 34, 120–1
United Kingdom 37, 44, 48, 75, 81, 87,
    101, 104–5, 108–9, 119, 123, 129, 136,
    138–40, 143, 166; relations with Russia
    159–64
United Nations 10, 22, 87, 107, 147, 169;
    UN Commission for Human Rights 23;
    UNHCR 164
'United Russia' 85

Urus-Martan 41
USA (United States of America) 22, 24,
    37, 44, 48, 51–2, 74, 81, 89, 93–4, 97–8,
    101, 103, 107–9, 114, 119, 128, 134,
    138, 143–4, 151, 164, 166, 169, 172–3;
    Puerto Rico 44; US State Department 99
Uzuev, Magomed 45

Validata 84
Vedeno x, 41
vertikal' xviii, 5, 11, 17, 19, 22, 50–1, 80,
    85, 87, 125, 128, 180n52
Victoria, Queen 37
Vietnam 3, 130; Viet Cong 130
Villepin, Dominique de 149
violence 100–1, 106, 109, 156–7, 159,
    169–71; cultural 10–11, 21, 154, 156;
    direct 10–12, 17, 89, 154, 156–7,
    169–70; structural 10–11, 16–17, 20–1,
    27, 55, 89, 125–7, 154, 156–7; 'violent'
    politics 157, 159
Vladikavkaz 62
Voina 37, 95, 202n34
Volgodonsk 74, 93, 95, 111
Volkodavy (wolfhounds) 63
Voloshin, Aleksandr 92
Vor 46
Vostok 130
VTsIOM xvi, 78, 144–5

Wahabbism xi, xviii, 23, 47, 93, 119, 125,
    197n70; *Wahhabites* 18, 55, 65, 76–7,
    86, 93, 97, 100, 109, 111–12, 125, 130,
    134, 165
Waal, Tom de 126, 139
Walsh, James 77
Walsh, Nick Paton 122
war of terror xii, 2, 7
war on terror xi–xii, 2–5, 7, 11–13, 15, 20,
    22, 24–7, 47, 74, 79, 89–92, 97–8, 101,
    105–9, 114, 126, 136, 143, 148, 151–2,
    157–8, 160, 162, 168–9, 170–3; on
    terrorism 25, 94, 97–8, 101, 107, 109,
    114, 143, 169
Ware, Robert Bruce 39
Washington, George 13
Washington Post, The 55
White, Hayden 38
White, Stephen 197n68
Wird xviii, 18
Workman, Judge Timothy 138–9, 142,
    213n43
World Chechen Congress 134, 138, 141,
    143

xenophobia 11, 20, 126

Yamadaev, Ruslan 85
Yamadaev, Sulim 27, 130
Yandirbiev, Zelimkhan 103, 135
Yarmuk 126
Yarysh-Mardy 112
Yastrzhembsky, Sergei 90, 98, 141
Yavlinsky, Gennady 76, 164
Yeltsin, Boris 4, 5, 22, 33, 41, 43, 55,
   59–60, 62–3, 69–77, 83, 90, 95, 111,
   127–8, 132, 152, 158, 167;
   administration 4, 21, 27, 30, 62;
   democrat 75; president 33, 69, 71, 73,
   76, 127- 8, 141
Yermolov, Aleksei 31, 33, 43, 86, 171
Yugoslavia (former) 150, 153, 155;
   Albanians 42; Bosnia 71, 110, 150;
   Croatia 110; Macedonia 42, 110;
   Montenegro 155; Sarajevo 71; Serbia
   110, 155
Yukos affair 163

zachistki (sweeps) xviii, 11–13, 27, 82, 84,
   106, 132, 136, 153, 178n17
Zakaev, Akhmed 6, 41, 48, 105, 108, 121,
   134–5, 144–6, 150, 164, 174, 205n87;
   extradition trial 6, 48, 82, 101, 137–43,
   173–4
Zapad 124, 130
Zavtra 63, 141
Zidane, Zinédine x-xii
Zikr xviii
zindan xviii, 37
Zürcher, Christoph 176n8
Zvereva, Galina 69
Zyuganov, Gennady 69